SHAKESPEAR

AND RENAISSA

POLITICS

THE ARDEN SHAKESPEARE

THE ARDEN CRITICAL COMPANIONS

GENERAL EDITORS

Andrew Hadfield and Paul Hammond

ADVISORY BOARD

MacDonald P. Jackson   Katherine Duncan-Jones   David Scott Kastan
Patricia Parker   Lois Potter   Phyllis Rackin   Bruce R. Smith
Brian Vickers   Blair Worden

Shakespeare and Renaissance Politics   *Andrew Hadfield*
Shakespeare and the Victorians   *Adrian Poole*

Forthcoming

Shakespeare and Comedy   *Robert Maslen*
Shakespeare and Language   *Jonathan Hope*
Shakespeare and Music   *David Lindley*
Shakespeare and Religion   *Alison Shell*
Shakespeare and Renaissance Europe   *ed. Andrew Hadfield and*
Paul Hammond

Further titles in preparation

THE ARDEN CRITICAL COMPANIONS

SHAKESPEARE AND RENAISSANCE POLITICS

ANDREW HADFIELD

The Arden website is at
http://www.ardenshakespeare.com

This edition of *Shakespeare and Renaissance Politics*
first published 2004 by the Arden Shakespeare

© 2004 Thomson Learning

Arden Shakespeare is an imprint of Thomson Learning

Thomson Learning
High Holborn House
50–51 Bedford Row
London WC1R 4LR

Typeset by LaserScript, Mitcham, Surrey

Printed in Croatia by Zrinski

British Library Cataloguing in Publication Data
A catalogue record for this book is available from the British Library

Library of Congress Cataloguing in Publication Data
A catalogue record has been requested

ISBN 1-90343-617-6

NPN 9 8 7 6 5 4 3 2 1

CONTENTS

FOR ALISON

PREFACE

I have wanted to write this book for a long time. It seemed to me that work on Shakespeare and politics, although much of it was fascinating and often incisive, fell into three distinct and rather limited categories. One type of argument, less frequently made now than some years ago, claims that Shakespeare did not really have a particular interest in politics because he was too concerned with more timeless and important questions of human nature. A second type, related to the first, asserts that he was a conservative and cautious thinker who was keen to accept the status quo; that, he may not have been overly keen on the charmless James I, but, like everyone else in the final years of Tudor England, he obviously loved Elizabeth. A third form of reading, appearing in the wake of New Historicist re-readings of Renaissance literature and culture, reversed this positive reading of Shakespeare and showed how his work was implicated in the history of class oppression, colonialism, misogyny, racism and other ideologies of exploitation.

I have a number of sympathies with the third of these ways of reading Shakespeare, although this seam of literary criticism is now close to being exhausted. The problem is that such an approach simply inverts the second form of argument outlined above and leaves Shakespeare's place within a cultural system as it was before, concentrating instead on a subsequent history of performance, reading and critical comment. Shakespeare's relationship to his literary, historical and cultural context remains the same. A serious consideration of his political thought and ideas, and the political significance of his work, involves reading his poetry and plays in terms of the political ideas, practices and systems of Tudor and Stuart England.

In this work I have set out to achieve this ambitious task. Friends, colleagues and critics often complain that I overuse the words 'clearly' and 'obviously', especially when matters are far from clear and obvious. Nevertheless, I do realize that it is both clear and obvious that I have produced a work which only just starts to tackle this significant intellectual task. I have tried to read Shakespeare's work in terms of sixteenth- and early seventeenth-century European and English political theory, classical political theory, court politics and intrigues, the theory and practice of parliamentary government, and political readings of British and European history, in order to outline and illuminate the range and diversity of early modern political ideas, forms and practices that are relevant to the study of Shakespeare's works. I don't think that I have been able to cover everything.

This study would not have been possible without the work of numerous scholars of Renaissance political ideas, history and literature. I owe an especial debt to the works of T.W. Baldwin, Patrick Collinson, John Guy, David Norbrook, Annabel Patterson, Markku Peltonen, J.G.A. Pocock, Quentin Skinner and Richard Tuck. Needless to say they cannot be held responsible for the use I have made of their ideas.

I am extremely grateful to the Department of English, University of Wales, Aberystwyth, and the Arts and Humanities Research Board. The former granted me a semester's research leave and the latter a second one as part of their research leave scheme (1999–2000), giving me a year in which to complete the writing of this book. Patrick Cheney, Martin Dzelzainis, Paul Hammond and Blair Worden have all read the complete typescript and have been exemplary in forcing me to rethink and rewrite various sections of the work, as well as saving me from numerous errors. I have presented some of the arguments contained within the book at the Universities of Durham and Glasgow, as well as at my own department in Aberystwyth. I am grateful to the audiences for their helpful comments on each occasion. Thanks also to my intellectual companions over the years, Patrick Cheney, Margaret Healy, Tom Healy, Claire Jowitt, David Scott Kastan, Paulina Kewes, Willy Maley, Jim Shapiro, Tim Woods and, especially, Paul Hammond, who has been an ideal co-editor, a model of meticulousness and an inexhaustible source of ideas. It has been a great pleasure to work with Jessica Hodge, Margaret Bartley and Jane Armstrong at Thomson Learning. Alison Hadfield compiled an excellent index at short notice. Jane Whitlock

Blundell has been an exemplary, and extremely tolerant, copy editor. Sections of Chapter One have appeared in Richard Dutton and Jean Howard, eds, *A Companion to Shakespeare, Volume II: The Histories* (Oxford, 2003); sections of Chapter Two in *Review of English Studies*; sections of Chapter Three in *Parergon*; and sections of Chapter Five in the *Kyushu Review* and *Shakespeare Survey*. I am grateful to the editors concerned for permission to reproduce the revised forms of the essays here.

My greatest debt, as it has been for some years now, is to my family. I have tried not to bore Alison, Lucy, Patrick and Maud with my peculiar obsessions, habits and propensity to fail to stop work when I should, but I realize that I do not succeed as well as I might. That they remind me of my failings less often than they might makes me realize how lucky I am to have them all.

February 2002

LIST OF ABBREVIATIONS

All references to Shakespeare are to the Arden editions, in Arden 3 when available, and otherwise in Arden 2.

AJLH	American Journal of Legal History
BJRL	Bulletin of the John Rylands Library
CQ	Critical Quarterly
CSPD	Calendar of State Papers, Domestic Series
DNB	Dictionary of National Biography
EIC	Essays in Criticism
ELH	English Literary History
ELR	English Literary Renaissance
HLQ	Huntington Library Quarterly
MP	Modern Philology
N & Q	Notes and Queries
OED	Oxford English Dictionary
P & P	Past and Present
PMLA	Publications of the Modern Language Association of America
RES	Review of English Studies
RQ	Renaissance Quarterly
SCJ	Sixteenth-Century Journal
SEL	Studies in English Literature, 1500–1900
SQ	Shakespeare Quarterly
SS	Shakespeare Survey
TP	Textual Practice
YES	Yearbook of English Studies

LIST OF ILLUSTRATIONS

Introduction

SHAKESPEARE AND THE VARIETIES OF EARLY MODERN POLITICAL CULTURE

I

What exactly did politics mean in England around the year 1600? How did people's conceptions of politics differ from our own? Obviously, then as now, definitions varied, overlapped and conflicted with each other, and people involved in the practice and theory of political life argued with one another.[1] Nevertheless, it is possible to provide a brief outline of the fundamental political issues and beliefs that occupied the minds of Elizabeth I, James I and their subjects.

The over-riding political issue of the time was the question of sovereignty and the legitimacy of the monarch. While it is undoubtedly true that most people – some historians would argue all – accepted the need for a sovereign as ruler, the question of which sovereign was a thorny one. The Tudor dynasty had no undisputed right to rule, and there were numerous other claimants to the throne. Henry VII was a usurper with a weak claim to the throne through his mother, Margaret Beaufort, who was descended from John of Gaunt, the son of Edward III. The same can be said for the Stuarts who succeeded the Tudors in 1603, although their claim was rather better. James secured the throne through the claim of his mother, Mary Stuart (Queen of Scots), who was the granddaughter of Margaret, daughter of Henry VII, who had married James IV of Scotland.[2]

Furthermore, there was a serious religious issue that affected the question of sovereignty.[3] As a result of Henry VIII's break with Rome (1533), his daughter, Elizabeth, who succeeded in line after her elder siblings Edward VI (1547–53) and Mary (1553–8), was declared a heretic and, therefore, a usurper by the Catholic Church, and there was considerable opposition to her reign in Europe as well as in Britain. In February 1570 Pope Pius V declared that the Catholic Church in Rome did not see Elizabeth as a legitimate ruler, and it was therefore the duty of her Catholic subjects to depose her. Many Catholics were forced to declare their loyalty or risk being fined, deprived of their lands, or worse still accused of treason. Many treatises were written defending the rights of Catholics to rebel and depose heretical rulers, ideas which mirrored a wave of Calvinist-inspired treatises which had argued that Protestants could depose tyrannous Catholic sovereigns (most English writers had in mind Mary Tudor, Elizabeth's elder sister).[4] Shakespeare's family may well have been Catholic, and the case has been made that Shakespeare himself could have been strongly influenced by Catholicism in his early career and possibly throughout his life.[5]

Other political issues assumed a lesser importance. There were no political parties as we understand them. Members were elected to parliament by a very small section of the populace. They did sometimes group themselves into factions, but would often act as independent members of a representative body.[6] In any case, parliament met only rarely in the reigns of Elizabeth and James, and, while it did undoubtedly have an important influence on English political life, real authority lay elsewhere.[7] Serious political power belonged to the circle that surrounded the monarch, those to whom he or she turned to for advice when necessary, the court and the royal councils.[8] It was at the court that most administrative and political offices were distributed, from the holding of lucrative monopolies and positions of enormous power and circumstance such as Lord Admiral of the Fleet and membership of the Privy Council, to minor regional and local positions granted as favours to powerful courtiers.[9] Indeed, an argument can be made that office-holding was the basis of political life in Elizabethan and Jacobean England rather than political representation.[10] Entertainments such as plays and masques were an important part of court life, and often these were an opportunity for a courtier to try to influence the monarch's political views.[11] The council that the monarch summoned at will was where decisions were made and political policy formulated.[12] In other words, proximity to the reality of politics was an even more distant prospect for most early modern English men and women than it is today.

It is important for us to realize that politics could not be easily separated from religion. While it is true that the cultural impact of the rediscovery of classical learning was immense, especially in terms of political ideas and philosophy, English society was dominated by religious questions and problems.[13] As has often been noted, both Protestants and Catholics developed 'resistance' theories and declared that they had the right to overthrow a monarch who persecuted their religion. Cardinal William Allen argued that Catholics had more right to resist an oppressive state that suppressed Catholicism than Protestants did because they had the authority of the true Church to support them whereas Protestants had to act alone with their deluded consciences.[14] The Protestants Christopher Goodman, John Knox and John Ponet argued that their allegiance to the true church gave them the same right to resist.[15] Despite the undoubted triumph of the defeat of the Armada in 1588, achieved just before Shakespeare began his career as a professional writer, fear of Catholic Spain dominated the last years of Elizabeth's reign.[16] For many writers, the European world could be divided into the two hostile camps of Protestantism and Catholicism. Not everyone accepted that this was an apocalyptic battle between good and evil, but the all-encompassing nature of the conflict could not be avoided as it affected political strategies devised at every level.[17] A central fear was that England could become divided and overrun with a sectarian civil war as France had been throughout the 1570s and 1580s.[18] Through careful diplomacy and an ecumenical religious policy James managed to establish a period of peace and stability after the shock of the Gunpowder Plot (1605) until the outbreak of the Thirty Years' War (1618).[19]

Early modern politics and political allegiances are a matter of considerable controversy. Political factions and groupings were never more than a loose alliance 'of people of varying experiences and outlooks who, while they agreed about some things, might disagree about others'.[20] Indeed, it is arguable that only after the failure of Robert Devereux, second Earl of Essex, to obtain the support and rewards at court that he demanded as his due, did a recognizable system of such groupings occur.[21] Even if this is disputed, it is still clear that the most significant divisions occurred towards the end of the 1590s, as political alliances started to become more pronounced. The hawkish Protestant lobby at court, who were keen to persuade Elizabeth to fight a more aggressive war with the Spanish than she was prepared to do, included both Sir Walter Raleigh and the Earl of Essex among its ranks. Yet it was also well known that these two men hated each other and competed for the Queen's favour, making political unity problematic.[22] Before that, Raleigh had opposed Robert Dudley, Earl of Leicester, even though it would seem that they had much in common, especially regarding their opposition to all things Catholic and Spanish.[23] At the same time, religious differences did not always preclude links with one's opponents. The staunchly Protestant Sidney family were closely linked with the Catholic martyr, Edmund Campion, even though Sir Philip Sidney, son-in-law of Sir Francis Walsingham, another prominent and vocal Protestant, often argued that any toleration of Catholicism would be disastrous for England.[24] Moreover, until the 1590s and the advent of a political language based on *ragion di stato* (reason of state), the language of politics was 'largely ethical', indicating that political theorists and actors agreed on a series of problems that demanded a certain form of behaviour rather than the choice of supporting one side against another.[25]

Politics also involved ideas and theories as well as a series of responses to events. Many people, of course, were prepared to accept the status quo, either through rational conviction that the middle way was the best way or through self-interest. Numerous political treatises written in the 1590s argued that monarchy was a divinely ordained institution and that it was the duty of subjects to obey the monarch without question because everyone and everything had its place in the natural order of things.[26] Edward Forset's *A comparative discourse of the*

FIGURE 1 Robert Devereux, second Earl of Essex as champion of the tilt-yard: miniature by Nicholas Hilliard, *c*.1595.

bodies natural and politique (1606) compares the commonwealth to a hive or a ship, but suggests that the analogy with a human body is best because it is vital that the head or the heart – the monarch – controls everything else.[27] For such theorists of government the worst of all possible evils was rebellion; this was clearly expressed in the 'Homilie

Agaynst Disobedience and Wylful Rebellion' (1570?), published in the aftermath of the 1569 Northern Rebellion and ordered to be read out in church services at key intervals throughout the year.[28] The 'Homilie' asks:

> From whom springeth such foul ruin of realms? Is not rebellion the greatest of all mischiefs? And who are most ready to the greatest of all mischiefs, but the worst men? Rebels, therefore, the worst of all subjects, are the most ready to rebellion, as being the worst of all vices, and furthest from the duty of a good subject: as, on the contrary part, the best subjects are most firm and constant in obedience, as in the special and peculiar virtue of good subjects.[29]

However, it would be wrong to assume that all Elizabeth's subjects felt that they should be quite as docile as this, even if few argued that violent rebellion was necessary and desirable. Most theories of government articulated in Tudor and Stuart England were derived from a mixture of Greek and Roman writings, the most important probably being Aristotle's *Politics*, Polybius' history of the rise of Rome and Cicero's orations on the forms and varieties of active life available for the good citizen.[30] A key notion was that the ideal government should take the form of a 'mixed' constitution, which incorporated all the elements of single rule (monarchy), a group of well-informed political advisers (oligarchy or aristocracy), and democracy (the wider participation of the lower orders).[31] Democracy, the most significant political form in the western world today, was not a serious possibility until the upheavals of the English Civil War.[32] At the end of the sixteenth and start of the seventeenth centuries, democracy, derived from the Greek term *demos*, a personification of the populace, could be used to mean a popular element within a larger political body, but was not used to describe a concept of a viable, self-contained mode of government.[33]

Of course, the notion of the 'mixed constitution' could be used for conservative ends, asserting that the monarch was the apex of the state and therefore the most important element within the constitution. Aristotle's authoritative survey of the varieties of possible political forms had concluded that monarchy was the best form of government because a single leader served the people most efficiently and this form of constitution was least prey to the evils of corruption and bribery.[34] It should also be recognized that supporters of the monarchy as the best possible form of government were keen to make sure that the ruler was virtuous and did not degenerate into a tyrant whose power went beyond the boundaries of the established laws. A keen supporter of the absolute powers of the monarch, James I, constantly warns his readers against the dangers of kings degenerating into tyrants.[35]

Equally, however, the concept of the 'mixed' constitution could be used by political theorists to argue that the people – or, more often, a select group of the people who constituted their representatives – had the power to restrain and limit the powers of the monarch. Few went as far as the Scottish humanist, George Buchanan (1506–82), who argued that kings were obliged to serve the people and if they failed in their duties could be overthrown by any of their subjects without further ado.[36] But many, such as Sir Edward Coke (1552–1634), James I's Chief Justice, who defended the validity of the common law against the King's assumption that royal prerogative always came first, did argue that the monarch's powers had to be limited by his or her subjects whose liberty and ability to enjoy their freedom without undue restraint was a key issue in early modern political discourse.[37] Those keen to limit the powers of the monarchy and those keen to preserve them often used the same sources and shared the same political language and assumptions, but there are important differences in the emphases of their arguments, not least the significance given in the writings of many constitutionalists to the need to oppose the monarch passively or actively should he or she transgress too far.[38] Many other influential treatises, such as Sir John Fortesque's *A Learned Commendation of the Politique Lawes of England*, translated from the Latin in 1567, and Sir Thomas Smith's *De Republica Anglorum* (published 1583, widely circulated earlier), were open to various readings. Such works could be understood to uphold an English tradition of limited monarchy and so preserve a generally accepted status quo, or read as implicitly critical of the excessive powers of the monarchy and its hold over all the offices of state, and in doing so providing arguments and evidence in favour of a more participatory mode of government.[39]

It is also possible to argue that republicanism and republican ideas had a crucial influence on Shakespeare's work (as I shall suggest in Chapter Three). This is a controversial subject because definitions of early modern republican ideas are hard to establish with any degree of consensus.[40] Many historians would dispute the importance of a serious strain of republicanism infiltrating English political thought before the 1640s, when subjects did actually rebel against the monarch and started to plot his execution.[41] However, a contrary case can be made that even if there were not a whole host of English republicans who believed in the necessity of establishing an English republic in the late sixteenth and early seventeenth centuries, there were many who were influenced by classical republican thought and its emphasis on the active virtue of the good citizen, who deserves to enjoy liberty under the protection of a benign state.[42]

Republicanism took many forms in early modern Europe. The Latin term *res publica* literally meant the 'public thing', but was most frequently translated as the 'common weal' or 'commonwealth'.[43] Accordingly, 'republicanism' was either directly or indirectly a central feature of English political life from the early sixteenth century onwards. The arguments of the 'commonwealth men', a group of reformers influenced by Italian humanist ideals and keen to reform administrative and constitutional structures, as well as public life in England, can be seen as the first significant entry of republicanism into English political thought.[44] As Markku Peltonen has reminded us, if English humanists took 'the princely context for granted, it did not prevent their adopting a number of "civic" and republican themes in their writings'.[45] Republicanism was not a monolithic concept indicating the participation of all citizens in the political process. Rather, it was a

> cluster of themes concerning citizenship, public virtue and true nobility ... Virtue was closely linked with the distinctively *republican* character of classical republicanism: to ensure that the

most virtuous men governed the commonwealth and to control corruption, magistracy should be elected rather than inherited. In this sense republicanism (in the narrow sense of a constitution without a king) could be an anti-monarchical goal: civic values required concomitant republican institutions, but monarchical arrangements were said to suppress these. Arrangements usually favoured by classical republicans were those of the mixed constitution, and the term republic was also used in the wider and more general sense of referring to a good and just constitution.[46]

I would suggest that a republican tradition was constituted of a number of different elements and languages, not all of which were exactly congruent or fitted together perfectly. Furthermore, these clustered beliefs, ideas and identifiable modes of writing do not necessarily indicate republicanism or republican thought if produced in isolation.[47] First, there is a rhetoric against tyranny, often derived from Tacitus' *Histories* and *Annals*, but which also often stemmed from Protestant resistance theorists such as John Knox, John Ponet and Christopher Goodman, writing in the 1550s.[48] Second, there is a strong commitment to the humanist programme of educational reform and a concentration on the study of the classics. Through the study of the texts of Cicero, Aristotle, Plato, Polybius, Thucydides and others, came an interest in the political ideas they espoused, as well as an understanding of the institutions and forms of political organization they advocated. Such study led to a select group of highly educated men possessing the means and the confidence to understand different constitutions in the ancient world and contemporary Europe and so debate alternative forms of government, including varieties of mixed rule made up of elements of monarchy, oligarchy and democracy, as well as republics such as Rome and Venice.[49] Third, there is a stress on the need for virtue in government officials or magistrates, often leading to the suggestion that hereditary monarchy was not the ideal form of government because it could not be guaranteed that the best would inherit the throne. Often such arguments praise the constitution of

Venice, where official positions were not held for life or at the whim of a monarch but rotated every few years. Equally important, other arguments, generally derived from Machiavelli, praise republics as best equipped to pursue wars, and claim that active virtue was best achieved in the trying conditions of battle.[50] Fourth, there is a keen interest in histories of the Roman republic and enthusiasm for Livy, who exhibited nostalgia for the lost republic and portrayed the opponents of and conspirators against Caesar – Brutus, Cassius and Pompey – in a positive light.[51] There is also enthusiasm for Lucan's *Pharsalia*, a key work in the grammar school curriculum, and certainly a work against tyrants and arguably a republican classic.[52] The very representation of the founding of the republic, the story of the rape of Lucrece – narrated in Livy's *History of Rome from its Foundation* – can, of course, be read as a republican gesture.[53] Fifth, the language of natural rights is employed, often derived from Huguenot treatises and the opposing arguments made by Catholic 'monarchomachs' such as Francisco Suarez.[54] This language grants citizens rights to relative autonomy and freedom from the oppressions of bad monarchs, whom they have the right to oppose if necessary. A treatise which argued this case and which had a significant influence in Elizabethan and Jacobean England is Innocent Gentillet's *A Discourse Upon the Meanes of wel Governing and Maintaining in Good Peace, a Kingdom, or other Principalitie … Against Nicholas Machiavell the Florentine*, translated by Simon Patericke in 1602.[55] Gentillet's defence of the rights of the individual against the 'policy' of the ruler defended and articulated in *The Prince* shows how complex and divided the republican tradition was (republicans concentrated far more on Machiavelli's political analysis in *The Discourses on the First Decade of Livy*).[56] The final element I would single out is the importance of offices and positions of responsibility held by ordinary citizens or subjects, which can be seen to constitute a public realm developing alongside that of formal political representation in parliament. According to Mark Goldie such active participation in public life constituted

> a republican tradition in which the active involvement of the
> citizen rather than the passive exercise of the franchise was

the essential feature of a good polity ... Early modern England
was neither a democracy nor, in our modern sense, a republic. It
was monarchical. Yet it could be said to be an unacknowledged
republic, or a monarchical republic.[57]

The most widely-read republican theorist was Niccolò Machiavelli,
whose work was probably known to Shakespeare.[58] Machiavelli was
well known as a historian of Florence (alongside Francesco Guicciardini)
and theorist of the art of war, as well as an analyst of both republican
and princely forms of government, which he discussed in *The Discourses
on the First Decade of Livy* and *The Prince*. Machiavelli's legacy and
influence is complex and controversial. He was studied in Renaissance
England as an advocate of oligarchical, republican government, which
he argued was the best and most stable form of political existence
(*Discourses*), as well as a sly adviser to princes, telling them how to
circumvent traditional ethical restraints and pursue their own interests
in the name of *realpolitik* (*The Prince*). Both, in very different ways, can
be seen as republican arguments, the latter because the state is
conceived in instrumental and practical terms amenable to dispassionate
political analysis. Machiavelli's argument in both works is that every
state needs a lawmaker 'who will give it such laws that it will maintain
itself even after his death'.[59] His concern is that the state functions in
the interests of all its inhabitants, which is why he places such
emphasis on the need for a constitution with properly instituted laws as
the best form of government.[60]

If this more inclusive definition of republicanism is allowed, then
Shakespeare's works – especially those written before the death of
Elizabeth – would seem to exhibit an interest in republican themes and
subjects. The emphasis throughout the tragedies and histories is placed
on the virtue and ability of the individual as qualifications for rule,
rather than simply inherited rights, a case I shall make in the first two
chapters of this book. Richard III, Macbeth and Claudius are all deposed
because they are not fit to rule, not simply because they are usurpers or
have a dubious claim to the throne in question. Other rulers do a rather
better job and are more obviously suited to the demands of high office,

Henry IV and to a greater extent Henry V being the obvious examples. But by far the largest category of rulers are presented to us as figures of flawed and limited virtue, whose ultimate worth it is up to us to judge. Henry VI and Richard II are monarchs who have certain personal virtues and charisma but who are not necessarily fit to govern countries (which then leads to the question of who should do so and how). King Lear has apparently been a successful king – though not one who has been particularly attentive to the needs of his humbler subjects – but fails to secure a workable succession (perhaps through the ill luck of having produced three daughters and no son). Leontes in *The Winter's Tale* nearly destroys his kingdom, along with his marriage, through his explosive temper. Prospero has proved a controversial figure: audiences have been unable to decide whether he has learned how to govern wisely on the island after his youthful neglect of Milan, or become a bullying tyrant. Rulers have to rule well, or disasters will follow. Exactly what such insights reveal about Shakespeare's political thought will be explored in this book.

II

Although no one would dispute that Shakespeare's plays and poetry have a political significance and are informed by contemporary political ideas, events and debates, few would be able to state with any confidence exactly what political position Shakespeare adopted. Shakespeare has been appropriated by conservative thinkers as one of their own, most famously in the influential reading of E.M.W. Tillyard, who wrote against the fear of chaos and the disintegration of civilization in the 1930s and 1940s.[61] Tillyard's interpretation of Shakespeare undoubtedly inspired the Chancellor of the Exchequer, Nigel Lawson, when he asserted in an interview that Shakespeare would have voted for the Conservative Party had he been alive in the 1980s, citing Ulysses' famous speech on 'degree' in *Troilus and Cressida* (1.3.75–137) as evidence. Needless to say, Lawson's comments were vigorously contested by academic readers alive to the weaknesses of Ulysses' argument and the ways in which his authority was undermined by events in the play.[62] Shakespeare has been hailed as a proto-democratic figure by some writers with left-wing political persuasions, or, more frequently, berated as a figure guilty of sowing the seeds of the reactionary culture established in subsequent centuries, a reading which neatly inverts that of Lawson.[63]

A more subtle and nuanced reading of Shakespeare's politics by Blair Worden claims that Shakespeare's politics are hard to pin down. Worden argues that it is difficult to relate the known facts of his life to his works. He also points out that there is less explicit interest in political debates and positions in his work than is shown in the writings of contemporary dramatists such as Ben Jonson, Samuel Daniel and George Chapman, or, as Worden has pointed out elsewhere, poets such as Sir Philip Sidney or Edmund Spenser.[64] For Worden, Shakespeare as a writer appears, like Hamlet, keen to 'preserve his mystery'.[65]

Worden's essay is a salutary warning to anyone foolish enough to assume that unravelling the complexities of the relationship between Shakespeare's works and political culture or political belief will be an easy task. One might add a whole host of additional problems to those emphasized by Worden. It is hard to argue that any given work is an exact expression of the author's personal conviction or belief. This problem applies especially to plays written for a professional company, as they had, of course, to be commercially successful and their subject matter had to be selected accordingly.[66] Shakespeare's history plays appear to have been very successful in the 1590s; but was this because their particular message appealed to the audiences who paid to see them, or was it simply the subject matter which provided the attraction?[67] In any case, we do not know how carefully audiences scrutinized plays, a problem which has led to the somewhat questionable assumption that fine speeches were for the educated in the audience and the low, comic scenes and fights for the 'groundlings'. Parallel evidence from court masques is not encouraging: spectators were often unable to hear the lines, were more interested in the spectacular effects than the message (the basis of the quarrel between Ben Jonson and Inigo Jones), and were often too relaxed and refreshed to concentrate on the performance.[68] Apprentices flocked to the theatres, and their rioting caused acute anxiety for the authorities, who closed the playhouses at various points in the 1590s, arguing, occasionally with good reason, that such gatherings could spread the plague. But as Barbara Freedman has pointed out, this was not due to the transgressive nature of the plays staged or the subversive role of the playhouse. Rather, such riots were to be expected when discontented and aggressive young men gathered together where beer was freely available and there were carnivalesque sports on show such as bear baiting.[69] Such evidence is not intended to argue the case that in the newly emerging public theatres developing outside the city walls of London – and so immune from some of the more stringent city regulations – political plays were insignificant in content or design, but simply that reconstructing their political *effect* in the absence of clearly available information is a challenging enterprise.

A further problem is determining exactly what Shakespeare would have read and known. We can safely conclude that he was interested in contemporary political events, given the clear echoes in his plays of recent incidents. A notable reference is the extravagant praise of the Earl of Essex's campaign in Ireland in 1599 and the confident prediction that the Earl would bring 'rebellion broached on his sword' (*Henry V*, 5.0.32) (a dangerous comment in the light of Shakespeare's connections with Essex and a splendid irony given that Essex did return bringing rebellion with him rather than preventing it).[70] It is equally hard to imagine that anyone who wrote *Macbeth* or *Coriolanus* was not aware of current affairs.[71] However, is it safe to assume that Shakespeare would have read political works by such influential continental thinkers as Jean Bodin, Niccolò Machiavelli or Justus Lipsius, or a Huguenot resistance treatise, *Vindicae Contra Tyrannos*? That he would have been versed in contemporary religious debate represented in the Marprelate pamphlets, the disputes over the martyrdom of the Jesuits Edmund Campion and Robert Parsons, or the scandalous Catholic dialogue, *Leicester's Commonwealth*? Or, that he would have carefully scrutinized and compared the different versions of British and classical history proliferating in the 1590s and early 1600s – notably those which made use of the sceptical historical method of

Tacitus, which was so much in vogue that in a poem published in 1616 Ben Jonson was able to satirize the precocious 'Ripe statesmen' who 'carry in their pockets Tacitus', as a key to all political wisdom?[72]

Shakespeare was clearly widely read, and his works demonstrate a grasp of classical works studied at school and later. Virgil, Plutarch, Ovid, Plautus, Terence and Livy are the most frequently cited, and form the basis of plays such as *Titus Andronicus*, *The Comedy of Errors*, *Antony and Cleopatra*, *The Tempest*, *Julius Caesar* and *A Midsummer Night's Dream*.[73] In fact, in *Timon of Athens* and *Titus Andronicus* he altered and adapted Latin and Greek history and literature to form his own works without any clear source, which indicates that he felt comfortable with and well-versed in at least one body of material (if one can assume that Latin and Greek texts can be said to form a coherent and distinct unit). His interest in British history and close reading of Holinshed's *Chronicles* (1577, 1587), the main source for the history plays, further suggests that Shakespeare was likely to have been knowledgeable about developments in history writing in the 1590s and early 1600s.[74] Such a conjecture is supported by the fact that the most Tacitean history of the period, John Hayward's *The Life and Reign of King Henrie IIII* (1599), recounted the same history that Shakespeare himself had dramatized earlier – the deposition of Richard II – in his play, *Richard II* (1595–6).[75] Both works became embroiled in the same dangerous political history, when they were used as justification for the attempted deposition of Elizabeth in the Earl of Essex's rebellion. Hayward's work was called in and suppressed in early 1599, after it had been dedicated to the Earl, the hostility of the authorities only seriously activated when Essex returned from Ireland in disgrace, having failed to quell the rebellion there.[76] Shakespeare's play was performed at the Globe at the request of the Earl's followers on 7 February 1601, the day before he attempted to raise the city of London in rebellion against the Queen.[77] When printed in the quarto of 1597, the play was carefully edited and the deposition scene cut (4.1.150–320), either at the insistence of the censors under John Whitgift, Archbishop of Canterbury, or by the publisher and/or author (see below, pp. 41–2).[78] Elizabeth herself was certainly in no doubt as to the contemporary significance of the play, lamenting to the antiquary, William Lambarde, that it had been 'played forty times in open streets and houses'. She demonstrated that she could read Tacitean history too: 'I am Richard II, know ye not that?'[79] Her secretary of state, Robert Cecil, confirmed the historical analogy: 'he [Essex] would have removed Her Majesty's servants, stepped into her chair, and perhaps treated her like Richard II'.[80]

The point to be made is that circumstantial evidence strongly suggests that Shakespeare could not have been ignorant of developments in the writing of political history and the use of historical parallels, given his own involvement in the events between 1599 and 1601. After all, his fulsome praise of Essex in *Henry V* appeared in print at almost exactly the same time that John Hayward was being aggressively interrogated for the dedication of his work to the Earl. How closely he read works of political history is a matter for conjecture, but three issues should be considered. First, Shakespeare clearly did read some key passages extremely carefully, as the use of Montaigne's essay, 'Of the Cannibals', in Gonzalo's speech in *The Tempest* (2.1.148–69), and the adaptation of an episode in Sidney's *Arcadia* to form the subplot of *King Lear* indicate. We should probably assume that passages in Renaissance works of literature which appear to be informed by political arguments and debates are consciously intended by the author in question, however controversial they might seem to us (although, of course, critics can mistakenly assume that something is there when it is not). Attacks by various characters on the abuse of power in *Macbeth*, a play which raises a series of questions about the legitimate rule of a bad king, demand to be read in terms of debates about the rights of resistance to tyranny, a problem which is also central to *Hamlet*, a work set at the court of an elective monarchy, in which the king has to be chosen rather than assuming the throne as a birthright.[81] The cynicism voiced towards the accumulation of wealth and the pursuit of pointless wars in *Timon of Athens* and *Troilus and Cressida*, respectively, or the hostile representation of a sycophantic and ineffective court in plays such as *Richard III* or *King Lear*, should also be seriously considered as interventions into contemporary politics, and not regarded as simply generated by the demands of the genre. As I hope to establish in this book, Shakespeare's plays contain criticisms of court life and behaviour that cannot simply be dismissed as conventional literary modes or devices. Details establish parallels with contemporary political events and encourage audiences and readers to enter into debates over issues and draw conclusions.[82]

Second, it is well attested that works of political history and theory were widely read in the late 1500s and early 1600s. Gabriel Harvey noted in his letter book for the 1570s and early 1580s the vogue for political works among Cambridge students: 'You can not stepp into a schollars studye but (ten to on) you shall litely finde open either Bodin de Republica or Le Royes Exposition uppon Aristotles Politiques or sum other like French or Italian Politique Discourses.' Harvey continued that 'sum good fellowes amongst us begin nowe to be prettely well acquayntid with a certayne parlous booke callid, as I remember me, Il Principe de Niccolo Machiavelli, and I can peradventure name you an odd crewe or tooe that ar as cuninge in his Discorsi sopra la prima Deca di Livio, in his Historia Fiorentina, and in his Dialogues della Arte della Guerra tooe.'[83] Harvey makes a case for a wide reading in European political theory and history among undergraduates. He also mentions Castiglione's *Il Cortegiano; or, the Courtier*, translated by Sir Thomas Hoby (1556); Stephan Guazzo's *Of Conversation*, translated by George Pettie (1586); French editions of Plutarch (1565, 1572); and Guicciardini's *History of Italy*, translated by Geoffrey Fenton (1579), the first two being important works which explain how a gentleman should behave, and the second two major works of history, which were much in vogue in the second half of the sixteenth century. Shakespeare was never a student at Oxford, Cambridge or the Inns of Court but, given that he lived in London and mixed with writers, courtiers and others who had received a higher education, it is unlikely that he was ignorant of such works. Furthermore, it is a testimony to the popularity of many of the longer works of political and religious history, that translators and writers with an eye on popular taste saw a market for collections of abbreviations and extracts, presumably for those who needed a key to help them copy out maxims into their commonplace books, or for those too busy to read a large folio of 600 or 800 pages. *A Collection of all the notable things in the hystorie of Guichiardinne* was published in 1591, dedicated to Sir Henry Brooke, Lord Cobham; Sir Robert Dallington published *Aphorisimes civill and militarie, amplified with authorities* (1613), which largely consists of extracts from Guicciardini; Henry Holland translated Piscator's abridgement of Calvin's *Institutes* (1596); and Thomas Gainsford published a volume of miscellaneous aphorisms, *The Rich Cabinet furnished with varieties* (1616). Hence readers who did not have enough time to read the most up-to-date works of history, political and military theory and religious doctrine were able to digest their significance in the form of readily available aphorisms.[84]

Analyses of Elizabethan reading practices have shown how readers were often extremely specific in the ways in which they approached texts, using them to extract the precise information they needed, concentrating on key passages to further their particular arguments (some aristocratic readers even paid scholars within their households to underline passages for them to scrutinize later).[85] Most educated readers copied out key extracts that they found especially useful into commonplace books for future use.[86] Abbreviations and collections such as those cited above were clearly designed to facilitate this process, saving readers and writers the trouble of performing the labour themselves. Longer works had sophisticated and carefully compiled indexes, enabling readers to look up and cross-reference points or material they required (examples being both editions of Holinshed's *Chronicles* (1577, 1587); Philemon Holland's translation of Livy, *The Romaine historie: also the breviaries of L. Florus* (1600); and Innocent Gentillet's *A Discourse Upon the Meanes of Wel Governing and Maintaining in Good Peace, a Kingdom, or other Principalitie ... Against Nicholas Machiavell the Florentine*, translated by Simon Patericke (1602)). Erasmus's *Adages* (1508, 1515, translated into English 1539) provided a compendious arrangement of reflections on a range of topics arranged thematically, and *England's Parnassus* (1600) provided a series of extracts from longer poems, also arranged in thematic groups.[87] Even if Shakespeare, a busy working dramatist, had little time to read important long works carefully, he could have accessed them in a more reader-friendly, abbreviated format, or searched out the required passages. In doing so, he would have been a typical rather than an unusual Elizabethan reader.

Third, as I shall attempt to demonstrate throughout this book, other dramatists wrote plays with obvious political purposes. As well as more overtly politically involved writers such as George Chapman, Samuel Daniel and Ben Jonson, mention needs to be made of dramatists such as Thomas Norton and Thomas Sackville, whose well-known play *Gorboduc, or, The Tragedy of Ferrex and Porrex*, arguably the first blank-verse tragedy in English, was produced in 1561 and published in 1565. This play, its plot taken from Geoffrey of Monmouth, shows Britain plunged into chaos after a disastrous civil war, with the royal line extinguished. The pirated edition of 1565 may well have appeared in response to Elizabeth's serious illness in 1563, the first of the succession crises which punctuated her reign and which inspired William Cecil, her chief minister, to draft a bill preparing for a 'vacation and interreigne' in the event of the Queen's death, a move which has been interpreted by some historians as a potentially republican document.[88] *Gorboduc* undoubtedly had an influence on later plays which adapted material from Geoffrey, such as the anonymous *The Tragedy of Locrine* (1595), and *King Lear*.[89] Thomas Kyd's pioneering work *The Spanish Tragedy* (*c.*1589) quite clearly combines a sectarian attack on the Catholic Spanish with a series of reflections on English foreign and domestic policy (it is also significant that Kyd is assumed by many commentators to be the author of a now lost version of *Hamlet*, which pre-dates Shakespeare's). Christopher Marlowe's *The Massacre at Paris* (*c.*1589) combined trenchant comments on the schismatic state of contemporary France with reflections on the problems of establishing stable government; and John Webster's later work, *The Duchess of Malfi* (*c.*1613), represents the corruption of Italian courts, but also reflects on the limitations of English political culture, specifically through the parallels made between the fictional life of the heroine and the real life of Arbella Stuart (1575–1615), a reluctant Stuart claimant to the throne, whose birth cost her dear.[90]

The Tudor and Stuart commercial theatre in which Shakespeare worked from the late 1580s onwards performed plays that were frequently concerned with political events. These were represented allegorically through the use of historical material drawn from English history, foreign settings – often Italian – or plots drawn from contemporary romances. Arguably, the theatre existed as a particular location or public space where political debates, commentary and allusion could be made by those who were excluded from the ordinary processes of political life. Texts for theatrical performances, which did come under careful scrutiny and control from the Master of the Revels in this period, were rarely heavily censored before they were produced on stage.[91] If a play offended enough influential and important people it would be closed down, the most notorious case being Thomas Middleton's *A Game at Chess* (1624), which satirically represented the current marriage negotiations with the Spanish, depicting the hated Spanish ambassador, the Count of Gondomar, as the evil Black Knight. After nine successive performances at the Globe theatre, a large number for the time, the play was prohibited and a warrant issued for Middleton's arrest.[92]

This is not to deny that there was significant – albeit limited – censorship of plays, often on political grounds, intervention which, in Janet Clare's words, 'could not have failed to interact with the creativity of practising dramatists and to have induced degrees of compromise, ambiguity and re-presentation of material'.[93] But it is now clear that many apparently problematic works, clearly hostile to the current policy of the crown, the general behaviour of important courtiers, the possibility of foreign alliances that many felt might undermine English independence and sovereignty, or even the unformulated and chaotic state of the political structures in England, were licensed and performed in the public theatres, as long as what they represented did not influence current events or trespass too closely on what was felt to be the prerogative of the monarch (such as Elizabeth's marriage plans, the Essex Rebellion, or important negotiations with other European powers).[94]

Political debate took place constantly in and around Shakespeare's London, and nowhere more so than in the variety of public performances on display. Court entertainments and masques were often aggressively polemical, trying to influence the behaviour of the monarch, and not simply excuses for lavish sycophancy as has all too often been assumed. For example, Sir Philip Sidney's entertainment, *The Lady of May* (*c*.1578), was an elaborate but hardly subtle attempt to persuade Elizabeth to marry Sidney's uncle, the Earl of Leicester; George Chapman's *The Memorable Masque* (1613), which emphasizes the wealth to be obtained from the Americas, appears to have been written as a defence of Chapman's friend, Sir Walter Raleigh, then languishing in the Tower of London and keen to get a last chance to find the fabled city of El Dorado in Guiana; and Ben Jonson's *Pleasure Reconciled to Virtue* (1617), was designed as a strenuous critique of the excesses of court spending.[95] From the 1560s onwards, plays performed at court, in public theatres and at the Inns of Court, commented, albeit often obliquely, on the Queen's marriage plans and her provision for the succession.[96] Some of Shakespeare's plays, notably *Macbeth*, *Measure for Measure* and *King Lear*, were performed at court as well as in the commercial theatres, when James I made his company, the Lord Chamberlain's Men, into the King's Men, a fact which does not appear to have drastically altered their content or significance. Furthermore, as Peter McCullough has recently argued, sermons preached at court throughout the reigns of Elizabeth and James were often explicitly critical of the monarch's religious policies, the divine in question seeing it as his duty to lecture the monarch on the ways and means of godly policy. This led to Elizabeth frequently losing patience with her ministers when they tried to foist a more radical Protestant agenda on her against her will and judgement. James was often in opposition to his more militantly Protestant son, Prince Henry, and courtly audiences would receive very different messages from the pulpits of the King and of his heir.[97]

Political decisions were generally made by a very small group of people. Parliaments did not meet frequently – in fact, they were summoned less often in the reigns of Elizabeth and James than they had been in the later Middle Ages.[98] As David Womersley has argued, 'in the late sixteenth century there was no domain of politics . . . the sphere of significant political life was contracted to the Court, from which information . . . might seep out to its satellites: the Inns of Court, the universities, the major religious centres of Lambeth, Canterbury, and

York, the provincial administration surrounding the Lord-Lieutenants'.[99] However, it is quite clear that by the second half of Elizabeth's reign, from 1580 onwards, increasing numbers of articulate citizens were becoming disenchanted with this state of affairs, felt that it was wrong that they were excluded from the political processes, and were prepared to criticize existing institutions, often casting an envious glance at those of other nations and city states past and present: Venice, republican Rome, Switzerland and ancient Greece being key examples.[100] Much criticism was contained in historical writing and literary works, including drama, which, in Mark Thornton Burnett's words, 'discharged a range of functions, both permitting a critical undercurrent to express itself and providing a forum within which contemporary anxieties were granted their most forceful and enduring statement'.[101] In the 1590s, when Shakespeare was first writing poetry and drama for performance and publication, there was considerable disquiet and vocal opposition to the regime, culminating in the Essex Rebellion.[102] Of course it would be naïve to suggest that the main bone of contention was the constitution itself or that political considerations lay behind all the unrest. The failure of consecutive harvests and resulting hunger, poor social conditions and religious opposition were significant factors too.[103] It would also be wrong to deny that Essex himself undoubtedly wished the outcome to be a restoration of the power of great magnates such as himself rather than forcing the Queen to implement a radical constitution.[104]

Nevertheless, questions of the constitution, political rights and representation assumed an increasing importance just at the time that Shakespeare was writing his first works.

> Writers became fascinated in and after 1591 by the themes
> of kingship, authority, and the acquisition of and retention of
> power, particularly in relation to humanist-classical definitions
> of 'virtue' in its civic and military aspects. The role of 'counsel'
> and 'counselling' in monarchies and republics, and the endemic
> problems of corruption and dissimulation, were put under the
> lens. The aim was to explain how 'vice', 'flattery' and 'ambition'

had to come to supersede the traditional values of 'wisdom', 'service' and *respublica*.[105]

Once James had ascended to the throne this critical impetus continued, inspired partly by nervousness at the advent of a new regime, and partly through a questioning of and opposition to James's theories of the divine right of kings.[106] Numerous types of work explore these questions and problems: histories such as Sir John Hayward's *The First Part of the Life and Raigne of Henrie IIII* (1599); works of travel writing such as Sir Robert Dallington's *The View of France* (1604) and *The Survey of the Great Dukes State of Tuscany* (1605), Fynes Moryson's *Itinerary* (1617) and Thomas Coryat's *Coryat's Crudities* (1611); translations such as Lewis Lewkenor's adaptation of Gasparo Contarini's *The Commonwealth and Government of Venice* (1599) and Edward Grimstone's rendition of Pierre d'Avity's *The Estates, Empires and Principalities of the World* (1615); as well as such major literary and dramatic works as Philip Sidney's *Arcadia* (first published in 1590), Edmund Spenser's *The Faerie Queene* (1590, 1596) and Christopher Marlowe's *Edward II* (1592).[107] Shakespeare's works need to be read in terms of this intellectual climate, and many of them, principally tragedies and histories, are clearly embroiled in the discussions and events of the 1590s and early 1600s.

The key debate, as I have already noted, centred on the question of the monarch's status and right to rule. It was generally agreed that the monarch ruled as sovereign through their authority as king or queen in parliament. But different emphases could be given to this constitutional position. Did the ruler have to rule in accordance with the dictates and conclusions reached in parliament, with the king or queen merely able to advise in their capacity as ruler but possessing no clear veto? Or, as Elizabeth and James argued, was parliament simply a body which could advise the monarch, who was obliged to listen but not necessarily to take heed of the counsel offered them? Parliament may have met infrequently in late Tudor and early Stuart times, and the centre of real power may have been the court and royal councils, but the significance of the debates it staged can be underestimated. A notable event occurred when a vocal puritan member of parliament, Peter Wentworth, made the case in the 1593 parliament that members should be accorded freedom of speech because they constituted the body that should really govern the land. Wentworth posed a series of ten questions to the house, asking, among other things, 'whether the Prince and state cann be mainteyned without this court of parliament', and whether it were actually lawful for the ruler to 'check, blame or punishe' any member of the house 'for any speache used in this place, except it be for trayterous wourds'.[108] Probably relatively few influential people supported Wentworth's stand, and he was imprisoned for his pains, but he exposed what was clearly a problematic and uneasy compromise. His intervention may not have featured very significantly in Shakespeare's consciousness or sphere of reference, but the fact that such a serious debate concerning the importance of parliament and the authority of the monarch occurred just before the second tetralogy was performed on stage (1595–9), is surely relevant. The four plays – *Richard II, 1 Henry IV, 2 Henry IV* and *Henry V* – which make up the sequence, debate and analyse the questions of sovereignty, legitimacy, the role of advisers and the status of established institutions, all issues raised by Wentworth's parliamentary intervention, making his words and actions a legitimate context for reading Shakespeare's works.

The problem of what subjects could and could not debate was related to the question of the legitimacy of the monarchy and how it derived its authority, an unavoidable issue since Henry VIII inaugurated the Reformation in England. Shakespeare lived through an unsettled and unstable era of English history, when it was generally accepted that rival factions would use the expanding medium of print culture to argue their case.[109] It was common practice also that works of literature would comment on political issues and events as part of these debates.[110] As I have already stated, the Tudors were never a securely established dynasty despite what has frequently been asserted about the 'golden age' of Elizabeth.[111] Although the brief reigns of Edward and Mary were not as disastrous as they have popularly been portrayed, each was beset by a number of major economic, political and social problems.[112] Most importantly, the two monarchs pursued diametrically opposed religious policies. Edward and his advisers attempted to inaugurate a Protestant revolution which, had it been carried through, would have transferred a great deal of political power to government institutions and reduced the church's ability to influence secular policy.[113] Mary sought to reverse this process, to return England to the papal fold and establish a heavily centralized state that could control the political and religious obedience of its subjects.[114] While Edward tried to sever all links with Rome and the major Catholic power in Europe, Spain, Mary sought to re-establish these ties, marrying Philip II (1554) in the hope of establishing a new Anglo-Spanish dynasty through issue which never came. Edward had to suppress two serious rebellions, Mary one.[115]

Elizabeth's accession, while relatively unproblematic, was not uncontested. Catholics had never accepted that Henry VIII's marriage to Catherine of Aragon had been properly annulled, as his wishes had not been granted papal sanction. Elizabeth was, therefore, illegitimate, and the throne should have passed to Mary Queen of Scots, who was also descended from Henry VII. This claim was announced by Henri II of France on Mary Tudor's death (17 November 1558), and formed the basis for the series of plots against Elizabeth throughout her reign.[116] Mary Queen of Scots was to prove a serious and troubling threat to Elizabeth, even after she was captured and held under house arrest at various locations in England, having fled Scotland in 1568. Elizabeth was left with the dilemma of whether to tolerate Mary's existence and so leave her as the focus for attempts to overthrow English Protestantism, or to risk the wrath of her fellow monarchs and have Mary executed as her more staunchly Protestant advisers desired. After the Babington plot in 1587, in which Mary was heavily implicated, Elizabeth reluctantly signed Mary's death warrant and she was executed on 8 February 1587.

But the execution of her chief rival solved little in terms of quashing speculation and making Elizabeth more secure. Elizabeth had successfully managed not to be seen to surrender English sovereignty to a foreign power (as her sister had done), and avoided favouring a particular faction within England by refusing all the marriage proposals and matches offered her. Opinion is divided as to whether she skilfully negotiated her way through a series of problems that could never be resolved harmoniously, and so kept her realm as stable as it could possibly be in difficult circumstances, or whether, as many of her more impatient subjects argued, she vacillated and dithered, preserving her virginity at the cost of her people's safety and happiness, and leaving them with no successor at her death.[117] By the time that Mary was executed, it was already likely that the Stuarts would accede to the English throne, either through James VI of Scotland, Mary Stuart's son, or, less plausibly, through his young cousin, Arbella Stuart.[118] Furthermore, the demands for Mary to be executed, which culminated in the Bond of Association (1584)

> enabled godly Englishmen from the ranks of the political nation to declare their allegiance to the commonwealth, on the queen's behalf and against her will. It encouraged political action that might extend to the assassination of a ruler judged – by the regime but not the queen – to be ungodly ... It called up the political *virtù* of godly Englishmen: their ability to act in a military capacity, as individual men and as members of the commonwealth, to preserve their own and other men's liberty, simultaneously religious and political.[119]

A political culture and language was developing which made a clear separation between the Queen as a ruler in person, and her role within the constitution. It was possible that subjects knew how to govern better than the monarch.[120]

Elizabeth was in a problematic position as queen, through her often-contested claim to the throne, through the problems precipitated by the short, troublesome reigns of her predecessors, and through her difficulties in securing the succession. It is little wonder that political issues featured largely in the minds of her subjects. Equally, it is hardly surprising that they continued to do so once James had assumed the throne, given the reputation of his mother in England, and the common image of Scotland as a divided and barbaric country, always beset by civil war.[121] And it is no exaggeration to claim that nearly all of Shakespeare's plays that deal with the question of kingship are centred

FIGURE 2 Queen Elizabeth I by an anonymous artist. This painting, now thought to have been painted in the early years of James's reign, shows how heavily the prospect of the Queen's death weighed on her and her subjects.

on problems of legitimacy and the succession. The first tetralogy (1589–94?) represents the course of the Wars of the Roses from the rapid disintegration of Henry V's triumph in France up to the establishment of the Tudor regime by the relatively uninspiring Henry VII (who does not feature as monarch in Shakespeare's sequence, although he does appear on stage in John Ford's late history play, *Perkin Warbeck* (1633)).[122]

The second tetralogy chronicles the deposition of Richard II, the painful and divided reign of Henry IV, and the controversial triumph of Henry V who, like his father, is always conscious that his claim to authority is dubious. Many plays – histories, tragedies and comedies – written before and after the accession of James confront similar issues. *Julius Caesar* (1599) is concerned with the rights and wrongs of rebellion against a charismatic potential dictator; *Hamlet* (1600–1) is set at the court of an elective monarchy at war with its neighbours, where the current king has murdered his predecessor; *Measure for Measure* (1602–3) imagines the issues presented when the legitimate ruler of a city state hands over the reins of power to a deputy in order to study his realm as a secret observer; *King Lear* (1605–6), concerns the disastrous attempt of one of Shakespeare's most powerful kings, who has united and pacified Britain, to secure the succession on his own terms;[123] *Macbeth* (1605–6) deals with the problems of re-establishing legitimate government after the reign of a bloody usurper, and directly confronts the question of what gives a monarch his authority. The list could be continued – it would have to include at least seven more plays, making a total of twenty, or more than half Shakespeare's plays.

No work of Shakespeare's deals as directly with the reign of either Elizabeth or James as Thomas Heywood's two-part *If You Know Not Me You Know Nobody, or, The Troubles of Queen Elizabeth* (1605). The first of these two plays, which must have been written after Elizabeth's death, shows her troubled accession, and the second, her triumph over the Armada.[124] Nevertheless, Shakespeare's plays are full of contemporary references which anchor them in the present and demand that playgoers and readers consider them in terms of current political issues. *Henry V* directly alludes to the rebellion of Hugh O'Neill, Earl of Tyrone, against the English crown in Ireland in the Nine Years' War, then about to reach its climax.[125] As is well known, in the folio Queen Isabel refers to Henry as 'brother Ireland' not 'brother England'. The editorial slip suggests that the play is as much about Ireland as it is about France.[126] The prophecies of the witches in *Macbeth* make reference to James's inheritance of the English throne via his descent from the murdered Banquo. The play also refers directly to a number of James's obsessions (the divine right of kings, witchcraft and the ability of the king to cure the 'king's evil' or scrofula).[127] The 'Mousetrap' play in *Hamlet* can be read as a retelling of Mary Stuart's alleged murder of her second husband, Lord Darnley.[128] *The Tempest* stages a series of issues relating to the question of the monarch's authority, from Gonzalo's pious meditation on governing the island (cynically undermined by Sebastian and Antonio), to Prospero's transfer of his power at the end of the play. It represents or alludes to dynastic matches and *realpolitik* in a European context, specifically the proposed marriage between Prince Charles and the Spanish infanta, plantation and colonization in Ireland and the Americas, and political repression in England.[129]

While it is easy to show, however, that many of his plays deal with such central political questions, it is hard to pinpoint exactly where Shakespeare's sympathies or political vision lay. He was undoubtedly influenced by the intellectual trends of the 1590s. His works appear to be indebted to the numerous attempts made in that decade to study history, politics and society in the detached and relatively objective manner pioneered by thinkers such as Lipsius, Montaigne, Livy and Tacitus, as well as their English disciples such as Francis Bacon and Sir John Hayward.[130] It would not be stretching a point to describe a number of Shakespeare's plays as 'Tacitean', in that they examine the merits and flaws of statesmen and rulers in the same way that Tacitus analysed the virtues and sins of Tiberius, Claudius, Vespasian and, most memorably, Nero, all in accounts translated into English in the 1590s. Tacitus was regarded throughout Europe as the most dispassionate of historians, whose work combined moral insight into the behaviour of political actors with an assessment of their value as governors. His histories were seen by some as exposures of the vices of the mighty and by others as warnings showing the powerful how to avoid the errors of their predecessors.[131] An anonymous play published in 1607, *The Tragedie of Claudius Tiberius Nero, Romes Greatest Tyrant*, makes use of Tacitus' account of Tiberius' reign as emperor in the first part of the *Annals*, which had been translated into English in 1598. Tacitus is referred to in the dedication to Arthur Mannering, one of Prince Henry's retinue, as 'our best approved historian'. The play indicates the importance of Tacitus for writers in the years before and after the accession of James, and it can be read in either of the ways suggested above.[132]

I shall explore this way of reading Shakespeare's works in the first chapter of this book.[133] The parts of *Edward III* which were definitely written by Shakespeare contain a devastating portrait of a king whose judgement and ability to rule are deformed by his inability to overcome his lust, a portrait that recalls Tacitus' account of the decline of Tiberius, as well as resembling the representation of Edward IV in *3 Henry VI*.[134] A more cynical work, *Troilus and Cressida* (1601–2), appears to reduce the course of the Trojan War to an argument over a 'whore and a cuckold', if we take the voice of the railing Thersites as the key to the play. Perhaps the most fully sustained example of all is Shakespeare's portrait of Henry V, a controversial figure still, who divides readers, playgoers and critics, some seeing him as a patriotic hero, others as a ruthless hypocrite.[135] In all these works the audience or reader is asked to sit in judgement on the action as it takes place, a process that parallels Tacitus' detached analysis of politics.

Other plays appear to go out of their way to present a sceptical and impartial analysis of historical events.[136] *Julius Caesar*, for example, exposes the weaknesses of Caesar, making it clear to the audience why his opponents resent what they see as his tyranny and usurpation of power. However, the play also points out the naïvety of Brutus, implying that although he may be a good man, he is an ineffective leader, with a weak grasp of the realities of popular politics. He makes two serious errors immediately after the assassination of Caesar: first, in having the conspirators wash their hands in the dead ruler's blood as a symbol of 'Peace, Freedom and Liberty' (3.1.110) (a detail added by Shakespeare), and second, in granting Mark Antony the right to deliver Caesar's funeral oration. Mark Antony does not emerge from the play with any more credit than Brutus or Caesar, given his complacent reaction to the violence he unleashes through his words: 'Now let it work. Mischief, thou art afoot: / Take thou what course thou wilt' (3.2.251–2). In the following scene we witness the brutal murder of Cinna the poet, mistaken for the conspirator of the same name, an example of the wretched fate of innocent writers trapped in the violent course of history. *Coriolanus* (1607–8) can be read as an equally dispassionate work. Coriolanus and his family adhere to an outdated, militaristic, aristocratic code of honour, a code that had been revived in late Elizabethan England.[137] While such beliefs enable them to defend Rome effectively from their enemies, they also isolate the patricians as an arrogant oligarchy at odds with the needs and desires of the mass of plebeians. At the same time, however, the plebeians are shown to be foolish and ignorant, easily swayed by the self-interested tribunes, Sicinius and Brutus. The key image of the play is undoubtedly Menenius's 'fable of the belly' (1.1.95–162), a political allegory that can be read in a variety of ways, and not necessarily as it is interpreted in the play.[138]

Such evidence, while it suggests that we cannot read Shakespeare's works as relatively simple expressions of belief in a providential world order, do not necessarily indicate that Shakespeare was critical enough of the status quo to provide an alternative vision. The 'new' humanism of the 1590s could be used to support or attack existing institutions; 'Tacitism' did not commit the historian or political commentator to a radical position, merely to observing that powerful rulers often failed to live up to the proper standards demanded by public life.[139] A powerful recent interpretation of the history plays argues that Shakespeare was in favour of a strong leader to unite the factions struggling for political control throughout Britain, placing little stress on the legitimate claim of the monarch in question and emphasizing instead the ruler's personal abilities and charisma. According to this view, Shakespeare opposed the claims of James VI of Scotland in his Elizabethan plays, but once James had shown himself to be a competent king, ceased to argue a case that might cause more harm than good.[140] Another argues that it would be surprising to find 'a Renaissance dramatist questioning the institution of monarchy', because although 'there was admiration for classical (and aristocratic) republican virtue', there was 'no suggestion that England could or should become a republic'.[141]

The question which needs to be asked is: does Shakespeare represent historically or geographically different forms of government in such a way as to suggest that they offer benefits that are not experienced by the inhabitants of England living under a hereditary monarchy? His works certainly demonstrate an interest in a variety of systems of government, even if they do not necessarily represent all of them with obvious approval. *Hamlet* represents an elective monarchy, and *King Lear* portrays a regime where the king decides who succeeds him. *Othello* and *The Merchant of Venice* are set in Venice, the former play showing a considerable interest in and knowledge of the republican constitution of the city.[142] *Coriolanus* is set in republican Rome and also shows considerable interest in the constitutional issues raised there.[143] *Titus Andronicus*, the one Roman play that has no clear and obvious source, also dramatizes a conflict between patrician rulers and the popular voice that could be construed as republican. The same might be said of *The Rape of Lucrece*.[144] Shakespeare was of course not alone in employing foreign settings in his plays and relating them to contemporary England. The stock setting for many Jacobean plays was a corrupt Italian city state which could stand as a version of a vaguely defined English court, as works by John Webster, Thomas Middleton and Cyril Tourneur demonstrate.[145] No other contemporary dramatist, however, explored the meaning and significance of such a wide variety of political and social systems, or established such a carefully nuanced relationship between examining alternative constitutions in their own right, and reading them in terms of English or British politics.

One final point needs to be considered when analysing Shakespeare's representation of politics. Were the plays only ever seen on stage by an audience or were they read as texts as well? Obviously, more people experienced the plays on stage as a spectacle than read them. The most recent estimate suggests that approximately 15,000 people went to the theatre weekly in London in 1595, out of a population of *c*.200,000, and that the figure had risen to 25,000 out of a population of 400,000 in 1625.[146] It is clear that Shakespeare's plays did also reach a reading public, first as quartos and later in the folio of 1623, which suggests that certain key political points may have assumed an added significance when they were accessed through the medium of the printed word.[147] It is possible that the deposition scene may have been omitted from the quarto of *Richard II* to prevent its circulation in print, and that it was actually performed on stage. After all, another printed book, Hayward's *Life and Raigne of King Henrie the IIII*, which also told the story of Richard's deposition, was called in by the authorities when it was read as an attack on Elizabeth's right to rule (see above, pp. 15–16).[148]

Why were plays printed? As literature they had little status until the publication in folio of Ben Jonson's *Works* in 1616, which collected together all his plays, masques and verse, presenting every item as of equal literary value.[149] The First Folio of *Mr. William Shakespeare's Comedies, Histories & Tragedies* followed in 1623. It used to be assumed that plays were published because the booksellers found them highly profitable, but this now seems implausible. As Peter Blayney has pointed out, plays made up a tiny part of the book trade in the second half of Elizabeth's reign. Most years saw the publication of between three and five plays, so that Shakespeare's plays made up a substantial proportion of those published. The two peak times were December 1593–May 1595 and May 1600–October 1601, when twenty-seven plays were published in each period. The first occurred when theatres were closed because of the fear of the spread of plague; the second is probably connected with a Privy Council order (22 June 1600) that the number of plays performed and the number of theatres in existence had to be restricted. The plays were undoubtedly issued as a form of advertising to persuade audiences to see them in the theatre, when that was possible.[150] As drama acquired a higher status as literature, so more plays were printed and read.

It is evident that a sizable audience existed for printed plays. It is notable that three of the best-selling of Shakespeare's printed plays from the 1590s were history plays: the quartos of *1 Henry IV* (1598: seven editions in twenty-five years); *Richard III* (1597: five editions in twenty-five years); and *Richard II* (1597: five editions in twenty-five years) (although it should be noted that *Venus and Adonis* went through eleven editions in the same period).[151] Greg Walker's research into the print runs for plays in the first half of the sixteenth century suggests that the run could be as high as 500–600 copies.[152] Assuming that later print runs were of a similar number, this suggests that many readers were keen to study material they had seen on stage, and also that there was a market among those who had not seen the play in performance. We can reasonably assume that printed playtexts were read carefully by a number of readers, a practice that became more widespread as the seventeenth century advanced.[153]

In this book I want to make the case that Shakespeare's analysis of politics ranged in two directions. He looked towards Europe and European thinkers' re-use of their classical political legacy. These included supporters of republican and absolutist forms of government, as well as proponents of a more 'mixed' constitution. Equally, he explored the English and British past, not simply to study examples from the wealth of chronicles available, but also to re-activate native traditions of counsel, advice and the influence of advisory bodies (principally parliament).[154] A monarch was frequently reminded by dramatists of his or her duties to the people, a tradition of political literature that was modified and expanded by the advent of the commercial theatre.[155]

Often political references in dramatic works amount to little more than a series of allusions to contemporary events, as might be expected. But just as often such references lead on to more sustained analysis of contemporary political issues and problems, indicating that dramatists had a clear interest in politics and realized that many in the audience would share their concerns. For example, Elizabeth's projected marriage to the Duke of Alençon in the late 1570s and early 1580s had a decisive impact on how writers discussed the interrelated problems of the rights of subjects and the question of the succession, notably in the works of John Lyly and Thomas Kyd, both of whom significantly influenced Shakespeare.[156] The same applies to the events of the protracted war with Spain from the 1580s to the early 1600s, which clearly had a decisive bearing on questions of sovereignty and national identity, and to the interrelated issues of religious denominations, schisms and toleration, which can be seen in the works of dramatists as diverse as Anthony Munday, Robert Greene, George Peele and Ben Jonson, as well as Shakespeare.[157]

In the chapters that follow I shall explore the use Shakespeare made of the legacy of political thought at his disposal, and how he used what

Chapter One

TRUE AND FALSE
SOVEREIGNS IN THE
ENGLISH HISTORY PLAYS

'Yet looks he like a king'

After he has just returned from his campaign in Ireland to face the rebellion that will soon overthrow him, Richard II salutes the ground of his native England and asserts that the forces of nature will preserve his legitimate rule:

> This earth shall have a feeling, and these stones
> Prove armed soldiers, ere her native king
> Shall falter under foul rebellion's arms ...
> Not all the water in the rough rude sea
> Can wash the balm off from an anointed king[.]
>
> *(Richard II*, 3.2.24–6, 54–5)

The lines are, of course, deeply ironic, not simply in the context of the play itself, but in terms of English history, recent as well as that of the fourteenth century. Richard is deposed by Bolingbroke, who becomes Henry IV despite the weakness of his claim to the throne, something he frequently admits after Richard's death. The sea and the land do not protect Richard, whose human qualities are emphasized in the two acts after his imprisonment and deposition.[1]

Richard is the only monarch represented in the cycle of eight plays that make up the first and second tetralogies who actually has a strong claim to be king of England. Henry IV is a self-confessed usurper,

FIGURE 3 The famous image of Richard in the Wilton Diptych (1392–5) suggests that Richard is a saintly and divine ruler. However, he had already offended a number of powerful nobles and was deposed and murdered soon after this was painted.

leaving his son, Henry V, with an equally problematic claim to the throne. After the murder of Richard, Henry IV promises to 'make a voyage to the Holy Land, / To wash this blood off from my guilty hand' (*Richard II*, 5.6.49–50), but he dies without undertaking this pilgrimage, repeating his recognition of his guilt to the future king: 'God knows, my son, / By what by-paths and indirect crook'd ways / I met this crown' (*2 Henry IV*, 4.5.183–5). His son, immediately after his reflections on the duties and nature of kingship before the Battle of Agincourt, when he seems most like the fallible, human Richard alone in his prison cell, reminds himself of his guilty debts to the murdered king:

> I Richard's body have interred new,
> And on it have bestowed more contrite tears
> Than from it issued forced drops of blood.
> Five hundred poor I have in yearly pay,
> Who twice a day their withered hands hold up
> Toward heaven to pardon blood; and I have built
> Two chantries, where the sad and solemn priests
> Sing still for Richard's soul. More will I do,
> Though all that I can do is nothing worth,
> Since that my penitence comes after all,
> Imploring pardon.
>
> (*Henry V*, 4.1.292–302)

At a crucial juncture in the play the audience is pointedly reminded on what unstable foundations the dynasty stands. The Bishop of Carlisle, on hearing of Richard's deposition, had prophesied that 'The blood of English shall manure the ground, / And future ages groan for this foul act' (*Richard II*, 4.1.138–9), a prediction that comes all too horribly true with the advent of the reign of the meek Henry VI and the subsequent Wars of the Roses. Like his father and his grandfather, Henry VI has to admit that his claim to the throne is insecure, and he is forced to concede that the logic of his possession of the crown enables Warwick to oblige him to name Richard Plantagenet, Duke of York, as his successor. In fact, Henry is only able to remain king because he accepts York's demand that he disinherit his own son and name Richard in his place (*1 Henry VI*, 1.1.124–90).

Edward IV has the same complicated claim as his father, Richard, Duke of York, claims that sixteenth-century chronicles invariably confused.[2] York makes his, which he asserts is 'infallible', to the Earls of Salisbury and Warwick, in *2 Henry VI*. He is descended from Edward III's third son, the Duke of Clarence, whose daughter married the Earl of March, Edmund Mortimer, and whose grandson, another Edmund Mortimer, 'laid claim unto the crown', but was imprisoned by Owen Glendower. His sister, Anne, married Richard, Earl of Cambridge, grandson of Edward III, and in York's own words:

> she was heir
> To Roger, Earl of March, who was the son
> Of Edmund Mortimer, who married Philippe,
> Sole daughter unto Lionel, Duke of Clarence.
> So, if the issue of the elder son
> Succeed before the younger, I am king.
>
> (*2 Henry VI*, 2.2.48–52)

Warwick, represented in the first tetralogy as an opportunist with more interest in self-promotion than questions of rights, obligations and duties, is persuaded by York's logic and responds with a rhetorical question: 'What plain proceeding is more plain than this?' (53).

York's claim, taken back several generations, is essentially that his line is descended from an older son of Edward III than Henry VI: the third son rather than the fourth, as Warwick neatly summarizes in the next two lines.[3] Dramatically, York's convoluted articulation of his rights indicates how much is at stake over such slender differences, ones that eventually create more problems than they solve. York himself is cast as a Machiavel, cunning, self-interested and scheming, and while he dies before he can seize the throne, his sons, Edward IV and Richard III, both reign briefly, the latter taking over his father's mantle as the stage villain.[4] Elsewhere in the play, York confesses his designs to the audience and shows that the other nobles have much to fear from him:

> My brain, more busy than the labouring spider,
> Weaves tedious snares to trap mine enemies ...
> I fear me you but warm the starved snake
> Who, cherished in your breasts, will sting your hearts.
>
> (2 *Henry VI*, 3.1.338–9, 342–3)

York's words prefigure the more brilliant and compelling rhetorical manoeuvres of his younger son, Richard. Edward and Richard, like their father, possess a claim to rule England that is insubstantial and can succeed only through military might and subtle manipulation. The nemesis of the York dynasty is the Earl of Richmond, later to be Henry VII, whose claim to the throne is through his mother, Margaret Beaufort, another descendant of John of Gaunt, the fourth son of Edward III. He completes the cycle of English kings after Richard II up to the advent of the Tudors, all of whom have weak or flawed claims to the throne.[5]

In short, Shakespeare's history plays written in the 1590s represent only one 'anointed king', Richard II, and he is deposed despite his faith in his status. (King John, despite having had a plausible claim to the throne, is constantly referred to as a usurper in a play obsessed with illegitimacy.)[6] This stubborn reality of English history, reproduced faithfully from Shakespeare's sources, Edward Hall's *The Union of the Two Noble and Illustre Famelies of Lancastre & Yorke* (1548), Raphael Holinshed's *Chronicles of England, Scotland and Ireland* (1577, 1587), Samuel Daniel's *The First Fowre Bookes of the civile warres betweene the two houses of Lancaster and Yorke* (1595) and *A Mirror for Magistrates* (1559, 1563, 1578, 1587), does not simply haunt the surviving records of the reigns of English kings, but was also directly related to the situation of the incumbent monarch, Elizabeth I. Elizabeth was the granddaughter of Henry VII, and so her claim was arguably as problematic as that of Henry VI, even though her grandfather claimed to unite the Houses of York and Lancaster and so end the bloody civil wars.[7] She had been declared illegitimate in her childhood in an attempt to prevent her from becoming queen when her mother, Anne Boleyn, was executed as a traitor after failing to produce a son.[8] When she assumed the throne, parliament was forced to declare her legitimate as a result of an unrepealed act from her sister's reign that had labelled her a bastard. Later, the Pope, in his papal bull of February 1570, granted her Catholic subjects the right to depose her, with violence if necessary. Furthermore, her most serious rival to the throne, Mary Queen of Scots, had been declared queen in France on Mary I's death in 1558, and Catholic Europe recognized her as the legitimate English queen.[9]

In the 1590s Shakespeare wrote ten plays – some of them in collaboration with other writers – based on English history, part of an expanding genre in that decade, and he produced only one later (*Henry VIII*, 1612–13). All of these, apart from one – *Edward III* (1592–3)[10] – used material from Edward Hall's *Chronicle*, which surveyed the reigns of Richard II to Henry VII, 'the period most dealt with in the literature of the time'.[11] Given Elizabeth's advanced age (she was fifty-seven in 1590), her contested claim to the throne, and the fact that, in the absence of an heir, the crown would in all likelihood be passed to the Stuarts, who had earlier been excluded by various acts of parliament for their Catholicism, it is little wonder that plays dealing with English history should prove so popular with a theatre public.[12] Nearly fifty history plays were composed between 1579 and 1606, and only seventeen more before 1650.[13] Once James had become king in 1603, English history plays, while still a major force on the stage, ceased to have such a central ideological importance.[14] Equally, it is easy to see why Elizabeth and her advisers were so wary of history plays. Shakespeare's *Richard II* appeared without the deposition scene, where Richard hands his crown over to Bolingbroke to make him Henry IV. The early quartos did not have the lines from the Earl of Northumberland's accusation that the Bishop of Carlisle's support for Richard amounts to treason (4.1.150–4), to Richard's jibe that Bolingbroke's supporters 'rise thus nimbly by a true king's fall' (318). The play was evidently popular, two editions appearing in 1597 and a further one in 1598. The 1608 quarto advertised itself as a restoration of the original performance text, indicating that the early quartos that appeared without the deposition scene could have been censored, given the sensitive subject matter of the material omitted: 'The Tragedie of

King Richard the Second: With new additions of the Parliament Sceane, and the deposing of King Richard, As it hath been lately acted by the Kinges Majesties servantes, at the Globe.'[15] Furthermore, as I have already noted, it was probably Shakespeare's play that was performed the day before the Essex Rebellion (see above, pp. 15–16).

Nobody writing in the 1590s could have had an unproblematic faith in the Tudors as a legitimate dynasty chosen by God to rule England; which, of course, is not to argue that many did not support the regime or had no belief in the need for the monarchy. The sacred aspects of Tudor kingship and the mystical symbolism surrounding the anointed monarch cannot be ignored. A whole array of potent symbols was created by artists, poets and other propagandists who were patronized by the crown, showing that the king or queen was the chosen deputy of God on earth.[16] Nevertheless it is hard to read a lot of this material as if it were simply the expression of generally accepted beliefs. As many historians have suggested, it is difficult to see much of it serving as successful propaganda, because too few people would get to see the paintings or read the books in question.[17] Moreover, as Machiavelli famously suggested, religion could be used in an instrumental way to try and manipulate people into accepting the legitimate authority, however dubious, of the ruling class. Tudor propagandists were not slow to realize the benefits of such advice, indicating that, for all the close links between religion and politics in the sixteenth century, political ideas could not be reduced simply to their religious significance.[18] In the seventeenth century the gap widened still further, even though the spread of printing meant that religious pamphlets proliferated.[19] More importantly still, religious ideas and doctrine often helped to foster opposition to the crown as much as obedience.[20] Shakespeare's history plays, along with many other Tudor and Stuart literary and historical texts, represent people making their own history, even if it is not always as they would please.

A work often cited by critics as though it were a statement of a general faith in the existing order, actually betrays a much more complex ideological position. 'An Homilie Agaynst Disobedience and Wylful Rebellion', was included in the collection of *Certain Sermons*

Appointed by the Queen's Majesty to be Declared and Read by all Parsons, Vicars, and Curates, every Sunday and Holiday in their Churches, issued in 1574.[21] As such, it was clearly often reproduced and would have been well known. This homily was composed in response to a series of events that threatened the stability of Elizabethan government: the last Tudor rebellion, the Northern Rebellion (1569–70), in favour of Mary Stuart's claim to the throne; the papal bull declaring Elizabeth to be illegitimate; and the execution of Thomas Howard, fourth Duke of Norfolk (1536–72), the leading Catholic courtier, for his part in the Ridolfi plot which aimed to install Mary as queen.[22] It was written at a desperate time, when Elizabeth and her advisers feared that there was a serious danger that the Tudor regime might be overthrown by the combined strength of English and European Catholics, inviting comparisons to the Pilgrimage of Grace (1536–7) in her father's reign.[23] The arguments the homily uses to vilify rebels and exhort ordinary citizens to obedience should be seen as propagandist responses to a crisis rather than statements of a reasoned and generally accepted political status quo. The homily castigates rebels for their actions and adopts the absolutist position that no rebellion is ever permissible, however tyrannical the king, an argument that James I later adopted in the late 1590s (see below, pp. 82–4).

> [A] rebel is worse than the worst prince, and rebellion worse than the worst government of the worst prince that hitherto hath been; both are rebels unmeet ministers, and rebellion an unfit and unwholesome medicine to reform any small lacks in a prince, or to cure any little griefs in government; such lewd remedies being far worse than any other maladies and disorders that can be in the body of a commonwealth ... *God giveth a prince in his anger,* – meaning an evil one, – *and taketh away a prince in his displeasure* (Hos. 13.11), meaning specially when he taketh away a good prince for the sins of the people: as in our memory he took away our good Josias, king Edward, in his young and good years, for our wickedness ... let us either deserve to have a good prince, or let us patiently suffer and obey such as we deserve.[24]

It does not follow that what was read out in church would be generally accepted as a political principle by the majority of the congregation, especially words designed to deal with a particular crisis. If rural and remote areas were more likely to be populated with Catholics where Protestant doctrines had not spread or had had little impact, then cities, especially London, afforded citizens access to alternative political ideas, especially if they were literate, as an expanding market for Protestant-inspired works indicates.[25] The declared focus of the sermon is Catholic-inspired rebellion, but the belief that rebellion against a tyrannical or illegitimate monarch could be sanctioned by God was as much a Protestant phenomenon as a Catholic one.[26]

The reference to Edward VI is especially ironic, as the radical Protestant thrust of his reign encouraged numerous thinkers keen to challenge the power of the monarchy and the rights assumed by Henry VIII after the Reformation.[27] These included John Ponet (1516–56), Bishop of Winchester, who died in exile after he had participated in Wyatt's Rebellion (1553–4), and author of *A Shorte Treatise of Politike Power* (1556), which urged the overthrow of tyrannical kings who broke the word of God; and Christopher Goodman, another Marian exile, whose treatise, *How Superior Powers Oght to be Obeyed* (1558), argued an identical case.[28] It is possible that such works may not have had a serious impact on a wider audience beyond the Puritan communities that developed from Edward's reign onwards – although it is likely that they did.[29] But as Shakespeare's editors have long realized, a major project from Edward's reign undoubtedly did have a significant impact on Shakespeare's history plays, namely, *A Mirror for Magistrates*.

A Mirror for Magistrates was one of the most popular works of the sixteenth century, going through six editions, often involving additions and the reconfiguration of the text, between its publication in 1559 and 1587 (1559, 1563, 1571, 1574, 1578, 1587).[30] It was written by a series of writers, led initially by William Baldwin, a prominent man of letters at Edward VI's court, but was suppressed on Mary's orders in 1555 after Edward's premature death (1553), by which time it was partially printed. Eventually it was published immediately after Mary died and Elizabeth became queen. The *Mirror* consists of a series of poetic narratives, most of them complaints spoken by unfortunate or wicked princes and nobles, who have come to a bad end. These are linked by prose passages in which the authors of the poems debate the significance of what they have just read. It was designed as an adaptation of the influential genre of *speculum principis* ('mirror for princes') literature, targeted at 'magistrates', a general term for those who held positions of office, from relatively humble justices of the peace to powerful counsellors of the monarch.

The *Mirror* was a conscious adaptation of lives and events from English history from the reign of Richard II to the fall of Henry VI, intended for a broad audience who could learn from it what had happened in the past and use the knowledge to make sure that England could be governed better and past mistakes avoided. William Baldwin's first preface emphasized the need for good government, the difficulty of finding suitable magistrates willing to perform duties for the state, and the pitfalls of high office. Baldwin cites Plato to argue that desire to govern is not necessarily an unqualified blessing:

> Well is that realme governed, in which the ambitious deseyr not to beare office. Wherby you may perceive ... what offices are, where they be duely executed: not gaynful spoyles for the greedy to hunt for, but payneful toyles for the heedy to be charged with. You may perceyve also by this sentence, that there is nothing more necessary in a common weale, than that officers be diligent and trusty in their charges. And sure in whatsoever realme such provision is made, that officers be forced to do their duties, there is it as harde a matter to get an officer, as it is in other places to shift of, and put by those, that with flattery, bribes, and other shiftes, sue and preace for offices.[31]

As these lines make clear, the *Mirror* is a work that concentrates upon the duties and problems encountered in establishing the forms of proper government. It is not an apology for the rights of kings, as even the most superficial acquaintance with its content will reveal, and, while it does condemn rebellion in the narrative of Jack Cade, it is really concerned with the problem of ruling in the interests of a wider community. The nineteen narratives included in the 1559 edition contain only four by kings (three English, one Scottish). The rest are by important aristocrats, except for one by a lower-class rebel, Jack Cade, and one by the Welsh prince and rebel, Owen Glendower. The fourteen additions up to 1587 contain only one more (that of James IV of Scotland), indicating that, as the title made clear, this was a work designed to foster good government, monarchs being only one part of the overall picture.

The work opens with the narrative of Robert Tresilian, Chief Justice during the reign of Richard II (but not included in Shakespeare's play).[32] The lesson to be learnt from Tresilian's story is made clear in the subtitle to his tragedy, which points out that he was hanged 'for misconstryuing the lawes, and expounding them to serve the Princes affections'. Tresilian admits that he and his fellow officers of the law deliberately misread and hid the clear meaning of the statutes:

> The lawes we interpreted and statutes of the lande,
> Not trulye by the texte, but nuly by a glose:
> And wurds that wer most plaine whan thei by us wer skande
> We turned by construction lyke a welchmans hose,
> Wherby many one both lyfe and lande dyd lose:
> Yet this we made a mean to mount aloft on mules.
> To serve kings in pointes men must sumwhile breke rules.

(71–7)

Tresilian is guilty of putting the interests of himself and the King before his duty to uphold the law for the benefit of the people: the last lines here are to be read as a confession of his sins, not an admission that omelettes cannot be made without eggs being broken. A few lines later, Tresilian admits that in office he venially served King Richard rather than his subjects:

> So wurkyng lawe lyke waxe, the subjecte was not sure
> Of lyfe, lande, nor goods, but at the princes wyll:
> Which caused his kingdome the shorter tyme to dure,
> For clayming power absolute both to save and spyll,

> The prince therby presumed his people for to pyll:
> And set his lustes for lawe and will had reasons place,
> No more but hang and drawe, there was no better grace.
>
> (85–91)

While Tresilian was guilty of manipulating and abusing the law so that it failed to mean what it stated, the *Mirror* cannot be accused of a similar sin. This stanza makes Tresilian's crimes explicit, implicates Richard, and forces the reader to ask whether Richard deserved the same fate as his Chief Justice. England should have been run by impartial laws beneficial to all, as Baldwin's preface makes clear; instead, the laws have been used to satisfy the greed of an unscrupulous king and his corrupt courtiers. Richard's assumption of 'power absolute' is both morally wrong and, ultimately, short-sighted, as it hastens his demise. The *Mirror* seems to be endorsing an understanding of sovereignty rooted in the will of the people, a radical Protestant belief prevalent in many intellectual circles at the court of Edward VI, and encouraged by the freedom granted to the press.[33] If so, did Richard deserve the same fate as Tresilian?

Richard's tragedy is the fifth included in the collection, the full title being, 'Howe kyng Richard the seconde was for his euyll gouernaunce deposed from his seat, and miserably murdered in prison'. This suggests that the authors of the *Mirror* again chose to concentrate on the effects of government and its benefit to the people it was designed to serve, rather than the rights of the monarch in question. The last sentence of the prose link asks the reader to picture the dead Richard 'al to be mangled, with blew woundes, lying pale and wanne al naked upon the cold stones in Paules church, the people standing about him, and making his mone in this sort' (p. 111). The people symbolically look down on the King, who tells them that the prince ought to follow virtue and uphold the rules of the land, a lesson he failed to heed while he was alive, when he was 'ruled all by lust', put his trust in 'false Flatterers', and paid more heed to the dictates of his will than 'faythful counsayle' (31–5). The tragedy does refer to the 'false faith' of the Earl of Worcester, who defected to Bolingbroke (71–80), but places little emphasis on the guilt of the King's enemies. The tragedy is a personal one, caused by Richard's vices, and the subsequent prose link concludes that it was 'to all Princes a ryght wurthy instruction' (p. 119). Significantly enough, there is no tragedy of Henry IV, who is described in the same prose link as 'a man more ware & prosperous in hys doynges although not untroubled with warres both of outforth and inward enemies'. As before, the emphasis is placed on the effects of a king's reign on his subjects rather than his rights over them. Henry is described here as 'a man', suggesting that he ruled through merit or power, not divine right.

But, as I have already pointed out, the *Mirror* was not a treatise advocating a subject's rights to overthrow an unpopular and unjust ruler. Richard's fate is deliberately mirrored in that of the rebel, Jack Cade (whose story is retold in *2 Henry VI*, 4.2–10). Cade's lament for his thoroughly deserved fate is made in precisely the same terms as Richard's, both admitting that they let their desires and lusts overcome their reason. Cade confesses that he is unsure exactly what causes men to behave as they do, but is certain that 'Our lust and wils our evils chefely warke' (7). Cade's sinful pride encourages him to aspire higher than is legitimate ('I am one / That would not stay my selfe in mine estate' (43–4)) and his rebellion against the King leads to the destruction of the valiant men of Kent (58–63). After their failure to cross Southwark Bridge, and the general pardon that leads to the dispersal of the rebels, Cade is run to ground, killed by Alexander Iden, and his body parts displayed on poles *pour encourager les autres*. The tragedy ends with an exhortation to subjects not to rebel against their princes, which deserves to be quoted at some length:

> Full litell knowe we wretches what we do.
> Whan we presume our princes to resist.
> We war with God, against his glory to,
> That placeth in his office whom he list,
> Therfore was never traytour yet but mist
> The marke he shot, and came to shamefull ende
> Nor never shall til God be forst to bend.

> God hath ordayned the power, all princes be
> His Lieutenauntes, or debities [deputies] in realmes,
> Against their foes still therfore fighteth he,
> And as his enmies drives them to extremes,
> Their wise devises prove but doltish dreames.
> No subject ought for any kind of cause,
> To force the lord, but yeeld him to the lawes.
>
> And therefore Baldwin warne men folow reason
> Subdue theyr wylles, and be not Fortunes slaves,
> A troublous ende doth ever folowe treason,
> There is no trust in rebelles, raskall knaves,
> In Fortune lesse, whiche wurketh as the waves:
> From whose assautes who lyst to stande at large,
> Must folowe skyll, and flye all wordly charge.
>
> (148–68)

Such lines appear as if they were an unequivocal endorsement of an established hierarchy, or 'Tudor orthodoxy', warning subjects never to rebel against their consecrated leaders, and, indeed, they have often been read as such.[34] However, the words cited are spoken by Cade himself. They describe the world as it appears to him after his rebellion, indicating that the complaint has a specific rather than a general focus. The appended prose links make the moral of the story rather more nuanced. The link before the tragedy emphasizes Cade's status, describing him as 'but base borne, of no abilitye, and lesse power ... he is one of Fortune's whelpes' (p. 170). The link that follows makes a careful distinction between rulers, who can be 'officers' as well as monarchs, and subjects such as Cade: 'howe uprightly ... and howe lyke a devine hath he [the author of the tragedy] determined the states of both officers and Rebelles. For in dede officers be gods deputies, and it is gods office which they beare ... And therefore whosoever rebelleth agaynst any ruler either good or bad, rebelleth against GOD' (p. 178). Given that *A Mirror for Magistrates* was targeted at those who held or wished to hold offices of state, the implication, while not explicitly stated, is clear. Subjects should never presume to alter government or their governors through rebellion, but magistrates (officers) were not bound by this dictate as they belonged to the class of God's chosen elite. Henry IV is criticized in the tragedies. Henry, Earl of Northumberland, who helped Bolingbroke overthrow Richard, confesses that, while Richard was a bad ruler, Henry 'becam in all poyntes wurse than he' (p. 58); and Owen Glendower laconically notes that 'Henry the fourth did then usurpe the crowne' (p. 64) (though whether this carries moral condemnation is not clear). Nevertheless, the *Mirror* does not rule out the possibility that bad kings like Richard may be deposed by magistrates. There is a marked contrast made between the rebellion of Jack Cade and the deposition of Richard in the text; the former is undoubtedly an evil act, the latter may well be justified but may not be the right thing to do. Indeed, both figures are represented as onerous problems with which magistrates have to deal.

The *Mirror* can be seen to draw on two central strands of political thought, both of which were crucial for the development of Shakespeare's history plays. The distinction made between magistrates and subjects is indebted to Presbyterian political thought.[35] Presbyterians generally argued that 'inferior' magistrates (those who held minor positions of office rather than important offices of state) had the right to resist bad monarchs and their evil advisers. Such distinctions were common in Protestant thought from the time of Martin Luther (1483–1546), but were most readily associated with the work of Jean Calvin (1509–64), the radical Geneva reformer, most famous for his doctrine of double predestination, but also influential for his analysis of government.[36] Calvin, like the authors of the *Mirror*, emphasized that the magistrate derived his authority from God, ruled for the benefit of the commonwealth, and 'that they that rule unjustly and wilfully are raised up by him [God] to punish the wickednesse of the people'.[37] Equally importantly, Calvin made a distinction between the political rights and duties of private citizens and magistrates exactly as the authors of the *Mirror* did:

For though the correcting of unbridled government bee the revengement of the Lord, let us not by and by thinke that it is committed to us, to whom there is given no other commandement but to obey and suffer. I speake always of private men. For if there bee at this time ... Magistrates for the behalfe of the people ... I doe not forbid them according to their office to withstand the outraging licentiousnesse of kings: that I affirme that if they winke at kings wilfully ranging over and treading downe the poore communalty, their dissembling is not without wicked breach of faith, because they decitfully betray the liberty of the people, whereof they know themselves to bee appointed protectors by the ordinance of God.[38]

It is evident that while private citizens could not revolt under any circumstances against their governors, the governors themselves were not so restricted. Such Presbyterian political thought had a massive impact on intellectual Protestants who gathered at the court of Edward VI, including the first Lord Protector, Edward Seymour, Duke of Somerset, and William Baldwin.[39] It is little wonder that Mary took exception to the *Mirror* and had it suppressed, especially if one considers that the proliferation of Calvinist-inspired resistance treatises produced by British Protestant exiles such as John Ponet, Christopher Goodman and John Knox during her reign were all targeted explicitly at her.[40]

Equally important was the example of Edward Hall's *Union*, the source of many of the tragedies contained in the *Mirror*, which was banned by the same proclamation that censored the later work.[41] Hall's history – which, like the *Mirror* has often been read as a defence of the status quo – emerged from the same intellectual, political and religious milieu as the *Mirror*, and is certainly hard to read as a work that supports kings however bad they are and condemns rebels however laudable their cause and motives. Hall, like Baldwin, was a committed Protestant who was enthusiastic about the new prospects of the Edwardian regime.[42] Hall's dedicatory epistle to Edward argues for the usefulness of history as a means of preserving a series of moral lessons.

Good rulers like Augustus and Trajan enable their successors to follow 'ther steppes in vertue and princely qualities'; without the histories of evil rulers such as Nero and Caligula 'young Princes and fraile governors might likewise have fallen in a like pit, but by redying their Vices and seying their mischevous ende, thei bee compelled to leave their evill waies, and embrace the good qualities of notable princes and prudent governors'. Hence 'writing is the key to enduce vertue, and represse vice'.[43]

Hall's opening paragraph is a plea for the need for unity and a warning of the destruction waged by civil wars in Rome, Italy, Scotland, Denmark and, worst of all, England: 'What mischiefe hath insurged in realmes by intestine devision, what depopulation hath ensued in countries by civill discencion, what detestable murder hath been committed in citees by seperate faccions, and what calamitee hath ensued in famous regions by domesticall discord & unnatural controversy' (p. 1). But it does not follow from this historically grounded lament that the *Union* launches a defence of anointed kings. Hall's account of the reign of Richard II and his deposition by Henry IV, given the subtitle 'An Introduction into the History of King Henry the Fourthe', follows the *Mirror* in laying much of the blame for his fall on Richard himself. Henry is tempted into revolt because Richard 'was now brought to that trade of livyng that he litle or nothyng regarded the counsaill of his uncles, nor of other grave and sadde persones, but did all thyng at his pleasure, setting his will and appetite in stede of lawe and reason' (p. 3). When Henry is banished alongside Thomas Mowbray, Duke of Norfolk (an event represented in Shakespeare's play), Hall notes that a large number of ordinary people 'ranne in every towne & streete, lamentyng and bewayling his departure. As who saie that when he departed, the onely shelde, defence & comfort of the comen people was vadid and gone, as though the sunne had fallen out of the spere' (p. 5).[44] Richard's suspicion of Henry's popularity leads him to seize the lands of John of Gaunt, Henry's father, on the latter's decease, defrauding Henry of his rightful inheritance '& geving to other that whiche was not his, distributed the dukes landes to his paresites, and flattering followers' (p. 5). Richard's rule is so corrupt that when he begins his campaign in Ireland, the opposition to him among those who hold offices of state is total:

> While king Richard was in Irelande, the grave persones of the nobilitee, the sage prelates of the clergy ye sad magestrates & rulers of the citees, tounes & comminailtie perceaving daily more & more the realme to fall into ruyne and desolacion (in maner irrecuperable as long as kyng Richard either lived or reigned,) after long deliberacion, wrote into France to duke Henry ... solicityng and requirying hym with all diligente celeritee to conveighe hym self into Englande, promisyng hym with all their aide, power and assistance, if he expellyng kyng Richard as a manne not mete nor conveniente for so princely an office and degree, would take upon hym the sceptre rule and diademe of his native countree and firste nutritive soyle.[45] (p. 6)

The Archbishop of Canterbury is sent off to Paris to convey the message directly to Henry, who can then return to England to restore law, order and justice. Henry is at pains to emphasize that he does not seek the throne through 'ambicion of wordly honour, nor for desire of Empire or rule' (p. 7), the Archbishop having made it clear that neither the nobles nor the commons can endure the 'yoke of wanton, unwitty kyng Richard' any longer, and have simply chosen him as a 'ruler whiche should excell and flourishe in wisedomee, policie and justice above all other' (p. 6).[46]

Henry comes to the throne as the people's choice, but as his rule starts to become an inevitability, Hall begins to shift the reader's sympathies, and provide a balanced account in which the sins and excesses of each monarch match those of the other. While it is true that all are in favour of Henry as king, and a long list of Richard's faults and crimes is brought before parliament to legitimize the abdication (pp. 8–11), Hall hints that now that Richard's fate is sealed, the easy moral distinctions made before Henry's campaign started are no longer applicable because the political situation in England has changed. Hall comments that Richard's faults 'ought to be imputed [more] to the frailtee of his wanton youth then to the malice of his heart or cankerdnesse of his stomache, but suche is the frayle judgement of mortall men' (p. 8). He describes the list of items against Richard as 'detestable' (p. 11), and shows how Henry proved not to be the saviour of England promised in the Archbishop's oration. Hall points out that the reign of Henry IV established new divisions which were not extinguished until much later, a reference to the cycle of English history that did not end until eighty-five years after the death of Henry IV with the victory of Henry VII at the Battle of Bosworth. He pours scorn on Henry's claims to have a better claim to the throne than Richard. Henry argued that his descent from the deformed eldest son of Henry III, Edmund Croucheback, gave him prior right over Richard, who was descended from Edward I.[47] As Henry knew, it was well attested that Edmund was, in fact, a younger son (who was also sound in body) (pp. 13–14). Hall describes how the new reign simply brought many new injustices inaugurated by the rebellion of the Earls of Huntingdon, Kent, Rutland and Salisbury (1400). This vain attempt to restore Richard to the throne was the first of many uprisings throughout Henry's reign, and a sign of what was to come (p. 15).

A key incident during this rebellion represents Hall's characteristic mode of analysis of historical events. The Duke and Duchess of Exeter are brother and sister of Richard and Henry respectively. The Duke is a keen supporter of the rebellion and raises troops, much to the consternation of the Duchess. Responding to her tears, the Duke presents her with an argument that is partly based on questions of rights and partly based on their self-interest:

> When the duke perceived her dolour, he said, Besse, how chaunseth this, when my brother king Richard was deposed of his dignitie, and committed to harde and sharpe prison which had bene kyng and ruled this realme noblie by the space of xxii. Yeres and your brother was exalted to the throne and dignitie imperiall of the same, then my hearte was heavie, my life stoode in jepordie and my combe was clerely cut [my fate was sealed], but you then rejoysed laughed and triumphed, wherfore I pray you be contente that I may aswell rejoyce and have pleasure at the deliveryng and

restoring of my brother justly to his dignitie, as you were jocond
and pleasaunt when your brother unjustly and untrulie deprived
and disseased my brother of the same. For of this I am sure. That
yf my brother prosper, you and I shal not fall nor decline: but if
your brother continue in his estate and magnificence I doubte not
your decay nor ruine, but I suspecte the losse of my life beside the
forfeyture of my landes and goodes. (p. 17)

Of course, the scenario outlined by the Duke is counterfactual, as the
rebellion fails; but the image of a family at war is a potent one, which
can be compared with the famous scene in *3 Henry VI*, where a son
discovers that he has killed his father and a father discovers that he has
killed his son (2.5). We will never know whether the Duke was correct
in his assessment of their situation. What the speech demonstrates is
Hall's concern with the effects of government on the king's subjects,
not the specific dynastic claims of rulers, which, in the case of Henry,
are shown to be propaganda designed to legitimize a *fait accompli*. In a
sense, there is no obvious political solution to the problem of the unjust
ruler, as the *Union* makes clear. Richard's reign was intolerable, as all
accounts available to Shakespeare – Hall, Holinshed, the *Mirror*,
Thomas of Woodstock – demonstrate, because of his extortion from his
subjects, disregard for the law, promotion of favourites and assorted
flatterers, and the murder of his uncle and protector, Thomas of
Woodstock, Duke of Gloucester.[48] But the cure could always be worse
than the disease.

What needs to be emphasized is that Shakespeare, while he may have
been innovative in terms of the development of the history play, was
working within a tradition of English history writing which was
specifically concerned with the effects of government on the wider
populace.[49] Hall, Holinshed and the authors of the *Mirror*, the three
principal sources not just for Shakespeare but for virtually all
adaptations of and works based on English historical sources produced
in the reign of Elizabeth, should not be read as upholders of a 'Tudor
myth', or of a simple providentialist reading of English history from
1399 to 1547.[50] Of course, all writers were relieved that the destructive

violence of the Wars of the Roses had finally come to an end with the advent of the Tudors, but this did not mean that they uncritically supported the Tudor regime or subscribed to a belief in the divine right of kings. History was invariably written with one eye on the present, and events were narrated for their relevance to current political issues. A case in point is the account of the deposition of Richard II in Holinshed's *Chronicles*, which, as Annabel Patterson has pointed out, focused on 'parliamentary resistance' in the confrontation between king and parliament, deliberately transforming what in Hall's *Union* had been 'largely a matter of personalities' in order to register a subsequent 'contraction in Parliament's role and a debasement of its principles'.[51] Holinshed's contributors, following and developing the ideas of Hall and the authors of the *Mirror*, used the example of English history to promote the notion of 'indifference', or impartiality, a principle that was designed to curb the excessive powers of monarchs who abused their subjects (like Richard II), as well as foster more sophisticated historiography and a fair judicial system.[52] Holinshed's *Chronicles*, like Hall's *Union* and the *Mirror*, were the focus of careful and hostile attention from the censors.[53]

Shakespeare's representation of kings in all his history plays is governed by the understanding that it is what kings do rather than what they are or claim to be that is important. That genealogical arguments are given little weight in the histories can be seen at the start of *Henry V* (1599), the play that completes the cycle of English history from the deposition of Richard II to the advent of the Tudors and, for the first time, represents a conspicuously successful king. The opening scene shows the Archbishop of Canterbury and the Bishop of Ely debating how to persuade the King to abandon a bill passed in his father's reign that would seize half the temporal wealth of the church.[54] The bishops praise the King for his newly acquired religious devotion and wisdom, and convince themselves that he can be made to listen to reason and that they will not have to face the awful prospect of losing half their revenue. The lines 'Turn him to any cause of policy, / The Gordian knot of it he will unloose' (1.1.45–6), seem to disclose the central issues of Henry's approach to the monarchy. The Gordian knot, tied by Gordius, the father of Midas, was proverbial for being impossible to untie, and it was prophesied that whoever managed to unloose it would rule Asia. Alexander the Great simply cut the knot with his sword. Henry is here implicitly compared to Alexander, the greatest conqueror of the ancient world, a prophetic allusion to what Henry will achieve in France and his reputation as the most successful warrior king in English history. Significantly enough, the comparison is repeated later in the play (3.1.19; 4.7.12–40).[55] But do the Archbishop's words indicate that Henry is able to go beyond Alexander and untie the most complex knots; or do they suggest that Henry, like Alexander, chooses to cut through them and use whatever information there is at his disposal to support the claims he would have made anyway? The comparison of Henry to Alexander – especially as it is made by the head of the English church – is double-edged. Alexander was admired for his military prowess, but was notorious for his cruelty and the fact that he had apparently learnt very little from having been taught by Aristotle.[56] Henry has undergone a different but equally important education in *1* and *2 Henry IV* through his dissolute life with the rogues in the Eastcheap Tavern, and his behaviour in France will show him to be a ruthless leader like Alexander or, even, the other famous conqueror of Asia, Tamburlaine, whose story had been one of the great dramatic successes of the 1590s.[57]

The conversation further heightens the importance – as well as the irony – of these lines. The Archbishop's calculation that the King will be inclined to their cause if they support his claims to the French crown, and his intention to 'give a greater sum / Than ever at one time the clergy yet / Did to his predecessors part withal' (1.1.79–81), show that he understands the world of political reality astutely, as his earlier use of the Machiavellian term 'policy' indicates.[58] The plan to give the money to Henry suggests that the decision to reveal 'The severals and unhidden passages / Of his true titles to some certain dukedoms, / And generally to the crown and seat of France, / Derived from Edward, his great-grandfather' (86–9), is a cynical manoeuvre that mirrors Henry's designs for personal and national aggrandisement. The church and the King speak the same political language.

In scene two Henry asks the Archbishop to expound his right to France, warning him that he must convince the King that his cause is just, given the high stakes of Henry's claim and the fearful consequences that will ensue:

> For never two such kingdoms did contend
> Without much fall of blood, whose guiltless drops
> Are every one a woe, a sore complaint
> 'Gainst him whose wrongs gives edge unto the swords
> That makes such waste in brief mortality.

(1.2.24–8)

Henry is effectively transferring the guilt of the campaign on to the advisers, making it clear that if he succeeds he will accept the glory himself, but if he fails then others can take the blame, a characteristic strategy.[59] In a lengthy and intricate speech (62 lines) the Archbishop explains that the French have unjustly assumed that the Salic Law stipulating that 'No woman shall succeed in Salic land' (39), applies to the whole realm of France, whereas the law really only applies to certain German principalities.[60] Hence Henry can claim the French crown through his descent from Edward III, who was the son of Isabella, the daughter of Philip IV of France. It is noticeable, however, that the Archbishop does not state the actual claim itself, appealing instead to the 'warlike spirit' of Henry's great-uncle, Edward the Black Prince, and his victories over the French at the battle of Crécy (1346) (103–10). The subsequent rallying cries by nobles and churchmen reveal a series of interchangeable bellicose sentiments and arguments (115–35).

It is hard to take Henry's claim seriously, especially when it is read alongside the bogus claims to crowns made throughout the first tetralogy – significantly enough, staging the bloody course of English history after Henry's death – and given the motives of the prelates supporting the campaign. There is a bitterly comic element to Henry's claims to France on the grounds that the incumbent dynasty has usurped his legitimate rights, given his dubious right to the English crown he possesses, acknowledged at key points in the play (see above, pp. 37–8). The invocation of the Salic Law by the French and the pious English desire to negate its use, cannot but seem ironic given the exclusion of Mary Queen of Scots from her rightful succession (see above, pp. 25–8; below, pp. 87–97), or the wealth of criticism against the female monarch on the grounds of her sex's natural unsuitability for government.[61] Furthermore, as the play makes increasingly clear, Henry's success in uniting the four nationalities of Britain, explicitly signalled in the scenes containing Fluellen, Gower, Jamy and MacMorris (3.2; 3.6) after the Siege of Harfleur and before the Battle of Agincourt, depends on a triumphant foreign war and is radically unstable.[62] The chorus's admission that the achievements of Henry came to nothing with the advent of his son – 'Whose state so many had the managing / That they lost France and made his England bleed, / Which oft our stage hath shown' (Epilogue, 11–13) – is a sharp reminder of the insubstantial nature of Henry's success, and an anticlimax after the bellicosity of the prologues to each act, the fabulous victories against all odds, and the carefully negotiated marriage alliance and peace treaty.[63] Like Alexander the Great's empire, in fact, which broke up when he died, prematurely (Henry was thirty-four when he died, Alexander, thirty-two).

One of the key images recurring throughout *Henry V*, as in many of the other history plays, is that of the king as player/actor. In *2 Henry IV*, Hal/Henry appropriated his father's crown, mistakenly thinking that the King was dead, and asserted: 'My due from thee is this imperial crown, / Which, as immediate from thy place and blood, / Derives itself to me' (4.5.40–2). The obvious irony of these lines is spelt out when Henry wakes up, and makes his last speech to his son, pointing out what care and trouble the crown has caused him because 'It seem'd in me / But as an honour snatch'd with boist'rous hand' (190–1). Henry hopes for better things for Hal but comments that 'all my reign hath been but as a scene / Acting that argument' (197–8), and he dies in the chamber called 'Jerusalem', not the real place, to complete his performance. Henry hopes that his son will be a real rather than a pretend king, as he feels that he has been:

> To thee it shall descend with better quiet,
> Better opinion, better confirmation;
> For all the soil of the achievement goes
> With me into the earth.

(187–90)

Henry's hopes of having dug and manured the ground ready for his son to rule properly refer back to the imagery of gardening prevalent throughout *Richard II* (Richard being another player king), although they obviously also mean that the dishonour of his usurpation should die with him.[64] However, such natural imagery ceased to be relevant once Henry had deposed Richard, and the notion of the king as actor assumes centre stage throughout the tetralogy. Equally, the stain of Henry's sin is the one thing that cannot be removed from the player king, who bears its indelible mark while all the trappings, marks and ceremonies that designate and define kingship are exposed as games that cannot hide the lack of real substance underneath.[65] The clothes are all 'soiled' and cannot be washed clean, even though, as *Richard II* demonstrates, the 'balm' can all too easily be washed off the anointed king. Henry's hope that he has established a dynasty proves as delusive as his hope that he will lead a crusade (the real 'crusade' turns out to be against the French). Henry IV's need to justify his rule by ceaselessly playing the role of king is a performative burden he bequeathes to his heir. Monarchs who have no natural right to rule – that is, all English monarchs after Richard – have to prove themselves worthy of the people's support, endlessly playing a part.[66] The theatre audience would have also have been aware of Elizabeth's desire to play the part of queen, and surround her role as majesty with sacred mystery, providing an obvious topical reference point and significance to the reproduction of English history on stage.[67] Henry's reputation as a king, as the chronicles available to Shakespeare made clear, was based not on the truth or falsity of his claim, which Shakespeare's play appears to treat as bogus, but on the purpose and success of his war in France and establishment of a secure peace.

Henry V is replete with scenes that reflect on the problem of the nation and its political identity, from the opening comments of the chorus and the machinations of the bishops to the final scene with its descriptions of France devastated by war, followed by the misunderstandings and broken macaronic dialogue of Henry and Katherine.[68] A key exchange takes place when Henry, repeating the cross-class transposition of his youth, disguises himself as a common soldier and mingles with three of his men, John Bates, Alexander Court and Michael Williams, at dawn before the Battle of Agincourt. This scene has no precedent in any of the sources. Henry introduces the question of the identity of the King, having suggested that the English commanders think they are doomed to defeat in combat. Henry argues that:

> the King is but a man, as I am: the violet smells to him as it doth to me; the element shows to him as it doth to me; all his senses have but human conditions; his ceremonies laid by, in his nakedness he appears but a man; and though his affections are higher mounted than ours, yet when they stoop they stoop with the like wing. Therefore when he sees reason of fears as we do, his fears, out of doubt, be of the same relish as ours are. Yet, in reason, no man should possess him with any appearance of fear, lest he, by showing it, should dishearten his army.

(4.1.102–12)

The sentiments are meant to appear democratic and egalitarian, but are actually authoritarian. Henry's argument is: the King has to lead the army; the King is a man like the men in his army; all these men feel fear; therefore, no one should show any fear as it will prevent the King from leading the army. The implication is that no one ought to question the King, a point made clearly when the disguised Henry asserts that he would willingly die for the King, 'his cause being just and his quarrel honourable' (127–8). Williams responds, 'That's more than we know' (129) (but, arguably, less than the audience does).

As the opening exchange in the play demonstrates, Henry's war with France is based on questionable grounds and is, in fact, plotted by the Archbishop of Canterbury and the Bishop of Ely, as a means of protecting church revenue and thwarting the demands of parliament, the elected body designed to represent the people.[69] Henry has to rely on Williams, Bates and Court to fight his wars, but he is effectively invoking the social analysis of Sir Thomas Smith, one of the key political theorists of Elizabethan England, in his influential *De Republica Anglorum* (published 1583, but in circulation from 1565). Like the authors of the *Mirror*, Smith divides society initially into two sorts of people: those 'that beare office, the other of them that beare none: the first are called magistrates, the second private men'.[70] He further divides English society into a hierarchy of four classes: gentlemen (including the king and nobles), citizens, yeoman artificers, and labourers (p. 31). Only the fourth sort or class, who include 'day labourers, poore husbandmen, yea marchantes or retailers which have no free lande, copiholders, and all artificers, as Taylers, Shoomakers, Carpenters, Brickemakers, Masons, &c', cannot become magistrates. Smith is somewhat ambivalent about their political role: 'These have no voice nor authoritie in our common wealth, and no account is made of them but onelie to be ruled, not to rule other, and yet they be not altogether neglected' (p. 46). Smith does not endorse this confused situation, merely describes it.[71]

This scene in *Henry V*, along with much of the two parts of *Henry IV*, could have been written with Smith's words in mind. Although it is not stated what Williams, Bates and Court do when they are not soldiers, they clearly belong to this fourth class, the class that Machiavelli argued produced the best soldiers.[72] And it might also be argued that Henry follows Smith's advice in refusing to neglect men who otherwise do not feature in the political landscape by moving among them before the battle. However, Henry is there to persuade them to fight loyally and to learn how to be a successful military commander, as manuals on military science urged.[73] We are always aware that we are not seeing an ideal of England, but England organized for military success. Henry's attention to the arguments of the men he commands is only partial, and he evades key issues, trying to manipulate them to follow his line of reasoning (as he himself has been manipulated by the bishops). Bates and Williams point out that the cause of war must be honourable, or else the crimes of war will be the King's responsibility and weigh on his conscience:

But if the cause be not good, the King himself hath a heavy
reckoning to make when all those legs and arms and heads
chopped off in a battle shall join together at the latter day and cry
all 'We died at such a place', some swearing, some crying for a
surgeon, some upon their wives left poor behind them, some upon
the debts they owe, some upon their children . . . Now if these men
do not die well it will be a black matter for the King, that led them
to it, who to disobey were against all proportion of subjection.[74]

(134–46)

Williams represents the King as responsible for the fate of his army on
the Day of Judgement, a theological image that, once again, reflects no
credit on the bishops who supported the King's claims for their own
ends, and stands in pointed contrast to Henry's attempts to remove the
hierarchies between rulers and subjects. Henry's response to Williams
misses the point. He argues that the King should not be held
responsible for the afterlife of his subjects should they die sinfully for
his cause (147–84). Henry is right, but his argument only serves to
emphasize the cynical manner in which the common people have been
used by the church and their leaders, who are prepared to risk the
people's deaths in a cause of dubious justice. As Williams notes in the
last line cited above, subjects are not permitted to disobey and, for all
the horizontal bonds formed here between men at war, the King still
rules and leads his men into battle. The scene can be read as a
carnivalesque interlude in the progress of war.[75] As in another play
which deals, albeit less explicitly, with Henry's French campaign,
Thomas Dekker's *The Shoemaker's Holiday* (1599), the horrors of war
can only briefly be suspended.[76] When Williams and Henry exchange
gloves as a sign that they will fight a duel if they survive the battle,
Bates urges them to 'Be friends, you English fools, be friends! We have
French quarrels enough' (219–20), a reminder that war was a
democratizing force only as long as everyone obeyed orders.

Henry's soliloquy can be read as a meditation on the notion of the
king's two bodies, whereby a monarch was deemed to have a private and
a public persona, his office and his person (so straddling the divide

between private citizens and magistrates articulated by theorists such as Smith).[77] Henry now feels the acute burden of office, and the personal responsibility for those he commands. He had previously passed the blame on to his enemies, in his speech to the governor of Harfleur (3.3.1–43), and, through his ambassador (his uncle, the Duke of Exeter), to the King of France, who is warned that unless he resigns his crown, on his head will be 'the widows' tears, the orphans' cries, / The dead men's blood, the pining maidens' groans, / For husbands, fathers and betrothed lovers / That shall be swallowed in this controversy' (2.4.106–9). It is only after his conversation with Bates and Williams that Henry acknowledges that all responsibility lies with him, suggesting that his education as a ruler is only now nearing completion, and indicating that, as Lear later admits on the heath, kings have to learn to govern through an understanding of the lower orders (those who Smith claims are not really fit to participate in the process of government):

> Upon the King! 'Let our lives, our souls,
> Our debts, our careful wives,
> Our children and our sins lay on the King!'
> We must bear all. O hard condition,
> Twin-born with greatness, subject to the breath
> Of every fool whose sense no more can feel
> But his own wringing! What infinite heart's ease
> Must kings neglect that private men enjoy!
> And what have kings that privates have not too,
> Save ceremony, save general ceremony?
> And what art thou, thou idol ceremony?
>
> (4.1.227–37)

This is Shakespeare's most sophisticated reflection on the problem of kingship in the English history plays, and concludes his historical sequence written in the 1590s.[78] There is no historical precedent for this scene or this speech in the chronicle sources or earlier plays. Henry finally starts to understand the power and responsibility of kingship – although even at this point he dismisses those who risk their lives for his cause as fools. His educational journey neatly reflects and inverts that taken by Richard II, who also realizes the burdens and duties of a king, but only when he has surrendered his crown. Henry, in contrast, is about to become the one successful king in Shakespeare's history plays, an achievement, significantly enough, founded on the pursuit of an aggressive foreign war.

The soliloquy draws our attention to what actually makes a king or gives him the right to rule, a question that has been reflected on at crucial moments throughout the sequence of the history plays. Henry is concentrating on the actions he must justify as ruler. In effect, he is answering the questions that Bates and Williams raised in their exchange – but only after they have departed, a detail that enables the mystery of kingship to be preserved for the characters within the play, while the audience is granted a more penetrating insight. Henry admits that only ceremony separates a king from his subjects, which, given his precarious claim to the throne, is a startlingly accurate assessment (and a revelation he is wise not to spread further afield). The remainder of the speech consists of Henry's thoughts on this thin line between subjects and rulers, and shows him to be self-absorbed and unaware of the full significance of his insight. He dismisses ceremony as a 'proud dream' (254) and lists the forms and manifestations that are used to justify and express the aura of majesty:

> I am a king that find thee [i.e., ceremony], and I know
> 'Tis not the balm, the sceptre and the ball,
> The sword, the mace, the crown imperial,
> The intertissued robe of gold and pearl,
> The farced title running 'fore the king,
> The throne he sits on, nor the tide of pomp
> That beats upon the high shore of this world,
> No, not all these, thrice-gorgeous ceremony,
> Not all these, laid in bed majestical,
> Can sleep so soundly as the wretched slave[.]

(256–65)

The list is a comprehensive survey of what transforms the private body of the king into his public body and supposedly singles him out as a sacred ruler. The lines would seem to reflect directly on the ways in which Elizabeth sought to preserve her mystery as ruler of state and anointed queen: ceremonies, pageants and costumes which, in the late 1590s, had come to attract severe criticism as means of disguising the dying body of a very old woman.[79] As is well known, *Henry V* was written at the height of the Nine Years' War in Ireland, and alludes to the war both directly, in the chorus to act four, with an optimistic prediction of the outcome of the Earl of Essex's campaign, and indirectly, through a 'Freudian slip' in act five of the folio text, when Queen Isabel of France opens her speech with 'So happy be the issue, brother Ireland' (5.2.12), instead of 'brother England'.[80] Henry's French wars have to be read in terms of Elizabeth's Irish wars, and, implicitly, his reflections on kingship reflect also on her role as queen.

The result of Henry's analysis of his duties as king before Agincourt is that he envies the lowest of his subjects ('the wretched slave'), because he, unlike the King, can sleep soundly. This seems a perverse conclusion to his thoughts, which can easily be read in a different way. The King's soldiers are, after all, drawn from the lower classes of society, and although they may sleep soundly, they are also likely to be killed in battle the next day. As Graham Holderness has pointed out, the list of the English dead read out after the battle (4.8.81–113) concentrates on all those with titles from Duke to esquire, but omits those of lower social status, 'None else of name' (106), effectively deleting them from the historical record. However, the list 'might have contained, among those nameless common soldiers, Henry's companions of the previous night, John Bates and Alexander Court, whose names he never sought to know'.[81] What really affects Henry's peace of mind, as he acknowledges later in the scene, is less the fate of the army he leads in pursuit of glory and success, than his guilty conscience because of the murder of Richard (4.1.289–302). Henry's meditations on the signs and images that single him out as king demonstrate the flimsy justification of his kingship, suggesting that he could easily be replaced by someone else, just as Richard was by his father. The 'anointed balm' has been transferred into a series of symbols and shows that must be reproduced and performed time and again to remind his subjects that they are in the presence of a king. By the same token, when Henry does not act like a king, he ceases to be one.

Henry V can be read as a play with republican undercurrents; or perhaps, more accurately, as a work that does not discount the possibility that England could be ruled better by a strong leader than a hereditary monarch, by someone who had no claim to govern apart from his intrinsic merit. The logic of Henry V's meditations on the question of his kingship is that a monarch should rule because he – or she – is the person best suited for the role. The play flirts dangerously with this reading in the notorious chorus to act five, which describes the triumphant return of Henry to London:

> But now behold,
> In the quick forge and working-house of thought,
> How London doth pour out her citizens.
> The Mayor and all his brethren in best sort,
> Like to the senators of th'antique Rome
> With the plebeians swarming at their heels,
> Go forth and fetch their conquering Caesar in;
> As, by a lower but as loving likelihood,
> Were now the General of our gracious Empress,
> As in good time he may, from Ireland coming,
> Bringing rebellion broached on his sword,
> How many would the peaceful city quit
> To welcome him!

(22–34)

Henry, albeit in carefully qualified terms, is compared to Robert Devereux, second Earl of Essex, imagined returning in triumph from his Irish campaign, a clear, if unsustained, suggestion that he might be a suitable king, as he and many of his supporters undoubtedly thought. The choruses were omitted from the folio – produced after Essex's disastrous failure to stem rebellion in Ireland and his abortive coup – and are only extant in the quarto. This suggests that they were performed on stage in 1599, but later removed, perhaps because of casting difficulties in subsequent productions, but also, through a wish to remove associations with a disgraced rebel.[82] Elizabeth, as I have already noted, acknowledged that she was represented as Richard II on stage (see above, pp. 15–16). Equally important is her recognition that the staging of that play before the uprising was not the only example of this identification. When Lambarde sought to comfort his Queen by isolating the comparison, 'Such a wicked imagination was determined and attempted by a most unkind Gent. The most adorned creature that ever your Majesty made', she responded with a more gloomy assessment of the situation: 'He that will forget God, will also forget his benefactors: this tragedy was played 40^{tie} times in open streets and houses.'[83] Elizabeth recognized that there was more general and aggressive disaffection with her rule, pointing to the proliferation of plays targeted at her at the turn of the century. If *Richard II* was used to represent Elizabeth as the feeble, corrupt and doomed monarch who lost a crown, *Henry V* cast her most ambitious courtier as England's most successful and popular king.

It is also worth noting that Henry is imagined here as Julius Caesar, entering Rome after his victory over Pompey's sons, with the mayor and citizens envisaged as the senators of Rome. This image invites comparison with the opening scene of Shakespeare's next play, *Julius Caesar*, produced later in the same year (1599) (see Figure 8). Here the tribunes, annually elected intermediaries between the plebeians and the senate, are shown disparaging Caesar's triumph, praising the dead Pompey, and urging the people to return to their houses.[84] Shakespeare was familiar with Caesar's career from reading Sir Thomas North's translation of Plutarch's *Lives* (1579), in preparation for writing the play. On the one hand, Caesar was famous for having reached his eminent position and achieved his successes through merit rather than birth, and for his spectacular military successes in Europe (58–49 BCE).[85] On the other, he had made a concerted effort to end the Roman republic and helped to plunge Rome into civil war. Just as Caesar was ruthless in his pursuit of personal glory, Henry was prepared to destroy besieged cities (3.3), slaughter prisoners (4.7), and lay waste vast areas of rural France (5.2.23–67), in order to further his ambitions.[86] While *Henry V* recognizes the merits of Essex, it also hints at the dangers of his ambitious rise to power.

FIGURE 4 The Battle of Agincourt, mid-fifteenth-century English illustration.
Showing one of England's most significant victories against the French.

More significant as evidence for a reading of the play's political
leaning is the representation of the British army at war. Henry's
rousing patriotic speech on the feast of St Crispian appeals to a
common experience among the soldiers, arguing that when the
survivors show their wounds, these will become signs of a glorious
moment in English history, one that will help define the nation.[87] Their
names will become synonymous with an ideal representation of
England, and

> we in it [the day] shall be remembered,
> We few, we happy few, we band of brothers.
> For he today that sheds his blood with me
> Shall be my brother; be he ne'er so vile,
> This day shall gentle his condition.

> And gentlemen in England now abed
> Shall think themselves accursed they were not here[.]
>
> (4.3.59–65)

Of course, the speech is propaganda and is undercut by the fact that the army is patently British rather than English, a point Shakespeare is at pains to make. Moreover, the promise that all men are in this moment equal does not prevent the lack of equality demonstrated when the lists of the dead are read out. Nevertheless, the play explores the idea, so familiar in Machiavellian republicanism, that the most actively virtuous state is one that is constantly at war, because only then can the worthiness of the citizens be put to the test. Put another way, the same logic decreed that a state forever at war would be able to enfranchise more of its citizens than one that remained constantly at peace. As J.G.A. Pocock comments on the arguments of Machiavelli's *The Art of War* and *The Discourses*:

> Military *virtù* necessitates political virtue because both can be presented in terms of the same end. The republic is the common good; the citizen, directing all his actions toward that good, may be said to dedicate his life to the republic; the patriot warrior dedicates his death, and the two are alike in perfecting human nature by sacrificing particular goods to a universal end. If this be virtue, then the warrior displays it as fully as the citizen, and it may be through military discipline that one learns to be a citizen and to display virtue.[88]

Such arguments could have been adapted from the translation of *The Art of Warre* published in 1560, and Shakespeare might also have consulted the relevant passages in the Latin or Italian editions of the *Discourses*.[89] But it is the analogous relationship between the texts that is important rather than an exact citation. Shakespeare could have gleaned such a straightforward argument from a variety of contacts, one of the most important sources being Lewis Lewkenor's translation of Gaspar Contarini's *The commonwealth and government of Venice* (1599), a work Shakespeare undoubtedly used (see below, pp. 154–6).

Furthermore, arguments had been made in the early 1590s that the best way to establish English freedoms and liberty was to pursue an aggressive conquest of Ireland, a political analysis that has an obvious bearing on *Henry V*.[90]

If war enfranchises and makes citizens or gentlemen of the army, it is a limited and unstable moment, a utopian hope that cannot survive the transition back to ordinary life. The active military emphasis of the republic could only preserve liberty for a relatively short space of time until military values transformed the republic into 'a tyranny, which may well be exercized by a Pompey or Caesar, once a citizen but now so far perverted as to use the sword as an instrument of political power'.[91] Machiavelli was acutely aware of this problem, and, as the startling juxtapositions in *Henry V* demonstrate, so was Shakespeare.[92] All men can be brothers in war, but not when the war draws to a close. At the outbreak of war leaders exhort citizens to act virtuously, inaugurating a more meritocratic form of government. But at the end of the campaign the old values are restored and often reinforced, strengthening the power of the crown.

Henry V, far from being a crudely patriotic play or, even, an exposé of conduct in war, is a sophisticated analysis of kingship which can be read alongside *Richard II*, the play which represents the deposition of the monarch that began the difficult cycle of late medieval English monarchy. The issues that are central to the last play of the tetralogy return us to those raised in the first.[93] *Henry V* forces the audience/reader to reconsider the career of England's most celebrated ruler, one who had been represented on the stage a few years previously in an uncritical light in the anonymous *The Famous Victories of Henry V* (early 1590s).[94] In the end, we have to judge the King on his merits.

The same is true of Shakespeare's other history plays which show unhappy kings behaving more or less badly and failing to gather the popular support they require to enable them to function as rulers. *King John*, perhaps one of Shakespeare's first plays, if the date of 1590/1 is correct, constantly emphasizes the problem of legitimacy. John's claim to the English throne is made more problematic than the sources indicated it really was.[95] John's notoriously difficult and uneasy reign is shown

alongside the conspicuous success of his subject, Philip the Bastard of
Faulconbridge, whose life parallels that of his king. While John suffers
torment and doubts, which prevent him from acting as effectively as he
might, the Bastard makes the most of his opportunities and dominates
the English campaign against the French (prefiguring Henry's triumphs
two hundred years later). At the start of act five, John is forced by the
Papal forces led by Cardinal Pandulph to surrender his crown and agrees
to accept his authority as king from the Pope in return for their help
against the French, who claim that John's nephew, Arthur, should rule
England.[96] John stresses the need for immediate action because he is in
danger of losing his crown through the lack of popular support:

> Our discontented counties do revolt;
> Our people quarrel with obedience,
> Swearing allegiance and the love of soul
> To stranger blood, to foreign royalty.
>
> (5.1.8–11)

The revolt against John reaches the proportions of a crisis after the
unfortunate death of Arthur. In contrast to the resigned gloom of John
is the ebullient confidence of the Bastard who has to urge John to
assume the proper mantle of a king:

> But wherefore do you droop? why look you sad?
> Be great in act, as you have been in thought;
> Let not the world see fear and sad distrust
> Govern the motion of a kingly eye!
> Be stirring as the time, be fire with fire,
> Threaten the threat'ner, and outface the brow
> Of bragging horror: so shall inferior eyes,
> That borrow their behaviours from the great,
> Grow great by your example and put on
> The dauntless spirit of resolution.
>
> (44–53)

King John emphasizes the need for rulers to act like kings, and so
transform themselves into monarchs. The play appears to draw attention

to the significant similarities between the reigns of John and Elizabeth, both rulers having had their titles undermined by papal decree (Elizabeth's through Pope Pius's bull of 1570, encouraging her Catholic subjects to rebel and overthrow her (see above, p. 2)).[97] However, the logic of the Bastard's ebullient bravado, his undoubted success in countering his own disadvantages as an illegitimate son, and his role in bolstering the reign of John, is that action is more important than a title. It is in keeping with the dramatic message of the play that the final lines in defence of England's independence and sovereignty are spoken by the Bastard: 'This England never did, nor never shall, / Lie at the proud foot of a conqueror' (5.7.112–13).

Throughout the history plays Shakespeare makes it clear that rulers depend either on popular support or on the good will of their mighty subjects, rather than on inherited titles for their survival in office. Richard II acknowledges that Bolingbroke is a danger to him because he has established a widespread base of support, and has a skilful enough common touch, whether sincere or false, to make himself seem like the next king:

> he did seem to dive into their hearts
> With humble and familiar courtesey ...
> Off goes his bonnet to an oyster-wench.
> A brace of draymen bid God speed him well
> And had the tribute of his supple knee
> With 'Thanks, my countrymen, my loving friends',
> As were our England in reversion his,
> And he our subjects' next degree in hope.
>
> (*Richard II*, 1.4.25–6, 31–6)

Similar comments are contained within the sources, notably Holinshed's *Chronicles*, but they are highlighted and elaborated in Shakespeare's play, with the addition of specific professions – craftsmen, oyster-wench, draymen – which serve to emphasize the extent of Bolingbroke's efforts and success.[98] Richard's haughty disdain for the aristocracy (shown in the first act of the play when he banishes Thomas Mowbray, Duke of Norfolk and Henry Bolingbroke, Duke of Hereford, having intervened to establish what judgement he pleases), his promotion of unsuitable favourites and neglect of the proper government of his people (shown in the discussion of the gardeners and the Queen (3.4)), are what lose him his crown.[99] His attempts at extortion and refusal to recognize the hereditary rights of his powerful subjects reveal him to be dangerously isolated. His actions are a pointed contrast to Bolingbroke's attempts to root his claims to the throne in terms of his popular appeal. Richard's uncle, the Duke of York, warns him not to seize the lands of the recently deceased John of Gaunt for his own benefit, because he only holds the throne by 'fair sequence and succession' (2.1.199). An inherited title which is not bolstered by more substantial support will never be an adequate basis for government. When Richard departs, the nobles discuss his plight. Northumberland observes that 'The king is not himself, but basely led / By flatterers' (241–2). Northumberland means that the King's true counsellors – such as himself – know better what is good for him than the bad ones he has chosen. They prevent Richard from performing his offices and duties as he should, misleading him into concentrating on his whims and desires.[100] Ross comments further that he has alienated all classes through his abuse of his powers: 'The commons hath he pill'd with grievous taxes, / And quite lost their hearts. The nobles hath he fin'd / For ancient quarrels and quite lost their hearts' (246–8). Their argument is reinforced by their decision to join Bolingbroke's army immediately. Like their future sovereign, whom they help to crown, Ross, Northumberland and Willoughby show that they regard sovereignty as unworkable without some form of consensus with a wider public, or, at least, the good will of the aristocracy. Shakespeare's political analysis seems to be in line with that of Sir Thomas Smith, who, in distinguishing between kings and tyrants, defined a king as someone 'who by succession or election commeth *with the good will of the people* to that government, and doth administer the common wealth by the lawes of the same [my emphasis]'.[101] Kings who lack the people's 'good will' not only have no stable basis for establishing government, but have no right to rule.

Equally pointed is the grotesquely comic process in *Richard III*, when Richard has to use Buckingham to fake popular support for him in order to assume the crown. Buckingham records that he is faced with silence when he proclaims 'God save Richard, England's royal King' (3.7.22), the people 'like dumb statues or breathing stones / Star'd each on other, and look'd deadly pale' (25–6), hardly an auspicious sign for the prospect of the new reign. After Richard's claim has been repeated by the Recorder, ten followers of Buckingham planted in the audience hurl their caps in the air and shout 'God save King Richard!' (36), enabling Buckingham to claim support for Richard's rule. This graphic demonstration of general hostility to Richard exposes the limits of his political skills, showing that he can succeed in outmanoeuvring corrupt and naïve nobles but cannot deceive the people. Furthermore, it indicates that without a wider basis of support he will not be able to rule for any length of time, as the play subsequently demonstrates.

The same is more poignantly the case for Henry VI, who yearns increasingly to be a private citizen rather than a king, a longing that culminates in his speech on a molehill where he voices his desire to be a shepherd while the chaotic violence of battle rages around him (3 Henry VI, 2.5.1–54). Shortly before his final imprisonment and murder, Henry reveals his bewilderment when faced with the issues and problems of kingship. After listing his good qualities to Exeter, he asks, 'why should they love Edward more than me?' (4.8.47). Exeter is spared having to answer by the entrance of Edward with his victorious forces, ready to re-establish the Yorkist dynasty, in itself an eloquent explanation of Henry's failure. Henry lacks the abilities of a king and so fails to be one. In 2 Henry VI, he is caught, as he observes himself (4.9.31–5), between the popular uprising of Jack Cade and the machinations of Richard, Duke of York, which culminate in York's invasion with his Irish army. Henry's remark to his wife that he will 'learn to govern better' (47) shows how ill-equipped he is to deal with the harsh realities of political leadership. Imprisoned later, Henry interrogates his gaolers and asks if they have not broken their oaths to act as 'true subjects' to the King (3 Henry VI, 3.1.78). Once again, the King is shown not to be the best judge of how he should perform his offices and duties. The first gaoler explains that they were only subjects while Henry was king (80), and that they now serve King Edward.

Henry accepts their logic, commenting that they would obey him again 'If he were seated as King Edward is' (95), but that, for now, 'what God will, that let your King perform; / And what he will, I humbly yield unto' (99–100). Henry's transition from ruler to subject is achieved with a minimum of effort, indicating that nothing separates Henry – who has, as he admits, a weak claim to the throne (*3 Henry VI*, 1.1.124–206) – from his lesser subjects. Richard, Duke of York, had earlier observed, accurately enough, that he was 'More like a king, more kingly in my thoughts' (*2 Henry VI*, 5.1.29) than the King himself. On learning of the release of the Duke of Somerset, later in the same scene, York exclaims, '"King" did I call thee? No, thou art not king, / Not fit to govern and rule multitudes' (93–4), words which are later echoed by Macduff on hearing the extensive list of Malcolm's supposed vices (see below, p. 80). York dies before he has the chance to claim the crown, but his sons, Edward IV and Richard III, both become kings in *3 Henry VI*, although they are no more answers to England's need for responsible kingship than Henry VI.

All fail because they are incapable of governing with wider horizons in mind than their own dynastic ambitions and factional conflict. Henry IV and Henry V study hard to justify their reigns and to learn how to govern, painfully aware that they must discover reasons other than legitimacy to rule successfully. Henry IV realizes that an external enemy will solve his problems, but he never has the luxury of a unified, peaceful realm which would enable him to risk overseas conquest. Henry V manages what his father planned in his French campaign, but the achievement of unity in war is unstable and the empire collapses with the accession of the pacific Henry VI. The Earl of Richmond's triumph at the Battle of Bosworth restores order. However, he succeeds not because of his claim to legitimate possession of the throne, which is barely mentioned in *Richard III*, and remains as shadowy as Richmond himself, but rather through his ability to govern, as his last speech demonstrates:

> Proclaim a pardon to the soldiers fled
> That in submission will return to us;

> And then, as we have ta'en the sacrament,
> We will unite the white rose and the red ...
> What traitor hears me and says not Amen? ...
> O now let Richmond and Elizabeth,
> The true succeeders of each royal House,
> By God's fair ordinance conjoin together ...
> Abate the edge of traitors, gracious Lord,
> That would reduce these bloody days again,
> And make poor England weep in streams of blood.
>
> (*Richard III*, 5.5.16–19, 22, 29–31, 35–7)

Richmond's words may not appear remarkable, but at the end of a sequence of four plays which have concentrated upon the bloody consequences of murderous factional conflict, an amnesty for former traitors and the plea for unity against future ones is clearly welcome. Richmond/Henry VII not only strives to end the slaughter England has endured, but reaches out to a public beyond an aristocracy notable mainly for its ingrained obsession with material gain and self-interest. Henry VII indicates that the Tudors have at least learned that government requires a wider base than their immediate peer group.

Chapter Two

THE POWER AND RIGHTS OF THE CROWN

'The King – the King's to blame'

———————————

In the last scene of act four of *Macbeth*, Malcolm, the oldest son of the murdered King Duncan, and Macduff, briefly retreat from the hectic action of the play to reflect on the dire fate of Scotland under Macbeth's tyranny and consider the land's future. Malcolm initiates the conversation by pointing out that Macbeth, now a 'tyrant, whose sole name blisters our tongues, / Was once thought honest' (4.3.12–13) and suggests that the same duplicity might continue in him: 'I am young; but something / You may discern of him through me' (14–15).[1] Malcolm explains that power can be corrupting: 'A good and virtuous nature may recoil, / In an imperial charge' (18–19), and warns Macduff that it can be impossible to tell the difference between good and evil: 'Though all things foul would wear the brows of grace, / Yet Grace must still look so' (23–4). The straightforward Macduff starts to lapse into despair ('I have lost my hopes' (24)), but the audience probably recalls Duncan's lament at his own failure to perceive the treacherous nature of Macdonwald: 'There's no art / To find the mind's construction in the face: / He was a gentleman on whom I built / An absolute trust' (1.4.11–14). Malcolm is about to show that his father's passive acceptance of the vicissitudes of fortune is naïve, and that there is more to the art of governing than Duncan realized. He will also have to experience the unpleasant reality of a political world where trust cannot be taken for granted.

Malcolm proceeds to test the loyalty of Macduff. He first asks the reasonable question why Macduff left his wife and child in Scotland to the mercy of Macbeth if he enjoys no protection from Macbeth's regime. We have just seen them murdered in the previous scene, so we know that Macduff is an honest – albeit not terribly thoughtful, bright or pragmatic – subject, although it is clear that Malcolm cannot be certain, as his cautious language demonstrates: 'you may be rightly just, / Whatever I shall think' (30–1). Macduff's explosive reaction is to abandon his hopes for revitalizing Scotland, castigating Malcolm for his inaction and declaring that his own honour matters more than the doubts and caution of a would-be saviour: 'I would not be the villain that thou think'st / For the whole space that's in the tyrant's grasp, / And the rich East to boot' (35–7).

Two approaches to the problem of Macbeth's tyranny and usurpation are juxtaposed in these few lines. Macduff argues in terms of the moral absolutes of good and evil, insisting that only resolute and immediate action by the righteous can hope to triumph. Malcolm deliberately undermines such theological terms by pointing out that the Devil is not easy to identify: 'Angels are bright still, though the brightest fell' (22). His approach might more properly be termed 'political', a cautious pragmatism that seeks to calculate the best way of dealing with a pressing problem and working out a solution.[2] Given the fate of Macduff's family, it is clear that his arguments are undercut by a dramatic irony that will become clear later in the scene. The audience also recall that Macbeth rose to prominence when he was instrumental in crushing Macdonwald's rebellion, a clear indication that the immediate solution to a problem is not necessarily the best or most lasting one.

The rest of the scene explores and elaborates this contrast between the moral and the political. Malcolm provides a series of his own tyrannical vices for Macduff to consider, suggesting that Scotland is better off under Macbeth's rule. He claims to be so addicted to sex that even an endless stream of Scottish wives, daughters, matrons and maids cannot 'fill up / The cistern of my lust' (62–3); so avaricious that he will deprive nobles of jewels, lands and houses, seeking even to foster quarrels between his subjects so that he can destroy them for their wealth; before finishing with a spectacular list of the kingly virtues that he lacks:

> the king-becoming graces,
> As Justice, Verity, Temp'rance, Stableness,
> Bounty, Perseverance, Mercy, Lowliness,
> Devotion, Patience, Courage, Fortitude,
> I have no relish of them; but abound
> In the division of each several crime,
> Acting it many ways.

(91–6)

Macduff's anguished response to Malcolm's question whether such a man is fit to govern is easy to endorse: 'Fit to govern? / No, not to live. – O nation miserable!' (102–3). At this point the language of moral absolutes appears to have triumphed over the political, with both interlocutors speaking in terms of polarized opposites.[3]

However, Malcolm subsequently admits that he has been lying, and that he is rather more suited for government than he has so far demonstrated, being chaste, temperate, loyal, 'and delight[ing] / No less in truth, than life: my first false speaking / Was this upon myself' (129–31). If it is Macduff who has been displaying his unsophisticated naïveté in the exchange so far, now it is Malcolm's turn. After this new revelation he asks why Macduff remains silent, and is met by the unsurprising riposte: 'Such welcome and unwelcome things at once, / 'Tis hard to reconcile' (138–9). Once doubt and uncertainty enter the realm of political discourse, it is impossible to go back to the security previously enjoyed.

This is a key passage, not just in terms of the play, but also in terms of Shakespeare's dramatic representation of politics. Macduff wants monarchs to be judged simply in terms of their saintliness, and he castigates the 'truest issue of thy [Scotland's] throne' because he 'blaspheme[s] his breed', unlike his father who was a 'most sainted King' and his mother who was 'Oft'ner upon her knees than on her feet' in devotion (106–10). Yet, as Duncan has demonstrated, the most pious kings do not necessarily make the best rulers. Moreover, Shakespeare's earlier English history plays had also shown that a saintly king could as easily lead to a serious national disaster as an evil one. Henry VI may be a better man than Richard III, but the effects of his rule are shown to be no less onerous for his unfortunate subjects.

Malcolm is portrayed here as a potentially successful ruler who is learning how to govern before he is ready to assume his rightful throne. By the end of the scene he has secured the loyalty of Macduff, albeit as much through the actions of Macbeth as his own. His tactics could be described as Machiavellian in their deliberate separation of morality from politics in order to achieve his goal. One of Machiavelli's most celebrated maxims was that the successful prince had to be capable of adopting the slyness of the fox as well as the strength of the lion, a key lesson of *The Prince* that was singled out by Renaissance readers:

> For heerby hee [Machiavelli] gaue to understand, that a prince ought to shew himselfe a man and a beast together. A prince then being constrained well to know how to counterfet the beast, hee ought amongst all beasts to chuse the complexion of the Fox, and of the Lyon together, and not of the one without the other: for the Fox is subtill, to keepe himselfe from snares, yet he is too weake to guard himselfe from wolves: and the Lion is strong enough to guard himselfe from wolves, but hee is not subtill enough to keepe himselfe from nets: A man must then bee a Foxe to know all subtilties and deceits, and a Lyon to bee stronger, and to make wolves afraid.[4]

This particular passage describes what takes place between Malcolm and Macduff fairly accurately. Malcolm is forced by his circumstances to act like a beast, the cunning fox. Macduff, in contrast, is the stupid lion, brave but foolhardy and totally unsuited for rule (having shown that he cannot 'protect' his family as a responsible father).[5] Malcolm, like Machiavelli's prudent ruler, has to tell lies and abandon the desirable standards of morality in order to assemble a loyal army that will enable him to rule at all, let alone well.

Macbeth ends with Malcolm's triumph and just rule re-established in Scotland. In the final speech in the play Malcolm makes all the higher-ranking Scottish nobles, thanes, into earls, perhaps reflecting James's desire to unify the British Isles, one of the clear subtexts of the play.[6] He recalls all exiles who have fled Macbeth's tyranny, a detail that would seem to parallel the return of the Protestant exiles when Elizabeth ascended the throne in 1558.[7] Scotland's future seems hopeful and Malcolm appears to be a good king whose aim is to heal divisions and establish a lasting peace (exactly as James I saw himself and his role as a ruler).[8] In showing this the play poses one of the central political questions of the sixteenth and seventeenth centuries: whether a monarch ruled through hereditary right, or through personal suitability for the role. If the latter was the case, under what circumstances were the people justified in deposing a wicked tyrant, and who was capable of making such a judgement?

Macbeth was undoubtedly written and first performed in 1605–6, soon after James's accession (1603). As commentators have often pointed out, the play is full of references to James's particular interests: witchcraft, the question of equivocation in the swearing of oaths, the ability – or inability – of the monarch to cure the king's evil (scrofula), and his own regal ancestry through Banquo, whose progeny are seen stretching 'out to th'crack of doom' (4.1.117).[9] It might be argued, however, that the central relevance of *Macbeth* to James is in terms of its representation of political problems, the succession and legitimacy of rulers. James had already published two important treatises outlining his conception, as King of Scotland, of monarchy and government, *Basilikon Doron* and *The Trew Law of Free Monarchies* (both 1598). James argued that hereditary rulers must be obeyed by their subjects whatever the character of the monarch and the effects of their actions. He distinguished between kings and tyrants, and had a stern conception of a king's duty to his subjects in office. He urged monarchs to obey the law: 'a good king will not onely delight to rule his subjects by the lawe, but even will conforme himselfe in his owne actions thereunto'. Nevertheless, he argued that monarchs must be obeyed no matter what crimes they commit.[10] A subject's duty was to obey the king because monarchy was the divinely ordained form of government. Rebellion was never permitted.[11] For James, a king was 'Gods Lieutenant in earth' and 'so is he Master over every person that

FIGURE 5 *King James I* by Daniel Mytens. The most imposing portrait of James, showing his sense of his majesty, as he towers over the viewer.

inhabiteth the same, having power over the life and death of every one of them'.[12] A king could never be deposed by the people as all kings rule as part of God's divine plan:

> The wickednesse therefore of the King can never make them that are ordained to be judged by him, to become his Judges ... a wicked king is sent by God for a curse to his people, and a plague for their sinnes: but that it is lawfull to them to shake off that curse at their owne hand, which God hath laid on them, that I deny, and may so do justly.[13]

James was, as he makes explicit in his treatises, making his case against the powerful and widely disseminated arguments of the 'resistance theorists' of monarchomachs such as John Knox, John Ponet and Christopher Goodman, who had argued that Protestants were justified in attempting to depose the Catholic Queen Mary Tudor because she oppressed the true religion.[14] Malcolm's description of his purported vices might have been written with a passage from *The Trew Law of Free Monarchies* in mind. James describes the worst that a monarch can do, as a pointed contrast to the greater evils caused by rebellion: 'tyrannizing over mens persons, sonnes, daughters and servants; redacting noble houses, and men, and women of noble blood, to slavish and servile offices; and extortion, and spoile of their lands and goods to the princes owne use and commoditie, and of his courtiers, and servants[.]'[15] James's imagined tyrant abuses his subjects by assuming that he can use them as his property, exactly the impression Malcolm gives of his future reign to Macduff.

But if James gave an unambiguous answer to the problem of tyranny (however bad a king may be, nothing can be done because any alternative is worse), *Macbeth*, in line with one of its principal themes, is much more equivocal. Immediately after Malcolm and Macduff's exchange, and before Macduff learns from Ross of the grim fate of his family, a doctor enters. He informs the Scots that the English King is about to appear, having just touched a number of his unfortunate subjects as a way of curing them of scrofula: 'With this strange virtue, / He hath a heavenly gift of prophecy; / And sundry blessings hang about his throne, / That speak him full of grace' (4.3.156–9). The English King and the ordered, peaceful land he rules serve as a pointed contrast to the chaos and anarchy of Macbeth's Scotland, a juxtaposition which could have seemed jingoistic and hostile to the new ruler and his countrymen.[16] Moreover, as Holinshed's *Chronicles*, the main source for *Macbeth*, reveal, Edward the Confessor's saintly rule was plagued by a series of wars, with the Welsh and the Danes as well as Macbeth's Scots, a disease of the body politic far more significant than scrofula. There were multiple and confusing claims to the throne, so that when Edward died, a series of foreign invasions and bloody wars erupted before William, Duke of Normandy became William I and inaugurated the Norman Conquest. Edward had prophesied these invasions. He could cure the king's evil, but could not solve the fundamental problems of government.[17] And, as anyone at all familiar with Shakespeare's work in the previous decade would have known, English history was not a straightforward tale of legitimate, good kings preserving stability and justly fighting off misguided, bad rivals.

The historical parallels between Britain in the middle of the eleventh century and Britain at the start of the seventeenth are uncomfortable ones which ask more questions about James's theories of government and right to rule than they answer. Holinshed portrays Duncan as an ineffective ruler who is too 'soft and gentle of nature', and who fosters anarchy and rebellion when his subjects perceive 'how negligent he was in punishing offendors'.[18] Macbeth, although cruel, was an effective and efficient ruler who successfully reformed the legal system and, in contrast to Duncan, quashed rebellion.[19] Malcolm may have been the legitimate king as Duncan's eldest son, but had he been a poor ruler, would the people have been obliged to obey him? And, as David Norbrook has pointed out, if primogeniture is the accepted norm, why does Duncan have to nominate his son as his successor, and why is Macbeth's rule accepted without demur by the nobles (including Banquo) if he is a usurper?[20]

It seems clear that Shakespeare is using *Macbeth* to explore the political problems of Britain immediately after the accession of James I. We are provided with contrasting images of saintly and tyrannical rulers in this one scene, and asked to assess, if not James I himself, then the basis for his claims to the English throne. James's mother, Mary Queen of Scots, had had the best claim to the English throne through her descent from her grandmother, Henry VIII's sister, Margaret Tudor. However, she had effectively been excluded because of her Catholicism (see above, pp. 25–6). Her case was argued in a widely circulating dialogue, *Leicester's Commonwealth* (1584). This polemical work also sought to expose the corrupt nature of England under Elizabeth, which the anonymous author argued was really ruled by self-interested Protestant nobles under the suzerainty of the Earl of Leicester.[21] If Mary could be excluded from the succession, then there could be no natural right of any candidate to assume that blood alone, apart from intrinsic virtue and suitability for power, would be enough. If James had an incontestable right to rule, then his legitimacy served also to highlight the undoubtedly weak claims of the Tudors, a dynasty whose history and pre-history Shakespeare had just so assiduously chronicled. There could be no easy escape from this particular cleft stick.

Macbeth is not the only one of Shakespeare's plays that raises the question of the legitimacy of the succession, one of the key issues confronting Elizabethan and Jacobean English citizens. Indeed, the problem became so pressing that Elizabeth forbade discussion of who would be her successor, and took drastic action against those like the puritan member of parliament Peter Wentworth, who refused to obey this dictate by raising the matter in parliament.[22] She was also prepared to resort to censorship on a number of occasions in the last years of her reign.[23] Nevertheless, for all the questions raised about James's right to rule, both before and after Elizabeth's death, there is a marked change in the nature and style of the debates after James's accession.[24] *Macbeth* is not a play that fights shy of awkward issues and problems. However, it is hard to read it as a work that expresses clear hostility to the monarch and questions his right to rule. Before James acceded to the throne, Shakespeare was far more sceptical of the worth and desirability of his becoming king of England.

I

A pointed contrast between the political subtext of plays written in Elizabeth's last years and those produced in the early years of James's reign is revealed through a comparison of *Hamlet* (1601–2) and *King Lear* (1605–6).[25] *Hamlet* represents a nation ruled by a murderous usurper; in Denmark, where government takes place in a paranoid and unstable court, which is threatened by aggressive and powerful enemies and haunted by a ghost from the past whose intervention, while legitimate, only brings destruction. When the royal family have destroyed themselves and extinguished their line, Denmark is inherited by Fortinbras, Prince of Norway. The splendid irony is that *Hamlet* opens with the Danes manning the battlements against the attempted invasion of Fortinbras, his aim being to recover the lands his father lost when he was defeated by Hamlet senior. The murder of Hamlet senior precipitates a chain of events which leaves Denmark not only deprived of its royal family, but in the same position they would have been in had Fortinbras senior defeated Hamlet.[26]

It would be a crude reading of the play that tried to relate its narrative mechanically to contemporary events. But, as Howard Erskine-Hill has pointed out, the play seems to contain numerous allusions to James VI of Scotland, his mother, Mary Queen of Scots and her part in the murder of her second husband, Lord Darnley.[27] The death of Hamlet senior bears an uncanny resemblance to the murder of Darnley, killed in 1567 by the Queen's lover Bothwell, whom she married four months later.[28] Darnley was, according to Holinshed, murdered in an orchard, exactly as the elder Hamlet was (1.5.59–79); the effect of poison on Darnley, as related by Buchanan, was to corrupt and disfigure his skin, just as Hamlet's ghost relates happened to him (71–3). Moreover, anti-Marian propaganda claimed that Mary slept with Bothwell before her husband's death, as Hamlet assumes that Gertrude has done with Claudius. The same material unfavourably contrasted the inferior 'appearance and character of Bothwell by comparison with Darnley', just as Hamlet confronts his mother with her bizarre trade in brothers for husbands (3.4.53–88).[29] Erskine-Hill suggests that in the portrait of the intellectual heir to the throne, 'Shakespeare ... seems to have dramatized the position of King James VI ... as the tragically incapacitated inheritor of the unnatural scene into which he had been born'.[30] Denmark, an unusual setting for an English Renaissance play, stands for Scotland, both being – or having been – elective monarchies.[31]

More pertinent than such a specific reading of the play – although Erskine-Hill's argument is persuasive and he is careful not to be reductive or formulaic in his subtle exposition of *Hamlet* – is the representation of a paranoid and unstable court in which the proper functions of advice, counsel and debate have degenerated to flattery, espionage and silence. Moreover, the court is one in which the problem of dynastic succession has not been tackled. Elsinore represents dying Tudor England two or three years before the end of that dynasty as much as embattled Stuart Scotland. Such allusions were legion in late Tudor and early Stuart literature, as numerous studies have pointed out.[32] Drama, especially, given the short runs of most plays and the need for commercial theatres to attract large audiences, was replete with contemporary topical and political allusions.[33] Courts, especially those of Italian city states, were routinely represented as vicious, luxurious and corrupt.[34] To give just one example: John Marston's *The Fawn*, written in 1604–5, launches a vicious attack on the corruption of James's court, using the setting of Urbino, famous as the city state where the dialogues that made up Baldisario Castiglione's *Book of the Courtier* purportedly took place.[35] In such plays the audience were invited to interpret the relationship between the foreign court and the court of their own monarch in London as they saw fit. The dramatist could, of course, deny that he intended any link between the two.[36]

Polonius, the chief counsellor of state (a role which had been occupied by William Cecil, Lord Burghley for most of Elizabeth's reign until his death in 1598) dispenses advice which is generally fatuous, long-winded and too generalized to be useful, as in his comments to his departing son, Laertes (1.3.55–81). He meets his end acting as a spy behind the arras, a just fate given his role in using his daughter to inform on Hamlet, a decision which leads to her madness and death.[37]

Contemporary political treatises routinely railed against the dangers of poor advice and urged rulers to select counsellors who could be critical without being subversive or treasonable in their comments. It is a sign of how ubiquitous a part of political discourse this was that both Machiavelli and his Huguenot critic, Innocent Gentillet, should devote key sections of their supposedly diametrically opposed treatises to warning princes of the dangers of tolerating bad advisers and flatterers.[38] A prince who failed to allow free and open counsel to operate would experience a surly, hostile and secretive court which would probably have to be controlled through the use of spies. Tacitus' account of the reign of Nero, a work which Shakespeare probably consulted in Sir Henry Saville's translation (1591), portrays Nero's court as a poisonous mixture of flatterers and conspirators who have to be rooted out by spies in order for the cruel and depraved emperor to survive in power.[39] Nero was duplicitous and could not be trusted by his subjects. The most infamous example of his crimes was the persecution of Seneca, who was forced to commit suicide after his involvement in a plot against the emperor.[40] Nero's tyranny encouraged a serious conspiracy which was eventually betrayed by those informers: all involved were either executed or forced to commit suicide.[41]

Polonius is also responsible for corrupting and poisoning other relationships at Elsinore. In act two, scene one, he is shown sending out his servant, Reynaldo, to spy on his son, Laertes, in Paris, instructing him so forcefully to go beyond the bounds of propriety that Reynaldo dares to protest (27, 36). He then abuses his parental relationship with his daughter, Ophelia, seeing her account of her disturbing encounter with Hamlet after she had returned his letters on her father's instruction as a matter to be referred further to the King rather than an indictment of his own inadequate counsel (110–20). The result is that Rosencrantz and Guildenstern, Hamlet's former school friends, are drawn into the plot by the King and Queen and sent to spy on the prince. Friendship, a relationship highly valued and frequently praised by Latin writers and their humanist followers, is corrupted at Elsinore, along with parenthood.[42] Eventually Hamlet exposes them, challenging

Guildenstern to play the recorder that one of the travelling players carries, explaining that 'It is as easy as lying' (3.2.348). When Guildenstern admits that he has not the skill, Hamlet counters, 'how unworthy a thing you make of me. You would play upon me, . . . you would pluck out the heart of my mystery, you would sound me from my lowest note to the top of my compass' (354–8). Hamlet asserts his own independence through his resistance: 'Call me what instrument you will, though you fret me, you cannot play upon me' (361–2). These words resemble a similar image employed by Francis Bacon, who argued that Elizabeth tempered her religious laws to insist on the outward obedience of her subjects only because she did not wish to 'make windows into men's hearts and secret thoughts' to discover their inner religious allegiances.[43]

One of Hamlet's most celebrated comments on the vicissitudes of the human condition, the speech where he reflects on 'What piece of work is a man', is probably best read as a comment on life at the dysfunctional court of Elsinore, rather than a general statement of existential angst. The words occur just after Guildenstern has admitted that he and Rosencrantz are in the service of the King, and are preceded by Hamlet's statement that his 'anticipation [shall] prevent your discovery, and your secrecy to the King and Queen moult no feather ["remain intact"]' (2.2.293–5). Hamlet's sardonic parody of optimistic accounts of man's abilities and God-like potential such as Pico della Mirandola's *Oration on the Dignity of Man* (1486), is conspicuously expressed as a means of describing and simultaneously disguising his madness, so refusing the corrupt and inadequate spies a window through to his soul.[44]

Hamlet appears to have been written with the classical histories of Suetonius, Seneca, Tacitus and, to a lesser extent, Plutarch, and their representations of the tyranny and cruelty of imperial Rome, very much at the forefront of the dramatist's mind. The play is clearly concerned with the same issues of government and the possibility of tyrannicide that were explored in *Julius Caesar*, written only one or two years earlier.[45] Polonius is responsible for the poisoning of all forms of human relationship – paternal, friendly, master/servant and political – only in so far as he is the chief counsellor. The real villain is the King, the usurper Claudius, as Laertes recognizes in the final, melodramatic denouement: 'The King – the King's to blame' (5.2.326). Claudius has murdered his brother, the legitimate king, and subsequently married his wife (an action that might well have reminded an audience as much of Henry VIII's union with his brother's wife, Catherine of Aragon, and the subsequent problems he encountered, as the story of Mary Stuart and the Earl of Bothwell), and in the process, disinherited his nephew, the probable successor.[46] In doing so he has destroyed any hope of a workable political process, which has degenerated into the standard combination of sycophancy and espionage found at the court of tyrants, and left his country open to invasion by the very forces his brother managed to defeat.

All this is not, of course, Claudius's intention – and we do not see him behaving in the manner of a tyrant unless he is protecting his own guilty secrets against the suspicions of his nephew – but his rule has these malign effects. He may not be a Nero, a Tiberius, a Caligula or even a Julius Caesar, but the similarities between his reign and theirs are uncomfortably close.[47] His name, an invention of Shakespeare's not found in any of the sources, is that of the Roman emperor whose reign preceded Nero's and was narrated by Tacitus in the *Annals*. Claudius, although not the most pernicious of Roman emperors, was nevertheless represented as brutal and conniving by both Tacitus and Suetonius.[48] Indeed, on the evidence of the two plays, there is far more justification for the assassination of Claudius than there is for that of Julius Caesar. In *Julius Caesar* the conspirators do not manage to provide any convincing evidence that Caesar is a tyrant, and rest their argument only on their own allegations and demands for liberty. Cassius, the instigator of the plot, simply asserts:

> And why should Caesar be a tyrant then?
> Poor man, I know he would not be a wolf
> But that he sees the Romans are but sheep.
> He were no lion, were not Romans hinds.
> Those that with haste will make a mighty fire

> Begin it with weak straws. What trash is Rome?
> What rubbish, and what offal? when it serves
> For the base matter to illuminate
> So vile a thing as Caesar?

(1.3.103–11)

Cassius's words demonstrate republican contempt for the masses as fickle and ill-educated, coupled with a desire for government that respects liberty, not legitimate criticism of a tyrant.[49] The speech is expressed in conditionals and subjunctives that concentrate on Cassius's haughty disdain for the citizens of Rome who support Caesar, rather than the supposed tyrant himself. We see Caesar as an isolated and ineffective ruler with poor judgement, cut off from the populace, and vain enough to refer to himself in the third person, but hardly a ruler who bears comparison to the worst tyrants represented in the pages of Tacitus or Suetonius.[50] In contrast, Claudius appears far more deserving of his brutal fate.

The issues raised in *Hamlet* can be read alongside the political philosophy expressed in the most infamous Huguenot monarchomach treatise, *Vindiciae, Contra Tyrannos: or, concerning the legitimate power of a prince over the people, and of the people over a prince*. The work, which is generally agreed to have been written by Hubert Languet and Philippe Duplessis Mornay, was published in Basle in 1579. It appeared under a false imprint (Edinburgh), and a pseudonym, Stephanus Junius Brutus, the Celt, a name which alluded to both Lucius Junius Brutus, the first consul of the Roman republic, who led the revolt against the last king of Rome, Tarquinius Superbus, and to Marcus Junius Brutus, assassin of Julius Caesar.[51] One of the key sources of *Hamlet* was Saxo Grammaticus's *Historiae Danicae*, a late twelfth-century work, first published in Latin in Paris in 1514. The hero, Amleth, eventually manages to revenge his murdered father, fooling his enemies by pretending to be stupid (his name signals a fool or simpleton). As Harold Jenkins has pointed out, 'Reduced to its bare outline this is the same story as the Romans told of Lucius Junius Brutus (a name which likewise signals a simpleton), who avenged the murder of his father when he drove the Tarquins out of Rome'.[52] This provides one of many links between Shakespeare's play and *Vindiciae, Contra Tyrannos*, which frequently refers to Tarquinius Superbus as the archetypal tyrant.[53] It concludes with a poem, the last lines of which are 'I believe that in vanquishing these huge monsters of evil, you will inscribe on the conquered: "O BRUTUS, YOU WERE MY TEACHER"'.[54]

The choice of Edinburgh as the fictitious place of publication and the transfer of the key figures of Roman republicanism to the Celtic fringe, emphasize the significance of Scotland in European political thought, a fact which strengthens the possible link between *Hamlet* and the Huguenot treatise. Scotland was most notable to European political commentators and theorists for the series of debates over the rights of resistance to tyrants written in response to the problems precipitated by the reign of Mary Queen of Scots.[55] The relevance of *Vindiciae, Contra Tyrannos* to *Hamlet*, and the likelihood of Shakespeare having consulted or read the work, is suggested by other contextual evidence. James VI's political reflections, published in 1598, were written in response to the arguments for regicide of his former tutor, George Buchanan, articulated in *De jure regni apud Scotos* (published 1579). The debate between the two draws attention to both sides of the argument raging in Scotland.[56] Not only was the Sidney family and its circle friendly with Buchanan and influenced by his ideas, but Sir Philip Sidney corresponded extensively with Languet and translated works by Duplessis Mornay.[57] *Vindiciae, Contra Tyrannos* was undoubtedly the key political text informing the arguments of Sidney's *Arcadia* concerning the limited power a monarchy should have and the rights of individual subjects, as Blair Worden has demonstrated.[58] The published *Arcadia* (1593), in turn, was the source for the subplot of *King Lear.*[59]

Vindiciae, Contra Tyrannos is divided into four sections, each based on a fundamental question of government. The first considers 'Whether subjects be bound, or ought, to obey princes who command anything against the law of God'; the second, 'Whether it be false to resist a prince wishing to abrogate the law of God and devastate the church: also by whom, how, and to what extent'; the third, 'Whether, and to what extent, it be lawful to resist a prince who is oppressing or ruining the commonwealth; also by whom, how, and by what right it may be allowed'; and the fourth, 'Whether neighbouring princes may by right, or ought, to render assistance to subjects of other princes who are being persecuted on account of pure religion, or oppressed by manifest tyranny'.[60] It will be clear that these questions are all relevant to the plot of *Hamlet*, although the relationship between the two texts is somewhat oblique.

The answer given to the first question in *Vindiciae, Contra Tyrannos* is straightforward, unequivocal and unsurprising. The author(s) state(s) that 'The king . . ., if he neglects God, if he goes over to his enemies, if he commits felonies against God, forfeits the kingdom by this very right and often loses it in practice'.[61] Moreover, 'subjects are not bound to obey a king against God'.[62] Claudius, although he shows no interest in ecclesiastical matters, is well aware of the theological significance of his actions. He admits that his 'offence is rank, it smells to heaven; / It hath the primal eldest curse upon't – / A brother's murder' (3.3.36–8), aligning him with the cursed race of Cain. His attempts to pray are futile – 'My words fly up, my thoughts remain below. / Words without thoughts never to heaven go' (97–8). Claudius's actions as king are violations of God's law. Hamlet's refusal to kill Claudius in this scene is not motivated by fear of breaking any religious or ethical code, but by the desire to prevent the victim's soul from ascending to heaven, and so escaping damnation.

Vindiciae, Contra Tyrannos asks that rulers be adjudged according to the effects of their rule and tyrants labelled accordingly:

> It can happen that someone who has occupied a kingdom by force rules it justly, and one to whom it is granted by right, does so unjustly. And clearly, since kingship is more a right than an inheritance, more a performance than a possession, he who performs his function badly seems more worthy of the name tyrant than he who has not received his function in the proper fashion.[63]

Although *Vindiciae, Contra Tyrannos* explicitly rejects the political philosophy of Machiavelli on numerous occasions, punning polemically on his name as 'Poxy Pelt' in the prefatory address to the reader, at this point the line of argument resembles his practical theories of rule rather than ones based on natural rights.[64] Many of the central questions that *Hamlet* poses derive from the particular problem which *Vindiciae, Contra Tyrannos* articulates. Is Claudius a good ruler and are the effects of his rule just? Would it be better on balance if Fortinbras were to take Denmark and rule instead (after all, England in 1600 faced a similar prospect)? Should dutiful subjects accept their lot and obey the ruler however he obtained power? Or is it their inevitable duty to oppose him?[65]

If the answer to the last question is yes, then is it, therefore, legitimate for Hamlet to resist, overthrow and depose Claudius, as the second and third questions in *Vindicae, Contra Tyrannos* ask? Hamlet's most famous soliloquy can be read as a response to this central political problem, as much as a meditation on the nature of existence:

> To be, or not to be, that is the question:
> Whether 'tis nobler in the mind to suffer
> The slings and arrows of outrageous fortune,
> Or to take arms against a sea of troubles
> And by opposing end them ...
> For who would bear the whips and scorns of time,
> Th'oppressor's wrong, the proud man's contumely,
> The pangs of dispriz'd love, the law's delay,
> The insolence of office, and the spurns
> That patient merit of th'unworthy takes,
> When he himself might his quietus make
> With a bare bodkin?

(3.1.56–60, 71–6)

The speech is nicely balanced in its hesitant embrace of violence as a solution. When Hamlet meditates on the nature of suffering and action, we cannot be sure whether he is planning 'to take arms against a sea of troubles' by ending his own life or that of the person or thing who has caused his misery. Equally, the desire to achieve 'quietus' (settling a debt) through the use of a 'bare bodkin' (dagger), does not indicate whether the intended target is his own breast or another's, and the mention of 'oppressor' and 'office' in the immediately previous build-up of phrases indicates that Hamlet's mind is at least partly on the sins of Claudius. Furthermore, political assassination, successful or not, invariably ended in the death of the assassin, as is the spectacular case at the end of the play.[66] Assuming the mantle of God's avenger against tyranny was, of course, a dubious honour because even if one was certain of one's right to kill, death undoubtedly awaited the perpetrator. Hamlet's anxiety and hesitation are understandable, especially as his only authority is a ghost claiming to be his father who urges him to kill the King. According to *Vindiciae, Contra Tyrannos*, private individuals were not handed the sword of justice to perform acts of revenge; only magistrates were entitled to wield it.[67]

Hamlet's status could not be more ambiguous: although an educated member of the royal family, he holds no particular office and is still a student in Wittenberg. Equally, kings had to remember who granted them their power. Citing David as the ideal king, the treatise argues:

> He was anointed twice: first by the prophet at the command of God as a token of election; then at the command of the people while he was being constituted as king. This was done in order that kings should always remember that it is from God, but by the people and for the people that they rule; and that they should not claim that they have received their kingdom from God alone and by the sword, as they say, since they were first girded with that very sword by the people.[68]

Claudius fails on both counts: he is described by Hamlet as having circumvented the normal process of establishing the succession by choice ('Popp'd in between th'election and my hopes' (5.2.65)) and is manifestly cut off from the voice of God.[69] There is, however, popular acclaim for Laertes, a significantly less tormented avenger than Hamlet, who is championed by the 'rabble' who want him to be king (4.5.102–8), and, to a lesser extent, for Hamlet, whom Claudius will not try for the murder of Polonius because of 'the great love the general gender bear him' (4.7.18).[70] Hamlet may be unsure of his rights, but Claudius, an 'incestuous, murd'rous, damned Dane' (5.2.332) masquerading as a legitimate king, is a ripe candidate for deposition.

Hamlet provides no obvious answers to the variety of political questions it raises. Nevertheless, it demands to be read in terms of the political anxieties of (very) late Elizabethan England, ruled by a decrepit, dying Queen who could no longer command the respect of many of her most influential subjects, with the uncertainty of being ruled by a new dynasty in prospect, surrounded by enemies (France, Spain, Ireland), divided in religious affiliation, and riven by factions at court.[71] Depending on the actual date of its composition – a problematic concept given the difference between the texts published as the first two quartos and the folio, which suggest that it was revised at various points[72] – it may have been written during or after the rebellion and execution of the Earl of Essex (February 1601).[73] The plot is, as I have already noted, in essence, a variation of the story of the banishment of the Tarquins, a narrative of republican liberation that haunted Shakespeare's working life and which he had first used in *The Rape of Lucrece* (1594). There is no straightforward way out of the political impasse at Elsinore as there was in Rome. But this may be a deliberate comment on the state of England in 1600.

II

King Lear, like *Hamlet*, represents the consequences of an undesirable succession and shows the disastrous events precipitated by the advent of the new reign. However, while the plot of *Hamlet* revolves around the question of whether to get rid of the incumbent monarch, *King Lear* is more concerned with how to restore what has been lost by a king's foolish actions. *Hamlet* looks towards an impending event; *King Lear* debates whether what has gone can be restored or rebuilt. The play, which surely looks back to the story of Oedipus, as dramatized by Seneca, represents the fall of a king from power and his subsequent path to enlightenment.[74] As Harry V. Jaffa has pointed out, at the start of the play, Lear is conspicuously 'the greatest of Shakespeare's kings ...

at the head of a united Britain (not merely England) and at peace, not only with all domestic factions, but with the outside world as well'.[75] The problem is that he then gives his kingdom away foolishly to his evil daughters, retaining the name of king and a supposed vestige of power, before his redemption begins on the heath with the poorest and least visible of his former subjects, a homeless beggar (albeit a fake). Unlike his sources, Geoffrey of Monmouth's *History of the Kings of Britain* and the chronicle play, *The History of King Leir*, Shakespeare grants Lear no ultimate redemption.[76] Just as it appears that Cordelia and France's invading army will restore the fractured dynasty, Cordelia is murdered and the grief-stricken Lear dies, leaving the kingdom in limbo with his heirs all dead.

The start and the conclusion clearly refer the audience back to the succession from Elizabeth to James and the extinction of the Tudor dynasty. But other details provided in the first scene link the play more specifically to the early rule of James and his grand plans for the unification of Britain, which, despite the adoption of the Union Jack as the official British flag in April 1605 and James's assumption of the title, 'King of Britain', was rejected by the English parliament in early 1607. While James saw only great possibilities, others opposed the union of the kingdoms through fear of being dominated by the Scots who came in James's wake, of the loss of English legal sovereignty, of the influence of the more austere Scottish Reformed Church (the 'Kirk'), and of loss of revenue through disadvantageous trade relations with Scotland.[77]

King Lear was undoubtedly first performed on the commercial stage some time in 1605–6, and was produced at court for the King 'during the Christmas period in 1606'.[78] Terence Hawkes has recently observed that Lear's attempted division of his kingdom into three portions would have appeared to contemporary playgoers, especially given that Lear's first imperious command is to ask for a map (1.1.36), as a breaking up of a unified Britain into its constituent nations. Goneril is to be married to the Duke of Albany, 'the old name for the area which a modern map terms Scotland', and Regan is to be married to the Duke of Cornwall, 'the old name for Wales and the West of England', which means that the 'third more opulent than your sisters' (86) offered to Cordelia 'appears as a cut-down, ragged, violated English remainder'.[79] Lear destroys Britain, while James was attempting – although unsuccessfully – to unite it. As if these parallels did not make the point obvious enough, James's two sons, Henry and Charles, had just been made Duke of Cornwall and Duke of Albany, the names of the husbands of Regan and Goneril.[80] *King Lear* both reflects and inverts the contemporary political situation of James, representing a king who tears Britain apart in the mistaken belief that he is handing over a secure and well-ordered kingdom to the next generation. His plan may be to ensure a balance of power in Britain, but the result is a destructive civil war.[81]

Lear's story can be read as a political odyssey; the dire fate he suffers, along with his family and subjects, stems from the errors he makes as a monarch. Like Duncan, he is – or has become – a poor judge of character, a key problem for a monarch who has to rely on advisers and counsellors. By the end of the first scene the damage has been done and the tragedy precipitated. Cordelia refuses to play the inheritance game demanded by her father, and speaks plainly in insisting on the language of natural rights rather than competitive court flattery, and stating that she loves her father 'According to my bond, no more nor less' (93) and will 'Return those duties back as are right fit, / Obey you, love you and most honour you' (97–8). Her bluntness is in direct contrast to the poetic effusions of Goneril and Regan. Goneril proclaims: 'I do love you more than word can wield the matter, / Dearer than eyesight, space and liberty, / Beyond what can be valued, rich or rare, / No less than life, with grace, health, beauty, honour' (55–8). Such words recall the language of sonnets and sonnet sequences of the 1590s, many composed as witty courtly exercises in order to win favour with Elizabeth, access to her person, her patronage and, most directly, material reward in the form of licensed monopolies.[82] They could be read as a warning to James, already notorious for his promotion of favourites, not to lapse into the errors of his predecessor in her final years.[83] As Curtis Perry has pointed out, when James became king 'he also became the object of hopes and frustrations which had previously been attached to Essex'.[84] Lear's blindness provokes an outburst from the loyal, but undiplomatic, Kent, who makes a desperate attempt to advise his king that his youngest daughter loves him best and that the other two are deceiving him, despite a regal warning not to come 'between the dragon and his wrath' (123):

> be Kent unmannerly
> When Lear is mad. What wouldst thou do, old man?
> Think'st thou that duty shall have dread to speak,
> When power to flattery bows? To plainness honour's bound
> When majesty falls to folly. Reserve thy state,
> And in thy best consideration check
> This hideous rashness.

(146–52)

Few kings would relish the prospect of being addressed as 'old man', but Kent's urgency is inspired by his sense that drastic action is required to bring the King to his senses before everybody suffers. Lear should 'reserve his state' and rule; but, crucially, he should listen to advice.

In *The Trew Law of Free Monarchies*, James referred to himself as a father and his subjects as his children:

> By the Law of Nature the King becomes a naturall Father to all his Lieges at his Coronation: And as the Father of his fatherly duty is bound to care for the nourishing, education, and vertuous government of his children; even so is the king bound to care for all his subjects. As all the toile and paine that the father can take for his children, will be thought light and well bestowed by him, so that the effect thereof redound to their profite and weale; so ought the Prince to doe towards his people.[85]

Such a conception of the relationship between ruler and subject allows little room for political intervention by the subject, who can never grow to meet the monarch on anything like equal terms and will always be a minor.[86] Kent's words, which do not derive from any of Shakespeare's sources, abruptly challenge James's political assumptions. Status and forms of address assume a central importance in the play, making the style as well as the content of Kent's intervention all the more provocative.[87] Kent is denied the right to speak and advise the ailing father of the people, who is showing himself to be wanting both as a parent and as a ruler; and it must have been clear to the audience, whether they knew the story or not, that Kent is right and Lear is wrong.[88] If Kent seems childish in his bluntness, is this not primarily because the political world of *King Lear* is childish, requiring family and subjects alike to compete for the father's affection when required, be seen and not heard when required, and obey the one who knows best? For James, kings should be 'the authors and makers of the Lawes', which they then ought to obey, even though they could not be challenged by their subjects.[89] Any assembled or elected body of representatives, such as parliament, could only advise the monarch. It was to be summoned when he desired to hear what it had to say, and dismissed when he had learnt what he needed to know, or, more pertinently, had been granted the money he wanted.[90]

In such states, political comment and advice has to be carefully coded or it risks incurring the 'dragon's wrath'. The word 'counsel' is used frequently throughout the play – more so than in any other work by Shakespeare – but it does not always simply mean the expression of advice.[91] When Kent returns in disguise to Lear's service, one of the ways in which he recommends himself to his king is through his ability to 'keep honest counsel' (1.4.32), meaning to keep secrets, a sign of how Kent's status as a loyal servant has changed, as well as how one should live in a state where free speech is circumscribed. Set against Kent's blunt attempt to advise the King while remaining loyal is the Fool, whose own advice consists of a series of cryptic maxims, or allegorical fables. Later in the same scene, the Fool makes his first entrance and criticizes Lear's folly, offering him his coxcomb (jester's hat) because Lear, not he, is the real fool. Fools at the English court in the sixteenth century were either dispensers of obliquely phrased wisdom – such as the Fool in *King Lear* – or simpletons – such as Lear in the Fool's eyes.[92] When Lear threatens to whip him, the Fool counters with 'Truth's a dog that must to kennel; he must be whipped out, when the Lady Brach [bitch] may stand by the fire and stink' (109–11). The King has exchanged the faithful hound for the sycophantic and false flatterer. Equally significant is the implication that just as James regarded his subjects as perpetual children incapable of assuming proper political rights and engaging in reasonable and sustained debate, so Lear sees his as animals (a key theme throughout the play).[93] That the Fool has in mind Goneril and Regan is further emphasized at the end of this exchange when the Fool, establishing himself as the figure of the truth teller, states, 'I marvel what kin thou and thy daughters are. They'll have me whipped for speaking true, thou'lt have me whipped for lying, and sometimes I am whipped for holding my peace' (173–6).

The political state established by *King Lear* is represented most clearly in act two, scene two via interrelated exchanges. First Kent challenges the authority of Oswald, Goneril's steward, hurling a spectacular series of insults before physically assaulting him. Kent describes Oswald as 'one that wouldst be a bawd in way of good service ... and the son and heir of a mongrel bitch' (2.2.19–22), indicating that the substance of his dislike of Oswald is Oswald's prostitution of the value of loyalty that Kent holds dear, as well as linking Oswald to the comments of the Fool when he alleged that the Lady Brach had won patronage and favour. Kent's defence of his actions to Cornwall and Gloucester culminates in a speech that appears to have contemporary political events in mind. Asked why he has become so violent with anger, Kent argues:

> That such a slave as this should wear a sword,
> Who wears no honesty. Such smiling rogues as these
> Like rats oft bite the holy cords atwain
> Which are too intricate t'unloose; smooth every passion
> That in the natures of their lords rebel,
> Bring oil to fire, snow to their colder moods,
> Renege, affirm and turn their halcyon beaks
> With every gale and vary of their masters,
> Knowing naught, like dogs, but following.
>
> (70–8)

Kent is placed in the stocks for his outburst.

King Lear was written and performed just over two years into James's reign. But already a series of events had started to sour the initial relief many felt at the accession of James after the bitter political struggles and uncertainty of Elizabeth's last years. James held his first parliament in 1604, and a dispute over the election established the tenor of the developing political struggle between the King and the House of Commons. Sir John Fortesque, the Chancellor of the Exchequer, was defeated in Buckinghamshire by a local gentleman with puritan sympathies, Sir Francis Goodwin. Fortesque would have been one of the members of the Privy Council in the Commons, so the Council tried to find if the election could be rendered invalid. Finding that Goodwin could be branded an outlaw, a second election was held and Fortesque was elected. The Commons responded by having Goodwin sworn in as a member, insisting that the first result should stand. Derek Hirst has pointed out the significance of the episode:

> The Buckinghamshire election dispute of 1604 was inter-preted by many members [of parliament] as being a blatant attempt on the crown's part to assert its judicial control over elections, and hence over who should sit. It pointed down the high road to packed and muzzled parliaments. The virulence of the protests, forcing the crown to concede, indicates that this apprehension was widespread.[94]

The resulting conflict became the first of many serious constitutional conflicts between parliament and crown in the next half-century. The Commons argued that they should be the judge of disputed elections, and pointed to a series of historical precedents; James claimed that his government had this right and also referred to a number of precedents. The issue centred on the question of who held ultimate authority, parliament or the monarch? The Commons were afraid that 'if the king could decide an election, enforce a proclamation, or raise a tax, once, then he might do it all the time, and liberty would be gone'.[95] During the dispute, James made the claim that 'the Commons only held their privileges by his grace', an ultra-royalist interpretation of the constitution in line with James's political statements elsewhere, which

FIGURE 6 Elizabeth opening parliament, from Sir Simonds D'Ewes, *The journals of all the Parliaments during the reign of Queen Elizabeth* (1682), frontispiece. A later picture, showing Elizabeth as Queen in parliament, governing with her elected subjects.

only served to reanimate the struggle between advocates of the 'mixed polity' and royal supremacy fought out in the second half of Elizabeth's reign.[96]

Kent can be seen as a Peter Wentworth figure (see pp. 23–4); Wentworth was imprisoned for arguing, in the Elizabethan parliaments of 1586–7 and 1593, that the House of Commons needed to be independent of the crown's demands and that members of parliament should possess freedom of speech.[97] Wentworth's son, Thomas, was a member of parliament in 1604 and was instrumental in raising the issue of the Buckinghamshire election.[98] Kent, as Wentworth had been, is rude, blunt and disrespectful in his attempt to advise Lear and censure those who have helped to erode the liberties of loyal subjects. But this does not invalidate his argument, one the play clearly endorses. Just as the House of Commons argued that its loyalty was to a constitution which governed the people, and of which the monarch was the head, rather than to the monarch independent of the constitution, so Kent argues that he knows better how Lear ought to govern himself in order to rule his people. Such arguments were familiar versions of the distinction made between the office and person of the king (see above, pp. 63–6). A conservative interpretation of this distinction – such as that made by James – regarded the two roles as virtually identical, the monarch ruling as head of state, his subjects only aspiring to be advisers who could be ignored if the monarch so chose. A more radical interpretation insisted on the importance of the distinction, arguing that subjects often knew better than the monarch how he should behave in the interests of both himself and his subjects.[99] *King Lear* would appear to support the second interpretation, against that of James, suggesting that Lear should have listened to his loyal followers who reserve the right to advise him for his own good – Cordelia, Kent and the Fool – and not the base flattery of Goneril and Regan.

Equally pointed is Kent's reference to Oswald as an undeserving servant who has been unfairly promoted through Lear's failure to perceive the self-serving nature beneath his flattery. James had already become notorious in England in the first years of his reign for ignoring loyal English courtiers and crown servants, and giving out wardships (the right to administer the estate and finances of orphans who had not yet come of age), pensions, and lucrative monopolies to his own Scottish entourage. That James acted as he did to help ease the debt of £422,000 he had inherited from his predecessor, did little to placate his critics. Those who benefited were generally attacked as sycophants, precisely the complaint that Kent makes of Oswald.[100]

Later in the same scene the Fool confronts Kent in the stocks, a symbolic juxtaposition of the two good subjects – Cordelia having gone into exile and Edgar having only just donned his disguise as Poor Tom – now marginalized by recent developments. When Kent asks 'How chance the King comes with so small a number?', the Fool responds with 'An thou hadst been set i'the stocks for that question, thou hadst well deserved it' (252–5), a sign that legitimate questions cannot be asked under the new authoritarian government of Goneril and Regan. Equally important, Kent's naïvety and the Fool's continued privilege show that under Lear such harsh repression was undoubtedly the exception rather than the rule. Indeed, the role of the Fool as a licensed court jester who is shown to be an astute, loyal adviser to the King, and who helps start the arduous process of Lear's recovery to sanity and better government, could well be read as deliberate defence of the value of a play such as *King Lear* and the role of drama in general to advise, warn and counsel the monarch. After all, this was exactly what plays such as *Hick Scorner*, John Skelton's *Magnificence*, and John Bale's *King Johan* had been designed to do at the Tudor court earlier in the century, in a tradition of giving counsel that continued in many of the court entertainments performed before Elizabeth.[101] The Fool gives Kent an analysis of the fate of Lear and his supporters:

> Let go thy hold when a great wheel runs down a hill lest it break thy neck with following it; but the great one that goes upward, let him draw thee after. When a wise man gives thee better counsel give me mine again; I would have none but knaves follow it, since a fool gives it. (261–6)

According to the Fool, fools like himself and Kent will stay and plummet into the depths alongside Lear, while knaves like Oswald will rise to the top with Goneril and Regan. The fate of the king who refuses to listen can be read as astringent advice, for James might well find himself neglecting and banishing his loyal critics, and promoting knaves and flatterers, if he cut himself off from his people (although, of course, Lear is tactfully represented as the inverse as much as the image of James). The word 'counsel' has again been diminished in significance, referring here to advice on whether to act ethically and foolishly, or sensibly and badly, rather than a public process of advising a king. The exchange ends when Kent asks the Fool where he learned such wisdom, to which the Fool replies 'Not i'the stocks, fool' (276). Freedom can only be achieved through disguise – physical or verbal – because criticism of authority inevitably results in punishment.

The rest of the play focuses primarily on the re-education of the old King and the attempts of the forces loyal to him and his good daughter to re-establish political order in Britain. Out on the heath in the storm, Lear rather belatedly starts to comprehend the reality of governing, through his newfound empathy with the lowest of his subjects:

> Poor naked wretches, whereso'er you are,
> That bide the pelting of this pitiless storm,
> How shall your houseless heads and unfed sides,
> Your looped and windowed raggedness, defend you
> From seasons such as these? O, I have ta'en
> Too little care of this.

> (3.4.28–33)

Later on, when Lear has descended into madness, his utterances start to resemble those of the Fool who has disappeared from the action of the play, and he directly criticizes the existing social and legal order:

> a dog's obeyed in office ...
> Through tattered clothes great vices do appear;
> Robes and furred gowns hide all. Plate sin with gold,
> And the strong lance of justice hurtless breaks;
> Arm it in rags, a pigmy's straw does pierce it.

> (4.6.154, 160–3)

Lear's education ultimately proves futile. At every point his redemption is undercut by subsequent dramatic events. His initial recognition of the suffering of the poor that has been tolerated in his state leads only to madness when he is confronted by Edgar disguised as Poor Tom; and the realization that injustice has generally prevailed is followed by an intense bout of insanity when the arrival of Cordelia's forces makes possible his restoration to the throne and so, were he mentally and physically capable, the solution to the problems he has recognized.

Shakespeare's transformation of the ending of the story of King Lear baffled subsequent readers, who generally restored a happy conclusion similar to that in Geoffrey of Monmouth's *History of the Kings of Britain* and the chronicle play, *King Leir*, or, like Samuel Johnson, could not bear to read the conclusion of Shakespeare's play.[102] *King Lear* has always had the reputation of being Shakespeare's most tragic play.[103] Yet, in political terms, *Hamlet* seems to be a far more pessimistic work, expressing doubts about the Stuart succession (which was the most likely outcome in 1600), and openly flirting with the arguments of the tyrannicides as a means out of a dangerous impasse.[104] *King Lear* ruthlessly exposes the political errors of a ruler who was both the image and opposite of James I, a reading strengthened by the Fool's prophecy in act three, scene two. Left alone on stage, the Fool proclaims a series of events, the first half of which refer to contemporary malpractice, the second to a utopian ideal, predicting: 'Then shall the realm of Albion / Come to great confusion' (3.2.91–2). This is a version of the famous sixteenth-century HEMPE prophecy, which decreed that England would come to an end after the reigns of Henry, Edward, Mary and Philip, and Elizabeth. The prophecy was fulfilled when James came to the throne and tried to 'end' England by attempting to establish a British kingdom in 1604–5.[105]

King Lear must surely, then, be read as pointing to the danger of a monarch cutting himself off from the people he rules, and so destroying what he has so carefully built up. The play does not represent a king who is ineffective or unimpressive, but one who has not taken enough care of his kingdom. The fact that he has ruled for so long and needs to secure the succession recalls the dilemmas faced by Elizabeth and her subjects rather than James and his. Of course, everything comes to nothing in *King Lear*, and Kent and Edgar, neither of whom has shown any particular aptitude or propensity for government, are left in charge of 'the gored state' (5.3.319). Nevertheless, the play is obsessed with the question of political advice or counsel and the need for government to be conducted with the consent of the people. Far from being radical, such views were entirely mainstream; it was James's argument that the monarch could take or leave the advice of powerful subjects that was a radical departure in terms of political discourse in England.[106]

To take one example: a work that may have influenced Shakespeare, given the date of its publication, its general impact in Britain, and the fact that it was the only published source of material from *The Prince* until the first full translation appeared in 1640, was Innocent Gentillet's *A Discourse Upon the Meanes of Wel Governing and Maintaining in Good Peace, A Kingdom, or other Principalitie ... Against Nicholas Machiavell the Florentine* (1602).[107] Gentillet's work was a Huguenot treatise, attacking Machiavelli as an apologist for tyranny seeking to undermine a tradition of mutual co-operation between rulers and subjects.[108] Gentillet argues that laws are more likely to be obeyed if they are established by a representative body; that such bodies are more stable than a prince (given the publication date of the translation, completed in 1577 and subsequently circulated in manuscript, this may be a rather pointed observation);[109] that freely-given counsel is best and that princes should encourage debate and differing advice as most helpful to them.[110] Most telling, perhaps, Gentillet argues, in response to Machiavelli's assertion that a prince is better off being feared than loved, that the Massacre of Saint Bartholomew's Day (23 August 1572), when Catholics slaughtered Protestants in Paris and throughout France, an event which sent shock waves throughout Protestant Europe, would not have occurred had the King had the respect and loyalty of the people.[111] Just as the massacre was frequently interpreted in apocalyptic terms, so *King Lear* signals an apocalyptic destruction of Albion/Britain.[112] Gentillet's treatise, written only four years after the massacre, carefully and deliberately refuses to discount the methods and practices of ordinary politics as a cure for the spectacular horrors of recent events. Similarly, Shakespeare, while representing a bleak universe and a depressing tragedy, never loses sight of the political manoeuvres that would have prevented the catastrophe from unfolding. Strange as it may seem, *King Lear* is an optimistic work, unlike *Hamlet*, because the ways and means of avoiding tragedy are explicit within the play, just as the fears accompanying the approaching end of the Tudor dynasty had been answered by the accession of James VI and I.

Chapter Three

REPUBLICANISM AND CONSTITUTIONALISM

'Tarquin's everlasting banishment'

In this chapter I want to make the case that Shakespeare's treatment of Roman material in his early work shows distinct evidence of republican leanings.[1] Taken together, *The Rape of Lucrece* and *Titus Andronicus* argue forcefully that hereditary monarchy may be an undesirable form of government. Both represent tyrants who are conspicuously less virtuous and competent as rulers than other prominent Roman citizens, implying that England might suffer from equally bad rule. Both works are also quite clear that alternative forms of government, which would involve either dispensing with or curbing the power of the head of state, are possible and desirable for Rome. While *Lucrece* alludes to the ways of reading a well-known and frequently represented story that was a central motif in European culture, *Titus*, a play with no antecedents or direct sources, provides a much more sustained and detailed analysis of political institutions and problems.

I

In the summer of 1592, a riot in Southwark began after the parties involved had 'assembled themselves by occasion & pretence of their meeting at a play'.[2] The Privy Council subsequently shut down the theatres. Although they re-opened at the end of December, they were closed again at the end of January because of an outbreak of the plague and fear of its spread. They remained closed for nearly a year, re-opening after Christmas in 1593.[3] Shakespeare's career as a dramatist in London was halted almost as soon as it had begun with only three co-written plays having been performed, *1, 2* and *3 Henry VI*.[4] Shakespeare evidently turned to writing poetry as one means of supplementing his lost income, and produced two narrative poems based on Roman subjects, *Venus and Adonis* (published 1593) and *The Rape of Lucrece* (1594). Both were dedicated to Henry Wriothesley, Earl of Southampton. The former belongs to the fashionable genre of epyllia, short epics dealing with erotic subject matter which were popular in the 1590s, and it may possibly have been written to justify the Earl's early fear of marriage, recounting as it does the unwelcome advances of an older woman towards her reluctant young lover.[5] The latter tells the most famous story from Livy's *Early History of Rome from its Foundation*, the rape of Lucrece by the son of the last king of Rome, Tarquinius Sextus, and his subsequent banishment by his nephew, Lucius Junius Brutus, which led to the establishment of the Roman republic.[6]

While *Venus and Adonis* can be read as a mixture of sophisticated erotic comedy and a lament for the passing of youth, *The Rape of Lucrece* was designed to appeal to Southampton's political leanings and persuasions. Wriothesley was intimately connected with the Earl of Essex's circle, and was developing 'the anti-absolutist ideas and oppositional views of history' that were 'openly discussed' by its members in the mid-1590s.[7] He went on to play a key part in the Earl's rebellion of 1601 (in which Shakespeare and his fellow actors played a minor role for which they were formally excused), spending two years in prison before being pardoned by James I. Wriothesley later became a relatively respectable figure at the Jacobean court.[8] He was a notable patron of writers, and had works dedicated to him by Barnabe Barnes, John Florio and Thomas Nashe, as well as Shakespeare, whom he probably met in the early 1590s at the Inns of Court, where plays were often performed for the students.[9] Barnes was noted for his anti-establishment views, as was the cynical Nashe, and Florio, given his Italian origin and linguistic skills, was clearly useful to anyone interested in Italian republican thought.[10]

Shakespeare's association with the Earl probably lasted into the reign of James, although how intimate their relationship was is hard to

FIGURE 7 *Henry Wriothesley, Third Earl of Southampton*, 1603, by John Decritz the Elder (attr. to).

determine.[11] While Shakespeare stands out as one of the few prominent writers who neglected to celebrate the accession of James with a poem, he seems to have marked the release of his erstwhile patron from prison in the same year. Sonnet 107 speaks of his 'true love' as 'forfeit to a confined doom', which may refer to the recent release of the Earl by James, very soon after the King's accession (see below, pp. 183–4).[12]

Of all the authors whom Wriothesley supported it was Shakespeare who produced a poem on the most obviously republican subject. Whether this expressed his own political views, or whether a needy writer composed a poem designed to engage the interest of a patron, is obviously a harder matter to determine.

The Rape of Lucrece is prefaced by a summary of the argument, derived from the versions of the story in Livy's *History* and Ovid's *Fasti*.[13] A key source may also have been the translation of Livy in William Painter's *Palace of Pleasure*, first published in 1566, a major source for many Elizabethan and Jacobean plays, including Webster's *The Duchess of Malfi* (*c*.1613), and a work that had clear republican sympathies.[14] Shakespeare, in his prefatory Argument, narrates the events immediately preceding the rape, describing how Tarquin had his father-in-law, Servius, murdered, and, 'contrary to Roman laws and customs, not requiring or staying for the people's suffrages, had possessed himself of the kingdom' (*Poems*, p. 65).[15] During the subsequent war against the Rutuli, their chief town of Ardea was besieged. One evening the Roman generals decided to determine whose wife was the most chaste, and planned to return to Rome in secret to surprise their spouses. Collatinus's wife, Lucrece, was adjudged the winner when she was discovered 'spinning amongst her maids', while the others were out 'dancing and revelling, or in several disports'. Tarquin became inflamed by Lucrece's beauty, and visited her at Collatium, where he 'treacherously stealeth into her chamber, violently ravished her, and early in the morning speedeth away'. Lucrece made her husband and his fellow officers, including Lucius Junius Brutus, swear revenge, before suddenly stabbing herself. They vowed to 'root out the whole hated family of the Tarquins', and Brutus 'acquainted the people with the doer and manner of the vile deed, with a bitter invective against the tyranny of the King' (p. 66). Moved by these words, the people exile the Tarquins 'with one consent and a general acclamation . . . and the state government changed from kings to consuls'.

Shakespeare's stated argument is not as explicitly political in its focus upon forms of government as William Painter's translation of Livy. Neither the poem nor the preface contains details of Brutus's speech to the people in the market place in Rome, where the act of rape is represented as the culmination of a series of brutal attacks on the citizens:

> And thereunto he added the pride and insolent behaviour of the king, the miserie and drudgerie of the people, and howe they, which in time past were victours and conquerours, were made of men of warre, Artificers, and Labourers. He remembered also the infamous murder of Servius Tullius their late kinge. These and such like he called to the people's remembraunce, whereby they abrogated and deposed Tarquinius, banishing him, his wife, and children.[16]

Instead, Shakespeare concentrates on the drama of the violation of Lucrece and her interaction with Tarquin and Brutus, rather than the public reaction to the event.[17] In doing so, he emphasizes the political significance of the encounter itself, specifically the injustice suffered by Lucrece and voiced in her lament.[18] Tarquin decides to violate Lucrece because another man, her husband, Collatine, controls her, a challenge to his rule which is represented in political terms: 'Perchance his boast of Lucrece' sov'reignty / Suggested this proud issue of a king' (36–7).[19]

Tarquin's sexual tyranny stems from a political motivation. His true desire is to be an authoritarian ruler commanding his subjects without restraint, a hypermasculinity that demonstrates a lack of rationality and so renders the tyrant effeminate. The tyrant's lack of self-government is then manifested in his inability to rule his subjects.[20] As he confesses to Lucrece, 'My will is strong past reason's weak removing' (243), a crucial admission given that the principal reason political theorists gave for excluding women from the class of rulers was their inability to let reason dominate their emotions.[21] Shakespeare explicitly labels Tarquin's projected actions as treason, a crime that predates the action itself: 'Thus treason works ere traitors be espied. / Who sees the lurking serpent steps aside' (361–2). His failure to control his senses leads him on, again reinforcing his 'womanly' inability to rule: 'Rolling his greedy eyeballs in his head; / By their high treason is his heart misled' (368–9). Shakespeare is clearly alluding to the standard legal doctrine and definition that imagining the king's death was high treason even before any actual act was committed.[22] However, here it is the king who is committing the treason by intending to rape one of his subjects. Significantly enough, Elizabethan statutes had gradually been expanding the number of crimes that fell within the definition of treason, bringing 'the Tudor era to a close with the establishment of a markedly royal interpretation of the scope of treason'.[23] For example, in 1581, when the crown lawyers were thwarted by parliament, which tried to limit the definition of the crimes committed by those who harboured Jesuits, a royal proclamation appeared in the following year declaring that anyone who knowingly aided a Jesuit or seminary priest was guilty of treason. The powers assumed by the crown increased as Elizabeth's reign progressed.[24] Tarquin also assumes legal authority and places his own actions beyond the laws required to control his subjects' actions. His actions cannot be defined as treason while he rules Rome, and his crime only emerges retrospectively with the establishment of the republic and the acceptance that sovereignty resides with the people.[25]

Tarquin's lack of self-control stands in direct contrast to Lucrece's self-sacrificing behaviour and ability to make decisions which benefit the commonwealth, allowing a relatively smooth transition to a form of government which undoubtedly benefits the majority of Rome's citizens. Lucrece becomes a Stoic, like Seneca, carefully determining her actions politically – deciding to help overthrow the tyrant and establish a more equitable form of government – before purging herself and the state through a death she has calmly accepted.[26] Her resistance leads to Tarquin's banishment and the establishment of the Roman republic. Shakespeare's poem casts Lucrece as a more important principal actor than Brutus, suggesting that she is the truly virtuous republican figure who liberates Rome.[27]

Perhaps the most politically charged passage in the poem is Lucrece's attempt to persuade Tarquin to come to his senses and return to the proper duties of a future monarch, a section that is unique to Shakespeare (582–672). Lucrece bases her argument on the fact that the creature she sees before her has left his proper form behind and adopted another identity antithetical to that of the heir to the throne: 'In Tarquin's likeness I did entertain thee: / Hast thou put on his shape to do him shame?' (596–7). Lucrece's words are an exploration of the familiar distinction between the office and person of the king:

> Thou seem'st not what thou art, a god, a king:
> For kings like gods should govern everything.
>
> How will thy shame be seeded in thine age,
> When thus thy vices bud before thy spring? ...
> O be remember'd, no outrageous thing
> From vassal actors can be wip'd away:
> Then kings' misdeeds cannot be hid in clay.
>
> This deed will make thee only lov'd for fear;
> But happy monarchs still are fear'd for love.
>
> (601–4, 607–11)

Lucrece's thoughts move rapidly from an understanding of Tarquin as an absolute monarch with godlike powers and rights, through the need to expose the crimes he has committed in language that is pointedly contrasted to his own attempts to keep them secret with her complicity (526–32), to a position that resembles a republican one.[28] The last lines seem to echo and invert Machiavelli's notorious words that it is better for kings to be feared (revered, as well as inspiring terror) than loved.[29] Lucrece argues that monarchs cannot rule happily without the support of their people, a substantial move from the political position she accepted as natural eight lines previously. Tarquin, as Livy, Painter and the Argument prefacing Shakespeare's work stated, was a usurper who had come to power 'contrary to the Roman laws and customs' (p. 65), and Lucrece is doing no more here than urging him to live within the accepted rules, laws and constitution of the city. Her speech is abruptly ended by Tarquin, just as her use of political imagery to describe his planned transgression is becoming threatening to his assumption of absolute power: 'So shall these slaves [i.e., "Black lust, dishonour, shame, misgoverning" (654)] be king, and thou their slave' (659); 'So let thy thoughts, low vassals to thy state' (666).

Tarquin's act of rape is intended as a hidden crime, associated with disguise and tyranny: 'Shame folded up in blind concealing night, / When most unseen, then most doth tyrannize' (675–6).[30] These lines prefigure Lucrece's denunciation of night after the act (764–833), as a means of keeping the vile behaviour of the King secret. Lucrece's speech charts a process of personal growth, in which she moves towards an understanding that bringing what is hidden out before the public gaze leads to happier citizens and better government. Initially, she worries that revealing Tarquin's crimes will shame her husband, but she immediately rejects these fears in acknowledging the impossible situation in which she has been placed: 'Yet am I guilty of thy honour's wrack; / Yet for thy honour did I entertain him' (841–2). Swiftly, she moves to a critique of the secretive system of government practised by the Roman monarchy, recognizing that 'no perfection is so absolute / That some impurity doth not pollute' (853–4). In one densely-packed stanza, she denounces Tarquin as guilty of a whole host of interrelated crimes, using a series of technical legal terms, alleging that he has committed murder, theft, perjury, subornation (bribing someone to commit a crime), treason, forgery, shift (trickery) and incest (Collatine was Tarquin's cousin) (918–24). Lucrece's speech concludes with her acknowledgement that Tarquin is not worthy to be a king. His crimes are worse because they have been committed by someone of supposedly noble blood: 'The baser is he, coming from a king, / To shame his hope with deeds degenerate' (1002–3). Her decision to reveal his crime explicitly acknowledges that in doing so she risks helping to overthrow the Roman constitution: 'For me, I force not argument a straw, / Since that my case is past the help of law' (1021–2). At this point in the poem, her arguments resemble those of works such as *Vindiciae, Contra Tyrannos* (see above, pp. 92–7).

Lucrece's complaint makes sense of her experience. The sexual act forced upon her will lead to the transformation of the Roman monarchy into a republic, a succession triggered by an act of copulation. But, whereas such acts were generally expected to lead to the production of an heir, Tarquin's rape leads to the birth of a new political system. Lucrece's complaint articulates and defines this political change, demonstrating that her violation is the key act, not the subsequent rebellion of Brutus. It is Lucrece who asks, 'Why should the private pleasure of some one / Become the public plague of many moe?' (1478–9), an unanswerable question that can only lead to a radical political transformation if acted upon. Furthermore, Lucrece points out that if Priam had 'check'd his son's desire, / Troy had been bright with fame and not with fire' (1490–1). The common representation of tyrants as men who cannot control their desires (wills) here points to legitimate rebellion, as Tarquin's crimes are viewed in the light of day. Shakespeare deals with this rebellion briefly, and the poem moves quickly to its inevitable conclusion after Lucrece's suicide. Collatine, initially paralysed, is soon galvanized into action by Brutus. Lucrece's blood becomes a symbol of freedom as 'The Romans plausibly did give consent / To Tarquin's everlasting banishment' (1854–5).

The Rape of Lucrece omits the subsequent struggle, described in Livy's *History*, between Tarquin and the newly established republic, when the exiled King sought to re-establish his rule, although it was reproduced in Painter's adaptation.[31] In doing so, Shakespeare's version of the story acquires an ostensibly less explicit political focus and concentrates instead on the role of Lucrece in effecting political change. In one sense this makes the poem a more obviously feminist text than its rival versions.[32] However, it is not clear that the poem is so uncritically sympathetic to its protagonist.[33] While Lucrece's actions help to inaugurate and establish the form and meaning of the republic, she not only 'never fully grasps the implications of the historical change which she initiates', but by her suicide she is precluded from participating in the new political world of the Roman republic.[34] Lucrece still adheres to the old culture of aristocratic honour, deciding that the jewel she has lost (her chastity) will be compensated for by the honourable overthrow of the Tarquins (1191–1211). In this sense the poem is unremittingly male; a dead woman's sacrificed corpse signals the transfer of power from male tyranny to the rather better male oligarchy of the republic.[35]

The question then arises as to how *The Rape of Lucrece* should be read in terms of Elizabeth's increasingly problematic rule in the 1590s.[36] I would suggest that the poem can be read in analogical rather than allegorical terms, as it relates clearly but obliquely to contemporary political developments, providing a series of hints rather than a sustained parallel. An obvious context to the poem would seem to be Elizabeth's cult of virginity, which took on a renewed importance in the late 1580s and early 1590s, after the failure of the Spanish Armada. The Ditchley portrait (c.1590), showed Elizabeth standing on a map of England, an imperial virgin defending her land and her body against attempted violation by a foreign tyrant (Philip II of Spain).[37] Shakespeare's poem shows a chaste wife honourably dying and letting a small group of men take over government, a political transformation that the poem endorses. Read this way, *The Rape of Lucrece* would appear to foreshadow the aims of the Essex Rebellion five years later, obliquely enough to escape censure and censorship, but clearly enough to signal this message to the initiated. In this case, the concentration on the role of Lucrece in the poem should be read as politically charged, a deliberate manoeuvre that relates the rape to the government of England in the late sixteenth century and suggests that a woman can point the way to republican government, a coded reading that might well have appealed to the Earl of Southampton.

II

The Rape of Lucrece suggests that Shakespeare was interested in republicanism and moved in republican political circles in the 1590s, even if it would be stretching a point to describe him as a committed believer in republican ideas. A work that provides further evidence of similar political leanings is *Titus Andronicus*. Jonathan Bate has persuasively argued that *Titus* was the first tragedy that Shakespeare wrote alone; that it was probably written in late 1593, at the end of the closure of the theatres; and that it was first performed in January 1594.[38] It should therefore be linked closely to *Lucrece*, and, if Bate's reconstruction is correct, 'emerges as *the* pivotal play in Shakespeare's early career'.[39]

There is no exact historical source or precedent for *Titus*, but Shakespeare makes use of stories from Livy's *History*, and Ovid's *Fasti* and *Metamorphoses*. The plot shows how the self-destructive tyranny of Rome's Emperors alienates both patricians and ordinary citizens, and delivers control of the city to the barbarous Goths. The most memorable image in a play saturated with disturbing violence and destruction is that of the mutilated and raped Lavinia, her tongue gouged out and hands lopped off in order to prevent her revealing who committed the crime.[40] The parallels to the fate of Lucrece are obvious; both are abused by tyrants – here the adopted sons of the Emperor, Demetrius and Chiron – who attempt to silence them, but are justly punished when their actions are revealed to the people.[41] Lavinia's physical dismemberment is a sign of the political effects of the tyrannous relationships and modes of government represented in the play.[42] She suffers as a literal result of her ill-treatment by her father, who refuses to acknowledge that she wishes to marry Bassianus rather than Saturninus, and of the evil designs of the husband he has chosen for her.

She also suffers as a direct consequence of the lack of proper government by consent in Rome, again, as a consequence of her father's actions, because he chooses to obey what he thinks is the will of the Emperor, rather than the people. The act also recalls the treatment meted out to John Stubbs, whose right hand was severed when he protested against the Queen's proposed marriage to the Duke of Alençon, suggesting an uncomfortable parallel between the cruel actions of the sons of the Emperor and those of Elizabeth.[43] Equally, it is important to recognize that the mutilated body of Lavinia serves to help restore the body politic to a more equitable state at the end of the play – albeit after a further orgy of blood-letting, which includes Lavinia's death at the hands of her father, so that her 'shame' (5.3.45–6) dies with her, a further reason to link her story to that of Lucrece.

The opening scene of the play shows Rome in a period of transition. The Romans have just defeated the Goths, but the people need to elect a new emperor. There are three principal candidates; Saturninus and Bassianus, elder and younger sons of the recently deceased (unnamed) emperor, and Titus Andronicus, a popular elected tribune, who has played a key role in the recent wars. Titus's brother, Marcus, another tribune, tries to persuade Titus to accept the position because of the swell of popular support he enjoys:

> safer triumph is this funeral pomp
> That hath aspired to Solon's happiness
> And triumphs over chance in honour's bed.
> Titus Andronicus, the people of Rome,
> Whose friend in justice thou hast ever been,
> Send thee by me, their tribune and their trust,
> This palliament of white and spotless hue,
> And name thee in election for the empire
> With these our late-deceased emperor's sons.
> Be *candidatus* then and put it on,
> And help to set a head on headless Rome.
>
> (1.1.179–89)

The fictional Rome of the play stands at the opposite point to the Rome of *Lucrece*; here, Marcus makes it clear that there is an opportunity to establish a workable and popular constitution under a leader who has the backing of the people. The wars are over, the old emperor is dead, and a new leader has emerged with a mandate to transform the political life of Rome. The reference to Solon, the legendary philosopher and lawgiver, familiar to Elizabethan readers through Plutarch's *Lives*, one of Shakespeare's key sources, reinforces our anticipation of imminent political change. Rome is a body politic without a head, as the last lines of Marcus's speech make clear, but it can be made whole again.[44] When Titus first refuses the honour of standing for election, Marcus makes the situation clear to him: 'Titus, thou shalt obtain and ask the empery' (204). Titus has the ability to rule Rome and direct it towards a better and fairer state.

However, Titus is shown making a series of key mistakes which reveal that he does not possess the ability or the imagination to break free of traditional, constricting conventions and ideas. First, he insists on the need to sacrifice Alarbus, son of the captured Queen of the Goths, Tamora, despite her pleas for mercy. Titus remains unmoved by a 'mother's tears in passion for her son' (109), and explains that as the

Goths have killed Romans, the citizens 'for their brethren slain, / Religiously they ask a sacrifice' (126–7). Not only does this sentiment blur the distinction between the supposedly civilized Rome and the barbarian Goths, showing the former to be as superstitious and pagan as the latter in their beliefs, but it also makes an enemy of the dangerous Tamora, soon to marry Saturninus and play her part in the cycle of destructive revenge.[45] Tamora and her two surviving sons, Chiron and Demetrius, comment on the 'cruel, irreligious piety' of Titus and suggest that Rome is less civilized than Scythia, a byword for barbarism from Herodotus' *Histories* (*c.*500 BCE) onwards.[46]

Second, Titus refuses to stand for election as emperor. When the patrician Saturninus tries to prevent Titus's candidacy, through an unsubtle mixture of scorn and the threat of violence, Titus again demonstrates that he has wholeheartedly adopted patrician values and is unable to think beyond them. Saturninus displays an opportunistic and confused notion of the people he intends to govern:

> Romans, do me right.
> Patricians, draw your swords and sheathe them not
> Till Saturninus be Rome's emperor.
> Andronicus, would thou were shipped to hell
> Rather than rob me of the people's hearts.
>
> (207–11)

Saturninus appeals to the physical force of the patricians to stake his claim as emperor, and acknowledges that Titus has deprived him of the support of a wider populace. For Saturninus, the desire for office comes before his legitimate right to govern; his sense of outrage stems from his belief that he was born to govern by hereditary right, not ability or worth. Saturninus is opposed by Lucius, Titus's eldest son, who eventually succeeds as 'Rome's gracious governor' (5.3.145) with popular support, and an army of Goths, at the end of the play. However, Titus, in deference to his social superior, promises to re-establish the traditional political order and restore to Saturninus 'The people's hearts, and wean them from themselves' (1.1.215). Despite appeals from Bassianus that Titus would be more sensible to support

Bassianus's faction if he is not going to stand himself, Titus appeals to his loyal supporters to elect Saturninus as emperor, which they promptly do.

Titus is represented as absolutely lacking in political sense in this scene. Saturninus has given a clear demonstration of his unsuitability for office, yet Titus has manipulated his followers to support Saturninus in order to preserve the status quo. The metaphor he employs (wean the people from themselves) shows that he sees the people as babies who have to be looked after by their social superiors.[47] Like Saturninus, he restricts the political class to the upper echelons of society, even though there are numerous signs that this may be a disastrous error. It soon becomes clear that Saturninus's need of popular support ceases when he has assumed power, and he reverts to an understanding of government as his sinecure. Titus is rewarded 'for thy favours done / To us in our election this day' (238–9), and the people are provided with a double-edged promise: 'when I do forget / The least of these unspeakable deserts, / Romans forget your fealty to me' (259–61). As Saturninus's words indicate, Titus's favours do not continue beyond the election; the second equivocation turns into a prophecy rather than a promise. Titus has failed to support the people at a point in their history when change for the better in the form of a more accountable and responsive government was a real possibility.

Saturninus's and Titus's subsequent language reveals how quickly the euphoric moment of victory and the promise of political transformation have become solidified into the hierarchical assumptions of an inherited tradition. Whereas Saturninus first speaks of his gratitude to Titus and his family for his 'election' (239), he now speaks of the 'fealty' (261) that Romans owe him. Tamora, about to replace Lavinia in Saturninus's affections, is referred to as 'prisoner to an emperor' (262) by Titus, and Saturninus declares that 'Princely shall be thy usage every way' (270). Titus's third error occurs when he acquiesces in Saturninus's short-lived desire to marry Lavinia and make her his empress, not bothering to ask her consent, a sign of his inability to escape from the values of the old patriarchy of imperial Rome. Saturninus declares that he will make Lavinia his 'empress, /

Rome's royal mistress, mistress of my heart' (244–5), illustrating that affectionate and political bonds are directly interrelated, and political power is regarded as a gift that the emperor can distribute as he desires. Lavinia, as the next few lines demonstrate, is ruled by the uncontrolled emotions of a tyrant, making her vulnerable to his whims and the constant vicissitudes that such an unstable position generates, a problem explored more fully in the relationship between Leontes and Hermione in *The Winter's Tale*.[48] Saturninus, like most tyrants represented on the Renaissance stage, cannot separate sexual and political desire.[49]

Lavinia has been silent until this point, but her facial expression clearly reveals her inner feelings. Saturninus asks her to 'Clear up ... that cloudy countenance' (267), and eventually inquires whether she is displeased with his promise to treat Tamora respectfully (a further signal that he is too self-regarding to rule Rome properly). Her response, that Saturninus is correct in his behaviour because 'true nobility / Warrants these words in princely courtesy' (275–6), indicates that her feelings and responses are circumscribed by the accepted political and personal codes that will dominate Saturninus's Rome.

The subsequent behaviour of Titus's sons and Saturninus's response to their actions reveal the extent of the tyranny that has been established in Rome and the dangers of living under such a regime. Bassianus, the younger brother of Saturninus, seizes Lavinia, claiming that he is already betrothed to her. His language is, yet again, as much political as marital. He asserts that 'this maid is mine' (280), and declares that he is 'resolved withal / To do myself this reason and this right' (282–3). Bassianus is supported by Titus's brother and sons. Marcus issues a gnomic statement when challenged by his brother: '*Suum cuique* [to each his own] is our Roman justice: / This prince in justice seizeth but his own' (284–5). Bassianus and Marcus appear as mirror images of Saturninus, as Marcus's selfish and anarchic interpretation of Roman law indicates. Saturninus relies on his person and will to rule; Bassianus, in asserting a prior right, relies on an unworkable, esoteric and patently unjust conception of the law that will only be of benefit to the powerful. As the factions visibly divide on stage, there is little to choose between the alliance of the Emperor and the Goths on one side, and the rebels on the other. If the former clearly represent cruelty and tyranny, the latter faction stands for the deformation of a republican tradition – in which rulers are accountable to the citizens, who are thereby given some limited control over the political institutions established in the city – into anarchy and chaos. Titus declares that Bassianus and his own sons are traitors (287–8), an accusation that is correct, but only if the law is seen from the position of Saturninus, who declares that all opposition to him is treachery. In the ensuing scuffle Titus kills his youngest son, Mutius, showing that he places his service to the state above the needs of his family, which arguably makes him a true citizen, of republican and Stoic virtue.[50] Lucius, his most articulate offspring, who becomes emperor at the end of the play, accuses Titus of being unjust and killing Mutius in a 'wrongful quarrel' (298). This prompts Titus to restate his allegiance to the Emperor and the values of old Rome, based on honour and bloodlines. He disowns his children as not worthy of him: 'My sons never would so dishonour me. / Traitor, restore Lavinia to the emperor' (300–1). Titus's reward is to be banished from political favour by Saturninus, who now chooses Tamora as his bride. Titus is ostensibly reconciled to Saturninus through the intervention of Tamora, but only because she fears his popularity and will move against his family as soon as an opportunity arises (439–63).

The long opening scene of *Titus* is carefully written and staged as a balanced exploration of opposing political languages and assumptions. Titus, who has the support of the people, is too conservative in his initiatives and assumptions, fails to heed the manifold warning signs that Saturninus is not a desirable ruler, and commits a series of fatal political errors that precipitate the tragedy. Lavinia, who only speaks once in the entire scene, is fought over by rival factions. Her role here prefigures her larger symbolic function in the play as Rome's body politic, mistreated and abused by its inhabitants to their own cost.[51] Lavinia's rape and dismemberment at the hands of Demetrius and Chiron, orchestrated by their mother, Tamora, is a metonymic representation illustrating how far Rome has degenerated from the high hopes for a more representative and accountable government only one act earlier; a parodic repetition of the fate of Lucrece.[52] The fact that two of Titus's remaining three sons, Quintus and Martius, should receive the blame for the murder of Bassianus, a crime committed at the same time, further indicates how quickly Rome has fallen prey to the anarchy of government by personal vendetta. Given Martius's foolish interpretation of the law, his death is not wholly undeserved or surprising. The two crimes demonstrate further how little separates the barbarity of the Goths from the violence endemic in ancient Roman values based on the cult of honour, which Titus himself was so keen to uphold, values that, significantly enough, were assuming increasing importance in late Elizabethan England.[53]

Titus, as the opening scene and its use of memorable and distressing physical images on stage demonstrate, stands out as a radical play keen to question belief in a hereditary monarchy as the only viable form of government. Lavinia's rape is represented in terms of Tereus's rape of Philomela in Ovid's *Metamorphoses*, and also the rape of Lucrece, which forms one of 'the play's patterning narratives'.[54] Aaron, inciting the sons of Tamora to violate Lavinia, asserts that 'Lucrece was not more chaste' (608) than Lavinia is; when the truth is revealed, Marcus has Lavinia kneel as he swears revenge on the Goths. He compares the vows of the assembled group to promises made by those who established the Roman republic: 'And swear with me – as, with the woeful fere [spouse] / And father of that chaste dishonoured dame, / Lord Junius Brutus swore for Lucrece rape' (4.1.89–91).[55] Titus's killing of Lavinia demands to be read in terms of Lucrece's suicide. Titus perceives her dismembered body as a sign of his own failure and wounded honour: 'Die, die, Lavinia, and thy shame with thee, / And with thy shame thy father's sorrow die' (5.3.45–6). In doing so, Titus reveals himself to be part of a moribund patriarchal, political order, and his own death fifteen lines later is both expected and a relief. Saturninus and Tamora are also killed. Immediately, Titus's brother, the tribune, Marcus, helps inaugurate what the play suggests could be a new political order and bring to a 'closure' (133) the bloody sequence of events that the audience has just witnessed. He appeals first for unity in the body politic, highlighting once again the key role of Lavinia, and her significance as a type of Lucrece whose death leads to the rejuvenation of the state: 'O let me teach you how to knit again / This scattered corn into one mutual sheaf, / These broken limbs again into one body' (69–71). Lucius is made emperor and helps to cure the wounds of civil war by revealing the evil plots and subterfuges of Saturninus's rule. While tyranny keeps everyone in the dark, more representative forms of government bring everything into the light and let the citizens decide.

Despite returning to Rome at the head of a foreign army, Lucius is shown to be a popular choice as ruler. Emillius declares that he is supported by the 'common voice' (139), and a few lines later, the Roman populace declare their support (145). While Aaron is led away to be buried up to his neck in the ground and starved to death, and Tamora's body is thrown to the wild beasts without a funeral ceremony, their baby remains as an ambiguous symbol of the new popular regime. The audience remains unsure whether he serves as a sign of its tolerance and forgiveness, or its inability to sever links with the past. Aaron's impending fate stands as a mirror image of Marcus's attempts to persuade Titus to accept the people's vote at the start of the play and rule as emperor. Titus's refusal leaves Rome 'headless' (1.1.189), and, as a result, Aaron's cruelty is allowed to flourish. Aaron's head will be left above ground as a primitive sacrifice to help complete the cycle of cruelty. While he is 'planted' in order to die, his seed has led to the harvest of the half-Moor and half-Roman-Goth baby. The baby may reveal that 'Rome has lost all vestiges of its political identity' and will be faced with equally violent episodes in the future, as Naomi Conn Liebler suggests.[56] Alternatively, the mixture of bloods and races he represents may point to a less rigidly divided state under Lucius's rule. In refusing to repent for the evils he has committed in life, Aaron distances himself from his child: 'I am no baby' (5.3.184). Furthermore, he revels in his evil and abjures any virtuous act he may have committed: 'If one good deed in all my life I did / I do repent it from my very soul' (188–9). It would not be too far-fetched a reading of the play to suggest that the baby stands as the one good deed he has committed – especially as the baby is visible on stage – and so points towards a more hopeful future for a Rome that can accommodate Romans and non-Romans alike.

Aaron, like Titus, stands for an old order that must be replaced for progress to occur. However, the seed they both sow should lead to the regeneration of the body politic. Lucius states that his aim is to 'heal Rome's harms and wipe away her woe' (147).

Titus is not a play that provides easy answers to the questions that it raises. Its representation of events, location in time and place, and allusions to other narratives, all make the play politically suggestive rather than definitive in its analysis. The first point that has to be made is that the fictional classical Rome created by the play cannot be ruled without the support of its citizens. The citizens appear only in the first and last scenes, and are absent from the development of the tragic and bloody action itself. Less visible than the citizens in *Julius Caesar* and *Coriolanus*, their presence nevertheless frames the play in terms of Rome's fictionalized political history. The first and last scenes deliberately associate Rome with representative government based on the crucial role of the tribunes as intermediaries between the aristocratic senate and a wider public.[57] The emperor cannot rule without paying heed to the popular will. Tyranny is seen as a destructive interlude that will eventually destroy itself. *Titus* implies that a mixed constitution is the most successful form of government, placing emphasis on the need for the citizens to participate in the political process.[58] The emperor can only govern with the consent and support of both the people and the aristocracy. The last scene shows all three parts of the state working together to re-establish political order after the trauma of civil war. After the death of Saturninus, Marcus, Lucius and Emillius assume control of Rome. They provide the assembled people with an explanation of the gory events they have just witnessed, prompted by a Roman lord who asks 'who hath brought the fatal engine in / That gives our Troy, our Rome, the civil wound' (85–6). Reference to Troy signals the establishment of Rome from the ashes of the Trojan empire by Aeneas, as narrated in Virgil's *Aeneid*, the most celebrated work of imperial Rome.[59] Rome stands at the crossroads and can either look to the future and re-create itself once more and establish a great civilization, or revert back to the destructive values of an old order. Any reference to Troy automatically triggers the familiar typological chain, Troy–Rome–

London (Troynovant), because Britain had supposedly been founded by the eponymous Brutus, descendant of Aeneas, after he was expelled from Rome, and so further cements the links between the events represented on stage and the political situation in contemporary England.[60]

Titus himself stands as a great warrior who cannot carry his success on the battlefield through to government precisely because, despite his obvious virtues, he is trapped inside a patriarchal culture of vengeance, blood and honour. Titus often echoes the words of Hieronimo in Thomas Kyd's *The Spanish Tragedy* (*c.*1589), among the most popular plays of the early 1590s and the one that established the figure of the frustrated revenge hero.[61] Kyd's protagonist became a byword for over-acting, and was often parodied or referred to in scathing terms, as Thomas Dekker's reference to Ben Jonson taking 'mad Hieronimoes part' indicates.[62] Just as Kyd's protagonist feels that he must resort to extensive, brutal revenge when he is denied justice for the murder of his son, so does Titus. Such values are arguably endorsed in *The Spanish Tragedy*, but are represented more problematically in *Titus*, especially given Titus's obvious limitations as a political and moral figure.[63] Both men follow courses of action that are heroic and dangerous, but can only lead to further murder and violence. Titus, more than Lavinia and Lucrece, has to die for a better order to be re-established. Lucius helped his father perform the sacrifice of Alarbus, but then stood up to Saturninus's attempts to silence Titus, before supporting the populist and democratic Bassianus and his prior right to Lavinia. His words and actions in this opening scene alone demonstrate that he is prepared to change, unlike his stubborn father.

Titus cannot be reduced to a simple political allegory or message, but engages with late Elizabethan political culture in a variety of ways. Thomas Smith argued that it was impossible for governments to remain the same over long periods of time because

> The nature of man is never to stand still in one maner of estate, but to grow from the lesse to the more, and decay from the more againe to the lesse, till it come to the fatall end and destruction, with many turnes and turmoyles of sicknesse and

recovering, seldome standing in a perfect health, neither of a mans bodie it selfe, nor of the politique bodie which is compact of the same.[64]

Shakespeare, of course, may not have known Smith's text, although it went through four editions between 1583 and 1594 and evidently reached a wide readership. If he did not know it directly, he undoubtedly encountered its arguments when they were incorporated into the second edition of Holinshed's *Chronicles* (1587), one of his key sources.[65] Smith's argument was illustrated with a potted history of Rome in one convoluted sentence, beginning with the line of kings established by Romulus, and continuing with the subsequent degeneration into tyranny, 'the rule of the best men, as in time when the first Consuls were', the 'usurping of a few' as with the rule of the senators after Tarquin's banishment, the decemvirate, the triumvirate of Caesar, Crassus and Pompey, and the 'ruling and usurping of the popular and the rascall'. Smith's ultimate point is that to avoid the equally dangerous peaks and troughs of tyranny and unstable popular rule – which inevitably led to tyranny – a mixed constitution made up of all three elements from society, king, nobility and commons, was the best safeguard. He uses the analogy of marriage and the establishment of a household as the first kingdom to argue that society developed through 'common and mutuall consent', handing over power to the father.[66]

There are significant points of comparison between Smith's argument and Shakespeare's play, especially in the use of Roman history to represent a wider truth about the development and decline of commonwealths. Both make extensive use of the ubiquitous analogy of the body politic, representing the state as ill, mutilated or healthy.[67] Both make a conspicuous effort to show that extremes of government are less desirable than a balanced and mixed constitution, which makes all the estates within society co-operate. In *Titus*, the people want to elect Titus at first, but will evidently be happier when they are directed to accept Lucius as their ruler at the end of the play.

Smith's work raises a crucial problem of political discourses and their influence. On the one hand, *De Republica Anglorum* is a product of a native political tradition, which developed out of the egalitarian thrust of Protestant thought, encouraging 'a politically significant section of the male elite to define themselves as "citizens", ambiguously of the True Church and of the godly nation called into existence (from the point of view of convinced Protestants) with England's break from Rome'.[68] The treatises of the 'resistance theorists', John Knox, John Ponet and Christopher Goodman, made up one strand of this complex whole (see above, pp. 3, 84). Equally important were the ideas and writings of the 'commonwealth men' who flourished at the court of Henry VIII, such as Thomas Starkey, Thomas Elyot and John Cheke, all of whom argued, in one form or another, for a balanced constitution and limited, or mixed, monarchy.[69] The most important expression of their views was Thomas Starkey's *A Dialogue Between Pole and Lupset*.[70] On the other, Smith's use of the word 'republic', and his allusions to the history of Rome as a means of examining English politics, also signal an interest in classical republicanism. Ann McLaren has pointed out how Smith's shuttling back and forth between a political language which attempts to include 'all men' in the body politic, and an exclusive, hierarchical language of monarchical rule expresses the contradictions of late Tudor thought.[71] Republicans also believed in the mixed constitution, and not all of them wished to depose the monarch.[72]

Titus Andronicus is a work that is evidently keen to engage in the representation and discussion of the question of the 'mixed monarchy'. For Shakespeare, like Smith, the comparison between transitional Rome, caught between empire and republic, and dying Elizabethan England, about to be ruled by a new, unknown dynasty, is there for the audience and readers of the published playtext to make. It is a sign of the play's aggressive stance that primogeniture, the usual means of maintaining power within a dynasty, is shown to be the least successful way of handing over power. Saturninus, Bassianus and Titus are all potential emperors of Rome at the start of the play. Of the three, Saturninus is clearly the least suited to rule. The opening exchange between the two sons of the dead emperor and the tribune, Marcus, shows Saturninus appealing to an exclusively aristocratic public to validate his right, a claim made in the most hierarchical terms possible:

> Noble patricians, patrons of my right,
> Defend the justice of my cause with arms.
> And countrymen, my loving followers,
> Plead my successive title with your swords.
> I am his first-born son that was the last
> That wore the imperial diadem of Rome:
> Then let my father's honours live in me,
> Nor wrong mine age with this indignity.
>
> (1.1.1–8)

Saturninus's words are meant to close off debate and legitimate his right to succeed as emperor. He appeals to the two classes in society, the nobility and the people, in his rhetorically balanced first four lines. Both are urged to use violence rather than argument: the aristocracy to support his personal right, indicating that Saturninus is employing the code of honour, asking them to defend one of their own; the people to support the more general principle of primogeniture. The last four lines make the appeal to the cult of honour more explicit – perhaps indicating that he is more concerned with his popularity among the powerful elite than among the public at large – and make the claim that anyone who disputes his right to rule is already in the wrong through violating the sacred principle of the succession of the first-born.

Bassianus's claim is more obviously populist:

> Romans, friends, followers, favourers of my right,
> If ever Bassianus, Caesar's son,
> Were gracious in the eyes of royal Rome,
> Keep then this passage to the Capitol,
> And suffer not dishonour to approach
> The imperial seat, to virtue consecrate,
> To justice, continence and nobility;
> But let desert in pure election shine,
> And, Romans, fight for freedom in your choice.
>
> (9–17)

Bassianus's speech directly contradicts Saturninus's in its assumption of principles of succession and rule. The opening line predicts the words of Mark Antony in *Julius Caesar* (3.2.74), in which he appeals directly to the populace as a means of overthrowing the oligarchic republic that Brutus and Cassius are attempting to establish. Bassianus does not appeal to the absolute right invoked by his elder brother, but articulates a lesser claim, calling on 'favourers of my right'. He asks to be elected only if he is thought to be the most worthy of the candidates standing for election. Whereas Saturninus relates honour to hereditary right, Bassianus links honour to virtue, indicating that the 'imperial seat' can only serve its true purpose if its occupant uses it properly by preserving the principles of 'justice, continence and honour'. Honour, like virtue, has to be earned, and cannot be assumed, making Bassianus's words republican in inclination, even if they do not refer directly to a political reality. The need to promote virtue was the principal concept of classical republicanism.[73] In asking that 'desert in pure election shine' and urging Romans to maintain their freedom in doing so, Bassianus is invoking republican principles to stand against the hereditary claims of Saturninus.

The claims made for Titus as a suitable governor are also based on his inherent virtue, albeit in war rather than government: 'A nobler man, a braver warrior, / Lives not this day within the city walls' (25–6). Shakespeare pointedly juxtaposes hereditary and republican arguments for government at the start of *Titus*. The play could be seen to possess a radical charge in that it shows the former to be the most unsuitable and dangerous form of government, one that immediately produces tyranny. In the context of England in 1594, with the succession likely to pass to a Scottish king of known autocratic political opinions, simply because of his ancestry, this can be read as a courageous – or foolhardy – beginning, especially as *Titus* has no obvious sources.[74]

However, if *Titus* can be read as a work that is openly suspicious of hereditary monarchy and exposes the vices of such a system of government (or, at least, the vices of those who argue for such forms of government), it does not provide an unproblematic endorsement of a republican system of elected offices. Titus shows that he does not deserve the support that he receives from the citizens of Rome. He is undoubtedly a successful and impressive warrior, but his judgement of character, and approach to the possibilities and consequences of decisions that determine how government should function, are both comically inept and constituent parts of the tragic action. Titus's response to the troubles that afflict Rome is notably less constructive and pragmatic than that of his son, Lucius. Confronted with the execution of his sons and the violation and mutilation of his daughter, Titus becomes an angel of revenge modelled on Hieronimo. Lucius plans to rescue his condemned brothers, while Titus concludes that 'Rome is but a wilderness of tigers' (3.1.54), and first threatens to chop his hands off because 'hands to do Rome service is but vain' (81), before determining his course of personal revenge. Lucius, in contrast, sees their campaign in terms of the expulsion of Tarquin, indicating that he has not lost sight of the political significance of their task.

The lesson of the electoral game of the opening scene – which can, perhaps, be read alongside the opening scene of *King Lear* – is that Bassianus is the most suitable candidate. An emperor who acknowledges the importance of the people's right to freedom and to participate in government, as well as the value of the 'imperial seat', can be seen to stand for 'mixed' government as advocated by a dominant strand in English political thought. Lucius's stated aims belong to a political tradition represented by Sir Thomas Smith, who had no difficulty in labelling England a republic, as well as thinkers more obviously indebted to a republican tradition such as Richard Beacon, whose *Solon His Follie*, heavily indebted to Machiavelli, appeared in 1594, the same year that *Titus* was first performed.[75] That this moderate approach to politics is neglected and a tyranny established illustrates the equal and opposite dangers of the extremes of unfettered populism and unrestrained monarchical rule. Saturninus illustrates the latter problem, as he does the standard vices of the stage tyrant.[76] He is only able to come to power because he has the support of the people, despite his stated faith in the rights of the nobility to select the emperor. They are shown to be fickle in transferring their allegiance to him, having initially supported Titus, principally because of his success in war, a theme later explored at greater length in *Coriolanus*.[77] Had the virtues of Bassianus been recognized, Rome might never have been drawn into a fractious and bloody civil war. Equally, had Titus not insisted on the ancient rites of blood sacrifice, the renewed conflict with the Goths might have been avoided.

In their different ways both *Lucrece* and *Titus* suggest that a more constitutional form of government, which relies on greater participation from a wider political class than is currently involved in making decisions, would be of benefit to any regime. Obviously such a class would not have to be drawn from all sections of the population and could still be fundamentally aristocratic in character, limiting the radical nature of any political demands made.[78] Nevertheless, it is hard not to feel that Shakespeare's early works, whether they can be read as a direct expression of his political opinions or whether they were written to pander to the whims of a republican patron, argued a case for limited monarchy and a mixed constitution.

Shakespeare was by no means the only celebrated writer who was unhappy with Elizabeth's regime in the 1590s. Edmund Spenser undoubtedly showed an interest in republican arguments in the last years of the 1590s. One of his posthumously published works was a sonnet prefacing Lewis Lewkenor's translation of Gasparo Contarini's *The commonwealth and government of Venice* (1599), a work that extols the virtues of republican Venice.[79] Shakespeare made extensive use of this work for his two Venetian plays.[80] Ben Jonson, whose rivalry with Shakespeare may have been even more important than has generally been assumed in forging the style and scope of early modern English drama, was also keen to represent republican Rome in his plays, with political implications that are – arguably – rather less oblique than those of Shakespeare's plays.[81] *Sejanus his Fall*, which adapts the story of Sejanus's failed coup against Tiberius, uses Tacitus' *Annals* in order to show that Elizabeth's court had become as servile and venial as that of Tiberius: 'tyranny prevails because the ruling class has allowed itself to be corrupted'.[82] Many other writers within the orbit of the Earl of Essex, such as Sir Henry Wotton and Henry Cuffe, wrote accounts of Roman and contemporary European history and political institutions in order indirectly to scrutinize late Elizabethan England.[83] Shakespeare's exploration of a variety of political forms in his works should not be seen as either unusual or surprising.

III

Shakespeare returned to the question of the transfer of power and the metamorphosis of one political system into another in *Julius Caesar*, which was probably the first play performed at the newly established Globe theatre, and most likely written just after *Henry V*.[84] These two plays can be read alongside each other as parallel lives, just as Plutarch joined the lives of Alexander and Julius Caesar.[85] The story of Julius Caesar's rise to power and subsequent assassination in the name of republican freedom was a *cause célèbre* that was frequently retold in the Renaissance as a means of justifying tyrannicide, or warning of its dangers.[86] *Vindiciae, Contra Tyrannos*, for example, explicitly justifies the actions of Brutus and Cassius as legitimate against a dictator. The author stresses the extent of opposition to Caesar and argues that it is the duty of the good citizen to bear arms against a tyrant and that those who fail or refuse to do so are culpable:

> Thus Pompey, Cato, Cicero, and others, performed the office of good citizens by snatching up weapons against Caesar when he was overturning the commonwealth; and there can be no excuse for those whose inactivity meant that these efforts resulted in no happy conclusion at all ... Brutus, Cassius, Casca, and others, who killed Caesar while the affair was still raging, could not be charged.[87]

In Athens, the ancient centre of liberty and democracy, bronze statues of Brutus and Cassius are erected 'by public decree', a sign that their actions meet the approval of the citizens of the home of political thought and just government.[88]

However, it would be misleading to assume that the assassination of Caesar was always represented by classical or Renaissance writers in the same terms as that of Tarquin.[89] Plutarch narrated the event three times in his lives of Caesar, Marcus Brutus and Mark Antony. He describes Caesar as a potential dictator, over-ruling the checks and balances of the Roman political system:

> the chiefest cause that made him mortally hated, was the covetous desire he had to be called king ... he still sitting in majesty, disdaining to rise up unto them when they came in, as if they had bene private men, aunswered them: that his honors had more neede to be cut of, then enlarged. This did not onely offend the Senate, but the common people also, to see that he should so lightly esteeme of the Magistrates of the common wealth.[90]

Plutarch, as translated by Thomas North, makes it clear that Caesar has alienated himself from both classes in a politically engaged and literate city. In doing so, he has made his ambition for higher office into a dangerous undertaking, and his lack of respect for the political offices and traditions of Rome has sealed his fate. Both *Vindiciae, Contra Tyrannos* and Plutarch's *Life of Julius Caesar* are keen to point out how engaged and active the citizens of Rome are, a legacy of the republic that they have lived in for the past four and a half centuries. Plutarch is at pains to emphasize that Brutus is chosen by the people to be their leader: 'Now ... they desired change, and wished Brutus only their prince and governor above all other'.[91] The parallels to *Titus* are evident: Caesar is like Saturninus, haughty and aloof; Brutus, like Titus, is the popular choice.

Even more significant still, I would suggest, is the pointed contrast between the rape of Lucrece and the subsequent banishment of Tarquin, and the assassination of Caesar. Plutarch opens his account of the life of Marcus Brutus with a substantial paragraph outlining the familial relationship between the two republicans, which, in the face of claims by defenders of Caesar that Lucius was not the ancestor of Marcus, he verifies. He also provides a careful consideration of their respective characters:

> Junius Brutus being of a sour stern nature, not softened by reason, being like unto sword blades of too hard a temper, was so

subject to his choler and malice he bore unto the tyrants, that for
their sakes he caused his own sons to be executed. But this
Marcus Brutus in contrary manner, whose life we presently
write, having framed his manners of life by the rules of virtue
and study of philosophy, and having employed his wit, which was
gentle and constant, in attempting of great things, methinks he
was rightly made and framed unto virtue. So that his very
enemies which wish him most hurt, because of his conspiracy
against Julius Caesar, if there are any noble attempt done in all
this conspiracy, they refer it wholly unto Brutus.[92]

This genuine praise of Marcus Brutus is, however, fraught with irony.
Whereas Lucius Junius Brutus's struggle against tyranny was
responsible for the establishment of the Roman republic, Marcus
Brutus's actions in the same cause resulted in civil war and the
destruction of the republic. Julius Caesar's death led ultimately to the rise
of Octavian, later Augustus, the most impressive of the dynasty of Roman
emperors he established. In one sense, the action of Shakespeare's play
takes place between the republican epic of civil war, Lucan's *Pharsalia* –
written during the reign of one of Rome's worst tyrants, Nero – which
represents the civil war between Caesar and Pompey referred to at the
start of Shakespeare's *Julius Caesar*, and the epic written in praise of
Augustus' imperial ambitions, the *Aeneid*.[93] The key point is that the
personalities and characters of the two Brutuses matter less than
the situations in which they are forced to act. The contrast between the
expulsion of Tarquin and the assassination of Julius Caesar stands as a
precise illustration of one of Marx's most celebrated analyses of history,
an insight anticipated by both Plutarch and Shakespeare:

Hegel remarks somewhere that all facts and personages of
great importance in world history occur, as it were, twice. He
forgot to add: the first time as tragedy, the second as farce ... Men
make their own history, but they do not make it just as they
please; they do not make it under circumstances chosen by
themselves, but under circumstances directly encountered,

given, and transmitted from the past. The tradition of all the dead generations weighs like a nightmare on the brain of the living. And just when they seem engaged in revolutionizing themselves and things, in creating something that has never yet existed, precisely in such periods of revolutionary crisis they anxiously conjure up the spirits of the past[.][94]

Lucrece's rape and suicide is a tragedy, but it leads to the establishment of the republic, a cathartic result for Rome. Brutus, good man that he undoubtedly is, allows himself to be misled by Cassius, who hated Caesar 'privately, more then he did the tyranny openly' (a pointed contrast to Lucius Junius Brutus).[95] Plutarch argues that Brutus, by allowing himself to be drawn into a conspiracy, damages both the republic, and also his own ability to rule and so lead Rome effectively:

> And surely, in my opinion, I am persuaded that Brutus might indeed have come to have been the chiefest man of Rome, if he could have contented himself for a time and have been next unto Caesar, and to have suffered his glory and authority, which he had got by his great victories, to consume with time.[96]

The example of Lucius Junius Brutus, Plutarch implies, misleads both Marcus Brutus and any readers who see their actions as equivalent. Brutus's sincere hatred of tyranny and its malign effects, ironically helps to hasten the end of the republic, rather than preserve it. Cassius, according to Plutarch, was no better than Caesar, his character being more clearly revealed by his behaviour after the assassination when 'it was certainly thought that he made war, and put himself into sundry dangers, more to *have absolute power and authority*, than to defend the liberty of his country [my emphasis]'.[97] Brutus, defender of republican liberty, has been taken in by a potential tyrant as bad as the one he has helped to overthrow.

Plutarch represents the people as divided, fickle and unsure of their political direction (a sign of a decaying political state and its institutions).[98] They are easily moved by skilful rhetoric and mutate according to circumstances. At first they 'desired change', but when

Brutus addressed the people in the marketplace, the morning after the assassination, they are divided in sympathy: 'by their great silence they showed, that they were sorry for Caesar's death, and also that they did reverence Brutus'.[99] Later, when Antonius (Mark Antony) delivers Caesar's funeral oration – also in the marketplace – 'his words moved the common people to compassion', because he 'framed his eloquence to make their hearts yearn the more', and, after they have been shown Caesar's blood-stained gown, full of holes, 'some of them cried out, "Kill the murderers!". Others plucked up forms, tables, and stalls about the market-place ... and having laid them all on a heap together, they set them on fire, and thereupon did put the body of Caesar, and burnt it in the midst of the most holy places'.[100] Caesar is effectively deified, a clear sign that the grand aims and ideals of the republic have already ceased to count for much with the populace. The looming anarchy leads to the murder of Cinna the poet because he shares a name with one of the conspirators, despite his having played no part in the conspiracy and having always been 'one of Caesar's chiefest friends'.

There are further twists in this complex and dangerous political situation, ruled by the power of the unrestrained populace. Brutus and then other conspirators flee, precisely because they are now afraid of the 'fury of the people', in whose name and for whose freedom they killed Caesar. The senate takes the side of the people, emphasizing its lack of political influence and the isolation of the conspirators. However, soon after the murder of Cinna, the mood of the people changes again, and they grow 'weary now of Antonius' pride and insolency, who ruled all things in manner with absolute power'. They 'desired that Brutus might return again'.[101] But, before Brutus can engineer a triumphant return to Rome, like that of Lucius in *Titus*, 'there fell out another change and alteration'; the rise of Octavius, the future Augustus, adopted as the heir of Caesar before his death. By distributing money, he is able to challenge the supremacy of Antony, and Rome is further divided up into two factions, with Brutus also gathering an army ready for the brutal civil war that will lead eventually to the establishment of imperial Rome. As any literate playgoer or reader would have known, Augustus, though a just – albeit flawed – ruler himself, precipitated a list of emperors more bad than good, who made the sins of Julius Caesar appear anodyne in comparison, as the histories of Tacitus and Suetonius revealed.[102]

Shakespeare's *Julius Caesar* is a play that, more than any other he wrote, adopts the political position of its main source, Plutarch.[103] In the three lives of Caesar, Brutus and Antony, Plutarch shows how far the ideals of the republic have decayed from its original inception and earlier days, to the point that political choice is between the over-ambitious and potentially tyrannical Caesar, and rule by the mob. In practice, there is nothing to distinguish either of them. Political advice has degenerated into conspiracy; the senate ends up aligned with the people, paving the way for the evils of unrestrained democracy; and civil war looms, as one of Brutus's friends, Faonius, predicted. He refused to join the conspirators, warning that 'civil war was worse than tyrannical government usurped against the law'.[104] The political institutions that made the republic a success and enabled Rome to integrate all political classes into its political system – the senate, the tribunate, the praetorship, the consulship – have collapsed into emperor and people. The mixed constitution, seen as the political ideal by so many Elizabethan writers, has degenerated into a false alternative between two equally undesirable states. Marcus Brutus may well be a better man than his namesake, Lucius Junius Brutus, but in such circumstances his spectacular and high-minded intervention into political life can only have malign consequences. When Lucius Junius Brutus is invoked in the play, it is as part of Cassius's attempt to persuade Brutus to replace Caesar, not as an unsullied political ideal: 'There was a Brutus once that would have brooked / Th'eternal devil to keep his state in Rome / As easily as a king' (1.2.158–60).[105] Later, Cassius fakes a prophetic letter which forces Brutus to make the same connection between the proposed assassination of Caesar and the actions of his ancestor against the Tarquins (2.1.46–58). Even the touchstones of republican liberty are parodied and abused, as a legitimate revolt against tyranny is transformed into a secretive plot. 'Rome, degenerate and decayed as it is' is 'the central protagonist of the play.'[106]

In *The Rape of Lucrece*, Collatine transforms the paralysing sorrow he feels at his wife's suicide to the manly action required to establish the republic when 'in key-cold Lucrece's bleeding stream / He falls, and bathes the pale fear in his face' (1774–5), transforming the anaemic, womanly fear and paralysis of the subject under a tyranny into the ruddy, bold and active citizen ready to establish the republic. Brutus attempts to repeat this symbolic change after the assassination:

> Stoop, Romans, stoop,
> And let us bathe our hands in Caesar's blood
> Up to the elbows and besmear our swords.
> Then walk we forth even to the market-place,
> And waving our red weapons o'er our heads
> Let's all cry, 'Peace, Freedom and Liberty.'
>
> (3.1.105–10)

The sentiment and honesty are admirable, yet not only is the pious hope obviously ridiculous, but the symbolism is far too easy to reverse. When Antony takes each of the conspirators by the hand (186–9), he is also touched by the blood of Caesar, but his purpose is to make Caesar's wounds speak, 'Which like dumb mouths do ope their ruby lips / To beg the voice and utterance of my tongue' (260–1), and so cause 'Woe to the hand that shed this costly blood' (258). The honest republican Brutus makes it far too easy for the cunning Mark Antony to 'Cry havoc and let slip the dogs of war' (273). That Mark Antony is able to do this through the use of the type of political forum that Brutus is so keen to re-establish, only shows how badly Brutus has misread the political temper of the time. The culture and symbols of republicanism are not potent enough to prevent their appropriation by their enemies, who see only murder and senseless violence.[107]

While *The Rape of Lucrece* and *Titus Andronicus* can be read as literary works which exhibit some sympathy for republican ideals and institutions, it is hard to regard *Julius Caesar* in the same way. Antony – publicly, at least – promises to join the conspirators if he is given reasons 'Why and wherein Caesar was dangerous' (222). Brutus's short prose speech to the assembled people is a series of rhetorical questions and hypothetical conundrums:

> If then that friend demand why Brutus rose against Caesar, this is my answer: not that I loved Caesar less, but that I loved Rome more. Had you rather Caesar were living, and die all slaves, than that Caesar were dead, to live all freemen? As Caesar loved me, I weep for him; as he was fortunate, I rejoice at it; as he was valiant, I honour him: but as he was ambitious, I slew him. (3.2.20–7)

In short, Brutus has no sensible answer to Antony's question, beyond a sincere but vague love for the ancient liberties of the Roman republic. When Antony enters with Caesar's body, Brutus reveals how little he has thought about how to re-instate the liberties he cherishes. He proclaims that although Mark Antony had no part in Caesar's death, he 'shall receive the benefit of his dying, a place in the commonwealth, as which of you shall not?' (42–4), a promise that has no meaning because it cannot articulate how the change from the projected monarchy of Caesar to the republic of Brutus can be achieved. The political vagueness of Brutus mirrors that of Caesar, a further sign of the decay of institutions and debate towards the end of the republic. This point is made and Brutus's hopes undercut when the third plebeian demands that Brutus 'be Caesar' (51). Antony is able to turn Brutus's hypothetical constructions against him with ease: 'The noble Brutus / Hath told you Caesar was ambitious: / If it were so, it was a grievous fault' (78–80), and so reveals the bankruptcy of the republican cause that fails to argue the case successfully, yet bases itself on the efficacy of public institutions and political argument. Within one scene Rome has been transformed from being a possible republic to being in a state of civil war.

Caesar is indeed open to criticism, but Brutus is unable to argue a coherent case against him. Cassius's criticisms made to Brutus to inaugurate the plot are, as Plutarch had suggested, based more on personal than political or intellectual grounds. Cassius tries to fuel Brutus's ambition by representing Caesar as feeble and cowardly, a contrast to the 'colossus' (1.2.135) he has become in Rome. The logic of his argument: 'The fault, dear Brutus, is not in our stars / But in ourselves, that we are underlings' (139–40), reduces republican idealism to envy.[108] Caesar appears foolish, isolated, self-absorbed and insulated from criticism, clearly an unsuitable choice for king. He claims to be suspicious of Cassius because he is too thin, reads alone, makes astute judgements and does not socialize as Antony does (197–209). Caesar is not wholly mistaken here, and he is clearly demonstrating good judgement in fearing Cassius. But the most crucial point is that whatever vestiges of sense remain in Caesar are being used not to rule Rome well, but to preserve his own position as the dominant figure within the republic. The speech ends with Caesar showing that his aim is to cut himself off from the people and become self-sufficient: 'I rather tell thee what is to be feared / Than what I fear: for always I am Caesar' (210–11). Fear is for those like Antony who are to protect Caesar, a sign that Caesar thinks of himself as divine rather than human. To proclaim oneself 'always . . . Caesar' is either a tautology (it is a name and everyone has one), or a further assertion of immortality, one cruelly exposed two acts later. Caesar's reference to himself in the third person when speaking to his wife, Calphurnia, his superstition and his faith in his own destiny, show how unsuitable a ruler he is.

The real problem, however, is not simply with Caesar as a potential ruler, and it would be wrong to read the play straightforwardly in terms of arguments for and against the tyrannicide of a bad monarch – as, I would suggest, is the case with other plays. Caesar's problematic status exposes the decay of the Roman body politic and the lack of alternatives available. Whereas Tarquin's expulsion, or the orgy of violence in the last act of *Titus*, lead to a real political solution in Rome, Caesar's death results only in protracted civil war, a series of unstable and undesirable alliances, and the eventual establishment of the Roman empire. That Caesar is supported by the plebeians, who would make him their king, and opposed only by a small band of conspirators with no popular base, exposes the political turmoil and lack of institutions and political ideas functioning in Rome.[109] But we have known that all is not well in Rome from the opening scene of the play, in which the tribunes, Flavius and

Murellus, remove scarves from the statues, angry at the inappropriate celebrations carried out to mark Caesar's triumphal return. When a cobbler argues that he was simply participating in a holiday 'to see Caesar and to rejoice in his triumph' (1.1.31–2), Murellus furiously replies:

> Wherefore rejoice? What conquest brings he home?
> What tributaries follow him to Rome
> To grace in captive bonds his chariot wheels?
> You blocks, you stones, you worse than senseless things!
> O you hard hearts, you cruel men of Rome,
> Knew you not Pompey? Many a time and oft
> Have you climbed up to walls and battlements,
> To towers and windows, yea, to chimney-tops,
> Your infants in your arms, and there have sat
> The livelong day, with patient expectation,
> To see great Pompey pass the streets of Rome ...
> And do you now strew flowers in his way,
> That comes in triumph over Pompey's blood?
>
> (33–43, 51–2)

Murellus's impassioned outburst makes a series of points which shadow the action of the play. The fickleness of the people is determined from the start of the play, a sign of a decaying state that cannot guide them, as much as of their own vice. Pompey has been replaced in their affections by Caesar, who is briefly replaced by Brutus, then Antony, and so on. In having to confront the people, Murellus also demonstrates the insignificance of the office he holds. Tribunes were supposed to be the representatives of the people, their protectors, not their moral guardians. We hear no more of Murellus and Flavius in the play, probably because they have been disposed of by the autocratic Caesar, as Casca reports ('Murellus and Flavius, for pulling scarves off Caesar's images, are put to silence' (1.2.284–5)). More importantly, their disappearance is a sign that they have no role to play in the last days of the Roman republic. Furthermore, Caesar's triumph is not against foreign powers, a victory that could be used to display the active virtue

FIGURE 8 *The Triumphs of Caesar*, canvas 9 by Andrea Mantegna. Mantegna shows Julius Caesar returning in triumph to Rome after his victories in Gaul (France) and Asia Minor. Caesar held a particular fascination for many Renaissance artists and scholars because he was effectively the first Roman Emperor and because of the extent of his military success.

of the Roman citizens, as in Livy's *History*, as read by Machiavelli.[110] Rather it is a triumph over his chief rival, ending a civil war condemned in Lucan's *Pharsalia*, the conflict that prefigures the variety of struggles Shakespeare represents in *Julius Caesar*, and continued in *Antony and Cleopatra*.[111]

Can we recognize a political stance adopted in *Julius Caesar*? If *Lucrece* and *Titus* can be read as works which represent republicanism sympathetically, does *Julius Caesar* mark a transformation in Shakespeare's political outlook? While superficially plausible, there are numerous objections to this interpretation. First, *Julius Caesar* represents a historical moment towards the end of the republic, when its fate was sealed, not a point when a revolutionary change of government seemed possible and desirable. Second, it would have been extremely problematic for Shakespeare to have produced a play which justified the assassination of Caesar in 1599, given the tense political circumstances accompanying the impending death of Elizabeth and the imminent change of dynasty, as well as the increasingly overt political sympathies of the Essex circle with whom Shakespeare was associated (see above, pp. 111–14).[112] Third, *Julius Caesar* can be read alongside *Henry V*, as a companion piece, recalling Plutarch's juxtaposition of the lives of Caesar and Alexander.[113] *Henry V* contains considerable evidence of republican sentiment, suggesting that it would be wrong to take one play in isolation as an expression of the author's political views (see above, pp. 56–71).

Julius Caesar is best read, I would suggest, in terms of the fears prevalent in late Elizabethan society. Caesar's death leads only to worse anarchy and tyranny, a message explicit in Plutarch's *Lives*. Elizabeth was extremely unpopular among many in the literate, articulate and politically frustrated sections of the public, those who felt they had a right to have political opinions and influence policy at the highest levels. But, as everyone knew, when she died, the succession would probably pass to James VI of Scotland, a prospect Shakespeare appears to have regarded with considerable foreboding.[114] In fact, Shakespeare's representation of the isolated conspirators and the disasters they inflict on Rome can be seen as a warning, that attempts to transform the political destiny of a nation without a proper plan, or a wider base of support, are doomed. Like other works produced at the *fin de siècle*, *Julius Caesar* exudes a resigned gloom at the impending fate of the nation.[115] Nevertheless, this is not to exclude the possibility that political change – or, rather, a reinforcement of the ideal of the mixed constitution – was desirable, as many of Shakespeare's other plays suggested.

Once Rome has started its slide into further civil war, there is a well-known short scene in which Cinna the poet is torn to pieces by a mob of plebeians, simply because he has the same name as one of the conspirators.[116] When Cinna protests that he is 'Cinna the poet', one of the plebeians responds 'Tear him for his bad verses, tear him for his bad verses' (3.3.30–1). While this brief scene graphically demonstrates the horrors of unbridled mob rule, it may also reflect on the dangerous status of the writer in 1599. *Julius Caesar* probably opened at the Globe theatre on 12 June 1599.[117] The Bishops' Ban, prohibiting the printing of satire and epigrams, and ordering the public burning of a number of works by Joseph Hall, John Marston, Thomas Middleton and others, was issued on 1 June.[118] On 28 May, all copies of John Hayward's *The First Part of the Life and Raigne of King Henrie the IIII* (1599) were called in and burnt, probably at the request of the Earl of Essex, the book's dedicatee, who was keen not to associate his name with 'a history representing an English monarch's failure in Ireland'.[119] Shakespeare had previously written three plays dealing with the events narrated in Hayward's *History*, so he had reason to feel nervous about the censorship carried out immediately before the production of *Julius Caesar*, as well as perhaps wanting to allude to recent topical developments in the play. He had also directly referred to Essex in his previous play, *Henry V*, and was later to be caught up in Essex's rebellion (see above, pp. 41–2). It is perhaps little wonder that *Julius Caesar* is a nervous play, fearful of change. It would be an error to read it – more so than making an equivalent case for *Lucrece* or *Titus* as youthful statements of Shakespeare's political sympathies – as a direct expression of the dramatist's political beliefs.

Chapter Four

ALTERNATIVE FORMS OF GOVERNMENT

'The great toe of this assembly'

If it is true that Shakespeare was frequently critical of hereditary monarchy as a defining form of government, the question that remains is whether he considered, or even promoted, alternative forms of rule in his poetry and plays. Or did he, as is generally assumed, accept the status quo through fear of change and of the potentially violent actions of the populace? As Anne Barton has noted, 'the settled conviction that Shakespeare's view of history was orthodox, conservative, rooted in the political theories expounded in the Homilies, has blinded the critic to what is actually there on the page'.[1] Indeed, for all the interest shown both in the history of republican Rome and its institutions and in the question of the monarch's legitimacy in Shakespeare's Elizabethan plays, a case can be made that the later plays, written after the accession of James I, demonstrate a much more sustained analysis of the varieties of possible and actual government, their mechanics and effects. After the accession of James, Shakespeare appears to have become more concerned with the existence and form of political and legal institutions, and placed less emphasis on the relationship between rulers and their subjects, and on the question of the personality of the monarch. It was much easier to develop such interests, I would suggest, after Elizabeth's death, when the ghost of the succession question was finally laid to rest. Moreover, the new monarch had to endure only one serious challenge to his rule, the Gunpowder Plot of 1605, and was generally prepared to argue with his subjects rather than silence them through the threat of force.

The Gunpowder Plot was precipitated by the disappointment of the hopes of leading recusants that the fines they had to pay for not attending church would not be enforced and that their religion would be tolerated.[2] Equally important was James's success in ending the protracted war with Spain, which effectively isolated militant English Catholics who demanded nothing less than the re-establishment of their religion as official state policy. When such hopes, encouraged by James's negotiations with the papacy to end the claim that the Pope had the right to depose monarchs, were dashed, a group of leading Catholics determined to overthrow both king and parliament by blowing them up at the state opening of the second session of James's first parliament, on 5 November 1605. The failure of the plot led to harsher penalties, rules for excluding Catholics from public offices and professions, and new laws that required recusants to swear under oath that the Pope could not depose monarchs. Equally importantly, these responses also signalled the increasing prominence of parliament and, consequently, of contested elections in English political life, because the conspirators recognized that their real enemy was parliament.[3] James had argued vigorously with his first parliament in the previous year, over the Goodwin–Fortesque case, and had strong views on the constitutional role of parliament, which would restrict it more than many of its members desired.[4] He continued to attempt to limit its role, though he accepted its central importance as the elected political body. At the same time, there was a growing sense of hostility towards the rigging of elections by the crown, and the concept of voters making up an electorate, whose support for candidates proposing a variety of political ideas and ideologies had to be wooed and won, began to develop significantly. The last years of Elizabeth's reign had helped to alienate many powerful and middle-ranking local figures who felt that the crown had handed power over to a corrupt elite, and that they should no longer tolerate such political abuses.[5] Elections were still rarely contested, and members of parliament were generally selected because of their social status rather than their political arguments and beliefs.[6] Nevertheless, 'hierarchical notions about social organisation need not make for a static society', and there was often tension between those who regarded the selection of

FIGURE 9 Engraving of the Gunpowder Plot Conspirators. This Protestant pamphlet represents the grisly fate of the conspirators, showing that Catholics were all traitors at heart.

members of parliament as a matter of bestowing honour on the local gentry or aristocracy, and those, like Edwin Sandys, who argued that the House of Commons ought to be independent.[7] One of the key areas where electoral unrest and contested elections took place was Warwickshire, Shakespeare's home town of Stratford-upon-Avon playing a major role.[8]

There was also pressure for political change nearer the centre of power. James's eldest son, Prince Henry, assembled an alternative court to rival that of his father. While James pursued a policy of *rapprochement* with Spain and encouraged religious toleration (despite the undoubted shock of the Gunpowder Plot), many of the radical and discontented Protestants who had favoured the pan-European policy of intervention in religious struggles advocated by the Sidney and Essex circles, gravitated towards the Prince.[9] While James saw himself as a pacific

Roman emperor, the British Augustus, Henry saw himself as 'the warrior-king leading his people in the field of battle'.[10] Given his links with the Essex circle through the patronage of the Earl of Southampton, and his close family links to Stratford, Shakespeare was connected to, and no doubt well-informed about, such forms of political opposition.[11]

One of the key political and cultural enthusiasms of Prince Henry's circle was an admiration for the political institutions and general liberty that existed in Venice, which in itself became a means of signalling criticism of English politics and England's constitution.[12] Praise for Venice had a long history in Renaissance England, effectively beginning when a number of the most distinguished thinkers at the court of Henry VIII went to Italy for their political education, drawn by the presence of Cardinal Pole, who established an influential household in Padua in the 1530s.[13] The first English work to establish the 'myth of Venice' as a symbol of cosmopolitan sophistication and the beacon of European liberty was Thomas Starkey's *Dialogue Between Pole and Lupset* (*c*.1529–32). Starkey argued that the constitution of Venice had remained steadfast for a thousand years because it was so well governed, and that its inhabitants were as healthy and wealthy as any in Christendom. One of its chief virtues was that offices of state could not be held for life, a key republican principle designed to foster active citizenship and prevent corruption and complacency. Equally important was the fact that no one wanted to accept the onerous position of duke (doge), because 'hye is restrained to gud order & polytyke'.[14] Starkey makes it clear that Venice stands as an enlightened contrast to the chaotic state of England with its piecemeal constitution, and that the English have much to learn from the Venetians, not least in limiting the power of the king: 'so wyth us also schold be of our kyng yf hys powar were tempered aftur the maner before descrybed'.[15] England was starting to see Venice as many Italian humanists perceived the city state: either as the locus of classical republicanism, the lone surviving example in the modern world and so a link between contemporary and ancient Europe, or as a proper mixed government, able to integrate all classes and so successfully combine the elements of monarchy, oligarchy and democracy, in a manner that no other state had managed.[16]

The myth was disseminated more widely with the publication in 1549 of William Thomas's *History of Italy*, a work that had a profound impact on English perceptions of Italy.[17] Thomas also lavishly praised Venice and its constitution, contrasting the city state to more negative political examples such as Naples, where tyranny rather than liberty flourished.[18] Thomas praises the wonderful buildings in the city and claims that everyone lives like a prince rather than a citizen (fos 74–5). Like Starkey he argues that one of the chief virtues of the Venetian constitution is that the doge is effectively an 'honourable slave' (fo. 77), his power limited by the citizens he governs. Every major decision requires a ballot of some form or other, which means that the Signori Capi, the three citizens who immediately advise the doge, are, in fact, more powerful than he is. In addition, there are six elected Signori from whose number the doge is selected, and together they deal with such crucial decisions as the declaration of war or peace, and any issue that will affect the constitution. Thomas argues that because the Venetians value liberty so highly they will not interfere with these offices (fos 77–8). Like Starkey, Thomas represents Venice as a model for England to copy, suggesting that the Great Council can be compared to the English parliament (fo. 80). He emphasizes the danger of concentrated power, and praises the Venetians' desire to use secret ballots whenever possible. In the narrative history of Venice, Thomas shows how the Venetians have consistently deposed tyrannical doges who have failed to respect their liberties. Yet, because of the strength and fairness of the constitution and laws, the city state has never degenerated into chaos or anarchy, and has always preserved the freedom of its subjects (fos 108–12).

Shakespeare may have known Thomas's *History*.[19] However, another work extolling the virtues of Venice that Shakespeare undoubtedly knew and made use of was Gasparo Contarini's *De Magistratibus et Republica Venetorum* (1543), which was translated as *The commonwealth and government of Venice* (1599) by Lewes Lewkenor.[20] Lewkenor's translation included extracts from other Italian writers and was intended as a guidebook for travellers, as well as a succinct and useful collection of all the information a reader would need to know about Venice.[21] Lewkenor/Contarini's conception of Venice is effectively

FIGURE 10 *Dogal Audience in the Sala del Collegio of the Doge's Palace* by Joseph Heintz the Younger. This late seventeenth-century print shows the grand, complex and ancient tradition of Venetian political processes, emphasizing stability, order and the possibility of debate.

identical to that of William Thomas. What makes the city state preeminent is not the inherent virtue of its citizens, but the constitutional, institutional and legal framework in which they live, whereby their liberties are protected and encouraged, and their vices are curbed.[22] Venice is an 'artificial angel', a miracle of human endeavour struggling against the ravages of time.[23] The five books of *The commonwealth and government of Venice* describe the general advantages of the city state; the duties of the doge and his councillors; the senate of 120 and the legal system; the financial networks and exchequer; and the advantages of Venice's government over other cities'. The picture provided is more detailed than Thomas's, but the argument is the same. Venice possesses a perfect constitution that has the ideal balance of monarchy, aristocracy and popular assembly (p. 37); everyone participates in government, so factions are avoided (p. 8); important offices and duties are spread around and rotated, so that no one can build up a level of power that might endanger the good of the state or other citizens (p. 33); the twin evils of tyranny and popular sedition are avoided (p. 11); laws are just and impartially administered (p. 25); taxes are fair (p. 109); and foreigners are keen to be governed by the Venetians because the city is ruled so much better than their own are (p. 147).

Lewkenor's text, which contains a number of marginal notes, is ambiguous about the status of monarchy as an ideal form of government, at times appearing to endorse Contarini's republicanism and criticisms of the monarchy; at others, tempering his enthusiasm for a political sovereignty rooted in the people and extolling monarchy as the best form of government.[24] Significantly enough, James I felt moved to criticize the constitution of Venice and, by implication, those who exhibited an enthusiasm for it, in *The Trew Law of Free Monarchies*, published the year before Lewkenor's translation. James contrasts the liberty subjects enjoyed under a hereditary monarchy to the perils endured by those living under an elective monarchy. Hereditary monarchies are able to protect the rights of ordinary subjects far better because they hand responsibilities to the monarch and so leave private citizens free to pursue their own lives and pleasures, unburdened by the cares of office, as well as promoting obedience and order. He contrasts the true freedom hereditary kingship establishes to that of constitutions with more superficial appeal: 'I meane alwaies of such free Monarchies as our king is, and not of elective kings, and much lesse of such sort of governors, as the dukes of *Venice* are, whose Aristocratick and limited government, is nothing like to free Monarchies.'[25] Opinions on Venice clearly signalled political persuasions.[26]

I

Shakespeare wrote two plays set in Venice, *The Merchant of Venice* (1596–7) and *Othello* (1601–2). Each demonstrates an interest in location that is far more developed than that in, for example, the Vienna of *Measure for Measure*, or the Bohemia of *The Winter's Tale*.[27] *The Merchant of Venice* shows more sustained interest in Venice as a cosmopolitan entrepôt than in the effects and influence of its social institutions on the population.[28] Each of its plots involves the relationship between European Christians and exotic aliens, and the attempts of the former group to accommodate or exclude the latter. Portia complains to Nerissa of the unstable mixture of styles adopted by the Europeanized English suitor, who has failed to fit in with the real significance of the varied peoples and races in Venice: 'You know I say nothing to him, for he understands not me, nor I him: he hath neither Latin, French, nor Italian ... How oddly he is suited! I think he bought his doublet in Italy, his round hose in France, his bonnet in Germany, and his behaviour everywhere' (1.2.66–8, 70–3). He stands as an example of the traveller who has lost his identity in aping all those he encounters.[29] The marriage casket game which ensues sees Portia reject princely suitors from Morocco and Aragon, before Bassanio wins her hand. By this means the threat of an unwanted union with Spanish Catholic Europe or North Africa is avoided, a danger alluded to comically in the advances of the ridiculous English suitor, which reminds the audience of the importance of such diplomatic matches.[30] The story of Antonio's failed commercial venture illustrates the dangers of high-risk capitalism, the variety of exotic locations serving to emphasize not only the lure and the glamour of merchant adventuring, but also the lack of security for the capitalist. As Shylock comments:

> yet his means are in supposition: he hath an argosy bound to Tripolis, another to the Indies, I understand moreover upon the Rialto, he hath a third at Mexico, a fourth for England, and other ventures he hath squand'red abroad, – but ships are but boards, sailors but men, there be land-rats, and water-rats, water-thieves, and land-thieves, (I mean pirates), and then there is the peril of waters, winds, and rocks[.]   (1.3.15–23)

And, of course, the plot hinges on Antonio's borrowing three thousand ducats on the bond of a pound of his own flesh from a Jewish moneylender, the largest alien group in Venice.[31] The resolution of this plot also helps to keep alien influences at a safe distance in Venice, but at the cost of a disturbing insularity and overt racism.

The two plots are intertwined through the issue of the operation of law in Venice, when Portia disguises herself as a lawyer in order to defend the friend of her husband-to-be. The play poses the question as to whether the marriage casket game and the formal court proceedings can be read in the same way and, if so, whether they both operate fairly and protect the liberties of everyone concerned. Venice was famous for its championing of liberty and ability to accommodate foreigners; but does Shakespeare's play reveal that such rights were distributed more by luck than judgement, and that intolerance was really the norm?[32]

The Duke and his main advisers – here simply labelled as 'Magnificoes' – oversee the trial scene in act four. The Duke pleads that Shylock exhibit mercy to Antonio, asking him to forgo his absolute rights and act in accordance with the spirit rather the letter of the law, suggesting that Shylock will, in fact, back down at the last minute:

> 'tis thought
> Thou'lt show thy mercy and remorse more strange
> Than is thy strange apparent cruelty;
> And where thou now exacts the penalty,
> Which is a pound of this poor merchant's flesh,
> Thou wilt not only loose the forfeiture,
> But touch'd with human gentleness and love,
> Forgive a moiety of the principal,
> Glancing an eye of pity on his losses[.]
>
> (4.1.19–27)

The Duke's appeal is echoed by Portia later in the same scene when she points to the wider significance of the 'quality of mercy', which is

> twice blest,
> It blesseth him that gives, and him that takes,
> 'Tis mightiest in the mightiest, it becomes
> The throned monarch better than his crown.
> His sceptre shows the force of temporal power,
> The attribute to awe and majesty,
> Wherein doth sit the dread and fear of kings:

> But mercy is above this sceptred sway,
> It is enthroned in the hearts of kings,
> It is an attribute to God himself[.]
>
> (4.1.182–91)

Portia argues that mercy is a royal prerogative.[33] Despite Shylock's insistence that his demands be met, Portia famously outmanoeuvres him on his own pedantic grounds, to save Antonio's life before invoking a previously unmentioned law that if an 'alien' seeks the life of a citizen, he will lose half his goods to the citizen in question and the other half to the state. The Duke duly pardons Shylock at the cost of all his wealth, half going to Antonio and half to the 'general state' (367).

Shakespeare's specific knowledge of Venice appears to be limited, and the legal system he represents has little to do with the one English travellers described.[34] Instead, the Venetian legal system functions as an ideal, one severely flawed by the behaviour of its citizens, indigenous and alien.[35] James Shapiro has pointed out that

> The trial scene offers a fantasy resolution to the conflicting and overlapping jurisdictions intrinsic to such trials by invoking a law that effectively supersedes the city's charter (a charter that more closely resembles the kind one would find in an English city under a feudal monarchy than in the Venetian Republic). As much as it might want to, given its charter, Venetian society cannot punish Shylock simply because he is a Jew. But in the terms of the play it can convict him as a threatening alien.[36]

The legal and political system Shakespeare represents as Venetian is one that is based on the principle of equity. In late sixteenth-century legal discourse and practice, equity, a concept originally derived from Aristotle's *Nicomachean Ethics*, was understood as a means of going beyond the letter of the law when the rules and ordinances of the common or civil law proved inadequate to deal with particularly tricky cases, or when legal principles came into conflict (both of which problems apply in *The Merchant of Venice*).[37] In Aristotle's words, equity is a vital component of good legal practice because 'all law is universal but about some things it is not possible to make a universal statement which shall be correct ... this is the nature of the equitable, a correction of law where it is defective owing to its universality'.[38] In English law the Court of Chancery was where cases that could not be resolved by the common law were referred because the 'chancellor is not strained by rigour or form of words of law to judge but *ex aequo* and *bono* and according to conscience'.[39]

Equity was an accepted practice within the English legal system, enabling lawyers to appeal to a higher principle than the list of codes and practices of the common law, when conflicts of interest occurred or specific cases demanded resolution.[40] The concept of equity was also one of the key political and legal terms developed by Jean Bodin (1529–96) in his influential *Six Books of the Republic* (1576), one of the most widely-read works of political theory in early modern Europe. A Latin version appeared in 1586 and an English translation by Richard Knolles (author of *The Generall Historie of the Turkes* (1603), a source for *Othello*) in 1606, entitled *The Six Bookes of the Commonweale*.[41] Gabriel Harvey witnessed its ubiquity in Cambridge in the late 1570s (see above, p. 17). Bodin formulated his ideas against the background of the vicious religious wars in France, most obviously manifested in the massacre of Saint Bartholomew's Day which took place only four years before the *Six Bookes* appeared. He has generally been read as a supporter of absolutism who felt that only a strongly centralized monarchy could prevent destructive sectarian conflict.[42] Nevertheless, Bodin used the term 'republic', or *res publica*, explicitly acknowledging, as Sir Thomas Smith had done, that there was no natural form of government, merely a variety of types that could be classified, as Aristotle had first attempted. Bodin not only suggested that economics and politics were not easily separable, but also argued that a *res publica* was no more than an *'artificial* family', or group of families, that need not be governed in the way that a family was generally governed (i.e., by the father). Richard Tuck has argued that 'because Bodin recognised that the *res publica* is in a way an *artificial* family, he was realistic about the non-natural character of political rulership, allowing democracies and aristocracies equal standing with monarchies'. Bodin clearly favoured 'an hereditary and legally absolute monarch', as the best solution to the universal problem of political formation, but the *Six Bookes* contain much material that supported other interpretations, as its subsequent history in France demonstrates.[43]

Bodin's political principles hinge on the role of the magistrates, whose function is to protect the authority of the state and enable it to operate smoothly. His earlier work, the *Methodus Ad Facilem Historiarum Cognitionem (Method for the Easy Comprehension of History)* (1566), had argued that the king's sovereignty should be limited by the law, and he had distinguished between hereditary monarchs such as the king of France, and the doge of Venice and the emperor of Germany who 'were little more than figureheads, and might even be deposed'.[44] Bodin's absolutism involves devolving considerable power to the magistrates, who have the right to overrule existing laws if there is a threat to the *res publica*. They can do this in the name of equity, and so both protect the authority of the monarch they represent and ensure that proper and fair government results. Magistrates can exceed their powers when necessary, sometimes increasing the severity of the laws, and sometimes making them more merciful and less punitive.[45] Bodin had little time for Calvinist or Huguenot resistance theorists, and he argued that an aristocratic state was more stable than a democratic one, preventing the twin evils of tyranny and anarchy.[46] Nevertheless, it is easy to see how his work could be used to support arguments that wished to emphasize the importance of the role of magistrates rather than defend the monarchical centre of the nation.

The trial scene in *The Merchant of Venice* not only shows lawyers resolving a problematic situation by going beyond the normal dictates of the law, but reveals the Duke devolving power to an individual lawyer – Portia – and accepting her solution. The Duke shows that he is keen to learn from public servants how he is to govern, and in his opening speech to Shylock he confesses himself unable to resolve the conflict between justice and mercy. Portia, in acting to defend Antonio from the accusations of an alien, can be seen as a magistrate serving the state, even if she has not been formally appointed to serve its interests. Her legal quibbling can be read as a form of equity, enabling justice and mercy to be resolved, at the cost of excluding the alien Jew, a problem that has shadowed readings of the play ever since.[47] When Shylock asserts, 'If you deny me, fie upon your law! / There is no force in the decrees of Venice', and asks, 'I stand for judgement, – answer, shall I have it?' (4.1.101–3), he is directly threatening to turn the law of the Venetians against itself, and so undermine the authority of the state. When Portia extols the quality of mercy and considers its relationship to the rigours of justice immediately after entering the courtroom dressed as a doctor of law, she demonstrates the stakes raised by the case Shylock has brought. The monarch has to devise a system of law that can accommodate both justice and mercy and so preserve his authority. Portia is on hand to save the Duke from the conflict of interests inherent in the city state he rules. In doing so she helps to unite the various people, customs and forces in Venice under the authority of the Duke, which she therefore acts to preserve. This is precisely the function of equity that Bodin advocated.

Nevertheless, Portia's success is qualified, and an audience cannot accept her victory as a straightforward triumph.[48] It is evident that the style of argument and the legal logic she applies to the case could win or lose any case in question regardless of their merit.[49] The considerable glee of the Christians when Shylock's threat is nullified has troubled the great majority of recent audiences and readers of the play, indicating that the harmony of the last act is hard to take at face value.[50] However, it is a solution to a pressing problem. The ability of Venice to accommodate strangers was still probably rather better than that of England in the 1590s, even though Jews like Shylock were sometimes forced to convert to Christianity. In 1596 Elizabeth issued an order that ten 'blackamoors' were to be deported, 'of which kind of people there are already here too many', following this up with further requests that her subjects get rid of black servants and make use of their 'own countrymen'.[51] There was considerable prejudice against the few Jews present in England after the case of Dr Roderigo Lopez, who was executed in 1593 for attempting to poison the Queen, an important context for Shakespeare's play.[52] Moreover, there were a number of riots targeted at foreigners who were deemed to have taken employment from English workers, most notably the Evil May Day riot of 1517 dramatized, almost certainly by Shakespeare, in *Sir Thomas More*.[53] Venice, in contrast, might have seemed a state blessed with rather better government, whose ruler did at least listen to the magistrates he relied upon and was prepared to learn from them how to uphold the law and govern. Before he exits, the Duke reminds Antonio that he is much 'bound' to Portia acting as a lawyer (4.1.403), a recognition of the important role played by articulate citizens in the running of the state. Admiration for such mutual dependence between governor and advisers was the staple of English observers of Venice throughout the sixteenth century.[54]

II

While Shakespeare's interest in the institutions of Venice is sketchy in *The Merchant of Venice*, it is far more clearly manifested in *Othello*, a play that first appeared on stage four to five years later (*c*.1602).[55] Shakespeare had evidently read Lewkenor's translation of Contarini, and used his fulsome praise of Venetian institutions when he represented Venice in the later play, notably Contarini's (and Lewkenor's) enthusiasm for the Venetian legal system.[56] Only the first act takes place in Venice, and the play depends for its dramatic effect, as well as the development of the plot, on the stark contrast between the well-ordered and reasonable state of Venice and the uncertainty experienced in the besieged and isolated colony of Cyprus. As in *The Merchant*, racial tension threatens to undermine the offices of the state. This time, however, hostility is directed at a high-ranking citizen who has been adopted by the city state as one of its own, not a barely tolerated alien, making the threat to Venice's equanimity all the more potent, as befits a tragedy. Equally important is the dramatic fact that while audience sympathies might be divided or troubled during a performance of *The Merchant*, there can be no doubt that sympathies must lie with Othello and Desdemona in *Othello*. No case has been made for Brabantio.

We observe Venetian justice in action in the third scene of the play. The first scene makes it clear that Brabantio's opposition to his daughter's secret marriage is based on racial prejudice stirred up by

Iago and Roderigo. When Iago boasts to Roderigo that he will 'poison his delight' and 'Plague him with flies' (1.1.67, 70), he does so by appealing to Brabantio's fear and hatred of black Africans: 'Even now, now, very now, an old black ram / Is tupping your white ewe!' (87–8), the insistent repetition of 'now' designed to produce an ekphrastic effect, so that the father can envisage his daughter hideously – as he feels – deflowered before his eyes.[57] When Brabantio complains of the noise that Roderigo and Iago are making, he points out that 'this is Venice: / My house is not a grange' (104–5). The image of an isolated farmhouse ('grange'), where the cacophony of livestock is constantly heard, in contrast to the cosmopolitan world of Venice, establishes a dichotomy between urban civilization and rural savagery. Iago is able to turn Brabantio's assertion against itself, by playing on the deep-seated fears of Desdemona's father: 'you'll have your daughter covered with a Barbary horse; you'll have your nephews neigh to you, you'll have coursers for cousins and jennets for germans!' (109–12), and then 'your daughter and the Moor are now making the beast with two backs' (114–15). Iago has simply carried through Brabantio's thoughts to their logical conclusion: his fear is that only his lineage protects him from the degeneration inherent in breeding with the aliens who inhabit Venice. Desdemona's forbidden marriage will – metaphorically – result in a new generation of uncivilized beasts. Brabantio's admission that 'This accident is not unlike my dream, / Belief of it oppresses me already' (140–1), reveals how astute Iago has been in assuming that paranoia haunts the Venetian upper classes. Brabantio evidently imagines that any serious intermingling with the races that surround them will undermine the main bulwark between Europe and the peoples on the other side of the Mediterranean, the powerful Ottoman empire and the unknown savages of black Africa.[58]

Brabantio then confronts Othello in the second scene; he accuses him of having bewitched his daughter, and would have him imprisoned. Othello points out that the Duke's officers are, in fact, with him, taking him to the Duke on some as yet unknown business of state. Brabantio feels that his cause will merit the attention of the Duke, 'Or any of my brothers of the state', and they will feel his wrong 'as 'twere their own'

(1.2.96–7). He is confident that the threat to his patriarchy cannot be less significant than the matter currently in hand, because the wrong he has suffered is symptomatic of the problems facing the Venetian state, as his last lines here indicate: 'For if such actions [i.e., Othello and Desdemona's marriage] may have passage free, / Bond-slaves and pagans shall our statesmen be' (98–9). For Brabantio, miscegenation is a direct challenge to the liberties that define Venice and a problem that will lead to the destruction of the republic. The parallel to the barbarian invasions of Rome, represented in *Titus*, is irresistible.[59] Equally significant is the fact that a retreat into cultural exclusion and isolation is against the spirit of Venetian society, ignores the basis of its wealth and success, and will probably help to transform it into a 'grange' rather than preserve its values.

The third scene of the play is entirely Shakespeare's invention, and has no counterpart in the principal source, Giraldi Cinthio's *Gli Hecatommithi* (1566), which Shakespeare probably used via the French translation (1584).[60] The councillors are revealed discussing the Turkish fleet currently sailing for Cyprus, 'the contemporary colonial outpost most vulnerable to invasion from the "barbarian" Turk'.[61] We witness the Venetian council having to act quickly and exercise its powers as a council of war. Shakespeare undoubtedly has in mind the powerful Council of Ten, who, according to Contarini, were responsible for the safety of the republic, often having to exercise their powers because of the constant threat from the Turks in the Mediterranean (p. 77).[62] The senators and Duke are seen reacting to information as speedily as it comes in, tracking the course of the Turkish fleet as it feints towards the island of Rhodes before heading for its real target, Cyprus. When it is discovered that Marcus Luccicos is unavailable to take command of Cyprus (1.3.46), because he is away in Florence, Othello is summoned. This detail alerts the reader or playgoer to the fact that scenes two and three are taking place simultaneously, inviting us to contrast the council's high opinion of Othello with the thoughts and actions of Brabantio. The council clearly feel able to put their trust in a successful black general, echoing Contarini's observations that Venetians had tremendous respect for strangers and foreigners, and that, consequently, many came to Venice because they would be better treated than they were in their own countries (pp. 105, 147).

Othello and Brabantio now enter the council chamber. The Duke's opening lines to the group which has disturbed their crucial meeting are designed to emphasize the democratic nature of Venetian government, showing that matters of public importance can be discussed openly, as Contarini claimed (pp. 34–5, 57–8). The Duke grants equal respect to Brabantio and Othello, as is reflected in the balance of his opening lines to them: 'Valiant Othello, we must straight employ you / Against the general enemy Ottoman. / [to Brabantio] I did not see you: welcome, gentle signior, / We lacked your counsel and your help tonight' (49–52). The Duke, who was elected by the citizens, treats valuable servants of the Venetian state equally, regardless of their origins.[63] When Brabantio makes his accusation that Desdemona has been abducted, the Duke promises that he will gain satisfaction, if he proves his charges: 'the bloody book of law / You shall yourself read, in the bitter letter, / After your own sense, yea, though our proper son / Stood in your action' (68–71). The Duke's aim is to make sure that justice is impartially administered, whoever is the perpetrator and whoever the victim.[64]

The scene shows that such impartial administration of the law does take place in Venice. When Brabantio repeats his allegations, the Duke reminds him of the proper process of law:

> To vouch this is no proof,
> Without more certain and more overt test
> Than these thin habits and poor likelihoods
> Of modern seeming do prefer against him.
>
> (107–10)

Once again, Brabantio, not Othello, is shown to be undermining the rules and spirit of Venice. Othello and Desdemona are each permitted to conduct a proper and lengthy defence of their actions, with Othello explaining that he was a welcome guest at Brabantio's house, a detail that further undermines Brabantio's case, illustrates the respect which is accorded Othello in Venice, and exposes the hypocrisy of the father.

Othello is so keen to be assimilated into Venetian society that he represents himself as a European traveller among the exotic wonders and marvels of Africa. In doing so he denies and expunges his African origins, and transforms himself into a loyal servant of the Venetian state, telling the Venetians exactly what they want to hear.[65] Therefore the seeds of the tragedy are partly sown by Desdemona's statement to the council that she fell in love with Othello because of the stories he told and that she 'saw Othello's visage in his mind' (253), a revelation that suggests that she too has not fully accommodated and accepted the identity of her new husband. That the Duke acknowledges the power of Othello's speech with another personal reflection on his offspring, 'I think this tale would win my daughter too' (172), perhaps indicates the strengths and limitations of Shakespeare's Venice, a society keen to accept foreigners within its boundaries, but not always fully aware of their different identities.

Nevertheless, Venetian government is shown to be remarkably successful. The Duke administers the law impartially, advising Brabantio to abandon a case he cannot hope to win: 'Good Brabantio, take up this mangled matter at the best: / Men do their broken weapons rather use / Than their bare hands' (173–5). Brabantio accepts the judgement of the Duke, albeit reluctantly. His words to his daughter indicate that his role as the bad, angry father has to be controlled by the state, and that the larger community or family overrules the limitations of the natural unit: 'For your sake, jewel, / I am glad at soul I have no other child, / For thy escape would teach me tyranny / To hang clogs on them' (196–9).[66] The Duke might well have promised Brabantio that 'the bloody book of law' will be used against whoever has bewitched his daughter, but the trial scene vindicates the newly-weds against the bigoted law of the father. The tyranny of the father submits to the liberty and wisdom of the Venetian republic.[67]

Mark Matheson has argued that 'There is a notable shift ... to a more explicitly republican discourse [in *Othello*] than he [Shakespeare] had used in *The Merchant of Venice*'.[68] Certainly it is true that we see the workings of the Venetian state in a very favourable light indeed, with the Duke patiently listening to advice before making a reasonable and assured judgement that settles the case, as far as it can be resolved, to everyone's satisfaction. Remarkably enough, both the outsider, Othello, and the tyrannical father, Brabantio, can be accommodated. Moreover, we see the council moving swiftly to resolve pressing military matters at the same time, using a loyal foreign general to repel the Turkish enemy. Balance and fairness are the hallmarks of Venice in *Othello*, just as Contarini suggested they were the qualities of a desirable constitution such as that of the real Venice:

> there cannot happen to a commonwealth a more dangerous or pestilent contagion, then the overweighing of one parte or faction above the other: for where the balance of justice standeth not even, it is unpossible that there should be a friendly societie and firme agreement among the citizens: which alwaies happeneth where many offices of the commonwealth meete together in one. For as every mixture dissolveth, if any one of the elements (of which the mixed body consisteth) overcome the other: and as in musicke the tune is marred where one string keepeth a greater noyse then hee should doe: so by the like reason, if you will have your commonwealth perfect and enduring, let not one parte be mightier then the other, but let them all (in as much as may bee) have equall share in the publique authoritie. (p. 67)

The Duke in *Othello* is prepared to listen to both sides of the argument before delivering a judgement, and, in doing so, can balance and control the divergent peoples and interest groups he rules. The tensions inherent in any society cannot be removed, but they are carefully integrated into the commonwealth to make up a functioning society, with no one possessing too much favour or power (it is clear that were Othello guilty of abducting Desdemona, he would be tried and punished as Brabantio demands).

It is significant that the tragedy unfolds not in Venice but in Cyprus, where the checks and balances of the Venetian constitution cannot be applied. Othello shows himself to be an able commander of the garrison, and capable of applying Venetian principles of justice to sort out problems, most notably after the drunken brawl when he punishes his second-in-command for his transgression (2.3). But he is undermined by the opportunism of Iago – like Brabantio, a man with his prejudices – and so cruelly transformed into the ferocious savage he so carefully defined himself against in the council chamber scene.[69] As in *Lucrece*, the contrast between lightness and darkness has an overtly political function. The visible legal and political processes of the republic, and especially the ways in which it deals with conflict and racial prejudice, stand in contrast to the sinister, untruthful and hidden methods of Iago, whose crimes are known only to the audience until near the end of the play. Iago's undoubted cleverness manifests itself only in cruelty and self-advancement, a common English view of the reality of Italian politics. If Venice shows Italian politics at their best, Iago, a scheming, Machiavellian stage villain, demonstrates much about Italy that was feared and hated in late sixteenth-century England.[70] As if to emphasize Shakespeare's positive image of Venice, the most notorious aspect of Venetian liberty, the proliferation of prostitutes in the republic, is transferred to Cyprus, in the form of Bianca, even though Iago is able to prey on Othello's fears as an outsider in suggesting that his chaste wife may be prepared to indulge in adultery.[71]

The representation of Venice in *Othello* is overwhelmingly positive. It is clear that Othello's tragedy would not have unfolded inside the republic and could only take place at the furthest reaches of the city's possessions. That Shakespeare chose to follow Lewkenor's lead in the very last years of Elizabeth's reign, in the midst of the confusion and uncertainty over the succession, indicates that he also saw the constitution of Venice as a desirable form of government which rewarded virtue and gave its prominent citizens a stake in the political process. Venice stands as a political ideal, as James I had complained in *The Trew Law of Free Monarchies*, providing a living example of the integrated and successful functioning of the mixed constitution. This was an ideal to which England supposedly aspired in works such as Sir Thomas Smith's *De Republica Anglorum*, but which, in reality, it did not match. Shakespeare, like so many other early modern Englishmen, seems to have found much to admire in Venice, and *Othello* suggests that

England could learn from her example.[72] The vulnerability of this ideal is emphasized by the fate of the Turks who perish at sea. The Ottoman empire was feared throughout Europe because it was perceived to be a cruel and brutal tyranny, representing everything that the liberties of Venice opposed.[73] Fortune could easily have engineered a different outcome and a vital part of Europe might have been destroyed. Shakespeare's play is acutely sensitive to the fine distinction between success and disaster, an awareness entirely in keeping with other plays he wrote immediately before Elizabeth's death. The provocative nature of *The Tragedy of Othello, The Moor of Venice* should not be underestimated.[74]

III

However, the play that demonstrates the most sustained interest in political institutions and processes is *Coriolanus* (*c.*1608–9), a work that has always divided critics concerned to establish Shakespeare's political persuasions.[75] *Coriolanus* dramatizes the conflict between patricians and plebeians, and so can be read in terms of class conflict and the discontented voices of Jacobean society.[76] It can equally plausibly be read in terms of more localized issues such as the process of parliamentary selection in London or Warwickshire. As Mark Kishlansky has pointed out, the account of the candidacy of Coriolanus is original to Shakespeare, a notable inclusion in a play that otherwise sticks quite carefully to its main source, Plutarch's *Life of Coriolanus*.[77] Furthermore, Kishlansky argues, 'these scenes so accurately portray the process by which officeholders were selected in the early seventeenth century that one must conclude that Shakespeare had first-hand experience, either of wardmote selections to the London Common Council or of parliamentary selections themselves'.[78] Given that the play begins with the famished, mutinous citizens discussing whether they wish to support the election of Coriolanus to the senate, such issues take centre stage at the start of the play, in the same way that the election of the emperor of Rome forms the dramatic opening of *Titus*.

The story of Coriolanus and his rebellion against Rome stood among the most significant failures of the Roman Republic.[79] One of the tribunes involved in turning the plebeians against Coriolanus is called Junius Brutus. Plutarch argues that Brutus and his fellow tribune, Sicinius Vellutus, were the 'causers and procurers of this sedition', although their office required them 'to defend the poor people from violence and oppression'.[80] Once again, the question of the overthrow of the monarchy and the establishment of the republic are central issues raised in the play. Whereas *Titus* and *Lucrece* dramatized the moment of change itself and concentrated on the contrast between tyranny and the mixed constitution, *Coriolanus* provides a much more substantial account of the institutions adopted by the Roman republic, giving us the opportunity to assess their value. In fact, as Anne Barton has observed, *Coriolanus* is the only one of Shakespeare's Roman plays that is set in a properly functioning republican Rome, 'in a mixed state of the kind that, for various reasons, was attracting considerable attention in Jacobean England'.[81]

The opening scenes of the play foreground political issues in a manner which also resembles the first act of *Othello*. The angry citizens enter as a large group, but unlike the mobs represented in *Julius Caesar* and *2 Henry VI*, they are concerned with political questions rather then violent revenge.[82] The articulate first citizen makes the case against Caius Martius, claiming that he is 'chief enemy to the people' (6–7), before demonstrating that he knows exactly how food is being distributed in times of dearth in the republic:

> We are accounted poor citizens, the patricians good. What authority surfeits on would relieve us. If they would yield us but the superfluity while it were wholesome, we might guess they relieved us humanely; but they think we are too dear: the leanness that afflicts us, the object of our misery, is an inventory to particularise their abundance; our sufferance is a gain to them.[83]

(14–21)

Not only does this speech accurately predict the argument of Menenius's fable of the belly, even though he is reputed to be 'one that has always loved the people' – in marked contrast to his friend, Coriolanus – but it also shows that the hunger of the citizens has been translated into political terms by their chief spokesman. One of the central arguments raised in the first scene is whether there is actually enough food to be distributed, as the citizens allege, or whether, in times of scarcity, certain citizens have first priority, as the senators claim. The last lines of the first citizen's speech show him struggling to articulate his sense of outrage and channel his anger into realistic and reasonable sentiments: 'Let us revenge this with our pikes, ere we become rakes. For the gods know, I speak this in hunger for bread, not in thirst for revenge' (21–4). The speech ends up by rejecting what it claimed was the motivation of the citizens – revenge – so that the citizens' march towards the Capitol is shown to be motivated by need and outrage at the injustice of their treatment by their social superiors, not the enraged violence of the mob. If anything, the first citizen's speech can be read as a warning that a starving people will resort to violence when they have no other means of political expression available to satisfy their basic needs.[84]

The arguments of the first citizen are met by Menenius in probably the most famous political confrontation in Shakespeare's works. Menenius attempts to defuse the violent threats of the citizens by arguing that 'most charitable care / Have the patricians of you' (64–5), and claiming that there is no solution to the problem of hunger because 'The gods, not the patricians, make it' (72). The first citizen confronts him with the claim that 'They ne'er cared for us yet. Suffer us to famish, and their storehouses crammed with grain' (78–80). The blame is also attached to war: 'If the wars eat us not up, they [the patricians] will; and there's all the love they bear us' (84–5).

As has often been pointed out, Shakespeare conflates two accounts of uprisings in Plutarch's *Life of Coriolanus*; the first caused by the 'sore oppression of usurers', and the second by famine brought about 'by reason of their warres which made extreme dearth they had among them'. Plutarch's account is neatly balanced: the first time, 'the senate did favour the rich against the people'; but the second, the 'flatterers of the people began to stir up sedition ... without any new occasion, or just matter offered of complaint', spreading 'false tales and rumours against the nobility'.[85] It is clear that the oppression caused by excessive usury is unreasonable, so that the riots that result are to a large extent justified. Indeed, many of those who suffer most are those who have defended Rome most valiantly:

> For those that had little, were yet spoiled of that little they had by their creditors, for lack of ability to pay the usury ... And such as had nothing left, their bodies were laid hold of, and they were made their bondmen, notwithstanding all the wounds and cuts they showed, which they had received in many battles, fighting for defence of their country and commonwealth ... of the which, they fought upon the promise the rich men had made them, that from thenceforth they would entreat them more gently.[86]

However, if the plebeians, who have served Rome so well in its necessary wars, are the victims the first time round, they are misled in the second case, when they fail to see that war can cause scarcity for everyone. For Plutarch, the central question is how the various classes and interest groups in the state work together against a common foe.

Coriolanus dramatizes the same social conflict, but instead of two parallel cases which point in opposite directions, we are presented with a complex series of confrontations that engage our sympathies in various ways. Menenius's argument with the first citizen employs the ubiquitous image of the body politic, the most frequently used metaphor for the state in early modern political discourse, but presents us with two diametrically opposed interpretations of its function.[87] For Menenius, the rebellious members are mistaken in regarding the belly as 'idle and unactive' (98) and should accept the argument that:

> The senators of Rome are this good belly,
> And you the mutinous members: for examine
> Their counsels and their cares, digest things rightly
> Touching the weal o'th'common, you shall find
> No public benefit which you receive
> But it proceeds or comes from them to you,
> And no way from yourselves.

> (147–53)

Menenius's argument – admittedly, produced in difficult circumstances – presents an authoritarian model of society, one that
corresponds neatly with the sentiments of James I in his published
writings. He sarcastically dismisses the first citizen as 'the great toe of this
assembly' (154) because he is 'one o'th'lowest, basest, poorest / Of this
most wise rebellion' (156–7). However, immediately before Menenius's
explanation, it is not at all obvious that the first citizen's ability to
manipulate the political metaphor is any less convincing or plausible
than that of Menenius, or that Menenius has the best of the argument.
The citizen parrots the explanation he expects Menenius to give after
his patrician adversary has introduced the image of the body politic:

FIRST CITIZEN   Your belly's answer – what?
    The kingly crown'd head, the vigilant eye,
    The counsellor heart, the arm our soldier,
    Our steed the leg, the tongue our trumpeter,
    With other muniments and petty helps
    In this our fabric, if that they –
MENENIUS   What then?
    'Fore me, this fellow speaks! What then? What then?
FIRST CITIZEN
    Should by the cormorant belly be restrain'd,
    Who is the sink o'th'body –
MENENIUS   Well, what then?
FIRST CITIZEN
    The former agents, if they did complain,
    What could the belly answer?

                                              (113–24)

The first citizen's notion of an integrated body politic, with different
parts of the body dependent on others, all working together to produce
a healthy whole, is more firmly in line with the usage of the metaphor
in early modern political discourse. Thomas Starkey, for example, saw
the body as the people, very much as the state is portrayed as a giant
body in the famous frontispiece to Thomas Hobbes's *Leviathan* (1651).
Whereas Hobbes saw the king as the head of state, Starkey argued that

the soul ruled the body and that the soul stood for civic law. Starkey saw the heart as the king (for the citizen it is a counsellor); the head and eyes as the officers of the prince (the citizen merely notes that the eye should be vigilant); the hands as craftsmen (the citizen sees the arms as soldiers); and the feet as agricultural labourers. He argued that the body had to be kept beautiful and in proportion, as well as sustained in health and strength. This is to be achieved through maintaining a careful balance of population in order to offset poverty. If there are too many people then the resources of the commonwealth will not be able to feed them properly, and if there are too few, then they will not be able to use the resources available to produce adequate food to feed everyone. Furthermore, man-made disasters, such as war, will have the same result.[88]

Starkey's analogy emphasizes the need for co-operation between the parts of the body, and their mutual dependence. It is notable that he privileges the law as the governing principle of the commonwealth, not the monarch, or a specific group within society. Starkey's text represents the point of contact between continental republicanism and English humanism in sixteenth-century political thought, imagining the state as an autonomous entity and the citizens within it as working together to make it function in the interests of everyone.[89] If the body politic analogy in *Coriolanus* is read in the ways that Starkey suggests, then Menenius is foolish in dismissing the first citizen as the 'great toe' of the state, and so as being of no worth. This 'great toe' might be seen in terms of Starkey's representation of agricultural labourers as feet, a crucial analogy in a play which shows that riots stem directly from hunger. Menenius's attempt to ridicule the citizen for having political opinions illustrates that he, like the other patricians in the play, underestimates and misreads the plebeians. More seriously, it suggests that he wants to restrict the political classes as much as possible, although this is an understandable reaction to a riot.[90]

There were, of course, other readings of the body politic. In *The Trew Law of Free Monarchies*, James I used the body analogy to read the state in a very different way:

The proper office of a King towards his Subjects, agrees very wel with the office of the head towards the body, and all the members therof: For from the head, being the seate of Judgement, proceedeth the care and foresight of guiding, and preventing all evill that may come to the body or any part thereof. The head cares for the body, so doeth the King for his people. As the discourse and direction flowes from the head, and the execution according to their office: so is it betwixt a wise Prince, and his people. As the judgement comming from the head may not onely imploy the members, every one in their owne office, as long as they are able for it; but likewise in case any of them be affected with any infirmitie must care and provide for their remedy, in-case it be curable, and if otherwise, gar cut them off for feare of infecting of the rest: even so is it betwixt the Prince, and his people.[91]

For James, all political power should descend from the king who cares for the good of his subjects, even to the extent of determining their right to live or die if they risk infecting the body politic with disease (generally an allusion to rebellion), as the last lines cited illustrate. Menenius's conception of the Roman republic is clearly in line with that of James, although he centralizes the belly as the commanding organ of the body, rather than the head. The effect of this, however, is to reinforce rather than diminish the simultaneously powerful and arbitrary nature of the analogy. The first citizen is able to manipulate the political rhetoric that Menenius employs to make his point and turn it against him, in the process exposing the authoritarian nature of Menenius's argument.[92] Menenius's fable, reproduced faithfully from Plutarch's *Life of Coriolanus*, succeeds in the short term, although this is as much to do with the imminent threat from the Volscians as with the force of Menenius's reasoning.[93] But the key point of the confrontation is to show that meanings are contested and that more than one political language can be spoken, whatever the patricians in the senate like to think.[94] It also highlights the problem of food and consumption: whether, when there is not enough to go around in times of war, priority should be given to those who rule, as Menenius's use of the body politic analogy asserts.

The plot of *Coriolanus*, as Janet Adelman has shown us, hinges on images of eating.[95] Coriolanus habitually describes the plebeians as though they were a huge collective mouth dependent on the bounty of the patricians. When asked to speak to the people in a conciliatory manner by the more politically astute Menenius, Coriolanus responds, 'Bid them wash their faces, / And keep their teeth clean' (2.3.62–3). When he later observes the two tribunes, Coriolanus refers to them as 'The tongues o'th'common mouth' (3.1.22), and comments, 'I do despise them: / For they do prank them in authority, / Against all noble sufferance' (22–4). When using similar metaphors to articulate his own thoughts and feelings, he tries to imagine himself as self-sufficient rather than dependent. For Coriolanus, it is a sign of weakness to ask for food: 'Better it is to die, better to starve, / Than crave the hire which first we do deserve' (2.3.112–13), he argues after an encounter with the citizens. In his first speech in the play he argues that the citizens' 'affections [inclinations] are / A sick man's appetite' (1.1.176–7), and, in his most compressed and powerful image, he claims that the plebeians should never be allowed to participate in government: 'at once pluck out / The multitudinous tongue: let them not lick / The sweet which is their poison' (3.1.154–6). Coriolanus's political opinions echo those of his mother, Volumnia, who regards any sign of dependence on others, including her own family, as a weakness. When asked by Menenius to share a meal, she responds, 'Anger's my meat: I sup upon myself / And so shall starve with feeding' (4.2.50–1).

Coriolanus's political journey leads to predictable personal and social catastrophe. He defects to the Volscians, becomes dependent on their leader, his *alter ego*, Aufidius, and returns to Rome at the head of an army. The plot echoes the conclusion of *Titus*, with an invading army threatening Rome; although, as readers of Plutarch would have known, the Romans subsequently defeated the Volscians to end the crisis.[96] Coriolanus's triumphs in war are what almost enable him to engineer the destruction of the Roman republic, establishing a pointed contrast between his success as a warrior hero and failure as an astute politician. Coriolanus seems to fail specifically because he has absorbed the militaristic creed of the aristocracy, and he learns that he is more dependent on others than his absurd dreams of self-sufficiency allow. He finally turns back to his native city when his mother admits her dependence on him and pleads for the safety and future of Rome. Coriolanus realizes the impossible conflict that has been established, and which he is powerless to resolve, between family and state. For Coriolanus, the Gods can now witness 'this unnatural scene' (5.3.184), as mother kneels before son.[97]

Coriolanus represents a crisis in authoritarian conceptions of the state, which has become a dysfunctional family. Just as Bodin conceived of the state as a family, so does Shakespeare, using the example of the relationship between Coriolanus and Volumnia to show the drastic effects of excessive control from above and its attendant illusion of self-sufficiency. As with so many of Shakespeare's Jacobean plays, *Coriolanus* appears to be strongly critical of the political conceptions of James I, as represented in his use of the analogy of the body politic.[98] However, the play has more often than not been read as a conservative work, principally because of the role of the tribunes, Sicinius and Brutus.[99]

It is undoubtedly true that the tribunes, those elected to represent the plebeians and mediate between them and the patrician senate, are unscrupulous, self-serving and keen to incite sedition and bring down Coriolanus. Shakespeare develops what he had found in Plutarch, where they are represented as those 'who had only been the causers and procurers of this sedition'.[100] The tribunes recognize that either they or Coriolanus must be defeated:

SICINIUS:

　　It shall be to him then, as our good wills,

　　A sure destruction.

BRUTUS:　　　　　　　So it must fall out

　　To him; or our authority's for an end[.]

　　　　　　　　　　　(2.1.240–2)

Nevertheless, as Brutus's speech continues, it is clear that there is a principled purpose to their actions that is not evident in Plutarch:

> We must suggest the people in what hatred
> He still hath held them: that to's power he would
> Have made them mules, silenc'd their pleaders, and
> Dispropertied their freedoms; holding them,
> In human action and capacity,
> Of no more soul nor fitness for the world
> Than camels in their war, who have their provand
> Only for bearing burthens, and sore blows
> For sinking under them.

(243–51)

The tribunes see themselves as acting to protect the people from the patricians, who do not have their best interests in mind and will use them to fight needless and unnecessary wars. Just as Coriolanus fears the mouths of the people, so the tribunes fear that their voices may support the cause of Coriolanus: 'All tongues speak of him' (203). They work later to have Coriolanus's election as consul revoked (2.3), in a scene that undoubtedly alludes to the Goodwin–Fortesque election of 1603/4 (see above, pp. 103–5). Sicinius admits that, like Mark Antony in *Julius Caesar*, they have goaded the people to act, foolishly believing that they have made their own minds up (2.3.260–1).[101] Their position is evidently problematic and open to challenge, as numerous critics have suggested.[102]

However, it is also true that they read the characters, beliefs and political actions of the patricians astutely and accurately. Martius's initial response to the citizens' complaints is 'Hang 'em!' (1.1.203), and he sees the election of the tribunes as the first sign of an unwelcome democratic shift in Roman politics, whereby the people 'will in time / Win upon power, and throw forth greater themes / For insurrection's arguing' (218–20). Menenius, a patrician who is markedly more popular among the plebeians than Coriolanus, voices similar opinions of the plebeians and the political institutions established by the republic to represent them. Menenius dismisses the tribunes by association: 'you wear out a good wholesome forenoon in hearing a cause between an orange-wife and a faucet-seller, and then rejourn [adjourn] the controversy of threepence to a second day of audience' (2.1.69–72), further demeaning their political role and integrity via references to colic, passing blood and chamber pots. For Menenius, the tribunes serve no proper political function: 'All the peace you make in their [the plebeians'] cause is calling both the parties knaves' (77–9), and he takes his leave with a comment worthy of Coriolanus: 'More of your conversation would infect my brain, being the herdsmen of the beastly plebeians' (93–5). For the patricians, the plebeians are no better then beasts.

Coriolanus reveals Rome in political turmoil, its institutions being undermined by the individuals who occupy them. It does not follow, however, that it is a play that invites an autocratic reading, showing a noble but seriously flawed warrior whose pride precipitates his tragic fate and enables society to bring him down. Rather, it presents us with two versions of the body politic at the start, and follows through the implications of each reading of the analogy.[103] Menenius, who expresses what patricians such as Coriolanus also believe, seeks not only to provide an authoritarian reading of the trope, but also to retain control of political language and prevent it being used by the lower classes. He is wrong-footed by the first citizen and shocked that his theories are being challenged by someone he feels should not possess a voice. In dismissing him as the 'great toe of this assembly', he shows that he has not thought carefully about how the body politic might best function or move forward. It is arguable that the decline of the metaphor took place when it was seized by those who, like James I, were keen to use it to undermine any notion of contract theory, and so rendered the analogy redundant even as they articulated their political positions.[104]

Coriolanus shows the patricians refusing to take the republic seriously and so forcing the plebeians and the tribunes to oppose them, creating a contested and divided society. Of course, they are not wholly to blame, as the war with the Volscians is the chief cause of the famine that spurs the citizens into action, making the Roman play a pointed counterpart to the English *Henry V*, where war serves as a means of uniting rather than dividing society (see above, pp. 56–71). Nevertheless, the first citizen's reading of the body politic analogy, one of Shakespeare's original additions to the story, indicates that both the tribunes and the citizens are more wholeheartedly in favour of the mixed constitution advocated by republicans and humanists alike than the patricians. The implication is that if their rights were taken more seriously and they were granted greater political influence, the Roman republic would function more justly and harmoniously. Given that the opening scene deliberately recalls contemporary English means of choosing candidates for elections, and that Menenius's arguments appear to represent those of James I, then the political message of the play appears, yet again, to be topical and pointed. English society will function better if there is wider participation in government by a range of estates or classes. The political institutions that make up the mixed constitution – parliament, councillors, magistrates, etc. – should be allowed to work properly without the destructive interference of a myopic oligarchy (or monarch), keen to preserve their own advantage at all costs.

Chapter Five

THE REALITY OF JACOBEAN POLITICS

'None that I love more than myself'

Shakespeare was obviously interested in the question of government throughout his writing career. However, the aspect of
government which interested him did not stay the same because
neither his own ideas nor the political situation in England, of course,
remained constant. James I's accession transformed the political
agenda: certain approaches and burning issues were put to one side
or disappeared altogether, and others came to the fore and assumed a
vital new importance. In some ways this change is self-evident.
Clearly the vexed question of the legitimacy of a female monarch and
the forms of political behaviour appropriate during her reign were
only relevant in so far as they impinged on issues of a nostalgic cult of
Elizabeth celebrated as a means of denigrating the rule of the present
monarch.[1] Equally, questions of the appropriateness of the Queen's
choice of potential marriage partner or her decision to remain a
virgin no longer applied as the new King brought his own family
with him. James's keen interest in theological debate, the theory of
the divine right of kings and the prerogative of the monarch, and the
unification of Britain under his sovereignty, were all new issues that
dominated parliamentary debate and political discussion elsewhere.[2]
In this chapter I want to show how three of Shakespeare's Jacobean
plays, *Measure for Measure*, *Timon of Athens* and *The Tempest*, can be
read as responses to the political practicalities of life in James's
England.

It surely cannot be a coincidence that Shakespeare's history plays, all of which date from the 1590s (except the late collaboration *Henry VIII*), deal extensively and obsessively with the question of the monarch's legitimacy and the problem of the succession. These were the issues that dominated political discussions and literary representations of Elizabeth, who actively forbade her subjects to talk openly about her – and their – future.[3] After 1603 Shakespeare produced three major plays all directly concerned with the 'matter of Britain', *King Lear, Macbeth* and *Cymbeline*, suggesting that his use of history had altered along with the new issues raised by James's reign.[4] More significantly still, as I shall argue in this chapter, Shakespeare appears to move away from the republican concerns and themes of works such as *Titus Andronicus* and *The Rape of Lucrece*, and from the more implicitly signalled political issues raised in *Richard II* and *Henry V*, towards an acceptance of the incumbent monarch's status and role as head of state.

Shakespeare's political progress would seem to mirror that of his erstwhile patron, the Earl of Southampton, who appears to have been influenced by republican ideas in the 1590s and who played a central role in the failed coup of 1601, but became a respectable – albeit relatively unimportant – member of the Jacobean court when released by James in his first action after his accession.[5] Shakespeare's sonnet 107 probably refers to Southampton's release, as well as marking the change in dynasty in grand political and metaphysical terms.[6] Shakespeare refers to 'the lease of my true love' as 'forfeit to a confined doom', but 'Now with the drops of this most balmy time / My love looks fresh', lines which seem to make best sense if read as the celebration of freedom after a period of incarceration. While the political, amatory and patronage-related significance of the ornate language of the sonnets is invariably ambiguous and has been contested by readers, it is hard not to see this sonnet as a comment on the merciful death of the Elizabethan regime:

> The mortal moon hath her eclipse endured,
> And the sad augurs mock their own presage;
> Uncertainties now crown themselves assured,

> And peace proclaims olives of endless age. ...
> And thou in this shalt find thy monument,
> When tyrants' crests and tombs of brass are spent.[7]
>
> (5–8, 13–14)

The image of the eclipsed moon surely refers to Elizabeth, who was most frequently represented as Diana, the goddess of the moon, in her final years.[8] The reference to the 'sad augurs' (soothsayers), indicates that anyone who predicted disaster when Elizabeth died – Shakespeare having been one of them (see above, pp. 78–97) – is now laughing at their earlier fears, as the time of uncertainty gives way to the new assurance of the Stuart dynasty and a male monarch at long last. The reference to peace suggests James's self-proclaimed status as an inaugurator of harmony and concord, and the words 'endless age' note that the dynasty will continue through James's two sons, Henry and Charles. The final couplet, with its reference to the brass tombs and crests of tyrants, would seem to be a direct attack on the recently deceased Queen. These are exactly the sort of sentiments that a poet closely connected to the remains of the Essex circle would have been likely to produce for his patrons on James's accession, given the care that Essex and his supporters had taken to help secure James's succession before Elizabeth's death, and the hopes they had of returning to political influence and office under his rule (hopes which were largely justified).[9]

Another obvious motive for Shakespeare's apparent change of allegiance and focus, from a disaffected figure to one more in tune with the regime, is apparent when we examine the progress of his professional career. Although Shakespeare is invariably represented as an Elizabethan dramatist – notably in John Madden's romantic comedy *Shakespeare in Love* (1999) – his receipt of direct court patronage was intermittent, and his position was probably straitened and uncomfortable in the last years of Elizabeth's reign.[10] His professional career was shaped by the fortunes of the companies for which he worked. In the 1590s he was employed by Strange's Men, possibly Pembroke's Men, and, most importantly, the Lord Chamberlain's Men. Only when the latter company received official patronage as the King's Men, in 1603, did Shakespeare have a direct and regular relationship with the monarch and the court (whatever the truth behind the story that the Queen's taste for Falstaff led to the production of *The Merry Wives of Windsor* (1596–7)).[11] Furthermore, the Lord Chamberlain's Men were fortunate to escape punishment after their ill-advised performance of *Richard II* before the Essex Rebellion.[12] Shakespeare, as is often noted, was one of the few dramatists who managed to escape punishment for his connection with the Essex Rebellion, but this episode can hardly have increased his sense of security in the last years of Elizabeth's reign.

It would be quite wrong to assume that supporting the right of the monarch to rule meant becoming an uncritical royal apologist, as has sometimes been argued.[13] James's assertion that parliament was only an advisory body and had no jurisdiction to restrict his actions as monarch, was not accepted by everyone. A number of civil lawyers and political analysts ('natural law theorists') reiterated the familiar argument that the monarch existed as part of a mixed constitution. They argued that the Houses of Parliament had a right to participate in debates and influence the monarch's actions.[14] The political significance of Shakespeare's plays lies in their often critical representations of the monarch, making them part of a long tradition of humanist works keen to advise and correct the monarch through providing counsel. Or, more likely, given that they were performed on the commercial stage, they show how the monarch might best be advised if he wished to listen to sensible counsel from his subjects.[15]

James himself made the case that a monarch should avoid flatterers and promote useful subjects who could provide helpful advice. While refusing to grant his subjects any right to challenge or circumscribe the king's actions, James explicitly advised his son, Prince Henry, to choose his court carefully and to avoid promoting flatterers to positions of responsibility and power because of the crucial role in government that advisers would play:

> But specially take good heed to the choice of your servants,
> that ye preferre to the offices of the Crowne and estate: for in
> other offices yee have onely to take heede to your owne weale; but

these concerne likewise the weale of your people, for the which yee must bee answerable to God. Choose then for all these Offices, men of knowen wisedome, honestie, and good conscience, well practised in the points of the craft, that yee ordaine them for, and free of all factions and partialities; but specially free of that filthie vice of Flatterie, the pest of all Princes, and wracke of Republicks … I fore-warned you to be at warre with your owne inward flatterer, how much more should ye be at war with outward flatterers, who are nothing so sib to you, as your selfe is; by the selling of such counterfeit wares, onely preassing to ground their greatnesse upon your ruines.[16]

In the political world according to James, the king's advisers and servants play a crucial role, even if they have no say in determining the actions of the king in a free monarchy. Throughout his political works, James stresses the need for the monarch to obey the laws he has established and to serve as an example to his people: 'for people are naturally inclined to counterfaite (like apes) their Princes maners' (p. 155). Book II of *Basilikon Doron*, fittingly enough, opens with a clear distinction between the 'lawfull good King' and 'an usurping Tyran', 'the one acknowledgeth himselfe ordained for his people … the other thinketh his people ordeined for him, a prey to his passions and inordinate appetites' (p. 155). The king had a duty to listen to advice and not surround himself with those – flatterers – who would fail to save him when he went wrong and would actually assist in turning him into a tyrant. In *The Trew Law of Free Monarchies*, James is clear that, as 'Gods Lieutenant in earth', the king makes the laws, not his subjects, but that he, 'although hee be above the Law, will subject and frame his actions thereto, for examples sake to his subjects, and of his owne free will'.[17]

James made sure that his key works, including *Basilikon Doron* and *The Trew Law of Free Monarchies*, were published in a new edition before he arrived in England in May 1603.[18] There could be no excuse for any of his powerful new subjects being ignorant of his political beliefs. If James was seeking to reassure his English subjects that they had nothing to fear from his views, he was also paving the way for any possible battle with parliament.[19] In *Basilikon Doron*, James referred to parliament as 'the Kings head Court', which should only meet when the king judged that the time was right to make new laws (p. 156). The first parliament of his reign opened on 19 March 1604. James made a speech outlining his view of his role as a divinely ordained king who would serve as the head of the kingdom, while the parliament made up the body.[20]

The clashes that took place in that first parliament are outlined above (see pp. 103–5). Nevertheless, it is clear that whatever disagreements James had with his subjects, his political vision left ample room for vigorous discussion and that he was prepared – at least, in theory – to take advice from trusted councillors.[21] Furthermore, he was at pains to stress this crucial aspect of his philosophy in his writings and make them available for all that wanted to read them. Francis Bacon enthused that *Basilikon Doron*, 'falling into every man's hand filled the whole realm as with a good perfume or incense before the King's coming in, for being excellently written and having nothing of affectation'. Bishop Montagu was equally fulsome in his praise and evaluation of the wide readership of the same work: 'What applause had it in the world … how did it enflame men's minds to a love and admiration of his Majesty beyond measure'.[22]

James was keen to be a patron of art, literature and philosophy. He adopted an existing troop of players, the Lord Chamberlain's Men, making them the King's Men, and had numerous plays performed at court throughout his reign. He helped to establish the masque as a vital form of court entertainment through the appointments of Inigo Jones and Ben Jonson, as set designer and masque writer respectively, and he also encouraged the preaching of sermons so that they became 'the pre-eminent literary genre at the Jacobean court'.[23] It is true that there were times when James seems to have been more keen on the appearance than on the content of the entertainment in question – especially in the case of masques – and he could be impatient if there was more verbiage than action on stage.[24] He was also quick to censor any work that exceeded the boundaries of what could legitimately enter the public realm. As King of Scotland he took offence at Edmund

Spenser's *The Faerie Queene*, which represented his mother, Mary Queen of Scots, in an unfavourable light; he called in Sir Walter Raleigh's *History of the World*; and he was keen to demonstrate his power as a monarch through a series of book burnings throughout his reign.[25] However, he was quite capable of promoting and censoring the same authors at different points. He took umbrage at the anti-Scots jibes and sneers at his plans for uniting the kingdoms in Ben Jonson, George Chapman and John Marston's *Eastward Ho*, and may also have been instrumental in having Jonson called before the Privy Council to explain the significance of his play *Sejanus his Fall*, at the very start of his reign.[26] Nevertheless, Jonson became a key figure at court soon afterwards. Some years later (1616), James was scandalized by John Barclay's satirical *Corona Regia* and its unfavourable portrait of kings, but later still (1622) wanted his political romance *Argenis* made more widely available, presumably because he approved of its political and moral sentiments.[27]

The evidence would suggest that James was keen to use and extend the venerable tradition of literature of counsel at court, encouraging lively debate and sponsoring performances and texts that he thought were of political value.[28] The list of plays that were staged by the King's Men, many of which were performed at court, as surviving dramatic records indicate, shows that James was certainly not averse to seeing plays that questioned and challenged his conception of how the monarch should behave and, often explicitly, his conception of kingship.[29] For example, Barnabe Barnes's rabidly anti-Catholic *The Devil's Charter* was performed at court in January and February 1607. This was undoubtedly part of a reaction to the Gunpowder Plot of two years earlier, but was clearly at odds with James's general policy of extending tolerance to loyal Catholics, enshrined in the Oath of Allegiance passed in the House of Commons in the session immediately prior to the performance of Barnes's play.[30] As I have already suggested, it is equally hard to read *Macbeth* and *King Lear* as works that simply accept and reinforce James's beliefs. And, although it was probably not performed at court, the King's Men were also responsible for producing Jonson's controversial *Sejanus his Fall* and, later, *Catiline his Conspiracy*.[31]

The central point that needs to be made is that Shakespeare did move more in royal and official circles in the first decade of the seventeenth century than he had done in the last decade of the sixteenth, and he did become much more respectable and affluent in the process.[32] Nevertheless, it would be a mistake to suggest that belonging to the King's Men and performing works at court meant that a straightforward acceptance of the King's political beliefs was a necessary prerequisite for such worldly success. A culture of lively critical debate existed in court literature, as it did elsewhere in James's realm (notably parliament, for all James's emphasis on the divine right of kings).[33] Shakespeare's plays written after 1603 concentrate far less on the legitimacy of the monarch than his earlier works had done, and far more on the behaviour of the monarch as a ruler in office. In doing so they are generally simultaneously more supportive of monarchy as an institution and equally – if not more – critical of the monarch's conduct. Furthermore, plays that are usually read as universalized comments on the vicissitudes and follies of human behaviour can often be seen in addition to possess a more specific political focus and charge. This mistaken excision of a historical dimension occurs because the relationship between politics and the dramas of everyday life – awkward moral decisions, insoluble dilemmas, appropriate and inappropriate behaviour, misunderstandings, marriage contracts – becomes much closer in Shakespeare's Jacobean plays.

I

Although *Measure for Measure* has often been read as a play designed to pander to James, it is hard to imagine a more confrontational work greeting an incoming monarch.[34] It is challenging and agonistic precisely because it deals with James's interests and concerns; the assumption that plays that dramatized issues close to the royal heart were automatically sycophantic and simply reproduced or expanded the monarch's ideas is wholly at odds with the reality of early modern English drama. *Measure for Measure* takes as its starting point a key motif used in *Henry V*, that of the disguised monarch mingling with his subjects to find out what they really think of him.[35] The effect of the manoeuvre in the earlier play was to point out how narrow the gap was between subject and monarch, making Shakespeare's decision to repeat the plot a brave one that also expressed confidence in the freedom he could expect on the early modern stage.[36] This makes the link between *Henry V* and *Measure for Measure* not only hard to ignore, but also positively provocative for a monarch who publicly argued for the divine right of kings. Yet all this did nothing to prevent its being staged in the banqueting hall of Whitehall before the King on 26 December 1604, probably in much the same form as the text preserved in the First Folio of 1623.[37]

It has often been noted that there are clear similarities between the concerns of Duke Vincentio and those of James, most significantly their confidence in their own powers to establish justice and proper government. The play does indeed end happily, when the Duke reveals himself and proceeds to sort out the related problems of the marriage contracts and the proper punishments, but this does not mean we have to be fully satisfied with the solutions provided or go so far as to see the Duke as a spiritual leader.[38] On the contrary, *Measure for Measure* is a work that challenges and frustrates expectations, raising questions that it declines to answer.[39] Its ostensibly comic form is continually interrogated, leaving the spectator unhappy with both developments and resolutions.[40] It is hard to believe that James would have recognized a resounding endorsement of his own ideas in a figure who passes his responsibilities over to a deputy, and spends most of the play deviously extracting information from those he is supposed to govern, before deciding that he has to appear and resolve the various plots he has initiated, consciously and unconsciously, at the end of the play. Nevertheless, there are definite echoes of James's works, most notably *Basilikon Doron*, throughout the play; the slanders that the Duke has to endure from the tongue of Lucio can be related to the rumours that surrounded James's sexual proclivities; and even relatively minor details such as the Duke's reclusiveness can be related to James's dislike of public performance and preference for reasoned argument.[41] When the Duke states 'I love the people, / But do not like to stage me to their eyes' (1.1.67–8), the sentiments echo those of James in 1603–4, and also remind the audience that the ruler is being 'staged' in *Measure for Measure*. Duke Vincentio is and is not James.[42]

The play opens with a dramatic example of the rhetorical figure of *occultatio* or *paralipsis* ('declining to say what you nevertheless do say'), when the Duke declares to Escalus: 'Of government the properties to unfold / Would seem in me t'affect speech and discourse'.[43] Given that the Duke is seen handing over the reins of power to Angelo this cannot be anything other than an irony. The Duke may not, as he says, ever deliver his oration on government, but the audience knows that the play will deal with precisely this issue, and in ways that the Duke has not intended. The effect is to place the politically literate viewer above the figure of the ruler represented on the stage, enabling the theatre audience to examine and analyse the purpose and actions of the monarch.[44] The play's discussions of justice, the operation of the law, moral behaviour, the ruler's prerogative and the rights of his subjects, are all staged for the audience to follow, encouraging them to adopt a particular viewpoint even if no definite answers are provided. *Measure for Measure*, its very title inviting a consideration of its purpose as drama, as well as the proper form that justice should adopt, stands as an interrogative play questioning the aims and ideals of the new dynasty.[45]

One of the key issues signalled in the early scenes of the play is the drastic change inaugurated in Vienna by the actions of the Duke. Angelo's first act is to decree that all the brothels in the suburbs of Vienna be pulled down. When Mistress Overdone learns of this threat to her livelihood she remarks, 'Why, here's a change indeed in the commonwealth' (1.2.96–7). Specifically, as Leah Marcus has pointed out, Angelo's actions resemble those of James immediately after his accession and his attempt to bring the independent civic laws of London under central control as part of his drive to assert the monarch's prerogative over the common law.[46] More generally, they signal the fear at the possibility of change that accompanies the advent of a new dynasty. Mistress Overdone's servant Pompey's response to her concern, 'good counsellors lack no clients: though you change your place, you need not change your trade' (98–100), refers pointedly to

James's accession and his change of place from Scotland to England.[47] The reference to 'good counsellors' is double-edged, reminding the ruler that any successful monarch could only function properly with a group of advisers to whom he was prepared to listen, but also referring to the widespread resentment of the advisers that James brought down with him from Scotland. The essayist Francis Osborne blamed what he saw as the deterioration of court values squarely on the Scots who arrived with James, employing a series of startling images to illustrate his point:

> The reason King James was so poorely followed, especially in his journies, was his partiality used towards the Scots, which hung like horseleeches on him, till they could get no more, falling then off by retiring into their owne country, or living at ease, leaving all chargeable attendance to the English. The harvest of the love and honour he reaped being sutable to the ill husbandry he used in the unadvised distribution of his favours: For of a number of empty vessels he filled to compleat the measure of our infelicity, few proved of use to him, unlesse such as, by reason of their vast runnings out, had daily need of a new supply.[48]

Pompey's lines indicate that catastrophic change can be controlled and marshalled in the right direction by the use of judicious counsellors. The question asked is whether James has managed to do this effectively, or whether he has simply relied on his familiars to protect him and make him feel at home, even if their presence is not in the interests of his subjects.

However, as the audience would have been well aware, many longed for drastic change under James, and hoped that his rule would signal the end of Elizabethan England. Shakespeare, given the events his company became involved in towards the end of Elizabeth's reign, may have been one of them. The fact that such arguments are put into the mouths of the Duke's more humble subjects not only recalls the scenes before the Battle of Agincourt in *Henry V*, but also gives the debate a confrontational and challenging edge. The exchange, if read in of James's accession, makes an explicit link between the behaviour at his court and the profession of prostitution, with the counsellors bringing in their wake a series of clients, suggesting that James runs his kingdom like a brothel. Francis Osborne's description of the lavish feasts that took place at court, meals which were 'unpractised by the most luxurious of tyrants', hint at sexual as well as gastronomic excess:

> I cannot forget one of the attendants of the king, that at a feast, made this monster in excesse, eate to his single share a whole pye, reckoned to my lord at ten pounds, being composed of amber-greece, magiseriall of perle, musk, &c. yet was so far (as he told me) from being sweet in the morning, that he almost poisoned his whole family, flying himselfe like the satyr from his owne stinck ... I am cloyd with the repetition of this excesse, no lesse then scandalized at the continuanace of it.[49]

The vocabulary and general terms of the description – 'excesse', 'sweet in the morning', 'satyr', 'cloyd' – and the author's profession that he is 'scandalized', make the connection between food and sex obvious for the reader, hinting at the links made in Ovid's *Elegies* and the Ovidian poetry fashionable in Elizabethan and Jacobean court circles.[50]

For Osborne, James's court resembles a giant brothel, a comparison also made in *Measure for Measure*. When the Duke imposes marriages on his subjects at the end of the play, he forces the slanderous courtier, Lucio, to marry Mistress Overdone. This punishment may have a symbolic resonance that exceeds its superficial righteousness as an act of justice. Lucio informs the Duke, disguised as a friar, that the Duke would exhibit sympathy for the disgraced Claudio if he were in Vienna, because he is a fine woodman (pursuer of women), who pardons others who have the same vice. The Duke's defence of himself must surely be a sly hit at James's reputation, bringing the audience's attention to the similarities between the staged court in Vienna and the real one in London: 'I have never heard the absent Duke much detected for women; he was not inclined that way' (3.2.118–19). Assuming we can see the Duke as a figure of James, albeit intermittently, this can be read as an ironic hint at James's homosexuality, further emphasizing the ludicrousness of Lucio's charges.[51] The joke surely continues when Lucio, trying to slander the Duke in the play, responds, 'O sir, you are deceived', to which the Duke responds ''Tis not possible' (120–1). In defending himself from the slander of promiscuity, the Duke is simultaneously confirming James's homosexuality in indignant tones.[52] Moreover, it is worth noting that the Duke is the only major character in the play who does not have a relationship with anyone of the opposite sex, which can be read as a sign of his self-control or of his secret preference for men. What seems like a spirited defence of chastity in the play only serves to confirm the liberal attitudes to sexuality that existed at James's court.

Nevertheless, whatever his personal failings, Lucio is surely right to complain of the lax moral behaviour in Vienna under the Duke. The Duke himself admits that this has been the general rule under his government, which is the principal reason that he feels he is unable to sort out the problems his liberal regime has precipitated: ''twas my fault to give the people scope, / 'Twould be my tyranny to strike and gall them / For what I bid them do' (1.3.35–7). Hence, Lucio's general complaints about the Duke's rule are valid in a broader sense and, given that the Duke conceives government in terms of his 'absolute power' (1.3.13), the confusion between ruler and court is understandable. In such a state, the general character of the court and those close to the head of state is the responsibility of the ruler. As Antonio states at the start of *The Duchess of Malfi* (1613–14):

> a prince's court
> Is like a common fountain, whence should flow
> Pure silver drops in general; but if t'chance
> Some curs'd example poison't near the head,
> *Death, and diseases through the whole land spread.*[53]
>
> (1.1.13–15)

When Duke Vincentio marries Lucio to Mistress Overdone, in a crucial sense he is punishing one of his courtiers for the sins of his court, not meting out true justice or trying to tackle the problem. If Lucio fails to see through the Duke's disguise as a friar, then the Duke also fails to perceive what are the real ills at his court. By implication the same problem also confronts James.

Measure for Measure is ostensibly concerned with the problem of sexual liberty and restraint. However, just as the image of the court as a brothel exists as part of a wider debate on the virtues and vices exhibited by those at the top of society, so the plot carefully links sexuality and government.[54] The play shows that the effects of the governments of the Duke and Angelo are remarkably similar. Claudio suggests that the ease and laxness of life under the Duke have led him astray and he will now have to suffer a period of restraint. When Lucio asks him what is the source of this restraint, Claudio replies:

> From too much liberty, my Lucio. Liberty,
> As surfeit, is the father of much fast;
> So every scope by the immoderate use
> Turns to restraint. Our natures do pursue,
> Like rats that ravin down their proper bane,
> A thirsty evil; and when we drink, we die.
>
> (1.2.117–22)

Claudio sees himself as a man who has not been properly governed and so has not learned to govern himself properly. The paradox is that the 'absolute authority' of the Duke has been used to run a city state notable for its liberty and the lax morals of its citizens. Claudio feels that he has been caught out and punished by 'the demi-god, Authority' (112), rather than reformed. The errors of the Duke are matched by the equal and opposite errors of Angelo, who wishes to impose order and restraint, but finds that he succumbs to the sexual temptation that undermines his authority and compromises his ability to rule. Claudio's speech, brought about by the actions of Angelo, later proves relevant to Angelo himself, in one of the many neat ironies in the play. Angelo learns to his cost that 'surfeit is the father of much fast'.

The problem of sexual control and restraint is also a political one. The Duke's plan is to have Angelo take his place so that Angelo can resolve the problems the Duke recognizes he has caused, without harming the Duke's reputation: 'Who may in th'ambush of my name strike home, / And yet my nature never in the fight / To do in slander' (1.3.41–3). By any criteria that can be applied, the plot is a failure. It bears a close resemblance to one of Machiavelli's key pieces of advice in *The Prince*. Machiavelli describes the brilliant strategy of Cesare Borgia, Duke Valentino, whose Italian name may be signalled in Vincentio, a name not used in any of Shakespeare's sources. He appointed 'a cruel, efficient man', Remirro de Orco, as governor of Romagna in his place when he acquired the province, because the weak lords who had ruled it previously had governed badly 'to such an extent that the province was rife with brigandage, factions, and every sort of abuse'. Having let Remirro establish firm government through his 'excessive authority', but in the process alienate the people, the Duke moved to win them back and re-establish himself as supreme governor:

> Knowing ... that the severities of the past had earned him a certain amount of hatred, to purge the minds of the people and to win them over completely he [Cesare Borgia] determined to show that if cruelties had been inflicted they were not his doing but prompted by the harsh nature of his minister. This gave Cesare a pretext; then, one morning, Remirro's body was found cut in two pieces on the piazza at Cesna, with a block of wood and a bloody knife beside it. The brutality of this spectacle kept the people of the Romagna for a time appeased and stupefied.[55]

However, the comparison of Duke Vincentio's mode of government with that of Cesare Borgia only serves to highlight the mistakes made by the Duke. At the end of the play he has to intervene to sort out the problems caused by his deputy, and act as a *deus ex machina* to bring the comedy to a conclusion; it has not been achieved without his guidance. The Duke's judgements are hasty and apparently arbitrary, especially when he changes his mind about the punishment of Lucio and decides not to have him whipped and hanged for his slanders. It is by no means clear that the marriages he arranges are desirable as acts of justice or for the couples involved. There is a further pointed irony in the fact that the Duke appoints Angelo so that his name will not become slandered, which is precisely what does happen under Angelo's rule. Angelo is innocent of slandering the Duke, just as the Duke is of promiscuity, but these respective sins flourish under their respective governments.

The end of the play is notable for its preservation of the status quo. The Duke returns to govern and nothing is changed from the start of the play. He is still in charge, dispensing judgements based on his sole authority, and still, presumably, suggesting that government is best administered as practice rather than theory, as he did in the opening speech of the play. While the rule of Remirro de Orco was an interlude that served to strengthen the hand of Cesare Borgia, the rule of Angelo functions only to emphasize the uncontrolled, authoritarian and arbitrary rule of the 'old fantastical duke of dark corners' (4.3.156), whose regime swings from one extreme to the other to the distress of his confused subjects.

But if *Measure for Measure* ends at the same point where it began, the central defining event it stages recalls one of the most significant and celebrated political changes of all. Angelo's attempt to force Isabella to sleep with him, his use of specious arguments and abuse of the pressure of authority, are a clear recollection and rewriting of the rape of Lucrece and the subsequent establishment of the Roman republic. Tarquin tries to persuade Lucrece to yield to him by arguing that if she keeps the crime secret nothing will happen to her husband, children, or Rome at large; Angelo tries Isabella's virtue by suggesting that no one will believe her anyway because he possesses absolute authority. Lucrece increases in moral and political stature and awareness as the battle of wills develops; Isabella also finds her resolve stiffened and certainty increased that her instincts are correct in the 150 lines they have on stage together. Most tellingly, Lucrece articulates what makes Tarquin a tyrant before Shakespeare uses the word (*Lucrece*, 676); Angelo declares that he will 'prove a tyrant' (2.4.168) to Isabella's brother unless she yields to him. By the end of the scene it has become clear to the audience that the reverse process of the establishment of the Roman republic has taken place and Tarquin is, in fact, restored. On one level this is a witty reminder that, as Shakespeare along with any literate reader of Tacitus or Suetonius knew, the republic eventually led to the autocratic imperial regime founded by Augustus. As the government in Vienna returned to the same point from which it started, so did ancient Roman history, and the Tarquins were eventually replaced by the likes of Nero and Caligula. In *Measure for Measure* the rape does not actually take place, through another process of substitution (the 'bed trick', whereby Mariana takes the place of Isabella, just as Angelo took the place of the Duke).[56] The prospect of cataclysmic change in the body politic disappears, and the Duke returns to restore the original order.

The plot of *Measure for Measure* is full of devices of substitution or repetition; the Duke is replaced by Angelo; Mariana substitutes herself for Isabella; the head of Ragozine takes the place of that of Claudio (making the planned 'head trick', whereby Barnardine's would be substituted for Claudio's, redundant), and so on. Such measures take the place of transformations, and give the title, *Measure for Measure*, its conservative charge. Much has been made of Shakespeare's debt to Ovid, the poet of transformation, exile and subversion. *Measure for Measure* should be read as an anti-Ovidian play, tantalizing the audience with exciting possibilities of change, only to frustrate and thwart such desires.[57] In political terms, we are back where we started, and no new form of government appears to transform the state.

Obviously, it would be a mistake to reduce the play to a political allegory, and the anti-Ovidian nature of the plot can be read as a generic experiment reversing the thrust of works full of Ovidian transformations, such as *A Midsummer Night's Dream*.[58] Nevertheless, *Measure for Measure* demands to be read as a polemical, controversial intervention into the state of politics in England at the start of James's reign.[59] The play quite studiously refuses to draw definite conclusions, instead pointing to a series of issues and problems that need to be resolved. The central conflict of liberty versus restraint on which the plot hinges is posed as a dilemma that requires proper resolution and careful government, but is something for which the Duke does not – or cannot – find a reasonable answer, other than leaving it to others to sort out (which they singularly fail to do).

Other issues are also left hanging in the balance, notably the contrast between the Duke and Angelo as governors. The Duke is slandered as a ruler who is rather too involved with his people and prone to personal attacks, something his judgements at the end of the play suggest is a weakness of his style of rule. Angelo is represented as 'a man whose blood / Is very snow-broth', making him unable to feel 'The wanton stings and motions of the sense' (1.4.57–9), or as a ruler who is too impartial and removed from the ordinary feelings of his fellow creatures to govern them effectively. The play does not conclude whether the best way to govern is to apply the rigour of the law or to show mercy, nor when, exactly, the monarch should exercise his prerogative to intervene and modify or halt the statutory code.[60] And we do not really know whether the Duke actually learns to govern better from interacting with his subjects in disguise. Like Henry V, he ought to have learnt something, but the evidence would suggest otherwise. The Duke spends his time frustrated at his inability to deal with slander, or to sort out the problems precipitated by Angelo's actions, until he reveals his true identity and returns like the *deus ex machina* of Old Comedy.[61]

Measure for Measure poses these political issues, I would suggest, as the work of a writer keen to help set the political agenda for the new king's reign. Given the attempts of the Essex faction – including Shakespeare and the Lord Chamberlain's Men – to perform the same act at the end of Elizabeth's reign, this is hardly a major surprise. Duke Vincentio is represented as a hapless – but not hopeless – monarch whose rule has precipitated a serious problem, the excessive liberty of his subjects, which he feels unable to control, and which has come to determine how he is seen by his subjects. The parallel to the early years of James's reign is obvious. Equally pertinent is the arbitrary and authoritarian style of the Duke's government, a style of rule that has reduced counsel to an irrelevance. The two main instances in the play of rulers interacting with their subjects as relative equals are Angelo's Tarquinian attempt to corrupt Isabella, and the Duke's extraction of slanderous comments from Lucio. Counsel has ceased to exist in this city state. Shakespeare's play, almost certainly the first he wrote after the accession of James and certainly the first new Shakespeare play performed at court by the King's Men, stands in the honourable tradition of 'mirrors for princes' literature. The Duke's aloof and egocentric style of rule is shown to be ineffective and unable to transform a moribund body politic. In this failure, he might be said to resemble Elizabeth in her last years, suggesting that James appeared to his subjects much like his fickle and irascible predecessor.[62] One of the chief fears expressed in *Measure for Measure* is that the change of ruler and dynasty will, in fact, bring no change at all. Instead of the major transformation that had been hoped for – and, of course, feared – there would simply be more of the same.

II

Timon of Athens (c.1607–8) is a play only occasionally read in terms of contemporary politics. Nevertheless, like *Measure for Measure*, it stages a number of issues relating to the practice of politics in James's reign.[63] *Timon* is most frequently read as an inferior *King Lear*, and certainly dates from around the same period, although I would like to argue for a later date – 1608 – than has often been proposed (see below, pp. 204–5).[64] The plot shows how the profligate generosity and susceptibility to flattery of a wealthy Athenian enable him to squander his vast fortune and give away his riches to a series of undeserving, petty-minded citizens. As a result of their myopic greed, the citizens leave Athens open to the invasion of the exiled general, Alcibiades. Timon, now a troglodyte hermit and dedicated misanthrope, pays the army of Alcibiades from a hoard of gold that he has just discovered, and refuses to listen to the pleas of the citizens. It is only when Alcibiades learns of Timon's death that he rethinks his plan to take revenge against his and Timon's enemies in Athens, although his last lines are open to a number of interpretations and do not necessarily guarantee peace.

As with many of Shakespeare's plays produced at court for James, there are frequent occasions when the behaviour of one of the central characters resembles that of the King.[65] While Timon is still enjoying the illusion of his wealth and the popularity it brings him, unaware that his coffers are actually empty, he is told by his steward, Flavius, that Lord Lucullus wishes to hunt with him and has presented him with 'two brace of greyhounds' (1.2.187). Greyhounds were expensive and important animals used in hunting, which was James's favourite pastime, as his contemporaries frequently noted. M. de Fontenay, envoy to James from his mother, Mary Stuart, observed in 1584 that 'He loves the chase above all the pleasures of this world, living in the saddle for six hours on end, running up hills and down dales with loosened bridle'.[66] James became notorious for refusing to attend to matters of state when it did not suit him and spending his time hunting at one of his – or his rich subjects' – country retreats.[67]

In 1603, James's nine-year-old son, Prince Henry, was represented with Sir John Harington, symbolically sheathing his sword after cutting the head off a deer, in a portrait by the court painter, Robert Peake. Next to him are the working animals most important to the hunter, his horse and his dog. The tableau indicates how significant hunting was as the official sport of James's court, and as a symbolic activity denoting manly achievement, physical prowess and power over nature.[68]

Literary references to hunting immediately referred the reader to the King and his court. Ben Jonson praises the 'seasoned deer' which the Sidneys possess at their seat in Penshurst, noting that they 'serve to feast or exercise thy friends'.[69] Towards the end of the poem, having described the bounty which is to be obtained at the Sidneys' table, Jonson comments:

> That found King James, when, hunting late this way
> With his brave son, the Prince, they saw the fires
> Shine bright on every hearth as the desires
> Of thy Penates had been set on flame
> To entertain them[.]

(76–80)

The sly irony is that the apparent serendipity of the encounter disguises a more exploitative relationship. The King was notorious for using his courtiers' country houses when he wished to find a retreat from the demands of court life, and forcing them to house his large retinue while he did so.[70] This relationship allowed the King to escape from the court, but it meant that his courtiers could not escape from their king as they might wish. 'To Penshurst', while ostensibly praising the delights of the country retreat, actually points out the problems and limitations of possessing one.[71] In 'The Sun Rising', probably written not long after

FIGURE 11   *Henry, Prince of Wales, and John, second Lord Harington of Essex* by Robert Peake, 1603.

James became king, John Donne berates the sun for waking the poet and his lover and urges him, among other things, to 'Go tell court-huntsmen, that the king will ride'.[72] The lyric relies on two related assumptions for its ironic effect. First, that hunting takes place every day, and it is the sun's duty to ensure that the king is able to follow this important pursuit; second, a point that becomes more obvious as the narrator starts to wake up, that he and his mistress have become the centre of the universe and so have replaced the king.[73] One of the central jokes in the poem is that the king is more often to be found calling for his hounds than dealing with crucial matters of state, exactly what James's contemporaries observed.

Shakespeare's reference to hunting in *Timon of Athens* is therefore pointed, especially when it is made clear in the second act that Timon, to the despair of his steward, is reluctant to turn from the pleasures of the hunt to deal with the pressing business of sorting out his bills and debts (2.2.1–8). Elsewhere in Shakespeare's work hunting is explicitly associated with tyranny; as when, for example, Prospero has Caliban hunted in *The Tempest*, or, when we witness a bloody 'ritual of death and dismemberment', in *Titus Andronicus* and *Julius Caesar*.[74] It is hard to believe that the audience failed to make the connection between Timon at this point in the play and the behaviour of their king.[75] In the lines that follow the offer of Lord Lucullus – which, we know, has only been made in anticipation of a greater gift in return from Timon – Flavius delivers a lengthy aside showing that he realizes the folly of his master's actions:

> He commands us to provide, and give great gifts,
> And all out of an empty coffer;
> Nor will he know his purse, or yield me this,
> To show him what a beggar his heart is,
> Being of no power to make his wishes good.
> His promises fly so beyond his state
> That what he speaks is all in debt; he owes for ev'ry word:
> He is so kind that he now pays interest for't[.]

> (1.2.190–7)

Timon then proves his steward right, and compounds the error in a significant manner: "'tis not enough to give: / Methinks I could deal kingdoms to my friends, / And ne'er be weary' (218–20).

Timon's words seem to point the reader towards an obvious metaphorical significance of the word 'state' (195), transforming it from its meaning as an individual's wealth or fortune into another common usage in early modern English political language, that of the realm or nation.[76] Interestingly enough, Donne's poem makes use of the identical word and metaphor in the last stanza, when the narrator asserts, 'She is all states, and all princes I' (21). In *Timon*, Shakespeare makes it obvious that the significance of the metaphor and its vehicle are reversible: Timon may be figuratively dealing in kingdoms in giving away gifts to friends and promising to bestow rewards on flatterers beyond his state, but the real king of England was accused by contemporaries of literally doing just that.

The essayist Francis Osborne provides a graphic link between James and Timon.[77] The story may well be apocryphal, but, whether true or not, it does date from the time that the play was written, as it describes Sir Robert Carr, the King's favourite, as being in the 'flower of his favour before he had either wife or beard'.[78] Carr came to London in the wake of James in 1603, was knighted in 1607, and married in 1613.[79] Cecil became Lord Treasurer in spring 1608 when the Earl of Dorset died. If there is a connection between *Timon* and the following anecdote – and I think it likely that there is – then the play was probably written and performed in mid- to late 1608.

Osborne alleges that the Lord Treasurer, Sir Robert Cecil, worried about James's lavish gifts to Carr, laid out the sum of £20,000, which James had given to Carr

> upon the ground in a roome through which his majesty was to passe: who, amazed at the quantity, as a sight not unpossibly his eyes never saw before, asked the treasurer whose money it was, who answered, 'Yours, before you gave it away;' whereupon the king fell into a passion, protesting he was abused, never intending any such gift: And casting himselfe upon the heap,

scrabled out the quantity of two or three hundred poundes, and swore he should have no more. However, it being the king's minion, Cecil durst not provoke him farther than by permitting him only the moiety [half].[80]

Osborne's anecdote shows how James only begins to understand the nature of money when he is confronted with the reality of it in the form of a huge pile. The lesson reduces James to a greedy miser, scrabbling in the pile to save his wealth from disappearing. The miser was represented frequently on stage, in figures such as Shylock, who laments the loss of his gold as much as his daughter (*Merchant*, 2.8.15–16), and Barabas in Christopher Marlowe's *The Jew of Malta*.[81] Yet, even after this humiliation, Cecil cannot face curtailing the King's expenditure as he would wish, and the King is too foolish to control his finances of his own accord. According to Osborne, the relationship between James and Carr is that between a doting monarch and an undeserving favourite.

The image of the undignified, prostrate James sorting through his displayed wealth may well be signalled in Shakespeare's darkly comic stage image of Timon digging for roots and finding gold. Timon, his wealth dissipated, has now left Athens and is searching for the most basic meal that the earth can provide him with. Instead he discovers gold, exactly what he has left Athens to avoid, and he curses the precious metal, which he now sees as the root of all evil, sent to tempt him:

> Gold? Yellow, glittering, precious gold?
> No, gods, I am no idle votarist.
> Roots, you clear heavens! Thus much of this will make
> Black, white; foul, fair; wrong, right;
> Base, noble; old, young; coward, valiant.
>   ... this
> Will lug your priests and servants from your sides,
> Pluck stout men's pillows from below their heads.
> This yellow slave
> Will knit and break religions, bless th'accurs'd,

> Make the hoar leprosy ador'd, place thieves,
> And give them title, knee and approbation
> With senators on the bench.
>
> (4.3.26–38)

This passage was praised by Karl Marx for its penetrating insight into the nature of money, as the fetishized commodity which possessed 'the property of buying everything, by possessing the property of appropriating all objects' and so mediating – falsely – between mankind and nature.[82] Whatever its value as a philosophical statement, it is clear that Timon's impassioned and angry reaction to his former worldly status is simply an inversion of his previous error, rather than a solution to the problem of his previous myopia. Timon allows his reaction to gold to determine his existence; in Athens he fails to notice that it distorts and undermines the ideal friendships he thinks he is establishing; in the woods he fails to understand that his undue trust in the benign effects of wealth have now led him to turn against mankind and become '*Misanthropos*' (4.3.54). The naïve community of the *polis* has been replaced by a body politic in which Timon and Apemantus snarl at each other, and Timon either repels intruders into their world or does what he can to bring the outside world to his level of misery.[83]

James, in Osborne's anecdote, also lets money dominate his life and also fails to grasp its essential nature. He either uses it to promote his favourites, satisfying his whims and enhancing his glory and status as ruler, or, horrified at his foolishness, seeks to protect his hoard. In desperately flinging himself on top of his heap of gold James abandons the regal dignity of the monarch, something he was obsessed with protecting in his writings. Just as Timon fails to learn the lesson of his folly, so does James, illustrating his fallible nature as a man, which is sharply at odds with his image of himself as a divinely-appointed ruler. Both Timon and James illustrate Marx's point that money determines the relationship between mankind and the wider world.

Anthony Weldon's description of James's character in his *The Court and Character of James I* also makes James sound very similar to Shakespeare's Timon:

He was very liberall of what he had not in his owne gripe, and would rather part with 100 *li*. hee never had in his keeping then one twenty shillings piece within his owne custody; he spent much, and had much use of his subjects purses, which bred some clashings with them in parliament ... and truly his bounty was not discommendable, for his rising favourites was the worst[.][84]

Weldon's critique of James, not published until 1650, is based on his support for the parliamentary cause in the civil war. It situates James's alleged inadequacies within a greater battle between the King and the institutions which represent the people and guarantee their liberties and their rights. In *Timon*, the profligacy of Timon and his ill-treatment by his friends and dependants ultimately leads to disaster for the city state, Timon's disillusionment helping to fuel the revenge of Alcibiades. Timon later refers to his remaining stock of gold as 'thou sweet king-killer' (4.3.384), again making a link between the play and the incumbent monarch (especially given that the Gunpowder Plot had nearly succeeded in killing the King only two years earlier).

The play ends with lines of studied ambiguity. Alcibiades, on hearing of Timon's death, appears to rethink his plans for sacking Athens, but the sense of his words is cryptic: 'Bring me into your city, / And I will use the olive with my sword, / Make war breed peace, make peace stint war, make each / Prescribe to other, as each other's leech' (5.4.81–4). The lines appear to mean that Alcibiades regards war and peace as symbiotic rather than opposite states of existence, both of them necessary for the public good as he sees it. However they are interpreted, the lines sound like a deliberate parody of James's self-fashioned image as the *rex pacificus*, the astute ruler capable of steering his subjects clear of the danger of destructive conflict.[85] Given that Timon's profligacy helps to secure the rise of Alcibiades, Shakespeare's play seems to be suggesting that a lack of control over the distribution of favours and gifts and the encouragement of a spendthrift culture in the body politic may undermine the legitimate aims of the governors.

Timon's riches undoubtedly fuel careless and dangerous profligacy, just as James's assumption that the financial restrictions placed on him as King of Scotland would be ended when he got his hands on England's bounty, earned him the enmity of some of his powerful subjects.[86] But the even more pernicious political effect of his attitude to wealth was the encouragement of flatterers, precisely the sort of courtiers and advisers James had urged Prince Henry to avoid in *Basilikon Doron*. *Timon* contains seventeen references to flattery and flatterers, more than any other Shakespeare play (*King Lear*, the work closest in style and scope to *Timon*, contains seven; *Coriolanus*, which can be read as a companion play based on Plutarch, twelve).[87] In the first scenes in the play, the 'churlish philosopher', Apemantus, detects the malign effects of Timon's foolish actions, and refuses to join in the festivities he organizes. Timon reproaches Alcibiades that he 'had rather be at a breakfast of enemies than a dinner of friends' (1.2.75–6), a quip which Alcibiades deliberately turns into a cannibalistic image, reminiscent of the gory cycle of revenge represented in a play such as *Titus Andronicus*, or the violent aristocratic honour and dysfunctional family relationships displayed in *Coriolanus*: 'So they were bleeding new, my lord, there's no meat like 'em; I could wish my best friend at such a feast' (77–9). Timon's witty antithesis is immediately transformed from a comic remark to a tragic irony. Apemantus, who aspires to be a self-sufficient cynic, completes the philosophical gloss, before a hypocritical guest proves the point and Timon shows that, despite the evidence at his disposal, he is still living in the enclosed comic world he has created for himself:

APEMANTUS   Would all those flatterers were thine enemies then, that then thou mightst kill 'em – and bid me to 'em.
FIRST LORD   Might we but have that happiness, my lord, that you would once use our hearts, whereby we might express some part of our zeals, we should think ourselves for ever perfect.
TIMON   O no doubt, my good friends, but the gods themselves have provided that I shall have much help from you: how had you been my friends else?

(80–8)

The dramatic irony of this exchange is straightforward: Timon refuses to leave the festive world that he has created and confront the truth that Apemantus, by no means an ideal friend, has shown him. Once again, the need for the powerful and mighty to listen to counsel they may not want to hear is highlighted, precisely the point made in Osborne's anecdote. Timon allows money to determine his relationship with his fellow man, as much after his descent into poverty as before. Apemantus, who is one of the few Athenians capable of giving Timon good counsel, gives up after the banquet scene when his comments go unheeded, and decides simply to resort to abuse. He concludes that advising a man like Timon is pointless: 'O that men's ears should be / To counsel deaf, but not to flattery' (1.2.250–1). The James who wrote *Basilikon Doron* would obviously have agreed, but the James observed by Francis Osborne and Anthony Weldon would have been too obsessed with rewarding adoring favourites from his imagined unlimited fortune to take proper heed.

The Athenian setting is clearly also relevant to a political reading of the play, given the importance of Athens as the city state where European political thought was conceived.[88] John Lyly, in *Euphues: the Anatomy of Wit* (1579), had represented Athens as an allegorical form of Oxford, deliberately drawing a parallel between the two centres of philosophical and political speculation. Given Shakespeare's knowledge of Lyly's comedies and the immense popularity of *Euphues*, it can be assumed that Shakespeare would have known of this precedent.[89] *Timon* makes use of the story of the famous misanthrope, Timon, which appeared in a variety of sources, but the story of Alcibiades is undoubtedly more important for reconstructing the political context of the play.[90] Alcibiades was a talented but unscrupulous Athenian who ignored the splendid education he received at the hands of his tutor, Pericles, the founder of the democratic Athenian constitution, and the good will of Socrates. Indeed, it was partly owing to Alcibiades that Pericles' plans to unite Greece as a democratic federation of states was abandoned and gave way to the revival of the imperialist designs of the Peloponnesian War. When he was summoned back to Athens to face trial for his violent crimes he fled to Sparta and supported revolts against Athens until he was recalled, serving the city as a military commander, before he was banished again and eventually assassinated on the order of his many enemies.

Shakespeare might have known the story of Alcibiades from reading Thucydides' *History of the Peloponnesian War*, an English translation of which was published in 1607 when he was probably at work on *Timon*.[91] It is more likely that he used North's Plutarch, given that he was going through what one critic has termed his '"Plutarchian" transitional period' between the great tragedies and late romances.[92] As Plutarch twins his *Life of Alcibiades* with that of *Caius Martius Coriolanus*, the source of *Coriolanus*, written within a year of *Timon*, it is hard to believe that Plutarch's comments on Alcibiades do not have a central relevance to Shakespeare's play.

Plutarch represents Alcibiades as a charismatic figure, a bold warrior and leader, as well as a persuasive orator, but ultimately addicted to pleasure and having no firm control over his undoubted talents. Alcibiades' essentially savage nature shows through in a story about a wrestling bout in his youth:

> One day wrestling with a companion of his, that handled him hardly, and thereby was likely to have given him the fall, he got his fellow's arm in his mouth, and bit so hard, as he would have eaten it off. The other feeling him bite so hard, let go his hold straight, and said unto him: 'What, Alcibiades, bitest thou like a woman?' 'No marry do I not', quoth he, 'but like a lion.'[93]

The cannibalistic image can be related to our initial impression of Alcibiades in *Timon*, keener to breakfast on his enemies than with his friends. Plutarch is clearly emphasizing the viciousness of Alcibiades and the fact that the educational training he receives from Pericles and the friendship of Socrates can only transform him to a limited extent. It is equally significant that one of his chief vices is vanity and he is highly susceptible to flattery, a word North uses frequently throughout his narrative. The story of his youth is that of a battle between vice and virtue. Socrates labours heroically to keep him away from 'strangers, seeking to entice him by flattery' and nurture his 'natural inclination to virtue' (p. 90). He generally succeeds, but on occasions his love of 'lust and pleasure' triumph and Alcibiades is 'carried away with the enticements of flatterers' (p. 92).

The adult Alcibiades is an equally ambiguous figure, sometimes leading the Athenians to heroic victories against all odds; at others, threatening to undermine the city state. Plutarch emphasizes the problematic relationship between the flawed general and the democratic body politic of Athens. Plutarch describes his plan to invade Sicily, a cherished dream of the Athenians, in suitably pointed terms: 'the only procurer of the Athenians, and persuader of them ... was Alcibiades; who had so allured the people with his pleasant tongue, that upon his persuasion, they built castles in the air' (p. 104). Alcibiades and the people of Athens have a symbiotic relationship: if he leads them astray through his dangerous oratory, they recognize that he is vital to their success. His second banishment, soon before his murder, is generally acknowledged a disaster, as the military successes he achieved disappear:

> The Athenians found themselves desolate, and in miserable state to see their empire lost ... they began together to bewail and lament their miseries and wretched state, looking back upon all their wilful faults and follies committed: among which, they did reckon their second time of falling out with Alcibiades, was their greatest fault. So they banished him only out of malice and displeasure, not for any offence himself in person had committed against them[.] (p. 134)

Timon links together the story of Timon with the story of Alcibiades to produce a moral fable with a political dimension.[94] The play, just like Plutarch's *Life of Alcibiades*, chronicles the failure of populace and leaders who between them manage to undermine the state they inhabit. Timon fails to see that he is squandering his wealth, because he is too foolish to see that his utopian ideal of friendship is actually based on the cash nexus he imagines is purely a reward for good fellowship. Alcibiades is banished because he cannot control his aggressive nature. His appeal for an equitable conception of the law based on mercy ('For pity is the virtue of the law, / And none but tyrants use it cruelly' (3.5.8–9)) does not sit well with the cause he pleads:

> It pleases time and fortune to lie heavy
> Upon a friend of mine, who in hot blood
> Hath stepp'd into the law, which is past depth
> To those that, without heed, do plunge into 't.
> He is a man, setting his fate aside,
> Of comely virtues;
> Nor did he soil the fact with cowardice
> (An honour in him which buys out his fault)
> But with a noble fury and fair spirit,
> Seeing his reputation touch'd to death,
> He did oppose his foe[.]

(10–20)

Alcibiades's conception of justice and mercy is so warped – suggesting that anyone who fairly owns up to a crime should be excused is hardly a reasonable principle of jurisprudence – that it is obvious that he is as unsuited for legal as Timon is for financial office.[95]

However, if Alcibiades has his faults, his banishment by the senate for pleading the case of a fellow soldier who has served Athens well in its military campaigns rather too vigorously is also unjust and short-sighted. His plan to loose his army of 'discontented troops' (116) on Athens is a potent threat and one that undoubtedly alludes to a central fear of Elizabethan and Jacobean society, whose members had suffered terrifying experiences of demobbed, unpaid armies wandering the countryside in search of the basic means of existence. Alcibiades's threat takes this fear a stage further.[96] There is an obvious sense of poetic justice when the deputation of senators tries to entice Timon back to Athens, presumably so that his new-found wealth can help to fund an army to defend Athens against Alcibiades. Timon is given an abject apology when the senate, 'which doth seldom / Play the recanter' (5.1.144–5), admits that it has treated Timon with a 'forgetfulness too general gross' (143), and now offers him 'absolute power' (161). Timon suggests to the senate that hanging themselves on the tree outside his cave will prevent further misery.

Timon cannot be reduced to a simple political allegory. It has often been suggested that it is a hybrid, experimental work, possibly written in collaboration with Thomas Middleton, and perhaps never even produced on stage in Shakespeare's lifetime.[97] Nevertheless, the fact that it is not simply a political work and cannot be decoded as a straightforward allegory of Jacobean politics in 1608, does not mean that the play possesses no political charge, nor that it does not contain allegorical representations which can easily be identified (such as Timon's profligacy and that of James).[98] While Timon and Apemantus are arguing in the woods, Apemantus tells Timon that he would give the world to the beasts, because he is so disgusted with the society made by men. Timon produces an elaborate analysis based on Apemantus's hypothesis to show the savage and competitive nature he sees as the essence of Athenian society:

> If thou wert the lion, the fox would beguile thee; if thou wert the lamb, the fox would eat thee; if thou wert the fox, the lion would suspect thee, when peradventure thou wert accus'd by the ass; if thou wert the ass, thy dulness would torment thee, and still thou liv'dst but as a breakfast to the wolf; if thou wert the wolf, thy greediness would afflict thee, and oft thou shouldst hazard thy life for thy dinner[.]

(4.3.329–36)

Apemantus articulates the inescapable moral they have already come to: 'the commonwealth of Athens is become a forest of beasts' (349–50).[99]

The arguments of each misanthrope owe much to traditional representations of men as animals in beast fables, most importantly, those of Aesop and Lucian, which Ben Jonson used to spectacular effect in *Volpone* (1605–6), a play that was part of the repertoire of the King's Men at the same time as *Timon*.[100] However, the choice of beasts – fox, lion and wolf – recalls Machiavelli's famous advice that a prince must know how to act like a beast if he is to retain power and govern effectively (cited above, p. 81). In the bestial world of modern politics, honour, trust, generosity and all the other qualities Timon exhibited in his former life in Athens are not principles that can be followed or valued.[101] Elsewhere Machiavelli asserts that a prince 'ought not to trust in the amitie of men' because they are 'full of ingratitude, variable, dissemblers . . . and covetous of gain . . . So that a prince which leaneth upon such a rampire, shall at the first fall unto ruine'.[102] Few maxims apply more obviously to both James and Timon.

Shakespeare, as I have suggested earlier, would have probably known Machiavelli from Innocent Gentillet's refutation of *The Prince*, popularly known as the *Anti-Machiavel*, translated into English in 1603 (the quotations are from Simon Patericke's translation of Gentillet), which included a translation of *The Prince* and extracts from the *Discourses*.[103] In linking the plot of Timon the misanthrope to the story of Alcibiades, *Timon* forges a bond between morality fable and political narrative (a link already implicit in the form of Plutarch's *Lives*). The argument of Gentillet's treatise is similar. He attempts to resist the amoral political world he saw in Machiavelli's writings and show that in a just world the right thing to do is the right thing to do, so putting political discourse back onto a moral basis. For Gentillet a prince must not only appear devout but must be so, and he must certainly always keep his word.[104]

Timon can be read as a play which represents the political world according to Machiavelli as a brutal fact. Athens, for all its philosophical sophistication, lurches chaotically from one extreme to another. Thucydides, the main source for its history, shows Athens veering between the perils of democracy and those of tyranny.[105] Shakespeare's Athens is in a state of degenerate chaos where flattery determines master–servant relations, and the law has lost its impartiality and become subject to the whims of a ruling elite who own it. Force ultimately holds sway in this world of beasts not men. In such a society the choice is between joining the corrupt body politic or retreating to the woods and becoming a misanthrope. Shakespeare implies that Machiavelli's conception of the world may be undesirable but true; Gentillet's desirable but false. The play's political message would appear to be that James in England, just like Timon in Athens, will need to adapt his relationship to others and his political practice to survive in such a world. In essence, he must become rather more realistic in his political ambitions and perceptions of others. *Timon* is not wholly negative in its implications, although it has often proved somewhat relentless as a piece of theatre.[106] The play ends with Alcibiades about to conquer Athens, an uncertain moment which presages disaster in the short term; but in the longer term the audience knows that Athens will become the bedrock of European thought. The implication is that people can learn from their mistakes, and the malign influences that cause a society to degenerate can be corrected. Perhaps, Shakespeare may have thought, this applied especially to a philosopher king like James, keen to encourage lively debate at his court.

III

A similar analysis of Jacobean politics is provided in *The Tempest* (*c.*1611–12), which takes place on an island location at the edge of the known European world. Shakespeare made use of William Strachey's unpublished account of his shipwreck in the Bermuda islands, the word 'tempest' itself signalling a New World setting.[107] Equally important is the fact that the drama unfolds on an unnamed Mediterranean island just off the North African coast, and makes considerable play of the mythic geography of Carthage and Tunisia. The Europeans are returning from the marriage of Claribel, the daughter of the King of Naples, to the King of Tunis, a dynastic match of considerable importance, especially given that Claribel becomes heir to the kingdoms of Naples and Milan, after her brother Ferdinand's supposed death (2.1.239–69).[108] Nevertheless, as an earlier exchange between the courtiers of Naples and Milan indicates, their knowledge of the history and geography of the region is limited (70–102).[109] The play has generated a whole series of debates concerning its relationship to the contemporary history and theory of colonialism.[110] However, the central point of the play may well be that Europeans cannot escape their political heritage, wherever they are and whatever they try to achieve. In this case the setting assumes a subtly different significance, as a symbolic location on the margins of the known world.[111]

The Tempest draws attention to itself as an Italian play, the leading protagonists all being Neapolitan and Milanese aristocrats or citizens:

Alonso, Sebastian, Prospero, Antonio, Ferdinand, Gonzalo, Trinculo and Stephano. Indeed, many of these names seem to have been taken from the historical actors represented in William Thomas's *Historie of Italie* (1549) and Geoffrey Fenton's translation of Francesco Guicciardini's *Storia d'Italia, The Historie of Guicciardini containing the warres of Italie and Other Partes* (1579, 1599).[112]

The first book of Guicciardini's *Historie* details the close relationship and bloody conflict between Naples and Milan. Naples is governed by Ferdinand I, a good but ambitious ruler, who is succeeded by Alfonso, and then by Ferdinand II. This second Ferdinand is betrayed to the King of France by a leading noble, Trinuulce, leaving Naples in the hands of the French after a series of further bloody wars (pp. 52–5). Not only are three names used that are adopted in *The Tempest*, but the actions of Trinuulce seem to prefigure the treacherous role of Trinculo, a servant in the Neapolitan household in Shakespeare's play, when he leads a rebellion against Prospero and Alonso. Later, an important counsellor named Gonzalo appears (p. 128), suggesting that Shakespeare may have been keen to signal the world of political intrigue and conflict represented in Guicciardini's *Historie*, while not wishing to write a play based on material directly from the work.[113]

Shakespeare might also have been keen to emulate the stated designs of Guicciardini, who has a directly practical understanding of the use of history, one reproduced by Fenton. On the opening page of the *Historie* he states that his aim is to reveal the lessons that can be learnt from history (p. 1).[114] In particular, it is vital to expose the mistakes made by rulers so that they can be avoided in future and better government may result. A marginal note laments, 'How harmful be the errors of Princes', beside comment on the damage done by those whose ambition and pride cause them to neglect and abuse the commonwealths they rule. Throughout the work Guicciardini evaluates the performance of various rulers, praising a few, but generally providing balanced criticism of their characters and period in office. The key figure in the early books is Lodovico Sforza.[115] Early on he is singled out as a threat to stability in northern Italy (p. 3). At the end of Book 4, Guicciardini suggests that he represents the human condition, being eloquent and industrious, and excellent in many ways, but vain and ambitious. When he is finally betrayed and imprisoned by the French, Guicciardini comments that 'the thoughts and ambitions of him, which earst could scarcely be contained within the limits of all *Italy* ... [were] now inclosed in one strait prison' (p. 183).

While such judgements have no specific bearing on the individual characters in *The Tempest*, it is easy to see that the performance of Prospero as the negligent Duke of Milan, or as the governor of the island, can be judged in similar terms, as indeed can the actions of Antonio and Sebastian and the ideas of Gonzalo. The same sort of historical and political analysis is provided in William Thomas's *Historie of Italie*, which was noted as a possible source of the play over a hundred years ago, and may have been used by Shakespeare when he was writing *Othello* (see above, p. 154).[116] Thomas's *Historie* contains an account of one Prospero Adorno, a Milanese officer who became Duke of Genoa, forged an alliance with King Ferdinand of Naples, and was eventually defeated and banished.[117] Thomas's stated aim is identical to that of Guicciardini. The book is advertised as one that is 'excedyng profitable to be redde; Because it intreateth of the astate of many and divers common weales, how thei ben, & now be gouerned'. The text itself shows a variety of different city states with their own distinctive political characteristics. The dedicatory letter to John, Viscount Lisle, Earl of Warwick, urges governors to study Italy and Italian politics because the various city states and principalities that constitute the nation serve either as models of good government to be imitated or bad government to be avoided. The text itself represents Venice as the ideal commonwealth. Genoa, Milan and Florence have chequered histories, oscillating between different forms of tyranny and liberty; Naples stands as the counter-example of bad government, a pointed contrast to the stability and freedom enjoyed by the citizens of Venice. Although Naples enjoys wealth that rivals that of Venice and is undeniably a beautiful city, the inconstancy of the people leads to endless civil wars, sedition and tyranny, epitomized in the factional struggles during the reign of King Alfonso, whose bastard son, Ferdinand, was heavily involved (fos 113–36).[118] Ferdinand and Alfonso are benign, legitimate figures in *The Tempest*, which prevents our reading Thomas's *Historie*, like Guicciardini's, as a direct source. Nevertheless, the world of intrigue, cruelty, plotting and divisive factions represented throughout these two histories haunts the play. Prospero has been usurped by his brother, Antonio, whose main ally is Sebastian, the brother of the King of Naples. In a play with no clear source, Shakespeare deliberately links the history of Milan, dominated by the notorious Sforza family, key figures in both Thomas's and Guicciardini's widely-read histories, with that of the worst Italian city state, Naples.

The political concerns of the play are emphasized in the opening scene. The ship, struggling in the tempest that eventually wrecks it, stands in the long line of political imagery as the ship of state, here an obviously unhappy and divided vessel that has little chance of surviving the storm.[119] The boatswain, the only figure who can actually rescue the stricken ship, is abused in turn by Gonzalo, Sebastian and Antonio when he refuses to defer to their superiority in the midst of the crisis and orders them below deck because they are impeding his efforts. Gonzalo, making a grim joke, suggests that they may all survive the storm because the boatswain's 'complexion is perfect gallows' (1.1.29) and so he must live to be hanged later. Sebastian and Antonio are more direct, the former uttering the curse, 'A pox o'your throat, you brawling, blasphemous, incharitable dog' (39–40), and the latter adding bravado to Gonzalo's taunt: 'Hang, cur! Hang, you whoreson, insolent noise-maker! We are less afraid to be drowned than thou art' (42–4).

The allegorical significance of the scene is made clear when we learn that the tempest has been conjured up by the magical powers of the deposed Duke of Milan, Prospero, in order to bring his enemies to justice. The crisis on board has been caused by the conflict resulting from the deposition of the lawful Duke, leaving the scheming aristocrats exposed to the mercy of forces beyond their control and so having to trust the apparently invisible lower classes for their safety. If the dynastic politics of marriage alliances, such as that between Claribel and the King of Tunis, help to determine the fate of states and nations, so also do the size and power of destructive forces less easy to manipulate and circumscribe. Prospero's tempest should be read in terms of the horrors of endless civil wars represented throughout the pages of Guicciardini and Thomas's histories. The boatswain's lament to the sea, 'What cares these roarers for the name of king?' (16–17), in which 'roarers' refers to the waves, but also metaphorically to rebellious subjects and crowds, indicates that no rule can ever be secure, but will depend upon good fortune and consent.

The opening scene of act two, in which we see the Milanese and Neapolitan aristocrats safely ashore, advances and complicates this political reading of the play. Here we see that the rulers are not simply set against the lower orders upon whom they are reluctantly dependent, but are divided among themselves. Gonzalo, using words that are derived from John Florio's translation of Michel de Montaigne's essay, 'Of the Cannibals', speculates on the possibilities of establishing perfect, unspoiled government.[120] His thoughts are cynically undercut by the asides of Sebastian and Antonio:

GONZALO

Had I plantation of this isle, my lord –

ANTONIO

He'd sow't with nettle-seed.

SEBASTIAN   Or docks, or mallows.

GONZALO

And were the king on't, what would I do?

SEBASTIAN

'Scape being drunk, for want of wine.

GONZALO

I'th' commonwealth I would by contraries
Execute all things, for no kind of traffic
Would I admit; no name of magistrate;
Letters should not be known; riches, poverty
And use of service, none; contract, succession,
Bourn, bound of land, tilth, vineyard – none;
No use of metal, corn, or wine or oil;
No occupation, all men idle, all;
And women, too, but innocent and pure;
No sovereignty –

FIGURE 12 *Land of Cockaigne* by Pieter Breughel the Elder (1567).

SEBASTIAN

              Yet he would be king on't.

ANTONIO

    The latter end of his commonwealth forgets the beginning.

                                        (2.1.144–59)

Gonzalo's reflections on his projected ideal state are a fantasy, one particularly appealing to someone who has had to live through the harsh realities of Milanese political life in the sixteenth century. All the trappings and vices of European civilization, from spectacular inequalities in wealth and the grind of daily work, to the confusions of the law ('contract'), land inheritance ('succession'), the falsehood of women and, most significantly given his own role, the layers of government, are to disappear.[121] Gonzalo's words bear a strong resemblance to the medieval vision of the Land of Cockaigne, where no one had to work, fruit fell from the trees and roast pigs ran around with carving knives stuck in their sides crying 'Eat me! Eat me!'.[122] Sebastian and Antonio undercut Gonzalo's argument in pointing out its obvious flaw: he wants to impose what he thinks is a state of nature. Not only are they clearly right that there is a contradiction inherent in the notion of a king abolishing sovereignty while overseeing the kingdom – a situation that resembles the absurdity of King Lear's supposed abdication – but their objections also point to the regressive nature of Gonzalo's fantasy and the impossibility of returning to the Golden Age.

The juxtaposition of political ideologies does not reflect well on Sebastian and Antonio either. While Gonzalo is naïve and unrealistic, they cannot see beyond the destructive factionalism and political calculation of contemporary Italian politics. They fail to realize that their behaviour is just as foolish as Gonzalo's because it leaves states open to a succession of rebellions and *coups d'état*. Power remains in the hands of a series of unstable elites. By the end of the scene they have established a plot to make Antonio ruler of Milan and Sebastian ruler of Naples (271–88), selfish political decisions that can benefit no one but themselves. The two views are equal and opposite in terms of their delusion and neither can lead towards the stability that the citizens of Venice have enjoyed for so long. If anything, the political lesson of this scene is similar to that of William Thomas's description of Genoa. There, a legitimate rebellion against the excesses of the tyrannous rule of their dukes and emperors led to power swinging too much in favour of the commons, leaving the city in an inconstant state of government. After the fall of the popular government, a powerful dukedom was re-established, inaugurating a harsh rule because liberty had been so badly misused (fos 161–87).

The plot of *The Tempest* centres around Prospero's plan for revenge on his enemies, whom he eventually holds in his power through his magic arts. One of the many splendid ironies of the play is that these arts, which enable Prospero to place himself in a position of unassailable power, have been acquired through his indifference to government when he was Duke of Milan. As he admits to Miranda, his brother was able to plot against him while he was 'neglecting worldly ends, all dedicated / To closeness and the bettering of my mind' (1.2.89–90). For Prospero, his 'library / Was dukedom large enough' (109–10), an unacceptable state of affairs for a governor. Just as Gonzalo's bookish reflections on government are of no serious use to anyone wishing to govern, neither was Prospero's learning, which benefited neither him nor his subjects, and left the city vulnerable to yet another *coup*. On the island, however, Prospero rules like an authoritarian European governor, employing Ariel and Caliban as slaves/servants who must obey him unconditionally – although he claims that this was not always the case with Caliban (345–9) – and controlling his daughter's affections as though her duty were to secure a marriage alliance (like Claribel).[123] The masque that Prospero has performed in act four, as part of the plot to entrap his enemies and expose their guilt, is a literal manifestation of the symbolic function of the masque as court entertainment. Masques, as lavish court spectacles, were originally designed to reinforce the power of the monarch, although, as often as not, they were used as vehicles for advising the ruler how to act or behave.[124] Prospero uses his masque as a means of reinforcing his own power. That he has to interrupt it to deal with the ridiculous plot against him by Trinculo, Stephano and Caliban, serves to emphasize the limits to his conception of authoritarian government, based, as it is, on literary and artistic models of perfection (exactly like Gonazalo's). Significantly enough, Prospero suggests that he will 'plague them all, / Even to roaring' (4.1.192–3), marking them out as dangerous rioters rather than aristocratic conspirators like Sebastian and Antonio, and forging a link with the comments of the boatswain in the opening scene.

Prospero proves himself to be a 'potent master' (34), and his magic art enables him to have all his enemies at his mercy (263). One of the central paradoxes of the play is that he has learnt how to operate within the given paradigms of European power politics on his isolated island, controlling Caliban and Ariel, before launching his counter-plot against those who usurped him. The play ends with a series of reconciliations and friendly alliances. When Prospero reveals himself as the 'wronged Duke of Milan' (5.1.107), Alonso immediately hands power over to him: 'Thy dukedom I resign and do entreat / Thou pardon me my wrongs' (118–19); Ferdinand and Miranda are betrothed; and Caliban promises that he will 'be wise hereafter / And seek for grace' (295–6). Gonzalo expresses the serendipity of the moment:

> Was Milan thrust from Milan that his issue
> Should become kings of Naples? O, rejoice
> Beyond a common joy, and set it down
> With gold on lasting pillars: in one voyage
> Did Claribel her husband find at Tunis;
> And Ferdinand, her brother, found a wife
> Where he himself was lost; Prospero his dukedom
> In a poor isle; and all of us ourselves,
> When no man was his own.
>
> (205–13)

But it is clear that this harmonious ending is a pleasant fiction, very like Gonzalo's utopian fantasy of the ideal island. In this new world of idealized political formations, Prospero can rule but also philosophize and meditate. He claims that he shall 'retire me to my Milan, where / Every third thought shall be my grave' (311–12). Like King Lear, he has made no proper arrangements to relinquish power. If Milanese politics are the same as they were when Prospero was forced to leave his native city, his intentions sound rather naïve. Overall, he appears to have learnt very little from his sojourn on the island. If he was potentially tyrannous as a ruler before his change of heart at the start of act five, he is now making few plans to protect what has been gained from his experiences, and the signs are that Milan is just as vulnerable to violent rebellion as it was when he ruled it earlier.

Prospero's mode of government might be linked to the sudden and dramatic swings of political modes represented in the histories of Guicciardini and William Thomas. Prospero is first overthrown for neglecting his dukedom; then he uses all his powers to regain what is rightfully his; and finally he forgives all his enemies and hopes for a new era. It is clear that he is taking a huge risk and that it is quite likely that such fine ideals – like Gonzalo's ideal commonwealth – have no place in the realities of messy European politics. An identical point was made in Montaigne's essay, which contrasted the benign and limited evils of the American savages to the horrors of the French wars of religion. Montaigne comments on the cannibalism practised by the Brazilians:

I am not sorie we note the barbarous horror of such an action, but grieved, that prying so narrowly into their faults we are so blinded in ours. I thinke there is more barbarisme in eating men alive, than to feed upon them being dead; to mangle by tortures and torments a body full of lively sense, to roast him in peeces, to make dogges and swine to gnaw and teare him in mammockes ... and which is worse, under pretence of pietie and religion ... than to roast and eat him after he is dead ... We may then well call them barbarous, in regard of reasons rules, but not in respect of us that exceed them in all kinde of barbarisme. Their warres are noble and generous, and have as much excuse and beautie, as this humane infirmitie may admit[.][125]

As Curtis Breight has argued, Prospero's treatment of Caliban, in particular, his torturing him with cramps, is represented in a language which seems to borrow terms from the tortures used to extract confessions from those accused of treason in Elizabethan England.[126] Prospero rules in a European fashion on the island and then returns to Europe as if it really were the 'brave new world' (5.1.183) his daughter imagines when she sees Europeans in numbers for the first time.

The play hints that Prospero's hopes will be dashed. He will return to a Europe which is the same as when he left it, dominated by intrigues and the cruelties of civil wars rather than the exotic transgressions of a Caliban.[127] When Miranda and Ferdinand are discovered playing chess, Ferdinand pledges that he would not play her false 'for the world' (173). Miranda's response has a symbolic resonance: 'Yes, for a score of kingdoms you should wrangle, / And I would call it fair play' (174–5). On one level the lines express their untainted love, but we remember that they met because of the dynastic marriage of Claribel and the King of Tunis, an event that, although not actually represented, overshadows the action of the play. Their union, like Gonzalo's vision of utopia and Prospero's pious hopes for the future of Milan, is a fairy tale at odds with the reality of contemporary Europe. It sets Miranda's wonder at the 'goodly creatures' – who include Sebastian and Antonio – in an ironic context, as we know that the reality of the Old World is more akin to that revealed in Montaigne's essay, 'Of the Cannibals', or the events that led up to the expulsion of Prospero from Milan. Sebastian and Antonio are still present at the end of the play. The reconciliation between Prospero and his brother is less than ideal and the words of forgiveness leave no room for doubt that Prospero's gesture is no more than a formality:

> For you, most wicked sir, whom to call brother
> Would even infect my mouth, I do forgive
> Thy rankest fault – all of them; and require
> My dukedom of thee, which perforce I know
> Thou must restore.

(130–4)

Antonio makes no response to these lines. The play ends with a clear sense that Europe contains far more creatures like Antonio and Sebastian who make sure that idealized visions of political interaction are never feasible alternatives to the murky reality of factional intrigue, dynastic alliances and vicious wars.

AFTERWORD

F or the reasons outlined in the introduction, it is not easy to recover the political perspectives and ideas contained within Shakespeare's plays and poetry. The first problem is that reconstructing the political ideology of a relatively remote period, with different conceptions of political action and belief as well as different political and social institutions, is a complicated and often confusing process; there is the constant danger of anachronistic reading and approximating alien statements to ones with which we are familiar. It is also hard to know, when analysing work produced within a fast-developing literary system in which writers wrote for hire or for patrons, what those writers actually believed themselves and what they produced with their masters' views in mind. Of course, such concerns particularly affect drama, an art form that is frequently topical and occasional in form and content.[1] But if such interpretative problems apply to the work of most writers of what we now term 'literature' in Elizabethan and Jacobean England, we have even more problems when we approach Shakespeare. Shakespeare's canonical status as the finest ever writer whose work transcends the limitations of its time has often meant either that the political significance of his plays has been ignored or that he has been appropriated as a conservative thinker.[2] More commonly still, such 'bardolatry' has often led to the assumption that Shakespeare was too enigmatic and brilliant a writer to have any political beliefs.[3]

Nevertheless, in spite of all these – not insignificant – factors that make a political reading of any early modern dramatist – let alone Shakespeare – problematic, I think that certain discernible patterns do emerge in his career and works. We know little enough about Shakespeare's political links, but he does appear to have been a client of Henry Wriothesley, Earl of Southampton, in the 1590s, and so linked to the large and powerful circle that gravitated towards Robert

Devereux, second Earl of Essex. The work Shakespeare produced in that decade seems to share the frustrations with the prevailing status quo and the over-lengthy reign of the aged Elizabeth characteristic of many other writers in the 1590s, especially those connected to the ambitious Essex. Shakespeare seems to toy with the idea that hereditary monarchy may not be the most obvious or best form of government, and his plays explore the merits and demerits of alternative political forms in practice. That many writers of literature and other forms of writing did not push such ideas further than they did and often merely hint at different forms of social and political existence may be put down to a variety of reasons: natural caution, fear of censorship or punishment, and a lack of obvious outlets for such beliefs in English society; probably a combination of all three factors.

While it is possible that Shakespeare was writing to please his patrons, it is noticeable that his interest in a variety of forms of government and politics continues into the next decade, after the accession of James, which would suggest that they were central concerns of his writing career, not merely imposed by the need to please. However, a clear change does take place in Shakespeare's political thinking after James becomes king. While the problem of the succession was the main concern of English political life in the last decade of Elizabeth's reign, a fact which is as apparent in Shakespeare's works as it is in those of many of his contemporaries, under James his work is more focused on the question of *how* to govern than of who had the right to do so. There is still a manifest interest in forms and types of government – as there was more generally in Jacobean England – but the legitimacy of the ruler is not the burning issue it was in earlier works. There is a significant difference between the politics of *The Rape of Lucrece*, written by a relatively impoverished man in his mid-twenties, and *The Tempest*, produced by a rather wealthier citizen in his mid-forties.[4] There was an equally large distance between English political life in 1594 and 1611. It is time that we cease to treat Shakespeare as a tantalizing enigma and read him alongside other writers of literary and non-literary works in one of the most fascinating periods of English writing and history.

THE PLANTAGENET DYNASTY

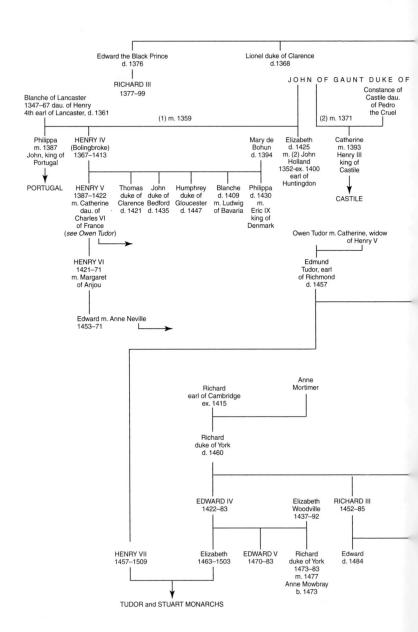

TUDOR and STUART MONARCHS

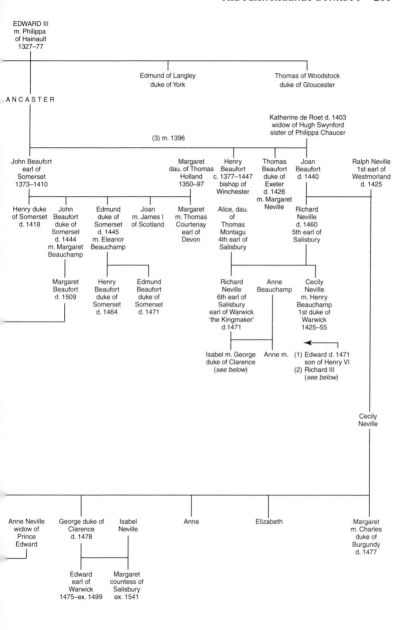

EDWARD III
m. Philippa
of Hainault
1327–77

Edmund of Langley
duke of York

Thomas of Woodstock
duke of Gloucester

ANCASTER

Katherine de Roet d. 1403
widow of Hugh Swynford
sister of Philippa Chaucer

(3) m. 1396

John Beaufort
earl of
Somerset
1373–1410

Margaret
dau. of Thomas
Holland
1350–97

Henry
Beaufort
c. 1377–1447
bishop of
Winchester

Thomas
Beaufort
duke of
Exeter
d. 1426
m. Margaret
Neville

Joan
Beaufort
d. 1440

Ralph Neville
1st earl of
Westmorland
d. 1425

Henry duke
of Somerset
d. 1418

John
Beaufort
duke of
Somerset
d. 1444
m. Margaret
Beauchamp

Edmund
duke of
Somerset
d. 1445
m. Eleanor
Beauchamp

Joan
m. James I
of Scotland

Margaret
m. Thomas
Courtenay
earl of
Devon

Alice, dau.
of
Thomas
Montagu
4th earl of
Salisbury

Richard
Neville
d. 1460
5th earl of
Salisbury

Margaret
Beaufort
d. 1509

Henry
Beaufort
duke of
Somerset
d. 1464

Edmund
Beaufort
duke of
Somerset
d. 1471

Richard
Neville
6th earl of
Salisbury
earl of Warwick
'the Kingmaker'
d.1471

Anne
Beauchamp

Cecily
Neville
m. Henry
Beauchamp
1st duke of
Warwick
1425–55

Isabel m. George
duke of Clarence
(see below)

Anne m.

(1) Edward d. 1471
son of Henry VI
(2) Richard III
(see below)

Cecily
Neville

Anne Neville
widow of
Prince
Edward

George duke of
Clarence
d. 1478

Isabel
Neville

Anne

Elizabeth

Margaret
m. Charles
duke of
Burgundy
d. 1477

Edward
earl of
Warwick
1475–ex. 1499

Margaret
countess of
Salisbury
ex. 1541

THE TUDOR DYNASTY

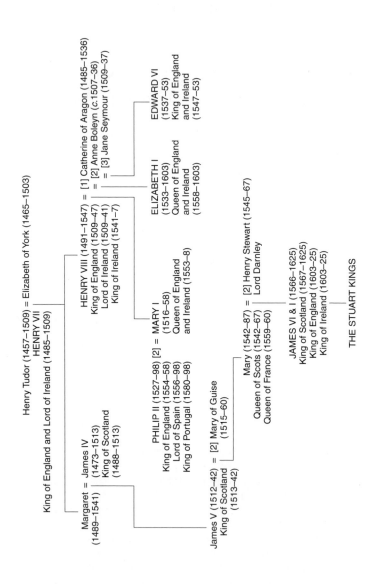

NOTES

INTRODUCTION: SHAKESPEARE AND THE VARIETIES OF EARLY MODERN POLITICAL CULTURE

1. The most comprehensive and readable survey of political thought in Renaissance Europe is Quentin Skinner, *The Foundations of Modern Political Thought*, 2 vols (Cambridge, 1978). See also Janet Coleman, *A History of Political Thought*, 2 vols (Oxford, 2000), II.

2. For details, see John Guy, *Tudor England* (Oxford, 1988), ch. 1; C.S.L. Davies, *Peace, Print and Protestantism, 1450–1558* (London, 1977), ch. 4. Useful reference guides are Rosemary O'Day, *The Longman Companion to the Tudor Age* (Harlow, 1995); C.R.N. Routh, *Who's Who in Tudor England* (rev. Peter Holmes) (London, 1990, rpt of 1964); C.P. Hill, *Who's Who in Stuart Britain* (London, 1988, rpt of 1965).

3. For further analysis, see above, pp. 24–6.

4. For discussion, see Skinner, *Foundations of Modern Political Thought*, II, pt 3.

5. For the evidence see E.A.J. Honigmann, *Shakespeare, The 'Lost Years'* (Manchester, 1998, rpt of 1985). For a more sceptical assessment, see Katherine Duncan-Jones, *Ungentle Shakespeare: Scenes from his Life* (London, 2001), pp. 193–8.

6. Although the usefulness of adopting the notion of 'factionalism' has been disputed, see Simon Adams, 'The patronage of the crown in Elizabethan politics: the 1590s in perspective', in John Guy, ed., *The Reign of Elizabeth I: Court and Culture in the Last Decade* (Cambridge, 1995), pp. 20–45.

7. See Mark A. Kishlansky, *Parliamentary Selection: Social and Political Choice in Early Modern England* (Cambridge, 1986). More generally, see J.E. Neale, *Elizabeth I and her Parliaments*, 2 vols (London, 1953, 1957), and *The Elizabethan House of Commons* (London, 1949); Jennifer Loach, *Parliament under the Tudors* (Oxford, 1991).

8. See David Loades, *Power in Tudor England* (Basingstoke, 1997), ch. 6; Penry Williams, *The Tudor Regime* (Oxford, 1979).

9. John Guy, 'Introduction: The 1590s: the second reign of Elizabeth I?', in Guy, ed., *Reign of Elizabeth I*, pp. 1–20, at pp. 1–2. For one example of a

great magnate in practice, see Paul E.J. Hammer, *The Polarisation of Elizabethan Politics: The Political Career of Robert Devereux, 2nd Earl of Essex, 1585–1597* (Cambridge, 1999).

10. See Mark Goldie's important essay, 'The unacknowledged republic: officeholding in early modern England', in Tim Harris, ed., *The Politics of the Excluded, c.1500–1850* (Basingstoke, 2001), pp. 153–94.

11. See Greg Walker, *Plays of Persuasion: Drama and Politics at the Court of Henry VIII* (Cambridge, 1991); Stephen Orgel, *The Illusion of Power: Political Theater in the English Renaissance* (Berkeley, 1975); David Lindley, ed., *The Court Masque* (Manchester, 1984).

12. See Loades, *Power in Tudor England*, ch. 3.

13. For a convenient guide to both forms of thought, see Isabel Rivers, *Classical and Christian Ideas in English Renaissance Poetry* (London, 1979). For a more extensive account see Charles B. Schmitt and Quentin Skinner, eds, *The Cambridge History of Renaissance Philosophy* (Cambridge, 1988).

14. William Allen, *A Treatise made in Defence of the lawful power and authoritie of Priesthood to remedie sinnes* (London, 1567), pp. 76–8. See Skinner, *Foundations of Modern Political Thought*, II, pt 3.

15. J.P. Sommerville, *Politics and Ideology in England, 1603–1640* (Harlow, 1986), ch. 6.

16. See R.B. Wernham, *After the Armada: Elizabethan England and the Struggle for Western Europe, 1588–1595* (Oxford, 1984); Carol Z. Weiner, 'The beleaguered isle: a study of Elizabethan and early Jacobean anti-Catholicism', *P & P* 51 (1971), 27–62.

17. See Guy, *Tudor England*, ch. 12.

18. See Andrew Hadfield, *Literature, Travel, and Colonial Writing in the English Renaissance, 1545–1625* (Oxford, 1998), pp. 34–40.

19. W.B. Patterson, *King James VI and I and the Reunion of Christendom* (Cambridge, 1997).

20. Blair Worden, *The Sound of Virtue: Philip Sidney's 'Arcadia' and Elizabethan Politics* (New Haven, 1996), p. xxii.

21. Simon Adams, 'The patronage of the crown in Elizabethan politics: the 1590s in perspective', in Guy, ed., *Reign of Elizabeth I*, pp. 20–45.

22. For discussion, see Hammer, *Polarisation of Elizabethan Politics*, ch. 9.

23. Conyers Read, *Lord Burghley and Queen Elizabeth* (London, 1960), pp. 394, 466.

24. Katherine Duncan-Jones, *Sir Philip Sidney, Courtier Poet* (New Haven, 1991), pp. 124–7, 216–7.

25. Worden, *Sound of Virtue*, p. 9.

26. See the examples collected in Robin Headlam Wells, *Shakespeare, Politics and the State* (Basingstoke, 1986), ch. 3.

27. Edward Forset, 'To the Reader', *A comparative discourse of the bodies natural and politique* (London, 1606), pp. 20–30. See also Kevin Sharpe, *Remapping Early Modern England: The Culture of Seventeenth-Century Politics* (Cambridge, 2000), pp. 52, 55. Such analogies did not go uncontested: see below, pp. 170–7.

28. See Wells, *Shakespeare, Politics and the State*, pp. 92–4. On the Northern Rebellion see Anthony Fletcher, *Tudor Rebellions* (3rd edn, Harlow, 1983), ch. 8. For further discussion see below, pp. 42–4.

29. Anon., An Homilie Agaynst Disobedience and Wylful Rebellion', in *Certain Sermons Appointed by the Queen's Majesty* (1574) (Cambridge, 1850), pp. 551–601, at p. 556. See above, pp. 42–4.

30. For discussion see Coleman, *History of Political Thought*, 1, chs 4–5.

31. Sommerville, *Politics and Ideology in England*, ch. 3; Patrick Collinson, *De Republica Anglorum: Or, History with the Politics put back* (Cambridge, 1990); John Guy, 'Tudor monarchy and its critiques', in John Guy, ed., *The Tudor Monarchy* (London, 1997), pp. 78–109; Wells, *Shakespeare, Politics and the State*, pp. 55–8.

32. See Christopher Hill, *Intellectual Origins of the English Civil War Revisited* (Oxford, 1997), pp. 342–3.

33. The principal theorist of democracy for Renaissance readers was Aristotle, who was hostile to it as a cause of instability leading ultimately to tyranny. See his *The Politics*, trans. Thomas Alan Sinclair (Harmondsworth, 1962), pp. 159–64, 235–46. See also Coleman, *History of Political Thought*, 1, pp. 4–5.

34. Aristotle, *Politics*, pp. 135–48, *passim*.

35. J.P. Sommerville, 'James I and the divine right of kings: English politics and continental theory', in Linda Levy Peck, ed., *The Mental World of the Jacobean Court* (Cambridge, 1991), pp. 55–70; J.H. Burns, *The Trew Law of Kingship: Concepts of Monarchy in Early Modern Scotland* (Oxford, 1996), ch. 7.

36. See Burns, *Trew Law of Kingship*, ch. 6; Roger A. Mason, 'George Buchanan, James VI and the Presbyterians', in Roger A. Mason, ed., *Scots and Britons: Scottish Political Thought and the Union of 1603* (Cambridge, 1994), pp. 112–37. For evidence that Shakespeare used Buchanan's *History of Scotland* when writing *Macbeth* see David Norbrook, '*Macbeth* and the politics of historiography', in Kevin Sharpe and Steven N. Zwicker, eds, *Politics of Discourse: The Literature and History of Seventeenth-Century England* (Berkeley, 1987), pp. 78–116; Alan Sinfield, '*Macbeth*: history, ideology and intellectuals', *CQ* 28 (Spring/Summer 1986), 63–77.

37. See J.G.A. Pocock, *The Ancient Constitution and the Feudal Law: A Study of English Historical Thought in the Seventeenth Century* (Cambridge, 2nd edn, 1987), *passim*; David Harris Sacks, 'Parliament, liberty, and the commonweal', in J.H. Hexter, ed., *Parliament and Liberty: From the Reign of Elizabeth to the English Civil War* (Stanford, 1992), pp. 85–121.

38. For divergent views, see Sharpe, *Remapping Early Modern England*, pt 1; Sommerville, *Politics and Ideology*, introduction. See also Guy, 'Introduction: the 1590s', in Guy, ed., *Reign of Elizabeth I*, pp. 11–12.

39. Constance Jordan, *Shakespeare's Monarchies: Ruler and Subject in the Romances* (Ithaca, 1997), pp. 23–5, 88–9; Collinson, *De Republica Anglorum*; A.N. McLaren, *Political Culture in the Reign of Elizabeth I: Queen and Commonwealth, 1558–1585* (Cambridge, 1999), ch. 7.

40. See the discussion in James Hankins, ed., *Renaissance Civic Humanism* (Cambridge, 2000).

41. See Blair Worden, 'English republicanism', in J.H. Burns and Mark Goldie, eds, *The Cambridge History of Political Thought, 1450–1700* (Cambridge, 1991), pp. 443–75.

42. See Quentin Skinner, *Liberty Before Liberalism* (Cambridge, 1998), chs 1–2.

43. Goldie, 'Unacknowledged republic', p. 154.

44. For discussion, see J.K. McConica, *English Humanists and Reformation Politics under Henry VIII and Edward VI* (Oxford, 1965); Collinson, 'The monarchical republic of Queen Elizabeth I', *BJRL* 69 (1987), 394–424, and Collinson, *De Republica Anglorum*.

45. Markku Peltonen, *Classical Humanism and Republicanism in English Political Thought, 1570–1640* (Cambridge, 1995), p. 9.

46. Peltonen, *Classical Humanism and Republicanism*, p. 2.

47. See Worden, 'English republicanism'. Worden, it should be noted, sees little that can be construed as republicanism in England before the 1640s.

48. See Rebecca W. Bushnell, *Tragedies of Tyrants: Political Thought and Theater in the English Renaissance* (Ithaca, 1990).

49. See Skinner, *Foundations of Modern Political Thought*, I, pt 2.

50. See J.G.A. Pocock, *The Machiavellian Moment: Florentine Political Thought and the Atlantic Republican Tradition* (Princeton, 1975), chs 7–9; Worden, 'English republicanism', p. 446.

51. Gian Biagio Conte, *Latin Literature; A History*, trans. Joseph B. Solodow, rev. Don Fowler and Glenn W. Most (Baltimore, 1999, rpt of 1994), p. 370.

52. See David Quint, *Epic and Empire: Politics and Generic Form from Virgil to Milton* (Princeton, 1993), ch. 4; David Norbrook, *Writing the English Republic: Poetry, Rhetoric and Politics, 1627–1660* (Cambridge, 1999), ch. 1.

53. As Shakespeare's version of the story suggests (see below, ch. 3).

54. W.M. Spellman, *European Political Thought, 1600–1700* (Basingstoke, 1998), ch. 3; Robert M. Kingdon, 'Calvinism and resistance theory, 1550–1580' and J.H.M. Salmon, 'Catholic resistance theory, ultramontanism, and the royalist response, 1580–1620', in Burns and Goldie, eds, *Cambridge History of Political Thought*, pp. 193–218, 219–53. See also Worden, 'English republicanism', p. 448.

55. See Felix Raab, *The English Face of Machiavelli: A Changing Interpretation, 1500–1700* (London, 1965), pp. 56–7, *passim*.

56. See Niccolò Machiavelli, *The Discourses*, trans. Leslie J. Walker, ed. Bernard Crick (Harmondsworth, 1970); Skinner, *Foundations of Modern Political Thought*, I, 158–62, 169–71.

57. Goldie, 'Unacknowledged republic', p. 154.

58. Anne Barton claims that 'it would be more surprising if it could be proved that Shakespeare had managed to avoid reading Machiavelli than if concrete evidence were to turn up that he had': 'Livy, Machiavelli and *Coriolanus*', in *Essays, Mainly Shakespearean* (Cambridge, 1994), pp. 136–60, p. 122. For a more sceptical view, see Stuart Gillespie, *Shakespeare's Books: A Dictionary of Shakespeare Sources* (London, 2001), pp. 311–16.

59. Coleman, *History of Political Thought*, II, p. 250.

60. Discussions of Machiavelli's political ideas are contained in Coleman, *History of Political Thought*, II, ch. 6; Quentin Skinner, *Machiavelli* (Oxford, 1981); Hankins, ed., *Renaissance Civic Humanism*; Pocock, *Machiavellian Moment*, chs 6–7. On Machiavelli in England, see Raab, *English Face of Machiavelli*, ch. 1.

61. E.M.W. Tillyard, *The Elizabethan World Picture* (Harmondsworth, 1972, rpt of 1943), pp. 17–19, and *Shakespeare's History Plays* (Harmondsworth, 1962, rpt of 1944).

62. Margot Heinemann, 'How Brecht read Shakespeare', in Jonathan Dollimore and Alan Sinfield, eds, *Political Shakespeare: New Essays in Cultural Materialism* (Manchester, 1985), pp. 226–54, at pp. 226–7.

63. For examples of the former reading, see Terry Eagleton, *William Shakespeare* (Oxford, 1986); Arnold Kettle, ed., *Shakespeare in a Changing World: Essays* (London, 1964). For the latter, see the essays in John Drakakis, ed., *Alternative Shakespeares* (London, 1985).

64. Blair Worden, 'Shakespeare and politics', *SS* 44 (1991), 1–15; *Sound of Virtue*, *passim*.

65. Worden, 'Shakespeare and politics', p. 15.

66. For analysis, see Douglas Bruster, *Drama and the Market in the Age of Shakespeare* (Cambridge, 1992); Andrew Gurr, *The Shakespearian Playing Companies* (Oxford, 1996); Rosalyn Lander Knutson, *Playing Companies and Commerce in Shakespeare's Time* (Cambridge, 2001).

67. See Andrew Gurr, *The Shakespearean Stage, 1574–1642* (Cambridge, 1992); Martin Butler, *Theatre and Crisis, 1632–1642* (Cambridge, 1984), appendix 2, 'Shakespeare's unprivileged playgoers, 1576–1642'; Scott McMillin and Sally-Beth MacLean, *The Queen's Men and their Plays* (Cambridge, 1998).

68. Lindley, ed., *Court Masque*, introduction, pp. 12–13.

69. Barbara Freedman, 'Elizabethan protest, plague and plays: rereading the "Documents of Control"', *ELR* 26 (1996), 17–45.

70. Annabel Patterson, *Shakespeare and the Popular Voice* (Oxford, 1989), pp. 83–5.

71. See Kishlansky, *Parliamentary Selection*, pp. 3–9; Henry N. Paul, *The Royal Play of 'Macbeth'* (New York, 1948).

72. 'The New Cry', in Ben Jonson, *Poems*, ed. Ian Donaldson (Oxford, 1975), lines 3, 15 (p. 48). See also Alan T. Bradford, 'Stuart absolutism and the "utility" of Tacitus', *HLQ* 46 (1983), pp. 127–55, at p. 137. 'Tacitean' history involved a sceptical and detached narrative of political events, in which the historian could analyse the foibles and limitations of rulers alongside those of their subjects. For a fuller discussion see above, pp. 89–92.

73. See, for example, T.W. Baldwin, *William Shakspere's Small Latine and Lesse Greeke* (Urbana, 1944); Jonathan Bate, *Shakespeare and Ovid* (Oxford, 1993); Robert S. Miola, 'Reading the classics', in David Scott Kastan, ed., *A Companion to Shakespeare* (Oxford, 1999), pp. 172–85; Robert S. Miola, *Shakespeare's Reading* (Oxford, 2000); Gillespie, *Shakespeare's Books*.

74. See D.R. Woolf, 'The shapes of history', in Kastan, ed., *Companion to Shakespeare*, pp. 186–205; Annabel Patterson, *Reading Holinshed's 'Chronicles'* (Chicago, 1994), *passim*; Ivo Kamps, *Historiography and Ideology in Stuart Drama* (Cambridge, 1996), ch. 4; Graham Holderness, *Shakespeare: The Histories* (Basingstoke, 2000).

75. *The First and Second Parts of John Hayward's 'The Life and Raigne of King Henrie IIII'*, ed. John J. Manning (London, 1991); Edwin B. Benjamin, 'Sir John Hayward and Tacitus', *RES* n.s. 8 (1957), 275–6.

76. See Cyndia Susan Clegg, *Press Censorship in Elizabethan England* (Cambridge, 1997), pp. 202–5.

77. Robert Lacey, *Robert, Earl of Essex: An Elizabethan Icarus* (London, 1970), pp. 282–3.

78. For discussion, see Janet Clare, *'Art made tongue-tied by authority': Elizabethan and Jacobean Dramatic Censorship* (2nd edn, Manchester, 1999), pp. 68–72.

79. J.E. Neale, *Queen Elizabeth* (London, 1934), p. 381.

80. Cited in Margaret Healy, *William Shakespeare, 'Richard II'* (Plymouth, 1998), p. 28.

81. For a reading of the play in terms of 'elective monarchy', see Stuart M. Kurland, '*Hamlet* and the Scottish succession', *SEL* 34 (1994), 279–300. I owe this reference to Willy Maley.

82. See Lawrence Danson, *Shakespeare's Dramatic Genres* (Oxford, 2000), for discussion of the relationship between generic form and subject matter. For a wider discussion of topical details and their significance, see David M. Bevington, *Tudor Drama and Politics: A Critical Approach to Topical Meaning* (Cambridge, Mass., 1968).

83. *Letter-Book of Gabriel Harvey, A.D. 1573–1580*, ed. Edward John Long Scott (London, 1884), p. 79. John Wilders argues that Shakespeare read Machiavelli; see *The Lost Garden: A View of Shakespeare's English and Roman Plays* (Basingstoke, 1978), pp. 48–9.

84. The most sustained analysis of an early seventeenth-century English reader is contained in Kevin Sharpe, *Reading Revolutions: the Politics of Reading in Early Modern England* (New Haven, 2000). Sharpe shows that his subject, Sir William Drake (1606–69) especially valued the works of Guicciardini, Machiavelli, Livy and Tacitus (p. 80).

85. Lisa Jardine and Anthony Grafton, '"Studied for Action": how Gabriel Harvey read his Livy', *P & P* 129 (1990), 30–78; Eugene R. Kintgen, *Reading in Tudor England* (Pittsburgh, 1996), pp. 182–3; Heidi Brayman Hackel, 'The "great variety" of readers and early modern reading practices', in Kastan, ed., *Companion to Shakespeare*, pp. 139–57. Similar conclusions are reached in D.R. Woolf, *Reading History in Early Modern England* (Cambridge, 2000).

86. See Ann Moss, *Printed Commonplace-Books and the Structuring of Renaissance Thought* (Oxford, 1996), ch. 6.

87. See Moss, *Printed Commonplace-Books*, pp. 209–10, *passim*.

88. See Marie Axton, *The Queen's Two Bodies: Drama and the Elizabethan Succession* (London, 1977), pp. 39–41, 45–7; Stephen Alford, *The Early Elizabethan Polity: William Cecil and the Succession Crisis, 1558–1569* (Cambridge, 1998), pp. 111–17. See also Greg Walker, *The Politics of Performance in Early Renaissance Drama* (Cambridge, 1998), ch. 6.

89. Anon., *The Tragedy of Locrine*, ed. Ronald B. McKerrow (Oxford, 1908).

90. See R.J. Mulryne, 'Nationality and language in Thomas Kyd's *The Spanish Tragedy*', in Jean-Pierre Maquerlot and Michèle Willems, eds, *Travel and Drama in Shakespeare's Time* (Cambridge, 1996), pp. 87–105; Hadfield, *Literature, Travel, and Colonial Writing*, pp. 202–17; Sara Jane Steen, 'The crime of marriage: Arbella Stuart and *The Duchess of Malfi*', *SCJ* 22 (1991), 61–76.

91. See Richard Dutton, *Mastering the Revels: The Regulation and Censorship of English Renaissance Drama* (Basingstoke, 1991), and *Licensing, Censorship and Authorship in Early Modern England* (Basingstoke, 2000).

92. For a recent analysis of the reasons for the play's suppression, see Richard Dutton, 'Receiving offence: *A Game at Chess* again', in Andrew Hadfield, ed., *Literature and Censorship in Renaissance England* (Basingstoke, 2001), pp. 50–71.

93. See Janet Clare, 'Censorship and negotiation', in Hadfield, ed., *Literature and Censorship in Renaissance England*, pp. 17–30, at p. 29. See also Clare, *'Art made tongue-tied by authority'*; Annabel Patterson, *Censorship and Interpretation: The Conditions of Writing and Reading in Early Modern England* (Madison, 1984).

94. See Clegg, *Press Censorship in Elizabethan England*.

95. Duncan-Jones, *Sir Philip Sidney*, pp. 148–52; David Lindley, ed., *Court Masques: Jacobean and Caroline Entertainments, 1605–1640* (Oxford, 1995), pp. 74–91; Martin Butler, 'Ben Jonson and the limits of courtly panegyric', in Kevin Sharpe and Peter Lake, eds, *Culture and Politics in Early Stuart England* (Basingstoke, 1994), pp. 91–116.

96. Axton, *Queen's Two Bodies*.

97. Peter E. McCullough, *Sermons at Court: Politics and Religion in Elizabethan and Jacobean Preaching* (Cambridge, 1998), chs 2–4.

98. J.S. Roskell, 'Perspectives in English parliamentary history', in E.B. Fryde and Edward Miller, eds, *Historical Studies of the English Parliament, II, 1399–1603* (Cambridge, 1970), pp. 296–323; Loach, *Parliament under the Tudors*, introduction. For more extensive details of Elizabethan parliamentary history, see Neale, *Elizabeth I and her Parliaments*.

99. David Womersley, 'Sir Henry Saville's translation of Tacitus and the political interpretation of Elizabethan texts', *RES*, n.s. 42 (1991), 313–42. Key accounts of Elizabethan 'high' politics are Conyers Read's two-volume biography of William Cecil, Lord Burghley, *Mr. Secretary Cecil and Queen Elizabeth* and *Lord Burghley and Queen Elizabeth*, 2 vols (London, 1955, 1960); Wallace McCaffrey, *Elizabeth I* (London, 1993).

100. For discussion, see Hadfield, *Literature, Travel, and Colonial Writing*, ch. 1. This topic is the subject of a forthcoming thesis by Rebecca Nesvett at the University of Wales, Aberystwyth.

101. Mark Thornton Burnett, *Masters and Servants in English Renaissance Drama and Culture: Authority and Obedience* (Basingstoke, 1997), p. 186. I have borrowed the term 'articulate citizen' from Arthur B. Ferguson, *The Articulate Citizen and the English Renaissance* (Durham, NC, 1965). For one version of this story, see Hadfield, *Literature, Travel, and Colonial Writing*. See also Patterson, *Reading Holinshed's 'Chronicles'*.

102. Guy, ed., *Reign of Elizabeth I*, introduction, pp. 6–7; Hammer, *Polarisation of Elizabethan Politics*.

103. Patrick Collinson, 'Ecclesiastical vitriol: religious satire in the 1590s and the invention of puritanism'; Jim Sharpe, 'Social strain and social dislocation, 1585–1603', in Guy, ed., *Reign of Elizabeth I*, pp. 150–70, 192–211.

104. Lacey, *Robert, Earl of Essex*, chs 28–9; Hammer, *Polarisation of Elizabethan Politics*, pt 2.

105. Guy, ed., *Reign of Elizabeth I*, introduction, p. 15.

106. Sommerville, *Politics and Ideology in England*, pt 1.

107. For details see Hadfield, *Literature, Travel, and Colonial Writing*, ch. 1; Worden, *Sound of Virtue*.

108. J.E. Neale, 'Peter Wentworth', in Fryde and Miller, eds, *Historical Studies of the English Parliament*, pp. 246–95, at p. 258. See also Neale, *Elizabeth I and her Parliaments*, pp. 251–66. More generally, see Guy, ed., *Reign of Elizabeth I*, pp. 11–12; McLaren, *Political Culture in the Reign of Elizabeth I*, pp. 189–94.

109. See, for example, David Zaret, *Origins of Democratic Culture: Printing, Petitions, and the Public Sphere in Early Modern England* (Princeton, 2000); Tessa Watt, *Cheap Print and Popular Piety, 1550–1640* (Cambridge, 1991).

110. Worden, *Sound of Virtue*, pt 1; Andrew Hadfield, *Literature, Politics and National Identity: Reformation to Renaissance* (Cambridge, 1994), introduction.

111. See, for example, A.L. Rowse, *The England of Elizabeth* (London, 1950); Neville Williams, *The Life and Times of Elizabeth I* (London, 1972). For comment, see Helen Hackett, *Virgin Mother, Maiden Queen: Elizabeth I and the Cult of the Virgin Mary* (Basingstoke, 1995).

112. For analysis, see Jennifer Loach and Robert Tittler, eds, *The Mid-Tudor Polity, c.1540–1560* (Basingstoke, 1980).

113. John N. King, *English Reformation Literature: The Tudor Origins of the Protestant Tradition* (Princeton, 1982); W.K. Jordan, *Edward VI: The Young King* (Cambridge, Mass., 1971).

114. David Loades, *The Reign of Mary Tudor: Politics, Government and Religion in England, 1553–58* (2nd edn, London, 1991).

115. David Loades, *Two Tudor Conspiracies* (Cambridge, 1965); Fletcher, *Tudor Rebellions*, chs 5–7.

116. Antonia Fraser, *Mary Queen of Scots* (London, 1969), p. 83.

117. Susan Doran, 'Why did Elizabeth not marry?', in Julia M. Walker, ed., *Dissing Elizabeth: Negative Representations of Gloriana* (Durham, NC, 1998), pp. 30–59, and *Monarchy and Matriarchy: The Courtships of Elizabeth I* (London, 1996).

118. *The Letters of Arbella Stuart*, ed. Sara Jane Steen (Oxford, 1994), p. 30. See also Susan Doran, '"Revenge her most foul and unnatural murder?": the impact of Mary Stuart's execution on Anglo-Scottish relations', *History* 85 (2000), 589–612.

119. McLaren, *Political Culture in the Reign of Elizabeth I*, p. 9.

120. Of course, it would be wrong to assume that such ideas developed suddenly in the late sixteenth century and that there was not a long medieval tradition behind attempts to control the public actions of the monarch; see Coleman, *History of Political Thought*, II, ch. 1.

121. See James Emerson Phillips, *Images of a Queen: Mary Stuart in Sixteenth-Century Literature* (Berkeley, 1964); J.O. Bartley, *Teague, Shenkin and Sawney: Being an Historical Study of the earliest Irish, Welsh and Scottish Characters in English Plays* (Cork, 1954), pt 4.

122. For analysis see Anne Barton, '"He that plays the king": Ford's *Perkin Warbeck*', in *Essays, Mainly Shakespearean* (Cambridge, 1994), pp. 234–60.

123. Harry V. Jaffa, 'The limits of politics: *King Lear*, Act I, scene 1', in Allan Bloom with Harry V. Jaffa, *Shakespeare's Politics* (Chicago, 1981, rpt of 1964), pp. 113–45.

124. Thomas Heywood, *If You Know Not Me You Know Nobody, Parts One and Two*, ed. Madeleine Doran, 2 vols (Oxford, 1935).

125. See Lisa Jardine, *Reading Shakespeare Historically* (London, 1996), pp. 3–14; Willy Maley, '"This sceptred isle": Shakespeare and the British problem', in John Joughin, ed., *Shakespeare and National Culture* (Manchester, 1997), pp. 83–108; Clare, *'Art made tongue-tied by authority'*, pp. 92–5.

126. See above, p. 66.

127. See above, p. 82.

128. On this reading of *Hamlet*, see Howard Erskine-Hill, *Poetry and the Realm of Politics: Shakespeare to Dryden* (Oxford, 1996), pp. 99–107.

129. Donna B. Hamilton, *Virgil and The 'Tempest': The Politics of Imitation* (Columbus, Ohio, 1990); Curtis C. Breight, '"Treason doth never prosper": *The Tempest* and the discourse of treason', *SQ* 41 (1990), 1–28; Hadfield, *Literature, Travel, and Colonial Writing*, pp. 242–54.

130. Martin Dzelzainis, 'Shakespeare and political thought', in Kastan, ed., *Companion to Shakespeare*, pp. 100–16, at p. 114.

131. Peter Burke, 'Tacitism', in T.A. Dorey, ed., *Tacitus* (London, 1969), pp. 149–71.

132. Anon. *The Tragedie of Claudius Tiberius Nero, Romes greatest Tyrant Truly represented out of the purest Records of those times* (London, 1607); Tacitus, *Annals*, pt 1.

133. *The Ende of Nero and Beginning of Galba: Fower Bookes of the Histories of Cornelius Tacitus. The Life of Agricola* (Oxford, 1591); *The Annales of Cornelius Tacitus. The Description of Germanie* (London, 1598). Markku Peltonen has pointed out the significance of translations in developing political ideas in early modern England; see *Classical Humanism and Republicanism*, introduction. See also Sharpe, *Reading Revolutions*, ch. 5.

134. William Shakespeare, *King Edward III*, ed. Giorgio Melchiori (Cambridge, 1998); Tacitus, *On Imperial Rome*, trans. Michael Grant (Harmondsworth, 1956), pt 1.

135. See John Sutherland and Cedric Watts, *Henry V, War Criminal? & Other Shakespeare Puzzles* (Oxford, 2000), pp. 108–16. For a recent account of the effect of the play on audiences, which attempts to determine how an original performance might have seemed to the first audience, see Pauline Kiernan, *Staging Shakespeare at the New Globe* (Cambridge, 1999), pt 2.

136. Some commentators have argued that Shakespeare's history plays are as
     much about the process of history as the events they represent. See, for
     example, Holderness, *Shakespeare: The Histories*; Paola Pugliatti, *Shakespeare
     the Historian* (Basingstoke, 1996). On the concept of 'impartiality' and its
     importance in the Renaissance, see Patterson, *Reading Holinshed's 'Chronicles'*.

137. On Elizabethan chivalry see Richard C. McCoy, *The Rites of Knighthood: The
     Literature and Politics of Elizabethan Chivalry* (Berkeley, 1989).

138. For a provocative recent analysis, see Ortwin de Graef, '"Sweet dreams,
     monstered nothings": catechresis in Kant and *Coriolanus*', in Andrew
     Hadfield, Dominic Rainsford and Tim Woods, eds, *The Ethics in Literature*
     (Basingstoke, 1999), pp. 231–47.

139. Bradford, 'Stuart absolutism'; Womersley, 'Sir Henry Saville'.

140. Erskine-Hill, *Poetry and the Realm of Politics*, pt 1.

141. Worden, 'Shakespeare and politics', p. 6. See also Wells, *Shakespeare,
     Politics and the State*.

142. See David McPherson, *Shakespeare, Jonson, and the Myth of Venice* (Newark,
     1990).

143. See C.C. Huffman, *Coriolanus in Context* (Lewisburg, 1971); Anne Barton,
     'Livy, Machiavelli and *Coriolanus*', in *Essays, Mainly Shakespearean*,
     pp. 136–60.

144. *Titus Andronicus*, ed. Jonathan Bate (London, 1995), introduction,
     pp. 17–21; Dzelzainis, 'Shakespeare and political thought', pp. 106–7.

145. See Jonathan Bate, 'The Elizabethans in Italy', in Maquerlot and Willems,
     eds, *Travel and Drama in Shakespeare's Time*, pp. 55–74; Hadfield, *Literature,
     Travel, and Colonial Writing*, ch. 4.

146. Gurr, *Shakespearean Stage*, p. 213.

147. See Thomas L. Berger and Jesse M. Lander, 'Shakespeare in print,
     1593–1640', in Kastan, ed., *Companion to Shakespeare*, pp. 395–413. See
     also the comments in Woolf, *Reading History in Early Modern England*,
     pp. 32–5.

148. For two very different interpretations, see Gurr, *Shakespearian Playing
     Companies*, p. 288, n. 21 (citing Leeds Barroll); Clare, *'Art made tongue-tied
     by authority'*, pp. 68–72.

149. See Richard Helgerson, *Self-Crowned Laureates: Spenser, Jonson, Milton and
     the Literary System* (Berkeley, 1983).

150. Peter Blayney, 'The publication of playbooks', in John D. Cox and David
     Scott Kastan, eds, *A New History of Early English Drama* (New York, 1997),
     pp. 383–422.

151. Blayney, 'Publication of playbooks', p. 388.

152. Greg Walker, 'Playing by the book: early Tudor drama and the printed
     text', in *Politics of Performance*, pp. 6–50.

153. Heidi Brayman Hackel, 'The "great variety" of readers and early modern reading practices', in Kastan, ed., *Companion to Shakespeare*, pp. 139–57. *The First Folio of Shakespeare: A Transcript of Contemporary Marginalia in a Copy of the Kodama Memorial Library of Meisei University*, ed. Akihiro Yamada (Tokyo, 1998), catalogues the annotations of one seventeenth-century reader. See also the comments in David Scott Kastan, *Shakespeare and the Book* (Cambridge, 2001), *passim*.

154. See McConica, *English Humanists and Reformation Politics*; Ferguson, *Articulate Citizen*; Glenn Burgess, *The Politics of the Ancient Constitution: An Introduction to English Political Thought, 1603–1642* (Basingstoke, 1992), ch. 2.

155. Walker, *Plays of Persuasion*. See also the useful debate staged in Dawson and Yachnin, *Culture of Playgoing in Shakespeare's England*.

156. See Axton, *Queen's Two Bodies*. See also Hadfield, *Literature, Travel, and Colonial Writing*, pp. 176–9; 'The Spanish Tragedy, the Alençon marriage plans, and John Stubbs's *Discoverie of a Gaping Gulf*', *N & Q* 245 (March 2000), 42–3.

157. See, for example, Axton, *Queen's Two Bodies*, *passim*; Kristen Poole, *Radical Religion from Shakespeare to Milton: Figures of Nonconformity in Early Modern England* (Cambridge, 2000), chs 1–2; Bevington, *Tudor Drama and Politics*.

158. See, for example, Louis A. Montrose, ''A Midsummer Night's Dream and the shaping fantasies of Elizabethan culture: gender, power, form', in Margaret W. Ferguson, Maureen Quilligan and Nancy J. Vickers, eds, *Rewriting the Renaissance* (Chicago, 1986), pp. 65–87.

159. On the possible reasons for Shakespeare's decision to write romantic rather than satirical comedies or comedies of humours, see James P. Bednarz, *Shakespeare and the Poets' War* (New York, 2001).

1: TRUE AND FALSE SOVEREIGNS IN THE ENGLISH HISTORY PLAYS

1. For analysis, see Phyllis Rackin, *Stages of History: Shakespeare's English Chronicles* (Ithaca, 1990), pp. 129–37; Margaret Healy, *William Shakespeare, 'Richard II'* (Plymouth, 1998), ch. 3.

2. As Ronald Knowles notes, the appearance of several Edmund Mortimers in the fourteenth and fifteenth centuries confused chroniclers, and the confusion was repeated in Shakespeare's *1 Henry IV*, and *1* and *2 Henry VI* (*2 Henry VI*, p. 213).

3. For details, see the genealogical charts in the Appendix I.

4. On the stage Machiavel, see Una Ellis-Fermor, *The Jacobean Drama* (London, 1965), pp. 11–16.

5. Convenient tables and summaries are provided in C.R.N. Routh, *Who's Who in Tudor England* (rev. Peter Holmes) (London, 1990, rpt of 1964), pp. xiv–xvii, 1–2.

6. For discussion, see Lily B. Campbell, *Shakespeare's 'Histories': Mirrors of Elizabethan Policy* (San Marino, Ca., 1947), ch. 12; Howard Erskine-Hill, *Poetry and the Realm of Politics: Shakespeare to Dryden* (Oxford, 1996), pp. 108–9.

7. See Sydney Anglo, *Images of Tudor Kingship* (Guildford, 1992), ch. 4.

8. J.E. Neale, *Queen Elizabeth* (London, 1934), pp. 17–18.

9. See Campbell, *Shakespeare's 'Histories'*, pp. 137–8; John Guy, *Tudor England* (Oxford, 1988), pp. 268–9; Antonia Fraser, *Mary Queen of Scots* (London, 1969), p. 83.

10. *King Edward III*, ed. Giorgio Melchiori (Cambridge, 1998), pp. 3–9.

11. Campbell, *Shakespeare's 'Histories'*, p. 70.

12. For a discussion of the rival candidates for the succession, see anon., *Leicester's Commonwealth: The Copy of a letter Written by a Master of Art of Cambridge (1584) and Related Documents*, ed. D.C. Peck (Athens, Ohio, 1985), introduction. On the exclusion of the Stuart line see G.R. Elton, *The Parliament of England, 1559–1581* (Cambridge, 1986), pp. 374–9.

13. Rackin, *Stages of History*, p. 31.

14. For an overview, see Alexander Leggatt, *English Drama: Shakespeare to the Restoration, 1590–1660* (Harlow, 1988); Benjamin Griffin, *Playing the Past: Approaches to English Historical Drama, 1385–1600* (Woodbridge, 2001). For analysis, see Ivo Kamps, *Historiography and Ideology in Stuart Drama* (Cambridge, 1996).

15. Campbell, *Shakespeare's 'Histories'*, pp. 192–3; Janet Clare, *'Art made tongue-tied by authority': Elizabethan and Jacobean Dramatic Censorship* (2nd edn, Manchester, 1999), pp. 68–72.

16. See John N. King, *Tudor Royal Iconography: Literature and Art in an Age of Religious Crisis* (Princeton, 1989).

17. Anglo, *Images of Tudor Kingship*, ch. 5; Greg Walker, *Persuasive Fictions: Faction, Faith and Political Culture in the Reign of Henry VIII* (Aldershot, 1996), ch. 4.

18. Felix Raab, *The English Face of Machiavelli: A Changing Interpretation, 1500–1700* (London, 1965), chs 1–3; Anglo, *Images of Tudor Kingship*, pp. 10–15, *passim*.

19. See David Zaret, *Origins of Democratic Culture: Printing, Petitions, and the Public Sphere in Early Modern England* (Princeton, 2000).

20. J.P. Sommerville, *Politics and Ideology in England, 1603–1640* (Harlow, 1986), ch. 6. On Elizabeth's establishment of a *via media*, see W.P. Haugaard, *Elizabeth and the English Reformation* (Cambridge, 1968). See above, pp. 25–6.

21. See, for example, Robin Headlam Wells, *Shakespeare, Politics and the State* (Basingstoke, 1986), pp. 92–4; Campbell, *Shakespeare's 'Histories'*, pp. 216–17; Catherine Belsey, *The Subject of Tragedy: Identity and Difference in Renaissance Drama* (London, 1985), pp. 94–6.

22. Anthony Fletcher, *Tudor Rebellions* (3rd edn, Harlow, 1983), pp. 82–96; Fraser, *Mary Queen of Scots*, ch. 21; Penry Williams, *The Tudor Regime* (Oxford, 1979), pp. 343–4, *passim*.

23. J.E. Neale, *Queen Elizabeth* (London, 1934), chs 11–12; Andrew Hadfield, 'The art of fiction: poetry and politics in Reformation England', *Leeds Studies in English*, n.s. 23 (1992), 127–56, at p. 144.

24. 'An Homilie Agaynst Disobedience and Wylful Rebellion', in *Certain Sermons Appointed by the Queen's Majesty* (1574) (Cambridge, 1850), pp. 551–99, at pp. 557–8.

25. Patrick Collinson, *The Birthpangs of Protestant England: Religious and Cultural Change in the Sixteenth and Seventeenth Centuries* (Basingstoke, 1988), ch. 4; Tessa Watt, *Cheap Print and Popular Piety, 1550–1640* (Cambridge, 1991). The development and spread of the Reformation is, of course, a contested issue among historians; for differing accounts, see A.G. Dickens, *The English Reformation* (rev. edn, London, 1986); J.J. Scarisbrick, *The Reformation and the English People* (Oxford, 1984). Nevertheless, my generalization holds true.

26. Dickens, *English Reformation*, chs 10–12; Quentin Skinner, *The Foundations of Modern Political Thought* (Cambridge, 1978), II, pt. 3. See above, pp. 92–7.

27. John N. King, *English Reformation Literature: The Tudor Origins of the Protestant Tradition* (Princeton, 1982).

28. On Wyatt's rebellion, see Fletcher, *Tudor Rebellions*, pp. 69–81.

29. Patrick Collinson, *The Elizabethan Puritan Movement* (Oxford, 1967) and *Birthpangs of Protestant England*, ch. 4.

30. For commentary, see William Baldwin *et al.*, *The Mirror for Magistrates*, ed. Lily B. Campbell (Cambridge, 1938), introduction; Andrew Hadfield, *Literature, Politics and National Identity: Reformation to Renaissance* (Cambridge, 1994), ch. 3.

31. Baldwin *et al.*, *Mirror for Magistrates*, ed. Campbell, p. 63. Subsequent references to this edition in parentheses in the text.

32. However, Tresilian does play a significant role in anon., *The First Part of the Reign of King Richard the Second or Thomas of Woodstock*, ed. Wilhelmina P. Frijlinck (Oxford, 1929), and he is led off to be hanged at the end as is his fate in the *Mirror*. A.R. Humphreys suggests that Shakespeare did make use of the *Mirror* for his portrayal of various aristocrats in the history plays; *2 King Henry IV* (London, 1966), introduction, pp. xxxvi–xxxvii.

33. W.K. Jordan, *Edward VI: The Young King* (Cambridge, Mass., 1971), ch. 3; King, *English Reformation Literature*, ch. 3.

34. Campbell, *Shakespeare's 'Histories'*, p. 215; E.M.W. Tillyard, *The Elizabethan World Picture* (Harmondsworth, 1972, rpt of 1943), pp. 65–6.

35. Sommerville, *Politics and Ideology in England*, pp. 190–2.

36. For Luther's political thought, see *Secular Authority: To What Extent It Should Be Obeyed* (1523), in John Dillenberger, ed., *Martin Luther: Selections from his Writings* (New York, 1961), pp. 363–402. On Calvin's political thought and its influence, see Skinner, *Foundations of Modern Political Thought*, II, pp. 235–8. On predestination, see François Wendel, *Calvin: The Origins and Development of his Religious Thought*, trans. Philip Maret (London, 1963), pp. 263–84.

37. Cited in Hadfield, *Literature, Politics and National Identity*, pp. 98–9.

38. Jean Calvin, *The Institution of the Christian Religion*, trans. Thomas Norton (1582), p. 748. Calvin's political and religious doctrines were also available in a condensed form in *Aphorismes of Christian Religion: Or, a verie Compendious abridgement of M.I. Calvins Institutions, set forth in short sentences methodically by M.I. Piscator*, trans. Henry Holland (London, 1596).

39. King, *English Reformation Literature*, pp. 114, 369.

40. Quentin Skinner, *The Foundations of Modern Political Thought*, 2 vols (Cambridge, 1978), II, pp. 210–11, 223–4, 234–5; Collinson, *Elizabethan Puritan Movement*, pt 3; Dickens, *English Reformation*, pp. 386–94, *passim*.

41. Annabel Patterson, *Reading Holinshed's 'Chronicles'* (Chicago, 1994), p. 251.

42. See the respective *DNB* entries.

43. Edward Hall, *The Union of the Two Noble and Illustre Famelies of Lancastre & Yorke* (1548) (London, 1809), pp. v–vi. Subsequent references to this edition in parentheses in the text.

44. Although earlier Hall had admitted that Henry was 'not so well beloved of all, as of some highly disdayned' (p. 3).

45. See also Raphael Holinshed, *Chronicles of England, Scotland and Ireland* (1587), III, pp. 497–8.

46. See also Holinshed, *Chronicles*, III, p. 501.

47. It may well be that the reference to a 'croucheback' contains a pointed reference to the eventual rule of Richard III, the nemesis of both the House of York and those who supported their claims. See also Holinshed, *Chronicles*, III, p. 505.

48. Holinshed, *Chronicles*, III, pp. 488–517; anon., *The First Part of the Reign of King Richard the Second*. Shakespeare's play assumes that the audience would know that Thomas Mowbray, Duke of Norfolk, was involved in Woodstock's murder; see Holinshed, *Chronicles*, III, pp. 493–5. See also R. Malcolm Smuts, *Culture and Power in England, 1585–1685* (Basingstoke, 1999), pp. 75–6.

49. See D.R. Woolf, *Reading History in Early Modern England* (Cambridge, 2000), pp. 32–5.

50. I have omitted John Foxe, author of *The Acts and Monuments of the Christian Church (Foxe's Book of Martyrs)* (1563, 1570, 1583), ed. David G. Newcombe and Michael Pidd (facsimile on CD-Rom) (Oxford, 2001). Foxe was used as a source for a number of literary works, most notably *Sir John Oldcastle, part one*; see *The Oldcastle Controversy: Sir John Oldcastle, Part I and The Famous Victories of Henry V*, anon., ed. Peter Corbin and Douglas Sedge (Manchester, 1991). Foxe's reading of history was much more obviously providentialist than Holinshed's, Hall's and the *Mirror*'s, but he was not a straightforward defender of the rights of kings, and was frequently critical of their oppressions of Protestants; see J.F. Mozeley, *John Foxe and his Book* (London, 1940).

51. Patterson, *Reading Holinshed's 'Chronicles'*, pp. 112–17. See above, pp. 15–16.

52. Patterson, *Reading Holinshed's 'Chronicles'*, p. ix, *passim*. See also her *Early Modern Liberalism* (Cambridge, 1997). Significantly enough, Hall makes a pointed reference to a seditious chronicle written by an abbot during the reign of Henry IV, that disparages the King and falsifies the historical record out of spite (*Union*, p. 16).

53. Patterson, *Reading Holinshed's 'Chronicles'*, ch. 11; Clare, *'Art made tongue-tied by authority'*, ch. 3.

54. As related in Holinshed, *Chronicles*, III, pp. 545–6. Holinshed does not show the machinations of the bishops, which is Shakespeare's invention. A recent analysis of Henry's claims is made in John Sutherland and Cedric Watts, *Henry V, War Criminal? & Other Shakespeare Puzzles* (Oxford, 2000), pp. 117–25. Watts concludes that Henry's claim is not valid.

55. Peter C. Herman, '"O, 'tis a gallant king": Shakespeare's *Henry V* and the crisis of the 1590s', in Dale Hoak, ed., *Tudor Political Culture* (Cambridge, 1995), pp. 204–25, at pp. 219–20.

56. The most likely source for information on Alexander was Plutarch. See his *Selected Lives of the Noble Grecians and Romans*, trans. Thomas North (1579), ed. Judith Mossman (Ware, 1998), pp. 385–465. For analysis of the comparison, see Judith Mossman, '*Henry V* and Plutarch's *Alexander*', *SQ* 45 (1994), 57–73.

57. On Henry's education, see Stephen Greenblatt, 'Invisible bullets', in *Shakespearean Negotiations: The Circulation of Social Energy in Renaissance England* (Oxford, 1988), pp. 21–65, at pp. 40–56. On Tamburlaine see Christopher Marlowe, *Tamburlaine the Great* (*c.* 1587, published 1590), in *The Complete Plays*, ed. Mark Thornton Burnett (London, 1999). Alexander's conquests are alluded to in *Tamburlaine* (e.g., at 1.1.152–4). For a fuller comparison between the two plays, see R.W. Battenhouse, 'The relation of *Henry V* to *Tamburlaine*', *SQ* 27 (1974), 71–9.

58. See Raab, *English Face of Machiavelli*, ch. 3.

59. See Herman, 'O, 'tis a gallant king'.

60. Based on Holinshed, *Chronicles*, III, pp. 545–6.

61. A.N. McLaren, *Political Culture in the Reign of Elizabeth I: Queen and Commonwealth, 1558–1585* (Cambridge, 1999); James Emerson Phillips, *Images of a Queen: Mary Stuart in Sixteenth-Century Literature* (Berkeley, 1964). As McLaren points out, such arguments clearly had uncomfortable implications concerning Elizabeth's right to rule.

62. For comment, see Philip Edwards, *Threshold of a Nation: A Study in English and Irish Drama* (Cambridge, 1979), pp. 74–86; Lisa Jardine, *Reading Shakespeare Historically* (London, 1996), pp. 7–11.

63. For a reading of these as deliberate ironies, see Herman, 'O, 'tis a gallant king', pp. 207, 219. The ironies in Shakespeare's play appear more pointed if it is read alongside *The Famous Victories of Henry V* (1598), one of its sources; see anon., *Oldcastle Controversy*, ed. Corbin and Sedge, pp. 21–8.

64. Caroline Spurgeon, *Shakespeare's Imagery and What it Tells Us* (Cambridge, 1965, rpt of 1935), pp. 220–3. On Richard II as a 'player king', see Margaret Healy, *William Shakespeare, 'Richard II'* (Plymouth, 1998), ch. 3.

65. For an excellent discussion see David Scott Kastan, 'Proud majesty made a subject: Shakespeare and the spectacle of rule', *SQ* 37 (1986), 459–75. See also Anglo, *Images of Tudor Kingship*, chs 1, 5.

66. Phyllis Rackin, *Stages of History: Shakespeare's English Chronicles* (Ithaca, 1990), pp. 71–2, 78.

67. See, for example, Roy Strong, *The Cult of Elizabeth: Elizabethan Portraiture and Pageantry* (London, 1977); Philippa Berry, *Of Chastity and Power: Elizabethan Literature and the Unmarried Queen* (London, 1989).

68. For recent commentary, see Michael Neill, 'Broken English and broken Irish: nation, language and the optic of power in Shakespeare's histories', *SQ* 45 (1994), 18–22; Claire McEachern, *The Poetics of English Nationhood, 1590–1612* (Cambridge, 1996), ch. 3; David J. Baker, *Between Nations: Shakespeare, Spenser, Marvell and the Question of Britain* (Stanford, 1997), ch. 1. On the dialogue between Henry and Katherine, see Jardine, *Reading Shakespeare Historically*, pp. 10–12.

69. On the status and role of later Tudor parliaments, see Norman Jones, 'Parliament and the political society of Elizabethan England', in Hoak, ed., *Tudor Political Culture*, pp. 226–42.

70. Thomas Smith, *De Republica Anglorum: A Discourse on the Commonwealth of England* (1583), ed. L. Alston (Shannon, 1972, rpt of 1906), pp. 30–1. Subsequent references to this edition in parentheses in the text.

71. For analysis, see McLaren, *Political Culture in the Reign of Elizabeth I*, pp. 210–11.

72. Niccolò Machiavelli, *The Arte of Warre* (1560), trans. Peter Whitehorne (London, 1905), p. 44. See also Barnaby Riche, *Allarme to England*,

foreshewing what perilles are procured, where the people live without regard of Martiall lawe (London, 1578), pt 3.

73. Machiavelli, *Arte of Warre*, pp. 80–1, *passim*; Riche, *Allarme to England*, pt 4.

74. This image might be read alongside Menenius's fable of the belly in *Coriolanus*; see above, pp. 172–7.

75. For an exploration of early modern conceptions of carnival in relation to Shakespeare, see Ronald Knowles, ed., *Shakespeare and Carnival: After Bakhtin* (Basingstoke, 1998).

76. Thomas Dekker, *The Shoemaker's Holiday*, ed. Anthony Parr (London, 1990), introduction, pp. xvii–xxv.

77. The classic study is Ernst H. Kantorowicz, *The King's Two Bodies: A Study in Mediaeval Political Theology* (Princeton, 1957). See also Marie Axton, *The Queen's Two Bodies: Drama and the Elizabethan Succession* (London, 1977). Cogent criticisms are made in David Norbrook, 'The Emperor's new body? *Richard II*, Ernst Kantorowicz, and the politics of Shakespeare criticism', *TP* 10 (1996), 329–57. Norbrook suggests that political criticism of the monarch was more often based on reading Greek and Roman political theory or actual study of the political institutions of England.

78. For analysis, see Jonathan Dollimore and Alan Sinfield, 'History and ideology: the instance of *Henry V*', in John Drakakis, ed., *Alternative Shakespeares* (London, 1985), pp. 206–27, at pp. 221–3.

79. See Frances Yates, *Astraea: The Imperial Theme in the Sixteenth Century* (London, 1975); Strong, *Cult of Elizabeth*; Helen Hackett, *Virgin Mother, Maiden Queen: Elizabeth I and the Cult of the Virgin Mary* (Basingstoke, 1995), ch. 6.

80. See *Henry V*, ed. Gary Taylor (Oxford, 1982), p. 18; Willy Maley, '"This sceptred isle": Shakespeare and the British problem', in John J. Joughin, ed., *Shakespeare and National Culture* (Manchester, 1997), pp. 83–108, at p. 98.

81. Graham Holderness, *Shakespeare: The Histories* (Basingstoke, 2000), p. 155; Rackin, *Stages of History*, pp. 228–9.

82. *Henry V*, ed. Taylor, p. 312; Annabel Patterson, *Shakespeare and the Popular Voice* (Oxford, 1989), pp. 76–7. It is also possible that they were never performed on stage.

83. Cited in *King Richard II*, ed. Peter Ure (London, 1961, rpt of 1956), introduction, p. lix. See also Kastan, 'Proud majesty made a subject', p. 468.

84. For a definition of tribune, see Sir Paul Harvey, *The Oxford Companion to Classical Literature* (Oxford, 1984, rpt of 1937), pp. 436–7.

85. See also Giovanni Botero, *Observations Upon the Lives of Alexander, Caesar, Scipio; newly Englished* (London, 1602), for another balanced assessment of Julius Caesar's controversial life, showing what an ambiguous figure he was for English readers in the late sixteenth and early seventeenth centuries.

86. A recent analysis of Henry's behaviour in war is John Sutherland, 'Henry V, war criminal?', in Sutherland and Watts, *Henry V, War Criminal?*, pp. 108–16.

87. Henry's exhortation to his men should be read alongside the debate over the merits of showing war wounds to the citizens in *Coriolanus* 2.3. Here, Coriolanus's refusal to show his wounds isolates him from the people he has saved from the Volscians.

88. J.G.A. Pocock, *The Machiavellian Moment: Florentine Political Thought and the Atlantic Republican Tradition* (Princeton, 1975), p. 201.

89. Machiavelli, *Art of Warre*, pp. 80–1, *passim*; *The Discourses*, trans. Leslie J. Walker, ed. Bernard Crick (Harmondsworth, 1970), pp. 274–81.

90. Markku Peltonen, *Classical Humanism and Republicanism in English Political Thought, 1570–1640* (Cambridge, 1995), pp. 101–2.

91. Pocock, *Machiavellian Moment*, p. 201.

92. Quentin Skinner, *Machiavelli* (Oxford, 1981), pp. 73–7.

93. See David Norbrook, '"A liberal tongue": language and rebellion in *Richard II*', in John M. Mucciolo, ed., *Shakespeare's Universe: Renaissance Ideas and Conventions: Essays in Honour of W.R. Elton* (Aldershot, 1996), pp. 37–51.

94. On the relationship between *Henry V* and *The Famous Victories of Henry V*, see William Shakespeare, *King Henry V*, ed. Andrew Gurr (Cambridge, 1992), appendix 1.

95. *King John*, ed. E.A.J. Honigmann (London, 1998, rpt of 1954), introduction, pp. xi–xxxiii, xliii–lix. See also Paola Pugliatti, *Shakespeare the Historian* (Basingstoke, 1996), ch. 6.

96. John was represented elsewhere as a proto-Protestant martyr after the Reformation, his treatment at the hands of the papacy being seen as a sign of the power of the Pope over pre-Reformation kings; see John Bale, *King Johan*, ed. Barry B. Adams (San Marino, 1969); Greg Walker, *Plays of Persuasion: Drama and Politics at the Court of Henry VIII* (Cambridge, 1991), ch. 6.

97. *King John*, ed. Honigmann, introduction, pp. xxvi–xxix.

98. Holinshed, *Chronicles*, III, p. 495.

99. See Norbrook, '"A liberal tongue"', pp. 41–6.

100. See Healy, *Richard II*, p. 8.

101. Smith, *De Republica Anglorum*, p. 14. See also Sir John Fortesque, *A Learned Commendation of the Politique Lawes of England* (London, 1567), and the comments in Constance Jordan, *Shakespeare's Monarchies: Ruler and Subject in the Romances* (Ithaca, 1997), pp. 23–5.

2: THE POWER AND RIGHTS OF THE CROWN

1. I have rejected Theobald's emendation of 'discern' to 'deserve', accepted in Kenneth Muir's Arden 2 edition (1951). Nicholas Brooke adopts 'discern' in his Oxford edition (1990).

2. For recent reflections on this problem, see Bernard Crick, *In Defence of Politics* (Harmondsworth, 1964); Michael J. Oakshott, *Rationalism in Politics and Other Essays* (2nd edn, London, 1981); A.J. Polan, *Lenin and the End of Politics* (London, 1984).

3. For an alternative reading of this episode, see Rebecca W. Bushnell, *Tragedies of Tyrants: Political Thought and Theater in the English Renaissance* (Ithaca, 1990), pp. 140–1.

4. Innocent Gentillet, *A Discourse Upon the Meanes of Wel Governing and Maintaining in Good Peace, A Kingdom, or other Principalitie ... Against Nicholas Machiavell the Florentine*, trans. Simon Patericke (1602) (New York, 1969), p. 222. I have used this translation because it is the version that Shakespeare may well have known; for discussion, see above, pp. 109–10. For a modern translation, see Niccolò Machiavelli, *The Prince*, trans. George Bull (Harmondsworth, 1961), pp. 99–100, or the more scholarly edition by Quentin Skinner and Russell Price (Cambridge, 1988), pp. 61–2. For comment, see Quentin Skinner, *The Foundations of Modern Political Thought* (Cambridge, 1978), I, p. 249. David Norbrook points out that Macbeth's soliloquy before he murders Duncan (1.7.1–28) presents him as 'motivated by Machiavellian virtù' ('*Macbeth* and the politics of historiography', in Kevin Sharpe and Steven N. Zwicker, eds, *Politics of Discourse: The Literature and History of Seventeenth-Century England* (Berkeley, 1987), pp. 78–116, at p. 101.

5. One of a king's primary duties was to protect his subjects; see, for example, Sir Thomas Smith, *De Republica Anglorum: A Discourse on the Commonwealth of England* (1583), ed. L. Alston (Shannon, 1972, rpt of 1906), p. 15.

6. Norbrook, '*Macbeth* and the politics of historiography', p. 95; Brian P. Levack, *The Formation of the British State: England, Scotland and the Union, 1603–1707* (Oxford, 1987), chs 1–2.

7. See Christina H. Garrett, *The Marian Exiles: A Study in the Origins of Elizabethan Puritanism* (Cambridge, 1938).

8. W.B. Patterson, *King James VI and I and the Reunion of Christendom* (Cambridge, 1997); D. Harris Willson, *King James VI and I* (London, 1956), ch. 15.

9. Henry N. Paul, *The Royal Play of 'Macbeth'* (New York, 1948); Bushnell, *Tragedies of Tyrants*, pp. 141–2; Norbrook, '*Macbeth* and the politics of historiography'. James (unlike his predecessors) did not believe that any monarch could cure scrofula, but was interested in the question as it related

to a monarch's powers and image; see Sydney Anglo, *Images of Tudor Kingship* (Guildford, 1992), p. 24.

10. James I, *Basilikon Doron*, in *The Workes* (1616) (Hildesheim and New York, 1971), pp. 137–89, at pp. 155–6; *The Trew Law of Free Monarchies*, in *Workes*, pp. 191–210, at p. 203.

11. James I, *Basilikon Doron*, p. 165; *Trew Law*, pp. 193–5.

12. James I, *Trew Law*, p. 203.

13. James I, *Trew Law*, p. 206.

14. For comment, see above, p. 9; pp. 92–7.

15. James I, *Trew Law*, p. 199; Bushnell, *Tragedies of Tyrants*, pp. 73–4.

16. For contemporary representations of Scotland on the English stage, see J.O. Bartley, *Teague, Shenkin and Sawney: Being an Historical Study of the earliest Irish, Welsh and Scottish Characters in English Plays* (Cork, 1954), pt 4.

17. Raphael Holinshed, *Chronicles of England, Scotland and Ireland* (London, 1587), I, pp. 748–65. A neat inversion of the priorities and claims of James VI and I; see Willson, *James VI and I, passim*.

18. Holinshed, *Chronicles*, V, pp. 264–5.

19. Holinshed, *Chronicles*, V, pp. 269–70.

20. Norbrook, '*Macbeth* and the politics of historiography', p. 94. The question of Scotland's monarchical system is complex and disputed. According to George Buchanan, Scotland was an elective monarchy until the reign of Kenneth III, but even then the succession usually fell to the eldest son of the reigning monarch as long as he was acceptable to the people; see George Buchanan, *The History of Scotland written in Latin by George Buchanan; faithfully rendered into English* (London, 1690), pp. 193–5. Buchanan's *History* was incorporated into Holinshed's *Chronicle of Scotland*, but it is also possible that Shakespeare knew the original Latin text; see Stuart Gillespie, *Shakespeare's Books: A Dictionary of Shakespeare Sources* (London, 2001), pp. 71–4.

21. Anon., *Leicester's Commonwealth: The Copy of a letter Written by a Master of Art of Cambridge (1584) and Related Documents*, ed. D.C. Peck (Athens, Ohio, 1985), pp. 40–1.

22. See Norman Jones, 'Parliament and the political society of Elizabethan England', in Dale Hoak, ed., *Tudor Political Culture* (Cambridge, 1995), pp. 226–42, at pp. 236–7.

23. Cyndia Susan Clegg, *Press Censorship in Elizabethan England* (Cambridge, 1997), pp. 81–9; James I, *Basilikon Doron*, pp. 176–7; Janet Clare, '*Art made tongue-tied by authority': Elizabethan and Jacobean Dramatic Censorship* (2nd edn, Manchester, 1999), chs 3–4.

24. See Howard Erskine-Hill, *Poetry and the Realm of Politics: Shakespeare to Dryden* (Oxford, 1996), pt 1, for discussion.

25. For the most sustained discussion of the two plays, traditionally regarded as rivals for the title of Shakespeare's greatest work, see R.A. Foakes, *Hamlet versus Lear: Cultural Politics and Shakespeare's Art* (Cambridge, 1993). For an argument that the political questions raised in the tragedies overlap with those in the history plays, and which further demonstrates the close links between the two generic forms, see Lawrence Danson, *Shakespeare's Dramatic Genres* (Oxford, 2000).

26. I have not included a discussion of the textual problems of *Hamlet*, for reasons of space and focus. I am assuming that, as with the history plays, the play was read as well as seen on stage. The passages that I discuss are common to both quarto and folio texts and I am assuming that the political significance of each version of the play is identical.

27. Erskine-Hill, *Poetry and the Realm of Politics*, pp. 99–111. I am much indebted to Erskine-Hill's incisive reading of *Hamlet*, even though I cannot fully agree with his conclusion that Shakespeare's political instinct was to side with the *de facto* ruler. See also Stuart M. Kurland, '*Hamlet* and the Scottish succession', *SEL* 34 (1994), 279–300.

28. For details see Antonia Fraser, *Mary Queen of Scots* (London, 1969), ch. 16. See also Jenny Wormald, *Court, Kirk, and Community: Scotland, 1470–1625* (London, 1981), ch. 9.

29. Erskine-Hill, *Poetry and the Realm of Politics*, p. 105.

30. Erskine-Hill, *Poetry and the Realm of Politics*, p. 107.

31. Erskine-Hill, *Poetry and the Realm of Politics*, p. 104. See above n. 20.

32. See, for example, Annabel Patterson, *Censorship and Interpretation: The Conditions of Writing and Reading in Early Modern England* (Madison, 1984); Clare, *'Art made tongue-tied by authority'*; J.W. Lever, *The Tragedy of State* (London, 1971).

33. See, for example, Curtis C. Breight, *Surveillance, Militarism and Drama in the Elizabethan Era* (Basingstoke, 1996); Andrew Hadfield, *Literature, Travel, and Colonial Writing in the English Renaissance, 1545–1625* (Oxford, 1998), ch. 4. Of course, drama at court was equally topical; see Graham Parry, 'The politics of the Jacobean masque', in J.R. Mulryne and Margaret Shewring, eds, *Theatre and Government under the Early Stuarts* (Cambridge, 1993), pp. 87–117.

34. See Lever, *Tragedy of State*; Swapan Chakravorty, *Society and Politics in the Plays of Thomas Middleton* (Oxford, 1996), ch. 5.

35. See Linda Levy Peck, 'John Marston's *The Fawn*: ambivalence and Jacobean courts', in David L. Smith, Richard Strier and David Bevington, eds, *The Theatrical City: Culture, Theatre and Politics in London, 1576–1649* (Cambridge, 1995), pp. 117–36. Castiglione's *Il Cortegiano* was the most influential courtesy book, showing readers how to behave well, in sixteenth-century

Europe; see Peter Burke, *The Fortunes of the Courtier: The European Reception of Castiglione's 'Cortegiano'* (Cambridge, 1995).

36. Annabel Patterson, *Censorship and Interpretation*, ch. 2.

37. On Burghley, see Conyers Read, *Mr. Secretary Cecil and Queen Elizabeth* and *Lord Burghley and Queen Elizabeth*, 2 vols (London, 1955, 1960).

38. Machiavelli, *The Prince*, ch. 23; Gentillet, *Discourse*, pp. 30–62.

39. David Womersley, '*3 Henry VI*: Shakespeare, Tacitus, and parricide', *N & Q* 280 (Dec. 1985), 468–73.

40. Tacitus, *On Imperial Rome*, trans. Michael Grant (Harmondsworth, 1956), p. 329. On Seneca's key influence on Renaissance writers, for his Stoic philosophy and drama, see Reid Barbour, *English Epicures and Stoics: Ancient Legacies in Early Stuart Culture* (Amherst, 1998), *passim*.

41. Tacitus, *On Imperial Rome*, ch. 15.

42. Ben Jonson, for example, was especially concerned with the question of true friendship in his writings; see David Riggs, *Ben Jonson: A Life* (Cambridge, Mass., 1989), pp. 284, 298, 312.

43. Cited in Christopher Haigh, *Elizabeth I* (Harlow, 1988), p. 37.

44. Pico della Mirandola, *Oration on the Dignity of Man*, in Ernst Cassirer, Paul Oskar Kristellar and John Herman Randall, Jr, eds, *The Renaissance Philosophy of Man* (Chicago, 1948), pp. 215–54, at pp. 224–5. For comment see Andrew Hadfield, *The English Renaissance, 1550–1620* (Oxford, 2000), pp. 239–40.

45. Robert S. Miola, '*Julius Caesar* and the tyrannicide debate', *RQ* 36 (1985), 271–90.

46. J.J. Scarisbrick, *Henry VIII* (London, 1968), chs 7–8.

47. Horatio compares the portent of the ghost to those which preceded the assassination of Julius Caesar (1.1.115–28).

48. Tacitus, *On Imperial Rome*, pp. 225–76; Suetonius, *The Twelve Caesars*, trans. Robert Graves (Harmondsworth, 1957), pp. 181–207.

49. On the aristocratic character of much early modern republicanism, see J.G.A. Pocock, *The Machiavellian Moment: Florentine Political Thought and the Atlantic Republican Tradition* (Princeton, 1975), pp. 100–3.

50. For an incisive analysis of the problem of rulers who are cut off from the people in Shakespeare's romances, see Constance Jordan, *Shakespeare's Monarchies: Ruler and Subject in the Romances* (Ithaca, 1997).

51. *Vindiciae, Contra Tyrannos*, ed. George Garnett (Cambridge, 1994), introduction, lv–lxxxvi, p. 3. See also Robert M. Kingdon, 'Calvinism and resistance theory, 1550–1580', in J.H. Burns and Mark Goldie, eds, *The Cambridge History of Political Thought, 1450–1700* (Cambridge, 1991), pp. 193–253, at p. 212. See also Blair Worden, *The Sound of Virtue: Philip Sidney's 'Arcadia' and Elizabethan Politics* (New Haven, 1996), *passim*.

52. *Hamlet*, ed. Harold Jenkins (London, 1982), introduction, p. 86.

53. *Vindiciae, Contra Tyrannos*, pp. 71, 161, 184.

54. *Vindiciae, Contra Tyrannos*, p. 187.

55. For a comprehensive survey of the literature produced in the wake of Mary's reign, see James Emerson Phillips, *Images of a Queen: Mary Stuart in Sixteenth-Century Literature* (Berkeley, 1964). See also Kurland, 'Hamlet and the Scottish succession'.

56. See Skinner, *Foundations of Modern Political Thought*, II, pp. 340–8; Kingdon, 'Calvinism and resistance theory', pp. 213–15.

57. James E. Phillips, 'George Buchanan and the Sidney Circle', *HLQ* 12 (1948–9), 23–55; Worden, *Sound of Virtue*, ch. 3.

58. Worden, *Sound of Virtue, passim*.

59. Text conveniently reproduced in Kenneth Muir's Arden 2 edition (1964), pp. 229–35.

60. *Vindiciae, Contra Tyrannos*, p. 5.

61. *Vindiciae, Contra Tyrannos*, pp. 20–1.

62. *Vindiciae, Contra Tyrannos*, pp. 33–4.

63. *Vindiciae, Contra Tyrannos*, pp. 140–1.

64. *Vindiciae, Contra Tyrannos*, p. 7; Machiavelli, *The Prince*, ch. 8.

65. Howard Erskine-Hill argues that this is the central tenet of Shakespeare's political thought, in *Poetry and the Realm of Politics*, chs 2–3.

66. See also Thomas Middleton (?), Cyril Tourneur (?), *The Revenger's Tragedy* (published 1608), which has a similarly gruesome conclusion: Thomas Middleton, *Five Plays*, ed. Bryan Loughrey and Neil Taylor (Harmondsworth, 1988), pp. 148–60.

67. *Vindiciae, Contra Tyrannos*, p. 60. This was a standard argument of 'resistance literature'; see, for example, John Ponet, *A Shorte Treatise of Politike Power* (London, 1556), pp. 71–2; Christopher Goodman, *How Superior Powers Oght to be Obeyed* (Geneva, 1558), p. 139.

68. *Vindiciae, Contra Tyrannos*, p. 69.

69. Hamlet's statement does not necessarily have to be taken at face value; as Harold Jenkins points out 'There was no [earlier] suggestion of any such "hopes" or of any discreditable manoeuvre on the part of Claudius' (*Hamlet*, p. 397). However one reads the line, it draws attention to Claudius's self-centred pursuit of power and authoritarian style of government.

70. Annabel Patterson, *Shakespeare and the Popular Voice* (Oxford, 1989), p. 104.

71. See John Guy, ed., *The Reign of Elizabeth I: Court and Culture in the Last Decade* (Cambridge, 1995).

72. For a discussion of the different texts and their significance, see *The First Quarto of Hamlet*, ed. Kathleen O. Irace (Cambridge, 1998).

73. Harold Jenkins concludes that the folio text dates from 1601, but that versions of the play may have been performed in 1599 and 1600 (*Hamlet*, p. 13). See also Patterson, *Shakespeare and the Popular Voice*, pp. 93–4.

74. Lucius Annaeus Seneca, *Oedipus*, in *Four Tragedies and Octavia*, trans. E.F. Watling (Harmondsworth, 1966). See also Barbour, *English Epicures and Stoics*; F.L. Lucas, *Seneca and Elizabethan Tragedy* (Cambridge, 1922).

75. Harry V. Jaffa, 'The limits of politics: *King Lear*, Act I, scene 1', in Allan Bloom with Harry V. Jaffa, *Shakespeare's Politics* (Chicago, 1981, rpt of 1964), pp. 113–45, at p. 113.

76. Geoffrey of Monmouth, *The History of the Kings of Britain*, trans. Lewis Thorpe (Harmondsworth, 1966), pp. 81–6; *The History of King Leir, 1605* (Oxford, 1907).

77. Levack, *Formation of the British State*, pp. 4–9, 42–4, *passim*.

78. *King Lear*, ed. R.A. Foakes (London, 1997), p. 90.

79. Terence Hawkes, *King Lear* (Plymouth, 1995), pp. 5–6.

80. William Shakespeare, *The Tragedy of King Lear*, ed. Jay L. Halio (Cambridge, 1992), p. 1; Patterson, *Shakespeare and the Popular Voice*, p. 107.

81. Jaffa, 'Limits of politics', p. 121. Jaffa argues that Lear's actions are 'not arbitrary or foolish', but a reasonable attempt to preserve unity (p. 122).

82. Arthur F. Marotti, '"Love is not love": Elizabethan sonnet sequences and the social order', *ELH* 49 (1982), 396–428.

83. Irene Carrier, *James VI and I: King of Great Britain* (Cambridge, 1998), pp. 100–1; Willson, *James VI and I*, pp. 175–6.

84. Curtis Perry, *The Making of Jacobean Culture* (Cambridge, 1997), p. 85. See also Michelle O'Callaghan, *The 'Shepheardes Nation': Jacobean Spenserians and Early Stuart Political Culture, 1612–1625* (Oxford, 2000).

85. James I, *Trew Law*, p. 195. Elsewhere James describes the people as apes who copy what the king does; *Basilikon Doron*, p. 155.

86. It would be a mistake, of course, to take this comment as the only expression of James's political views. Elsewhere he articulates a less restrictive notion of the relationship between rulers and subjects. See above, p. 82.

87. For one analysis, see Lisa Jardine, 'Reading and the technology of textual affect: Erasmus's familiar letters and Shakespeare's *King Lear*', in *Reading Shakespeare Historically* (London, 1996), pp. 78–97.

88. For an invaluable assessment of the significance of the debates over 'the matter of Britain' in the sixteenth century and the wider knowledge of them, see T.D. Kendrick, *British Antiquity* (London, 1950).

89. James I, *Trew Law*, p. 203. See above, pp. 83–4.

90. James I, *Basilikon Doron*, p. 156; *Trew Law*, p. 202. A convenient overview of James's parliaments is contained in Conrad Russell, *The Crisis of Parliaments: English History, 1509–1660* (Oxford, 1971), pt 5, ch. 3. See also Menna

Prestwich, 'Constitutional ideas and parliamentary developments in England, 1603–1625', in Alan G.R. Smith, ed., *The Reign of James VI and I* (London, 1973), pp. 160–76.

91. On 'counsel' and its ambiguities, see John Guy, 'The rhetoric of counsel in early modern England', in Dale Hoak, ed., *Tudor Political Culture* (Cambridge, 1995), pp. 292–310.

92. Enid Welsford, *The Fool: His Social and Literary History* (London, 1935), ch. 7.

93. Caroline Spurgeon, *Shakespeare's Imagery and What it Tells Us* (Cambridge, 1965, rpt of 1935), pp. 214, 341–2.

94. Derek Hirst, *The Representative of the People? Voters and Voting under the Early Stuarts* (Cambridge, 1975), p. 9.

95. Russell, *Crisis of Parliaments*, p. 267. See also Wallace Notestein, *The House of Commons 1604–1610* (New Haven, 1971), pp. 60–78.

96. Russell, *Crisis of Parliaments*, p. 268; Guy, *Reign of Elizabeth I*, pp. 11–12. For a reading of the episode in terms of *Pericles*, see Constance Jordan, *Shakespeare's Monarchies*, ch. 2.

97. On Wentworth see J.E. Neale, 'Peter Wentworth', in E.B. Fryde and Edward Miller, eds, *Historical Studies of the English Parliament: II, 1399–1603* (Cambridge, 1970), pp. 246–95; J.E. Neale, *Elizabeth I and her Parliaments: II, 1584–1601* (London, 1957), pt 4, ch. 2.

98. Russell, *Crisis of Parliaments*, pp. 266–7; David Mathew, *James I* (London, 1967), p. 132.

99. See John Guy, 'Tudor monarchy and its critiques', in John Guy, ed., *The Tudor Monarchy* (London, 1997), pp. 78–109; David Norbrook, '"A liberal tongue": language and rebellion in *Richard II*', in John M. Mucciolo, ed., *Shakespeare's Universe: Renaissance Ideas and Conventions: Essays in Honour of W.R. Elton* (Aldershot, 1996), pp. 37–51.

100. Carrier, *James VI and I*, pp. 100–1; David Harris Sacks, 'The countervailing of benefits: monopoly, liberty, and benevolence in Elizabethan England', in Hoak, ed., *Tudor Political Culture*, pp. 272–91.

101. Greg Walker, 'Household drama and the art of good counsel', in *The Politics of Performance in Early Renaissance Drama* (Cambridge, 1998), pp. 51–75; Walker, *Plays of Persuasion*; Graham Parry, 'Entertainments at court', in John D. Cox and David Scott Kastan, eds, *A New History of Early English Drama* (New York, 1997), pp. 195–211.

102. Brian Vickers, ed., *Shakespeare: The Critical Heritage*, 6 vols (London, 1974–81), I, pp. 344–86; *Samuel Johnson on Shakespeare*, ed. H.R. Woudhuysen (Harmondsworth, 1989), pp. 219–23.

103. The most influential interpretation for modern readers has been A.C. Bradley, *Shakespearean Tragedy: Lectures on Hamlet, Othello, King Lear, Macbeth* (London, 1904), lectures 7 and 8.

104. Although James's accession was by no means inevitable, see Susan Doran, '"Revenge her most foul and unnatural murder?": the impact of Mary Stuart's execution on Anglo-Scottish relations', *History* 85 (2000), 589–612.

105. Howard Dobin, *Merlin's Disciples: Prophecy, Poetry, and Power in Renaissance England* (Stanford, 1990), pp. 89, 194–6. Doubts have been raised about the passage's authenticity, as it does not exist in the quarto. But it seems most likely that it was added later by Shakespeare himself.

106. Bushnell, *Tragedies of Tyrants*, pp. 69–70.

107. Felix Raab, *The English Face of Machiavelli: A Changing Interpretation, 1500–1700* (London, 1965), pp. 56–7.

108. Kingdon, 'Calvinism and resistance theory', p. 208; Skinner, *Foundations of Modern Political Thought*, I, pp. 250–1; II, pp. 308–9.

109. Raab, *English Face of Machiavelli*, p. 56.

110. Gentillet, *Discourse*, pp. 15–16, 21, 29–30.

111. Gentillet, *Discourse*, pp. 65–6; Machiavelli, *The Prince*, ch. 27. On the massacre and its effects, see Robert M. Kingdon, *Myths about the St Bartholomew's Day Massacre, 1572–1576* (Cambridge, Mass., 1988).

112. See Hadfield, *Literature, Travel, and Colonial Writing*, p. 100; Joseph Wittreich, '"Image of that horror": the Apocalypse in *King Lear*', in C.A. Patrides and Joseph Wittreich, eds, *The Apocalypse in English Renaissance Thought and Literature* (Manchester, 1984), pp. 175–206.

3: REPUBLICANISM AND CONSTITUTIONALISM

1. On republicanism see above, pp. 8–12.

2. Cited in E.K. Chambers, *The Elizabethan Stage*, 4 vols (Oxford, 1923), IV, p. 310.

3. Chambers, *Elizabethan Stage*, IV, p. 313.

4. For arguments that Shakespeare's dramatic career may have begun earlier than is often assumed, see E.A.J. Honigmann, *Shakespeare, the 'Lost Years'* (2nd edn, Manchester, 1998); Katherine Duncan-Jones, *Ungentle Shakespeare: Scenes from his Life* (London, 2001), ch. 2.

5. See Anthony Mortimer, *Variable Passions: A Reading of Shakespeare's 'Venus and Adonis'* (New York, 2000); William Keach, *Elizabethan Erotic Narratives: Irony and Pathos in the Ovidian Poetry of Shakespeare, Marlowe and their Contemporaries* (New Brunswick, NJ, 1977), ch. 10; G.P.V. Akrigg, *Shakespeare and the Earl of Southampton* (London, 1968), p. 195.

6. See Livy, *The Early History of Rome from its Foundation*, trans. Aubrey De Sélincourt (London, 1960), pp. 82–5.

7. Margot Heinemann, 'Rebel lords, popular playwrights, and political culture: notes on the Jacobean patronage of the Earl of Southampton', *YES* 21 (1991), 63–86, p. 64; Paul E.J. Hammer, *The Polarisation of Elizabethan Politics: The Political Career of Robert Devereux, 2nd Earl of Essex, 1585–1597* (Cambridge, 1999), ch. 7.

8. Akrigg, *Shakespeare and the Earl of Southampton*, chs 10–12.

9. Akrigg, *Shakespeare and the Earl of Southampton*, p. 31; Park Honan, *Shakespeare: A Life* (Oxford, 1998), ch. 10.

10. See the respective *DNB* entries. On Florio, see also Warren Boutcher, '"A French dexterity, & an Italian confidence": new documents on John Florio, learned strangers and Protestant humanist study of modern languages in Renaissance England from *c*.1547 to *c*.1625', *Reformation* 2 (1997), 39–109.

11. For a recent assessment see Duncan-Jones, *Ungentle Shakespeare, passim*. Duncan-Jones suggests that Shakespeare and Southampton's relationship diminished in importance towards the end of the 1590s.

12. William Shakespeare, *Shakespeare's Sonnets*, ed. Katherine Duncan-Jones (London, 1997), pp. 107–8; Heinemann, 'Rebel lords', p. 69; Akrigg, *Shakespeare and the Earl of Southampton*, pt 2, ch. 2.

13. T.W. Baldwin, *On the Literary Genetics of Shakspere's Poems and Sonnets* (Urbana, 1950), pp. 108–12. Philemon Holland's translation of Livy's *History of Rome* did not appear until 1600. For an analysis of the history and development of the story, see Ian Donaldson, *The Rapes of Lucrece: A Myth and its Transformations* (Oxford, 1982).

14. Painter's work was originally entitled *The Cytie of Cyvelitie*, giving a sense of its political focus; for discussion, see Andrew Hadfield, *Literature, Travel, and Colonial Writing in the English Renaissance, 1545–1625* (Oxford, 1998), pp. 147–62.

15. Livy, *Early History of Rome*, p. 71.

16. William Painter, *The Palace of Pleasure*, 3 vols, ed. Joseph Jacobs (Hildesheim, 1968, rpt of 1890), I, p. 25; Livy, *Early History of Rome*, p. 84.

17. See Donaldson, *Rapes of Lucrece*, pp. 40–56.

18. Philippa Berry, 'Woman, language, and history in *The Rape of Lucrece*', *SS* 44 (1992), 33–9, p. 34.

19. Jane O. Newman points out that women in the poem are the means whereby power is transferred from a single male ruler to a group of male rulers: '"And let mild women to him lose their mildness": Philomela, violence, and Shakespeare's *The Rape of Lucrece*', *SQ* 45 (1994), 304–26, pp. 317–18.

20. Rebecca W. Bushnell, *Tragedies of Tyrants: Political Thought and Theater in the English Renaissance* (Ithaca, 1990), ch. 4.

21. Ian MacLean, *The Renaissance Notion of Woman: A Study in the Fortunes of Scholasticism and Medical Science in European Intellectual Life* (Cambridge, 1980), p. 63; A.N. McLaren, *Political Culture in the Reign of Elizabeth I: Queen and Commonwealth, 1558–1585* (Cambridge, 1999), ch. 1.

22. John Bellamy, *The Tudor Law of Treason: An Introduction* (London, 1979), p. 15.

23. Bellamy, *Tudor Law of Treason*, p. 48.

24. Bellamy, *Tudor Law of Treason*, p. 72.

25. See also the discussion in Curtis C. Breight, '"Treason doth never prosper": *The Tempest* and the discourse of treason', *SQ* 41 (1990), 1–28.

26. Reid Barbour, *English Epicures and Stoics: Ancient Legacies in Early Stuart Culture* (Amherst, 1998), p. 16.

27. Berry, 'Woman, language, and history', p. 35.

28. In effect, the sins of the two Tarquins are different sides of the same coin. As Ian Donaldson comments, 'The political tyranny of Tarquinius Superbus is mirrored in the sexual tyranny of his son, Sextus Tarquinius' (*Rapes of Lucrece*, p. 8).

29. Niccolò Machiavelli, *The Prince*, trans. George Bull (Harmondsworth, 1961), ch. 17.

30. See Jocelyn Catty, *Writing Rape, Writing Women in Early Modern England: Unbridled Speech* (Basingstoke, 1999), p. 57.

31. Livy, *Early History of Rome*, pp. 92–112. See also Georgina Masson, *A Concise History of Republican Rome* (London, 1973), pp. 18–22.

32. See Berry, 'Woman, language, and history', for a balanced, persuasive case along these lines.

33. See Catty, *Writing Rape*, p. 67.

34. Berry, 'Woman, language, and history', p. 35. For a more extended discussion of the iconography of the portraits of Elizabeth, see Andrew Belsey and Catherine Belsey, 'Icons of divinity: portraits of Elizabeth I', in Lucy Gent and Nigel Llewellyn, eds, *Renaissance Bodies: The Human Figure in English Culture, c.1540–1660* (London, 1990), pp. 11–35.

35. Newman, '"And let mild women"', pp. 317–18.

36. For another retelling of the story and its political significance, see Paulina Kewes, 'Roman history and early Stuart drama: Thomas Heywood's *The Rape of Lucrece*', *ELR* 32 (2002), 239–67. I am grateful to Dr Kewes for allowing me to consult this important essay before its publication.

37. See Roy Strong, *The Cult of Elizabeth: Elizabethan Portraiture and Pageantry* (London, 1977), p. 154. See also Frances A. Yates, *Astraea: The Imperial Theme in the Sixteenth Century* (London, 1975), pp. 118, 218–19; Helen Hackett, *Virgin Mother, Maiden Queen: Elizabeth I and the Cult of the Virgin Mary* (Basingstoke, 1995), pp. 134–5, 165.

38. *Titus Andronicus*, ed. Jonathan Bate (London, 1995), p. 78.

39. *Titus Andronicus*, ed. Bate, p. 79.

40. For readings of the violence and its significance, see Gillian Murray Kendall, '"Lend me thy hand": metaphor and mayhem in *Titus Andronicus*', *SQ* 40 (1989), 299–316; Katherine A. Rowe, 'Dismembering and forgetting in *Titus Andronicus*', *SQ* 45 (1994), 279–303.

41. See Jonathan Bate, *Shakespeare and Ovid* (Oxford, 1993), pp. 81–2.

42. For a different reading of Lavinia's rape and dismemberment, see Leonard Tennenhouse, *Power on Display: The Politics of Shakespeare's Genres* (London, 1986), pp. 106–12.

43. For analysis and comment see Sid Ray, '"Rape, I fear, was root of thy annoy": the politics of consent in *Titus Andronicus*', *SQ* 49 (1998), 22–39, pp. 22–3. Although the circumstances are quite different – Elizabeth acted because her authority was questioned and to prevent a diplomatic incident, Demetrius and Chiron to hide their crime – both are examples of the powerful brutally limiting the speech of their opponents.

44. On the use of this image, see Sir John Fortesque, *A Learned Commendation of the Politque Lawes of England*, trans. Robert Mulcaster (London, 1567), fo. 30. For analysis in relation to Shakespeare, see Constance Jordan, *Shakespeare's Monarchies: Ruler and Subject in the Romances* (Ithaca, 1997), pp. 88–9.

45. Naomi Conn Liebler, *Shakespeare's Festive Tragedy: The Ritual Foundations of Genre* (London, 1995), pp. 137–8.

46. Herodotus, *The Histories*, trans. Aubrey De Sélincourt, rev. A.R. Burn (Harmondsworth, 1972), bk 4.

47. Just as James did on occasion; see above, p. 100.

48. Jordan, *Shakespeare's Monarchies*, ch. 3.

49. Bushnell, *Tragedies of Tyrants*, p. 118.

50. Markku Peltonen, *Classical Humanism and Republicanism in English Political Thought, 1570–1640* (Cambridge, 1995), pp. 10–11, *passim*; Barbour, *English Epicures and Stoics*, ch. 4.

51. Ray, '"Rape, I fear, was root of thy annoy"', p. 22.

52. Two powerful analyses of the play's representation of violence and dismemberment are Kendall, '"Lend me thy hand"'; and Rowe, 'Dismembering and forgetting in *Titus Andronicus*'.

53. See Richard C. McCoy, *The Rites of Knighthood: The Literature and Politics of Elizabethan Chivalry* (Berkeley, 1989).

54. *Titus Andronicus*, ed. Bate, p. 164; Ovid, *Metamorphoses*, trans. Mary M. Innes (Harmondsworth, 1955), pp. 146–53. Newman points out that the rape of Philomela also forms a key subtext in *The Rape of Lucrece*; '"And let mild women"'.

55. For further comment, see *Titus Andronicus*, ed. Bate, pp. 18, 92.

56. Liebler, *Shakespeare's Festive Tragedy*, p. 147.

57. On the republican constitutions established in Rome, see M. Cary and H.H. Scullard, *A History of Rome down to the Reign of Constantine* (3rd edn, Basingstoke, 1975), pp. 62–3, 97.

58. On the 'mixed' constitution and the political possibilities associated with this form of government, see above, pp. 6–8.

59. Although it needs to be acknowledged that the *Aeneid* is by no means a straightforward work of imperial propaganda; see R.J. Tarrant, 'Poetry and power: Virgil's poetry in contemporary context', in Charles Martindale, ed., *The Cambridge Companion to Virgil* (Cambridge, 1997), pp. 169–87.

60. For the use of the Trojan legend in the play, see Heather James, *Shakespeare's Troy: Drama, Politics, and the Translation of Empire* (Cambridge, 1997), ch. 2. For further comment on another use of the legend in late Elizabethan England, see Andrew Hadfield, *Literature, Politics and National Identity: Reformation to Renaissance* (Cambridge, 1994), pp. 198–9.

61. *Titus Andronicus*, ed. Bate, pp. 285–6; Thomas Kyd, *The Spanish Tragedy*, ed. Philip Edwards (Manchester, 1977, rpt of 1959).

62. Kyd, *Spanish Tragedy*, pp. lxvi–lxvii; David Riggs, *Ben Jonson: A Life* (Cambridge, Mass., 1989), p. 20.

63. For a representative reading of *The Spanish Tragedy*, see Peter B. Murray, *Thomas Kyd* (New York, 1969), ch. 2. On the representation of revenge in *Titus*, see, for example, Kendall, '"Lend me thy hand"'.

64. Sir Thomas Smith, *De Republica Anglorum: A Discourse on the Commonwealth of England* (1583), ed. L. Alston (Shannon, 1972, rpt of 1906), p. 12.

65. Smith, *De Republica Anglorum*, introduction, p. xvi; Raphael Holinshed, *Chronicles of England, Scotland and Ireland* (London, 1587), I, p. 292; Annabel Patterson, *Reading Holinshed's 'Chronicles'* (Chicago, 1994), pp. 100–4.

66. Smith, *De Republica Anglorum*, p. 24.

67. For a wider discussion, see D.G. Hale, *The Body Politic: A Political Metaphor in Renaissance England* (The Hague, 1971).

68. McLaren, *Political Culture in the Reign of Elizabeth I*, p. 80.

69. See W. Gordon Zeeveld, *Foundations of Tudor Polity* (Cambridge, Mass., 1948); J.K. McConica, *English Humanists and Reformation Politics under Henry VIII and Edward VI* (Oxford, 1965); Thomas F. Mayer, *Thomas Starkey and the Commonweal* (Cambridge, 1989).

70. Thomas Starkey, *A Dialogue Between Pole and Lupset*, ed. Thomas F. Mayer (London, 1989).

71. McLaren, *Political Culture in the Reign of Elizabeth I*, pp. 205, 210–11.

72. Peltonen, *Classical Humanism and Republicanism*, p. 2. See above, pp. 6–7.

73. Peltonen, *Classical Humanism and Republicanism*, p. 2. See above, pp. 8–11.

74. For a discussion of the wider dramatic context to which *Titus* should be linked, see Marie Axton, *The Queen's Two Bodies: Drama and the Elizabethan Succession* (London, 1977), ch. 7.

75. For analysis, see Peltonen, *Classical Humanism and Republicanism*, pp. 76–102; Sydney Anglo, 'A Machiavellian solution to the Irish problem: Richard Beacon's *Solon his Follie* (1594)', in Edward Chaney and Peter Mack, eds, *England and the Continental Renaissance: Essays in Honour of J.B. Trapp* (Woodbridge, 1990), pp. 153–64; Vincent Carey, 'The Irish face of Machiavelli: Richard Beacon's *Solon his Follie* and republican ideology in the conquest of Ireland', in Hiram Morgan, ed., *Political Ideology in Ireland, 1534–1641* (Dublin, 1999), pp. 83–109.

76. Bushnell, *Tragedies of Tyrants*, ch. 1.

77. Emillius compares Titus to Coriolanus because he 'threats in course of this revenge to do / As much as ever Coriolanus did' (4.4.66–7), showing that Shakespeare had already read this life from Plutarch.

78. For details, see Peltonen, *Classical Humanism and Republicanism*, ch. 2.

79. See Andrew Hadfield, 'Was Spenser a republican?', *English* 47 (1998), 169–82, at 171–2.

80. See above, pp. 153–70.

81. On Shakespeare's rivalry with Jonson, see Ian Donaldson, '"Misconstruing everything": *Julius Caesar* and *Sejanus*', in Grace Ioppolo, ed., *Shakespeare Performed: Essays in Honour of R.A. Foakes* (Newark, 2000), pp. 88–107; James P. Bednarz, *Shakespeare and The Poets' War* (New York, 2001). On Jonson's representation of republican Rome, see Blair Worden, 'Ben Jonson among the historians', in Kevin Sharpe and Peter Lake, eds, *Culture and Politics in Early Stuart England* (Basingstoke, 1994), pp. 67–89; and 'Politics in *Catiline*: Jonson and his sources', in Martin Butler, ed., *Re-Presenting Ben Jonson: Text, History, Performance* (Basingstoke, 1999), pp. 152–73.

82. Worden, 'Ben Jonson among the historians', pp. 83–6.

83. See Hammer, *Polarisation of Elizabethan Politics*, ch. 7.

84. An eccentric reading of the significance of first staging of *Julius Caesar* is given in Steve Sohmer, *Shakespeare's Mystery Play: The Opening of the Globe Theatre, 1599* (Manchester, 1999). *As You Like It* is the other possible candidate for first play performed at the Globe.

85. Judith Mossman, '*Henry V* and Plutarch's *Alexander*', *SQ* 45 (1994), 57–73.

86. A recent analysis is contained in Paulina Kewes, '*Julius Caesar* in Jacobean England', *The Seventeenth Century* 17 (2002), 155–86. I am grateful to Dr Kewes for allowing me to see this important article in typescript.

87. Anon., *Vindiciae, Contra Tyrannos*, ed. George Garnett (Cambridge, 1994), pp. 152–3.

88. *Vindiciae, Contra Tyrannos*, p. 153.

89. See Robert S. Miola, '*Julius Caesar* and the tyrannicide debate', *RQ* 36 (1985), 271–90. *Vindiciae, Contra Tyrannos* treats the two assassinations equally; pp. 71, 161, 184.

90. Plutarch, *The Life of Julius Caesar*, in Plutarch, *Selected Lives of the Noble Grecians and Romans*, trans. Thomas North (1579), ed. Judith Mossman (Ware, 1998), pp. 467–530, at p. 521.

91. Plutarch, *Life of Julius Caesar*, p. 523.

92. Plutarch, *Life of Marcus Brutus*, in *Selected Lives*, pp. 813–61, at p. 813.

93. Lucan, *Civil War*, trans. Susan H. Braund (Oxford, 1992); Virgil, *The Aeneid*, trans. David West (Harmondsworth, 1990). For analysis, see David Quint, *Epic and Empire: Politics and Generic Form from Virgil to Milton* (Princeton, 1993), chs 2, 4; R.J. Tarrant, 'Aspects of Virgil's reception in antiquity', in Charles Martindale, ed., *The Cambridge Companion to Virgil* (Cambridge, 1997), pp. 56–72, at pp. 65–7. *The Aeneid* can also be read as a more complex and less straightforward celebration of the Roman empire than simple Augustan propaganda (see above, note 59). However, it was often read in this way, especially in the late sixteenth century.

94. Karl Marx, *The Eighteenth Brumaire of Louis Bonaparte*, in *Selected Writings*, ed. David McLellan (Oxford, 1977), pp. 300–25, at p. 300. Marx was a studious reader of both Plutarch and Shakespeare; see S.S. Prawer, *Karl Marx and World Literature* (Oxford, 1976), pp. 28–9.

95. Plutarch, *Life of Marcus Brutus*, p. 819.

96. Plutarch, *Life of Marcus Brutus*, p. 819.

97. Plutarch, *Life of Marcus Brutus*, p. 839.

98. See Barbara L. Parker, '"A thing unfirm": Plato's *Republic* and Shakespeare's *Julius Caesar*', *SQ* 44 (1993), 30–43, at pp. 32–3; Miola, '*Julius Caesar* and the tyrannicide debate', p. 288.

99. Plutarch, *Life of Caesar*, p. 839; *Life of Marcus Brutus*, p. 528.

100. Plutarch, *Life of Marcus Brutus*, p. 830.

101. Plutarch, *Life of Marcus Brutus*, p. 831.

102. Plutarch, *Life of Marcus Brutus*, p. 832.

103. For a discussion of Shakespeare's sources, see Robert S. Miola, 'Shakespeare and his Sources: observations on the critical history of *Julius Caesar*', *SS* 40 (1988), 69–76.

104. Plutarch, *Life of Marcus Brutus*, p. 822.

105. For comment, see Robert S. Miola, *Shakespeare's Rome* (Cambridge, 1983), pp. 81–2.

106. Miola, *Shakespeare's Rome*, p. 76.

107. See the related argument of Kevin Sharpe, '"An image doting rabble": the failure of republican culture in seventeenth-century England', in Kevin

Sharpe and Steven N. Zwicker, eds, *Refiguring Revolutions: Aesthetics and Politics from the English Revolution to the Romantic Revolution* (Berkeley, 1998), pp. 25–56, at pp. 26–7.

108. Plutarch represents Caesar as vigorous and brave, indicating that Cassius is probably lying to Brutus, as he is elsewhere; Plutarch, *Life of Julius Caesar*, pp. 480–3. See also Miola, *Shakespeare's Rome*, pp. 81–6.

109. The staging of the second scene 'enforces the sense of conspiratorial isolation'; Miola, *Shakespeare's Rome*, p. 81. See also Emrys Jones, *Scenic Form in Shakespeare* (Oxford, 1971), pp. 18–23.

110. Niccolò Machiavelli, *The Discourses*, trans. Leslie J. Walker, ed. Bernard Crick (Harmondsworth, 1970). See also Quentin Skinner, *The Foundations of Modern Political Thought*, 2 vols (Cambridge, 1978), I, pp. 131–8; J.G.A. Pocock, *The Machiavellian Moment: Florentine Political Thought and the Atlantic Republican Tradition* (Princeton, 1975), ch. 7.

111. Lucan's poem was often used in schooling, and parts of it had been translated only a few years earlier, by Christopher Marlowe. On Lucan's use in school, see T.W. Baldwin, *William Shakspere's Small Latine and Lesse Greeke*, 2 vols (Urbana, 1944), I, pp. 103–5; II, pp. 549–51, *passim*. Marlowe's translation was entered in the Stationers' Register in 1593, but not published until 1600 by Thomas Thorpe (who later published Shakespeare's *Sonnets*); Christopher Marlowe, *The Poems*, ed. Millar McLure (Manchester, 1968), p. xxxiv.

112. Katherine Duncan-Jones suggests that *As You Like It*, often read as 'the gentlest and most relaxed of Shakespeare's comedies', was also intimately bound up with the Essex uprising; *Ungentle Shakespeare*, pp. 123–6.

113. Mossman, '*Henry V* and Plutarch's *Alexander*'; Parker, '"A thing unfirm"', p. 43.

114. Howard Erskine-Hill, *Poetry and the Realm of Politics: Shakespeare to Dryden* (Oxford, 1996), pt 1. See above, pp. 87–97.

115. See Andrew Hadfield, 'Spenser, Drayton, and the question of Britain', *RES*, n.s. 51 (2000), 582–99, at 599.

116. The fact that Cinna's name leads to his fate suggests that this scene ought to be read alongside Caesar's unshakeable faith in his name and identity (see above, p. 145). The story is told in Plutarch, *Life of Marcus Brutus*, pp. 830–31. For comment, see Robin Headlam Wells, *Shakespeare, Politics and the State* (Basingstoke, 1986), pp. 48–9.

117. *Julius Caesar*, ed. David Daniell (London, 1998), pp. 15–16.

118. Cyndia Susan Clegg, *Press Censorship in Elizabethan England* (Cambridge, 1997), pp. 198–9.

119. Clegg, *Press Censorship*, pp. 202–8 (quotation, p. 207).

4: ALTERNATIVE FORMS OF GOVERNMENT

1. Anne Barton, 'Livy, Machiavelli and Shakespeare's *Coriolanus*', in *Essays, Mainly Shakespearean* (Cambridge, 1994), pp. 136–60, at p. 160.

2. The term 'recusant' refers to those, invariably Catholic, who refused to attend Church of England services and so broke the law, risking large fines or worse; see Arnold Pritchard, *Catholic Loyalism in Elizabethan England* (London, 1979), pp. 3–4.

3. Conrad Russell, *The Crisis of Parliaments: English History 1509–1660* (Oxford, 1971), pp. 264–6; D. Harris Willson, *James VI and I* (London, 1956), pp. 223–7. On the increasing importance of contested elections, see Derek Hirst, *The Representative of the People? Voters and Voting under the Early Stuarts* (Cambridge, 1975).

4. See, for example, 'A Speech to the Lords and Commons of the Parliament at White-Hall, on Wednesday the XXI. Of March. Anno 1609', in King James VI and I, *Political Writings*, ed. Johann P. Somerville (Cambridge, 1994), pp. 179–203. For details of the debates about the status and role of parliament in the early 1600s, see J.P. Kenyon, ed., *The Stuart Constitution: Documents and Commentary* (2nd edn, Cambridge, 1986), bk 1, ch. 2. On the Goodwin–Fortesque case, see above, pp. 103–5.

5. Hirst, *Representative of the People?*, pp. 2–10.

6. Mark A. Kishlansky, *Parliamentary Selection: Social and Political Choice in Early Modern England* (Cambridge, 1986), ch. 1.

7. Kishlansky, *Parliamentary Selection*, p. x; Hirst, *Representative of the People?*, ch. 4.

8. For an elaborate discussion of the relationship between events in Warwickshire and *Coriolanus*, see Richard Wilson, 'Against the grain: representing the market in *Coriolanus*', in *Will Power: Essays on Shakespearean Authority* (Hemel Hempstead, 1993), pp. 88–125.

9. Roy Strong, *Henry Prince of Wales and England's Lost Renaissance* (London, 1986), pp. 71–85.

10. Jonathan Goldberg, *James I and the Politics of Literature* (Baltimore, 1983), pp. 31–55; Leah S. Marcus, *Puzzling Shakespeare: Local Reading and its Discontents* (Berkeley, 1988), pp. 121–3, 135–6; Strong, *Henry Prince of Wales*, p. 73.

11. For details of Shakespeare's connections with Stratford in the early 1600s, see Park Honan, *Shakespeare: A Life* (Oxford, 1998), pp. 288–94; Samuel Schoenbaum, *Shakespeare's Lives* (Oxford, 1970), pt 1, chs 4–5; Wilson, 'Against the grain'. For an account of the development of opposition politics in James's reign, see Curtis Perry, *The Making of Jacobean Culture* (Cambridge, 1997).

12. See Andrew Hadfield, *Literature, Travel, and Colonial Writing in the English Renaissance, 1545–1625* (Oxford, 1998), ch. 1.

13. Felix Raab, *The English Face of Machiavelli; A Changing Interpretation, 1500–1700* (London, 1965), pp. 26–8; W. Gordon Zeeveld, *Foundations of Tudor Polity* (Cambridge, Mass., 1948), chs 3–5; Hadfield, *Literature, Travel, and Colonial Writing*, pp. 19–24.

14. Thomas Starkey, *A Dialogue Between Pole and Lupset*, ed. Thomas F. Mayer (London, 1989), p. 123.

15. Starkey, *Dialogue Between Pole and Lupset*, p. 123.

16. J.G.A. Pocock, *The Machiavellian Moment: Florentine Political Thought and the Atlantic Republican Tradition* (Princeton, 1975), p. 100; Markku Peltonen, *Classical Humanism and Republicanism in English Political Thought, 1570–1640* (Cambridge, 1995), pp. 106–7, 112–18, *passim*; Howard Erskine-Hill, *Poetry and the Realm of Politics: Shakespeare to Dryden* (Oxford, 1996), ch. 4.

17. Erskine-Hill, *Poetry and the Realm of Politics*, pp. 127–9; David McPherson, *Shakespeare, Jonson, and the Myth of Venice* (Newark, 1990), p. 21; Hadfield, *Literature, Travel, and Colonial Writing*, pp. 24–31.

18. William Thomas, *The Historie of Italie* (London, 1549), fo. 8. Subsequent references in parentheses in the text.

19. For discussions of Shakespeare's reading about Venice, see J.R. Mulryne, 'History and myth in *The Merchant of Venice*', and Leo Salingar, 'The idea of Venice in Shakespeare and Ben Jonson', in Michele Marrapodi, A.J. Hoenselaars, Marcello Cappuzzo and L. Falzon Santucci, eds, *Shakespeare's Italy: Functions of Italian Locations in Renaissance Drama* (Manchester, 1993), pp. 87–99, 171–84.

20. *The commonwealth and government of Venice. Written by the Cardinall Gaspar Contareno*, trans. Lewes Lewkenor (London, 1599). All subsequent references in parentheses in the text. For discussion of Lewkenor's translation, see Pocock, *Machiavellian Moment*, pp. 320–30; Hadfield, *Literature, Travel, and Colonial Writing*, pp. 46–58.

21. David McPherson, 'Lewkenor's Venice and its sources', *RQ* 41 (1988), 459–66; McPherson, *Shakespeare, Jonson, and the Myth of Venice*, pp. 22–3, *passim*.

22. Pocock, *Machiavellian Moment*, p. 321.

23. Pocock, *Machiavellian Moment*, p. 324; McPherson, 'Lewkenor's Venice', p. 461.

24. Hadfield, *Literature, Travel, and Colonial Writing*, pp. 56–8. Aristotle argued that monarchy was the most stable form of government; *The Politics*, trans. Thomas Alan Sinclair (Harmondsworth, 1962), pp. 135–48.

25. James I, *The Trew Law of Free Monarchies*, in *The Workes* (1616) (Hildesheim and New York, 1971), pp. 193–210, at p. 203.

26. Venice was also well known for its protracted quarrel with the papacy, which received considerable sympathy in Elizabethan and Jacobean England, where Venice was often seen as a quasi-Protestant city state. James softened his attitude enough to cultivate Venice when he became King of England, as Venice was a Catholic state which opposed Spain; see Willson, *James VI and I*, ch. 15.

27. On *Measure for Measure*, see McPherson, *Shakespeare, Jonson, and the Myth of Venice*, p. 67. For a contrary view, see Thomas Healy, 'Selves, states, and sectarianism in early modern England', *English* 44 (1995), 193–213, at 206. On *The Winter's Tale*, see Michelle Marrapodi, '"Of that fatal country": Sicily and the rhetoric of topography in *The Winter's Tale*', in Marrapodi *et al.*, eds, *Shakespeare's Italy*, pp. 213–28.

28. On Venice's role in European commerce and culture, see Lisa Jardine, *Worldly Goods: A New History of the Renaissance* (Basingstoke, 1996), pp. 18–19, 45–9. For a contemporary description, see Thomas, *Historie of Italie*, fo. 76.

29. For the most influential account of this fear, see Roger Ascham, *The scholemaster or plaine and perfite way of teachyng children, the Latin tong* (London, 1570), fos 25–7, 29–30.

30. For an overview, see Garrett Mattingly, *Renaissance Diplomacy* (London, 1955).

31. On the Jews in Venice, see Thomas, *Historie of Italie*, fo. 77; Thomas Coryat, *Coryat's Crudities, Hastily gobled up in five Monethes travells* (1611) (rpt Glasgow, 1905), 2 vols, I, pp. 372–80; McPherson, *Shakespeare, Jonson, and the Myth of Venice*, pp. 61–7; James Shapiro, *Shakespeare and the Jews* (New York, 1996), *passim*.

32. On Venice and liberty, see Thomas, *Historie of Italie*, fos 78, 85–6. Jane Donawerth suggests that there is a logic to the selection of caskets endorsed by Shakespeare; *Shakespeare and the Sixteenth-Century Study of Language* (Chicago, 1984), ch. 6.

33. See Stephen A. Cohen, '"The quality of mercy": law, equity and ideology in *The Merchant of Venice*', *Mosaic* 27.4 (Dec. 1994), 35–54, at 44–6. I owe this reference to Melanie Williams.

34. Thomas, *Historie of Italie*, fos 81–2; Contarini, *Commonwealth and government of Venice*, pp. 22–5.

35. See McPherson, *Shakespeare, Jonson, and the Myth of Venice*, pp. 67–8.

36. Shapiro, *Shakespeare and the Jews*, pp. 188–9.

37. Aristotle, *Nicomachean Ethics*, trans. David Ross (Oxford, 1980, rpt of 1925), pp. 132–4; Donald R. Kelly, 'Law', in J.H. Burns and Mark Goldie, eds, *The Cambridge History of Political Thought, 1450–1700* (Cambridge, 1991), pp. 66–94.

38. Aristotle, *Nicomachean Ethics*, p. 133.

39. Sir Thomas Smith, cited in G.R. Elton, ed., *The Tudor Constitution: Documents and Commentary* (Cambridge, 1972, rpt of 1960), p. 155.

40. Stuart E. Prall, 'The development of equity in Tudor England', *AJLH* 8 (1964), 1–19.

41. So indicating the close relationship between the terms 'republic' (*res publica*) and 'commonwealth' in contemporary political discourse. On the problem of translation of republican theory, see Thomas F. Mayer, *Thomas Starkey and the Commonweal* (Cambridge, 1989), ch. 4; Peltonen, *Classical Humanism and Republicanism*, introduction.

42. See Julian H. Franklin, *Jean Bodin and the Rise of Absolutist Theory* (Cambridge, 1973); Quentin Skinner, *The Foundations of Modern Political Thought*, 2 vols (Cambridge, 1978), II, pp. 184–301; Julian H. Franklin, 'Sovereignty and the mixed constitution: Bodin and his critics', in Burns and Goldie, ed., *Cambridge History of Political Thought*, pp. 298–328.

43. Richard Tuck, *Philosophy and Government, 1572–1651* (Cambridge, 1993), p. 27.

44. Franklin, 'Sovereignty and the mixed constitution', p. 306; Jean Bodin, *Method for the Easy Comprehension of History*, trans. Beatrice Reynolds (New York, 1945), ch. 6.

45. Jean Bodin, *The Six Bookes of the Commonweale out of the French and Latine Copies, done into English, by R. Knolles* (London, 1606), Bk 3, ch. 4.

46. Bodin, *Six Bookes*, Bk 4, ch. 1.

47. Shapiro, *Shakespeare and the Jews, passim*.

48. A pointed contrast to the unproblematic conclusion of Shakespeare's principal source, Ser Giovanni Florentino's *Il Pecorone*; see Geoffrey Bullough, *Narrative and Dramatic Sources of Shakespeare*, 8 vols (London, 1957–75), I, pp. 463–76, at pp. 474–5.

49. See Cohen, '"The quality of mercy"', p. 48, for comment.

50. See, for example, Leslie A. Fiedler, *The Stranger in Shakespeare* (London, 1973), ch. 2; Shapiro, *Shakespeare and the Jews*, ch. 5. A contrary reading can be found in Joan Ozark Holmer, *The Merchant of Venice: Choice, Hazard and Consequence* (Basingstoke, 1995).

51. Cited in Julia Briggs, *This Stage-Play World: Texts and Contexts, 1580–1625* (2nd edn, Oxford, 1997), pp. 95–6. For further discussion see Kim F. Hall, *Things of Darkness: Economies of Race and Gender in Early Modern England* (Ithaca, NY, 1995).

52. Shapiro, *Shakespeare and the Jews*, pp. 71–3, *passim*; Briggs, *Stage-Play World*, p. 100.

53. Anthony Munday *et al.*, *Sir Thomas More*, ed. Vittorio Gabrieli and Giorgio Melchiori (Manchester, 1990), 2.3. See Briggs, *Stage-Play World*, p. 250.

54. Shakespeare's – relatively – positive representation of Venice is in pointed contrast to that of Ben Jonson, who in *Volpone* (1605–6) represents Venice as a corrupt, soulless place where men are transformed into beasts; see Douglas Duncan, *Ben Jonson and the Lucianic Tradition* (Cambridge, 1979), ch. 7; McPherson, *Shakespeare, Jonson, and the Myth of Venice*, ch. 5. Jonson's representation of Venice may have been made in response to Shakespeare's, but there is no evidence to prove this.
55. On the date, see *Othello*, ed. E.A.J. Honigmann (London, 1997), appendix 1.
56. McPherson, *Shakespeare, Jonson, and the Myth of Venice*, pp. 20, 36, 48; Kenneth Muir, 'Shakespeare and Lewkenor', *RES* 7 (1956), 182–3.
57. On ekphrasis and the importance of visual culture in Shakespeare, see Alison Thorne, *Vision and Rhetoric in Shakespeare: Looking through Language* (Basingstoke, 2000).
58. See Patricia Parker, 'Fantasies of "race" and "gender": Africa, *Othello* and bringing to light', in Margo Hendricks and Patricia Parker, eds, *Women, "Race", & Writing in the Early Modern Period* (London, 1994), pp. 84–100; Virginia Mason Vaughan, *Othello: A Contextual History* (Cambridge, 1994), ch. 3.
59. On the 'barbarian invasions' of Rome, see Michael Grant, *History of Rome* (London, 1978), ch. 17.
60. For details of Shakespeare's use of Cinthio, see *Othello*, ed. Norman Sanders (Cambridge, 1984), introduction, pp. 2–10; Vaughan, *Othello: A Contextual History*, pp. 83–4. Sanders comments that 'the changes made by Shakespeare as he refashions the tale', are more striking than the similarities (p. 8).
61. Parker, 'Fantasies of "race" and "gender"', p. 95.
62. Contarini refers to Venice's constant fear of the Ottoman empire and the strategic importance of Cyprus throughout *The commonwealth and government of Venice*; see pp. 109, 171–2, 175, 223–9.
63. Contarini, *Commonwealth and government of Venice*, p. 51
64. Contarini, *Commonwealth and government of Venice*, p. 25.
65. On Othello's racial identity and its role within the play, see G.K. Hunter, '*Othello* and colour prejudice', in *Dramatic Identities and Cultural Traditions* (Liverpool, 1978), pp. 31–59; Karen Newman, '"And wash the Ethiop white": femininity and the monstrous in *Othello*', in Jean E. Howard and Marion O'Connor, eds, *Shakespeare Reproduced: The Text in History and Ideology* (London, 1987), pp. 143–62; John Gillies, *Shakespeare and the Geography of Difference* (Cambridge, 1994), pp. 25–30.
66. Jean Bodin represents the state in similar terms: see Tuck, *Philosophy and Government*, pp. 26–7.
67. For a different reading of this scene, see Gillies, *Shakespeare and the Geography of Difference*, pp. 138–9.

68. Mark Matheson, 'Venetian culture and the politics of *Othello*', *SS* 48 (1995), 123–33, at 124.

69. When preparing to kill Desdemona in 5.2, Othello represents his actions as a judicial execution, transforming himself into a parody of a Venetian judge, a different and conflicting sign of his cruel fall from grace.

70. Robert Hapgood, '*Othello*', in Stanley Wells, ed., *Shakespeare: A Bibliographical Guide* (Oxford, 1990), pp. 223–40 at p. 228; More generally, see Raab, *English Face of Machiavelli*, ch. 2; J.L. Livesay, *The Elizabethan Image of Italy* (Chapel Hill, NC, 1964), *passim*.

71. See Vaughan, *Othello: A Contextual History*, pp. 16–19.

72. See McPherson, *Shakespeare, Jonson, and the Myth of Venice*; Hadfield, *Literature, Travel, and Colonial Writing*, pp. 49–67.

73. See Andrew Hadfield, ed., *Amazons, Savages & Machiavels: Travel & Colonial Writing in English, 1550–1630: An Anthology* (Oxford, 2001), pp. 166–78.

74. For further discussion, see Vaughan, *Othello: A Contextual History*; Hall, *Things of Darkness*.

75. For diverging readings, see Marcus, *Puzzling Shakespeare*, pp. 202–12; Barton, 'Livy, Machiavelli and Shakespeare's *Coriolanus*'; Brian Vickers, '*Coriolanus* and the demons of politics', in *Returning to Shakespeare* (London, 1989), pp. 135–93; W. Gordon Zeeveld, '*Coriolanus* and Jacobean politics', *MLR* 57 (1962), 321–34.

76. See, for example, Robin Headlam Wells, *Shakespeare, Politics and the State* (Basingstoke, 1986), pp. 39–41; Barton, 'Livy, Machiavelli and Shakespeare's *Coriolanus*'.

77. Kishlansky, *Parliamentary Selection*, p. 4. See also Wilson, 'Against the grain', pp. 98–104; Plutarch, *Life of Coriolanus*, in *Selected Lives of the Noble Grecians and Romans*, trans. Thomas North (1579), ed. Judith Mossman (Ware, 1998), pp. 137–78. Shakespeare also made use of Livy, *The Early History of Rome from its Foundation*, trans. Aubrey De Sélincourt (Harmondsworth, 1960), pp. 126–35. For comparative analysis of Shakespeare's use of Plutarch and Livy, see Barton, 'Livy, Machiavelli and Shakespeare's *Coriolanus*', pp. 136–9; Vickers, '*Coriolanus* and the demons of politics', pp. 140–3.

78. Kishlansky, *Parliamentary Selection*, p. 5.

79. C.C. Huffman, *Coriolanus in Context* (Lewisburg, 1971), p. 172.

80. Plutarch, *Life of Coriolanus*, p. 142.

81. Barton, 'Livy, Machiavelli and Shakespeare's *Coriolanus*', p. 138.

82. As noted by Barton; 'Livy, Machiavelli and Shakespeare's *Coriolanus*', p. 140.

83. As D.G. Hale points out, later events show that 'there was truth in the citizens' first charges against the senate'; '*Coriolanus*: the death of a political metaphor', *SS* 22 (1971), 197–202.

84. For discussion of the contemporary background, see *Coriolanus*, ed. Lee Bliss (Cambridge, 2000), introduction, pp. 17–27.

85. Plutarch, *Life of Coriolanus*, pp. 140, 148.

86. Plutarch, *Life of Coriolanus*, p. 140.

87. For further examples and discussion, see D.G. Hale, *The Body Politic: A Political Metaphor in Renaissance English Literature* (The Hague, 1971); Peter Burke, 'Tacitism, scepticism, and reason of state', in Burns and Goldie, eds, *Cambridge History of Political Thought*, pp. 479–98, at pp. 482, 486.

88. Starkey, *Dialogue Between Pole and Lupset*, pp. 31–3. See also Smith, *De Republica Anglorum: A Discourse of the Commonwealth of England* (1583), ed. L. Alston (Shannon, 1972, rpt of 1906), p. 49; Andrew Gurr, '*Coriolanus* and the body politic', *SS* 28 (1975), 63–9.

89. Peltonen, *Classical Humanism and Republicanism*, p. 9.

90. Especially given the circumstances in which 'An Homilie Agaynst Disobedience and Wylful Rebellion', was produced; see above, pp. 42–4.

91. James I, *Trew Law*, p. 204. See also Gurr, '*Coriolanus* and the body politic', pp. 64–6.

92. See Marcus, *Puzzling Shakespeare*, p. 205.

93. Plutarch, *Life of Coriolanus*, p. 142.

94. More generally, see Glenn Burgess, *The Politics of the Ancient Constitution: An Introduction to English Political Thought, 1603–1642* (Basingstoke, 1992).

95. Janet Adelman, *Suffocating Mothers: Fantasies of Maternal Origin in Shakespeare's Plays, 'Hamlet' to 'The Tempest'* (London, 1992), pp. 146–64.

96. Plutarch, *Life of Coriolanus*, p. 178.

97. Shakespeare's representation of the encounter is significantly more dramatic than Plutarch's; see Plutarch, *Life of Coriolanus*, pp. 173–5.

98. See Shannon Miller, 'Topicality and subversion in William Shakespeare's *Coriolanus*', *SEL* 32 (1992), 287–310; Annabel Patterson, *Shakespeare and the Popular Voice* (Oxford, 1989), ch. 10.

99. See, for example, E.C. Pettet, '*Coriolanus* and the Midlands Insurrection of 1607', *SS* 3 (1950), 34–42; Vickers, '*Coriolanus* and the demons of politics'.

100. Plutarch, *Life of Coriolanus*, p. 142.

101. Miller, 'Topicality and subversion', pp. 290–5.

102. Vickers, '*Coriolanus* and the demons of politics', pp. 142–3; Huffman, *Coriolanus in Context*, pp. 188–9, 195. For an alternative view, see Kenneth Muir, 'In defence of the tribunes', *EIC* 4 (1954), 331–3.

103. D.G. Hale provides a slightly different interpretation, '*Coriolanus*: the death of a political metaphor', p. 202.

104. Hale, *Body Politic*, pp. 112–13.

5: THE REALITY OF JACOBEAN POLITICS

1. For one aspect of this cult, see Michelle O'Callaghan, *The 'Shepheardes Nation': Jacobean Spenserians and Early Stuart Political Culture, 1612–1625* (Oxford, 2000). See also Helen Hackett, *Virgin Mother, Maiden Queen: Elizabeth I and the Cult of the Virgin Mary* (Basingstoke, 1995), ch. 7.

2. Convenient overviews of early Stuart political culture and parliaments can be found in Conrad Russell, *The Crisis of Parliaments: English History 1509–1660* (Oxford, 1971), pp. 256–84; Roger Lockyer, *James VI and I* (Harlow, 1998), ch. 4. Relevant documents are contained in J.P. Kenyon, ed., *The Stuart Constitution: Documents and Commentary* (2nd edn, Cambridge, 1986), pp. 7–73. The most thorough analysis is Wallace Notestein, *The House of Commons 1604–1610* (New Haven, 1971); see also Roger Lockyer, *The Early Stuarts: A Political History of England, 1603–1642* (Harlow, 1989).

3. Hackett, *Virgin Mother, Maiden Queen*, ch. 6.

4. For further discussion, see Andrew Hadfield, *Shakespeare, Spenser and the Matter of Britain* (Basingstoke, 2003), ch. 10.

5. For details, see G.P.V. Akrigg, *Shakespeare and the Earl of Southampton* (London, 1968), pt 1, ch. 12.

6. For discussion, see Akrigg, *Shakespeare and the Earl of Southampton*, pt 2, ch. 9; *Shakespeare's Sonnets*, ed. Katherine Duncan-Jones (London, 1997), pp. 21–4.

7. A good example is John Barrell's reading of sonnet 29: see *Poetry, Language & Politics* (Manchester, 1988), pp. 18–43.

8. Hackett, *Virgin Mother, Maiden Queen, passim*; Philippa Berry, *Of Chastity and Power: Elizabethan Literature and the Unmarried Queen* (London, 1989), ch. 3.

9. Lockyer, *James VI and I*, pp. 159–60.

10. On *Shakespeare in Love*, see Tony Howard, 'Shakespeare's cinematic offshoots', in Russell Jackson, ed., *The Cambridge Companion to Shakespeare on Film* (Cambridge, 2000), pp. 295–313, at pp. 309–11.

11. For details, see Peter Thomson, *Shakespeare's Professional Career* (Cambridge, 1992), chs 5–7; Andrew Gurr, *The Shakespearian Playing Companies* (Oxford, 1996), chs 15–16. On the story of *The Merry Wives of Windsor*, see Katherine Duncan-Jones, *Ungentle Shakespeare: Scenes from his Life* (London, 2001), p. 97. Duncan-Jones accepts its truth.

12. Duncan-Jones, *Ungentle Shakespeare*, pp. 127–8. See above, pp. 15–16.

13. For examples of such readings, see Josephine Waters Bennett, *'Measure for Measure' as Royal Entertainment* (New York, 1966); David L. Stevenson, 'The role of James I in Shakespeare's *Measure for Measure*', *ELH* 26 (1959), 188–208; Henry N. Paul, *The Royal Play of 'Macbeth'* (London, 1950).

14. See J.P. Sommerville, *Politics and Ideology in England, 1603–1640* (Harlow, 1986), pt 1 ('natural law theorists' is Sommerville's term); Glenn Burgess, *The Politics of the Ancient Constitution: An Introduction to English Political Thought, 1603–1642* (Basingstoke, 1992); Constance Jordan, *Shakespeare's Monarchies: Ruler and Subject in the Romances* (Ithaca, 1997).

15. See, for example, Greg Walker, *Plays of Persuasion: Drama and Politics at the Court of Henry VIII* (Cambridge, 1991); L.K. Born, 'The perfect prince: a study in thirteenth- and fourteenth-century ideals', *Speculum* 3 (1928), 470–504. I hope it is clear that I am not trying to conflate the significance of the performance of court entertainments and the development of the public stage, but trying to show important similarities between the two.

16. James I, *Basilikon Doron*, in *The Workes* (1616) (Hildesheim and New York, 1971), pp. 137–89, at p. 169. Subsequent references to this edition in parentheses in the text.

17. James I, *The Trew Law of Free Monarchies*, in *Workes*, pp. 191–210, at pp. 200, 203.

18. Roger Lockyer, *James VI and I*, p. 34; Jenny Wormald, 'James VI and I, *Basilikon Doron* and *The Trew Law of Free Monarchies*: the Scottish context and the English translation', in Linda Levy Peck, ed., *The Mental World of the Jacobean Court* (Cambridge, 1991), pp. 36–54, at pp. 51–2.

19. Lockyer, *James VI and I*, p. 35.

20. The text of the speech is conveniently reproduced in James VI and I, *Political Writings*, ed. Johann P. Somerville (Cambridge, 1994), pp. 132–46.

21. Lockyer, *James VI and I*, p. 27. Lockyer points out that 'James was amenable to learned argument'.

22. D. Harris Willson, *King James VI and I* (London, 1956), p. 166.

23. Gurr, *Shakespearian Playing Companies*, chs 6–7; Martin Butler, 'Ben Jonson and the limits of courtly panegyric', in Kevin Sharpe and Peter Lake, eds, *Culture and Politics in Early Stuart England* (Basingstoke, 1994), pp. 91–115; Peter E. McCullough, *Sermons at Court: Politics and Religion in Elizabethan and Jacobean Preaching* (Cambridge, 1998), p. 125.

24. See the descriptions in Robert Ashton, ed., *James I by his Contemporaries: An Account of his Career and Character as seen by some of his Contemporaries* (London, 1969), pp. 237–44.

25. Richard A. McCabe, 'The masks of Duessa: Spenser, Mary Queen of Scots, and James VI', *ELR* 17 (1987), 224–42; Robert Lacey, *Sir Walter Raleigh* (London, 1975), pp. 365–7; Cyndia Susan Clegg, 'Burning books as propaganda in Jacobean England', in Andrew Hadfield, ed., *Literature and Censorship in Renaissance England* (Basingstoke, 2001), pp. 165–86.

26. Blair Worden, 'Ben Jonson among the historians', in Sharpe and Lake, eds, *Culture and Politics*, pp. 67–89; David Riggs, *Ben Jonson: A Life* (Cambridge,

Mass., 1989), ch. 7; George Chapman, Ben Jonson and John Marston, *Eastward Ho!*, ed. R.W. van Fossen (Manchester, 1979); Ben Jonson, *Sejanus his Fall*, ed. W.F. Bolton (London, 1966), introduction, p. xii.

27. William Trumbull, *HMC 75: Downshire Manuscripts, VI, Papers of William Trumbull, Sept. 1616–Dec. 1618*, pp. 211–12. I owe this reference to Rebecca Moss.

28. Walker, *Plays of Persuasion*; Born, 'The perfect prince'.

29. Complete listings of the plays performed at court are given in Gurr, *Shakespearian Playing Companies*, pp. 304–5, 386–93.

30. Notestein, *House of Commons*, pp. 146–8; Lockyer, *James VI and I*, ch. 6. More generally, see Antonia Fraser, *The Gunpowder Plot: Terror and Faith in 1605* (London, 1996).

31. Gurr, *Shakespearian Playing Companies*, pp. 299–300; Jonson, *Sejanus his Fall*, introduction, pp. xi–xii; Riggs, *Ben Jonson*, pp. 176–7.

32. On Shakespeare's increasing affluence and respectability, see Duncan-Jones, *Ungentle Shakespeare*, ch. 7.

33. Lockyer, *James VI and I*, pp. 159–77.

34. There is a long tradition of this type of argument, up to and including much new historicist work. See, for example, Bennett, *'Measure for Measure' as Royal Entertainment*; Stevenson, 'The role of James I'; Jonathan Goldberg, *James I and the Politics of Literature* (Baltimore, 1983), pp. 231–9; Leonard Tennenhouse, *Power on Display: The Politics of Shakespeare's Genres* (London, 1986), pp. 154–9.

35. On the disguised ruler plays, all produced in the early 1600s, see Frank Whigham, 'Flattering courtly desire', in David L. Smith, Richard Strier and David Bevington, eds, *The Theatrical City: Culture, Theatre and Politics in London, 1576–1649* (Cambridge, 1995), pp. 137–56, at p. 139.

36. Especially given the earlier staging of *Richard II* (assuming that it was Shakespeare's play) and the praise of Essex in *Henry V*.

37. *Measure for Measure*, ed. J.W. Lever (London, 1965), introduction, pp. xxxi–xxxv; Gurr, *Shakespearian Playing Companies*, p. 304. For a discussion of possible differences between the text performed in 1603 and the printed text, see *Measure for Measure*, ed. Brian Gibbons (Cambridge, 1991), pp. 193–211. For a further analysis of the context of its first production, see John H. Astington, 'The Globe, the Court and *Measure for Measure*', *SS* 52 (1999), 133–42.

38. See Roy Battenhouse, *'Measure for Measure* and the Christian doctrine of atonement', *PMLA* 61 (1946), 1029–59.

39. See also Deborah Kuller Shuger's interesting analysis of the play, *Political Theologies in Shakespeare's England: The Sacred and the State in 'Measure for Measure'* (Basingstoke, 2001).

40. See Paul Hammond, 'The argument of *Measure for Measure*', *ELR* 16 (1986), 496–519, at 496.

41. Bennett, *'Measure for Measure' as Royal Entertainment*, ch. 6; M. Lindsay Kaplan, 'Slander for slander in *Measure for Measure*', in *The Culture of Slander in Early Modern England* (Cambridge, 1997), pp. 92–108; Stevenson, 'The role of James I', pp. 198–9.

42. For a nuanced discussion of the relationship between Duke Vincentio and James, see Leah S. Marcus, *Puzzling Shakespeare: Local Reading and its Discontents* (Berkeley, 1988), pp. 160–202. More generally see David Scott Kastan, 'Proud majesty made a subject: Shakespeare and the spectacle of rule', *SQ* 37 (1986), 459–75.

43. Quotation from Brian Vickers, *In Defence of Rhetoric* (Oxford, 1988), p. 397. For a further analysis of these opening lines, see Hammond, 'Argument of *Measure for Measure*', pp. 496–7.

44. Kastan, 'Proud majesty made a subject', p. 464.

45. On interrogative texts, see Catherine Belsey, *Critical Practice* (London, 1980), ch. 4; Boika Sokolova, *Shakespeare's Romances as Interrogative Texts: Their Alienation Strategies and Ideology* (Lewiston, 1992), pp. 29–31.

46. Marcus, *Puzzling Shakespeare*, pp. 165–84.

47. On the motif of 'change' in the play, see Jacques Lezra, 'The appearance of history in *Measure for Measure*', in *Unspeakable Subjects: The Genealogy of the Event in Early Modern Europe* (Stanford, 1997), pp. 257–96, at p. 260. I owe this reference to Claire Jowitt.

48. Cited in Ashton, ed., *James I by his Contemporaries*, p. 232. Lady Anne Clifford also commented that she and her mother 'saw a great change between the fashion of the Court as it is now and of that in the Queen's time' (loc. cit.). See also Willson, *King James VI and I*, ch. 10. For details of Osborne's importance as a source for the life of James, see Lockyer, *James VI and I*, pp. 2–4.

49. Ashton, ed., *James I by his Contemporaries*, p. 233.

50. See Jonathan Bate, *Shakespeare and Ovid* (Oxford, 1993), *passim*; Gordon Braden, 'Ovid, Petrarch, and Shakespeare's *Sonnets*', in A.B. Taylor, ed., *Shakespeare's Ovid: 'The Metamorphoses' in the Plays and Poems* (Cambridge, 2000), pp. 96–112. See also Christopher Marlowe's translations of Ovid's *Elegies* in *The Poems*, ed. Millar Maclure (London, 1968), pp. 105–217.

51. For evidence that another of Shakespeare's works was thought to contain an indelicate allusion to the King's sexuality, see Paul Hammond, 'James I's homosexuality and the revision of the Folio text of *King Lear*', *N & Q* 242 (March 1997), 62–4.

52. For discussion see Michael B. Young, *James VI and I and the History of Homosexuality* (Basingstoke, 2000).

53. John Webster, *The Duchess of Malfi*, ed. John Russell Brown (London, 1964).

54. See also Shuger's argument; *Political Theologies*, *passim*.

55. Niccolò Machiavelli, *The Prince*, trans. George Bull (Harmondsworth, 1961), pp. 57–8. See also Innocent Gentillet, *A Discourse Upon the Meanes of Wel Governing and Maintaining in Good Peace, a Kingdom, or other Principalitie ... Against Nicholas Machiavell the Florentine*, trans. Simon Patericke (1602) (New York, 1969), pp. 184–5. I have abandoned my preferred practice of citing Patericke's translation because Gentillet does not cite this whole episode.

56. On the 'bed trick', see Marliss C. Desens, *The Bed Trick in English Renaissance Drama* (Newark, 1994).

57. See Jonathan Bate, *Shakespeare and Ovid*; A.B. Taylor, ed., *Shakespeare's Ovid*.

58. For analysis, see Niall Rudd, 'Pyramus and Thisbe in Shakespeare and Ovid', in Taylor, ed., *Shakespeare's Ovid*, pp. 113–25.

59. In addition to the evidence already cited, Isabella's speech to Angelo about mercy for prisoners (2.2.59–63) may allude to the imprisonment of Sir Walter Raleigh; the confusion over the planned execution of Claudio appears to refer to the dispute over the execution of James's mother, Mary Queen of Scots, when Elizabeth publicly blamed her secretary, William Davison, for sending off the warrant without her permission (5.1.455–67) (for details, see J.E. Neale, *Queen Elizabeth* (London, 1934), ch. 16).

60. Precisely what was being debated in parliament and more widely among lawyers; see Notestein, *House of Commons*, ch. 1; J.G.A. Pocock, *The Ancient Constitution and the Feudal Law: A Study of English Historical Thought in the Seventeenth Century* (2nd edn, Cambridge, 1987), ch. 2. For the political background, see also G.R. Elton, ed., *The Tudor Constitution: Documents and Commentary* (Cambridge, 1972, rpt of 1960), ch. 5.

61. On the structure of Old Comedy, see Philip Whaley Marsh, *A Handbook of Classical Drama* (Stanford, 1944), pp. 258–63.

62. On the slow process of change from Elizabethan to Jacobean England and the resulting frustration, see Curtis Perry, *The Making of Jacobean Culture* (Cambridge, 1997).

63. Three important recent articles are Robert S. Miola, 'Timon in Shakespeare's Athens', *SQ* 13 (1980), 21–30; John M. Wallace, '*Timon of Athens* and the Three Graces: Shakespeare's Senecan study', *MP* 83 (1985–6), 349–63; Coppélia Kahn, '"Magic of bounty": *Timon of Athens*, Jacobean patronage, and maternal power', *SQ* 38 (1987), 34–57.

64. *Timon of Athens*, ed. H.J. Oliver (London, 1959), introduction, pp. xl–xlii. On *Timon* as an inferior *King Lear* see Nicholas Greene, *Shakespeare's Tragic Imagination* (Basingstoke, 1992), p. 147; John Dover Wilson, *The Essential Shakespeare* (Cambridge, 1932), p. 131.

65. For an incisive discussion, see Kahn '"Magic of bounty"', pp. 41–50.

66. Ashton, ed., *James I by his Contemporaries*, p. 2.

67. Lockyer, *James VI and I*, p. 200.

68. For commentary, see Edward Berry, *Shakespeare and the Hunt: A Cultural and Social Study* (Cambridge, 2001), pp. 1–3; Roy Strong, *Henry Prince of Wales and England's Lost Renaissance* (London, 1986), p. 114.

69. Ben Jonson, 'To Penshurst' (published 1616), in *Poems*, ed. Ian Donaldson (Oxford, 1975), ll. 20–1.

70. Compare *King Lear*, 1.4, for a similar account of the monarch's exploitation of his powerful subjects.

71. For further analysis, see Don E. Wayne, *Penshurst: The Semiotics of Place and the Poetics of History* (London, 1984).

72. John Donne, *The Complete English Poems*, ed. J.C. Smith (Harmondsworth, 1971), l. 7.

73. For analysis, see John Carey, *John Donne: Life, Mind and Art* (2nd edn, London, 1990), pp. 94–6.

74. See Berry, *Shakespeare and the Hunt*, chs 3, 7 (quotation at p. 94).

75. Commentators appear not to have made this connection, although Rolf Soellner alludes to a link between Timon and James, in *Timon of Athens: Shakespeare's Pessimistic Tragedy* (Columbus, Ohio, 1979), p. 124.

76. See the *OED* definition, p. 3025, no. 29.

77. For details of Osborne's importance as a source for the life of James, see Lockyer, *James VI and I*, pp. 2–4. The anecdote is alluded to in Alvin Kernan, *Shakespeare, the King's Playwright: Theater in the Stuart Court, 1603–1613* (New Haven, 1995), pp. 126–7.

78. Cited in Ashton, ed., *James I by his Contemporaries*, p. 69.

79. Lockyer, *James VI and I*, p. 168; David Lindley, *The Trials of Frances Howard: Fact and Fiction at the Court of King James* (London, 1993), ch. 4.

80. Cited in Ashton, ed., *James I by his Contemporaries*, p. 69.

81. A further analogue is Malbecco in Edmund Spenser's *The Faerie Queene*, ed. A.C. Hamilton (London, 1977), Bk II, canto x.

82. Karl Marx and Friedrich Engels, *On Literature and Art* (Moscow, 1976), p. 135.

83. On the significance of the Athenian setting of the play, see Miola, 'Timon in Shakespeare's Athens'.

84. Cited in Ashton, ed., *James I by his Contemporaries*, p. 14. On Weldon, see Lockyer, *James VI and I*, pp. 2–4.

85. Willson, *King James VI and I*, ch. 15; Ashton, ed., *James I by his Contemporaries*, ch. 8; W.B. Patterson, *King James VI and I and the Reunion of Christendom* (Cambridge, 1997).

86. Lockyer, *James VI and I*, pp. 78–80. See also Kahn, '"Magic of bounty"', pp. 42–7.

87. See John Bartlett, *A Complete Concordance to Shakespeare* (London, 1997, rpt of 1894), p. 539.

88. See Harry V. Jaffa, 'Nature and the city: *Timon of Athens*', in John E. Alvis and Thomas G. West, eds, *Shakespeare as Political Thinker* (Wilmington, Delaware, 2000), pp. 177–201, at pp. 199–200; Miola, 'Timon in Shakespeare's Athens'. Nicholas Greene suggests otherwise, claiming that Athens 'is an indeterminate place with the vaguest of classical associations' (*Shakespeare's Tragic Imagination*, p. 126). It is true that Shakespeare's representation of Athens lacks the historical and geographical specificity of his representation of Rome, but this does not mean that we can assume that Athens has no significance as a location.

89. See G.K. Hunter, *John Lyly: The Humanist as Courtier* (London, 1962), p. 59.

90. For details of the sources, see Geoffrey Bullough, *Narrative and Dramatic Sources of Shakespeare*, 8 vols (London, 1957–75), VI, ch. 3. Bullough suggests that Shakespeare made use of Lyly's *Campaspe* (pp. 339–45).

91. Thucydides, *History. Tr. into Englishe* (1607) (trans. anon.). A previous translation by T. Nicolls had appeared in 1550.

92. A.D. Nuttall, *Timon of Athens* (Boston, 1989), p. xix.

93. Plutarch, *Life of Alcibiades*, in *Selected Lives of the Noble Grecians and Romans*, trans. Thomas North (1597), ed. Judith Mossman (Ware, 1998), pp. 87–136, at p. 88. Subsequent references to this edition in parentheses in the text.

94. On *Timon* as a fable, see Wallace, '*Timon of Athens* and the Three Graces', p. 361.

95. On Alcibiades as a furious anti-Stoic figure, see Wallace, '*Timon of Athens* and the Three Graces', p. 361.

96. See A.L. Beier, *Masterless Men: The Vagrancy Problem in England, 1560–1640* (London, 1985), pp. 93–5.

97. Greene, *Shakespeare's Tragic Imagination*, p. 147; *Timon of Athens*, ed. Karl Klein (Cambridge, 2001), introduction, pp. 61–6; Nuttall, *Timon of Athens*, ch. 3; Luke Wilson, *Theaters of Intention: Drama and the Law in Early Modern England* (Stanford, 2000), pp. 177–83.

98. The political charge of a Jacobean play for the public stage might be usefully contrasted to contemporary court masques, such as those which reflect on the significant incidents in the life of Frances Howard; see Lindley, *Trials of Frances Howard*, pp. 17–19, 58–60.

99. See Miola, 'Timon in Shakespeare's Athens', p. 26.

100. Gurr, *Shakespearian Playing Companies*, p. 304. On *Volpone* and beast fables, see Douglas Duncan, *Ben Jonson and the Lucianic Tradition* (Cambridge, 1979), ch. 7. John M. Wallace argues that *Volpone* and *Timon* 'are competitive studies of the same subject': '*Timon of Athens* and the Three Graces', p. 350.

101. For comments on Shakespeare and Machiavelli as a representative of 'modern politics', see John E. Alvis, 'Introductory: Shakespearean poetry and politics', in Alvis and West, eds, *Shakespeare as Political Thinker*, pp. 1–27.

102. Gentillet, *Discourse*, p. 218.

103. Felix Raab, *The English Face of Machiavelli: A Changing Interpretation, 1500–1700* (London, 1965), pp. 56–7; Quentin Skinner, *The Foundations of Modern Political Thought*, 2 vols. (Cambridge, 1978), I, pp. 250–1.

104. Gentillet, *Discourse*, pp. 92–9, 222–7.

105. Thucydides, *The History of the Peloponnesian War*, trans. Rex Warner and M.I. Finley (Harmondsworth, 1972), *passim*.

106. For stage history, see *Timon*, ed. Klein, introduction, pp. 35–52.

107. See *The Tempest*, ed. Virginia Mason Vaughan and Alden T. Vaughan (London, 1999), pp. 287–303; Francis Barker and Peter Hulme, 'Nymphs and reapers heavily vanish: the discursive con-texts of *The Tempest*', in John Drakakis, ed., *Alternative Shakespeares* (London, 1985), pp. 191–205; Paul Brown, '"This thing of darkness I acknowledge mine": *The Tempest* and the discourse of colonialism', in Jonathan Dollimore and Alan Sinfield, eds, *Political Shakespeare: New Essays in Cultural Materialism* (Manchester, 1985), pp. 48–71.

108. See Richard Wilson, 'Voyage to Tunis: new history and the Old World of *The Tempest*', *ELH* 64 (1997), 333–57.

109. See *The Tempest*, ed. Stephen Orgel (Oxford, 1987), pp. 40–3.

110. A convenient overview is R.S. White, ed., *The Tempest* (Basingstoke, 1999). See also Donna B. Hamilton, *Virgil and 'The Tempest': The Politics of Imitation* (Columbus, Ohio, 1990).

111. For analysis, see Peter Hulme, *Colonial Encounters: Europe and the Native Caribbean, 1492–1797* (London, 1986), ch. 3; John Gillies, *Shakespeare and the Geography of Difference* (Cambridge, 1994), pp. 140–55; Andrew Hadfield, *Literature, Travel, and Colonial Writing in the English Renaissance, 1545–1625* (Oxford, 1998), pp. 242–54.

112. *The Historie of Guicciardini containing the warres of Italie and Other Partes* (1579), trans. Geoffrey Fenton (London, 1599), p. 3. Subsequent references to this edition in parentheses in the text. There is a convenient modern translation of most of the text with helpful summaries; Francesco Guicciardini, *The History of Italy*, trans. Sidney Alexander (Princeton, 1969).

113. The one English play based on Guicciardini's *Historie* is Barnabe Barnes's *The Devil's Charter* (see above, p. 188).

114. For an analysis of the work, see Rudolf B. Gottfried, *Geoffrey Fenton's 'Historie of Guicciardini'* (Indiana, 1940).

115. The Sforza family also play a vital role in Machiavelli's *The Prince*. For comparative analysis of Guicciardini and Machiavelli as political theorists and historians, see Felix Gilbert, *Machiavelli and Guicciardini: Politics and History in Sixteenth-Century Florence* (Princeton, 1965); J.G.A. Pocock, *The Machiavellian Moment: Florentine Political Thought and the Atlantic Republican Tradition* (Princeton, 1975), chs 5–8.
116. *Tempest*, ed. Orgel, p. 42.
117. William Thomas, *Historie of Italie* (1549), p. 181. Subsequent references to this edition in parentheses in the text.
118. For further details, see Hadfield, *Literature, Travel, and Colonial Writing*, pp. 124–32.
119. For comment, see David Norbrook, '"What cares these roarers for the name of king?": language and utopia in *The Tempest*', in Jonathan Hope and Gordon McMullan, eds, *The Politics of Tragicomedy: Shakespeare and After* (London, 1992), pp. 21–54.
120. *The Essayes of Michel Lord of Montaigne*, trans. John Florio (1603), 3 vols (London, 1910), I, pp. 215–29.
121. See *Essayes of Montaigne*, I, p. 220.
122. A.L. Morton, *The English Utopia* (London, 1954), ch. 1.
123. Prospero is represented as a tyrant in much recent criticism. See the essays collected in White, ed., *The Tempest*, for examples.
124. See Stephen Orgel, *The Illusion of Power: Political Theater in the English Renaissance* (Berkeley, 1975); David Lindley, ed., *The Court Masque* (Manchester, 1984).
125. *Essayes of Montaigne*, pp. 223–4.
126. Curtis C. Breight, '"Treason doth never prosper": *The Tempest* and the discourse of treason', *SQ* 41 (1990), 1–28. See also John Bellamy, *The Tudor Law of Treason: An Introduction* (London, 1979), pp. 109–21.
127. *Measure for Measure* is a play that also shows how stasis triumphs over change; see above, pp. 189–200.

AFTERWORD

1. See Guy Finch Lytle and Stephen Orgel, eds, *Patronage in the Renaissance* (Princeton, 1981); Richard Helgerson, *Self-Crowned Laureates: Spenser, Jonson, Milton and the Literary System* (Berkeley, 1983).
2. For comment see the interesting essay by Gary Taylor, 'Bardicide', repr. in Richard Wilson, ed., *Julius Caesar: Contemporary Critical Essays* (Basingstoke, 2002), pp. 188–209.

3. The literature on 'bardolatry' is now immense. Two recent works which show how Shakespeare's status has distorted readings of his works are Michael Keevak, *Sexual Shakespeare: Forgery, Authorship, Portraiture* (Detroit, 2001); Graham Holderness, *Cultural Shakespeare: Essays in the Shakespeare Myth* (Hatfield, 2001).

4. For biographical details, see Katherine Duncan-Jones, *Ungentle Shakespeare: Scenes from his Life* (London, 2001), chs 3, 9.

BIBLIOGRAPHY

References to Shakespeare are to the Arden editions of the poetry and plays, in Arden 3, when available, and otherwise in Arden 2.

Adams, Simon, 'The patronage of the crown in Elizabethan politics: the 1590s in perspective', in Guy, ed., *The Reign of Elizabeth I*, pp. 20–45

Adelman, Janet, *Suffocating Mothers: Fantasies of Maternal Origin in Shakespeare's Plays, 'Hamlet' to 'The Tempest'* (London, 1992)

Akrigg, G.P.V., *Shakespeare and the Earl of Southampton* (London, 1968)

Alford, Stephen, *The Early Elizabethan Polity: William Cecil and the Succession Crisis, 1558–1569* (Cambridge, 1998)

Allen, William, *A Treatise made in Defence of the lawful power and authoritie of Priesthood to remedie sinnes* (London, 1567)

Alvis, John E., and Thomas G. West, eds, *Shakespeare as Political Thinker* (Wilmington, Delaware, 2000)

Anglo, Sydney, 'A Machiavellian solution to the Irish problem: Richard Beacon's *Solon his Follie* (1594)', in Edward Chaney and Peter Mack, eds, *England and the Continental Renaissance: Essays in Honour of J.B. Trapp* (Woodbridge, 1990), pp. 153–64

— *Images of Tudor Kingship* (Guildford, 1992)

anon., *The First Part of the Reign of King Richard the Second or Thomas of Woodstock*, ed. Wilhelmina P. Frijlinck (Oxford, 1929)

— *The History of King Leir, 1605* (Oxford, 1907)

— 'An Homilie Agaynst Disobedience and Wylful Rebellion', in *Certain Sermons Appointed by the Queen's Majesty* (1570?) (Cambridge, 1850), pp. 551–99

— *Leicester's Commonwealth: The Copy of a letter Written by a Master of Art of Cambridge (1584) and Related Documents*, ed. D.C. Peck (Athens, Ohio, 1985)

— *The Oldcastle Controversy: Sir John Oldcastle, Part I and The Famous Victories of Henry V*, ed. Peter Corbin and Douglas Sedge (Manchester, 1991)

— *The Tragedie of Claudius Tiberius Nero, Romes greatest Tyrant Truly represented out of the purest Records of those times* (London, 1607)

— *The Tragedy of Locrine*, ed. Ronald B. McKerrow (Oxford, 1908)

— *Vindiciae, Contra Tyrannos*, ed. George Garnett (Cambridge, 1994)

Aristotle, *Nicomachean Ethics*, trans. David Ross (Oxford, 1980, rpt of 1925)

— *The Politics*, trans. Thomas Alan Sinclair (Harmondsworth, 1962)

Ascham, Roger, *The scholemaster or plaine and perfite way of teachyng children, the Latin tong* (London, 1570)

Ashton, Robert, ed., *James I by his Contemporaries: An Account of his Career and Character as seen by some of his Contemporaries* (London, 1969)

Astington, John H., 'The Globe, the Court and *Measure for Measure*', *SS* 52 (1999), 133–42

Axton, Marie, *The Queen's Two Bodies: Drama and the Elizabethan Succession* (London, 1977)

Baker, David J., *Between Nations: Shakespeare, Spenser, Marvell and the Question of Britain* (Stanford, 1997)

Baldwin, T.W., *William Shakspere's Small Latine and Lesse Greeke* (Urbana, 1944)
— *On the Literary Genetics of Shakspere's Poems and Sonnets* (Urbana, 1950)

Baldwin, William, *et al.*, *The Mirror for Magistrates*, ed. Lily B. Campbell (Cambridge, 1938)

Bale, John, *King Johan*, ed. Barry B. Adams (San Marino, 1969)

Barbour, Reid, *English Epicures and Stoics: Ancient Legacies in Early Stuart Culture* (Amherst, 1998)

Barker, Francis, and Peter Hulme, 'Nymphs and reapers heavily vanish: the discursive con-texts of *The Tempest*', in Drakakis, ed., *Alternative Shakespeares*, pp. 191–205

Barnes, Barnabe, *The divils charter: a tragedy conteining the life and death of pope Alexander the sixt* (London, 1607)

Barrell, John, *Poetry, Language & Politics* (Manchester, 1988)

Bartlett, John, *A Complete Concordance to Shakespeare* (London, 1997, rpt of 1894)

Bartley, J.O., *Teague, Shenkin and Sawney: Being an Historical Study of the earliest Irish, Welsh and Scottish Characters in English Plays* (Cork, 1954)

Barton, Anne, '"He that plays the king": Ford's *Perkin Warbeck*', in *Essays, Mainly Shakespearean* (Cambridge, 1994), pp. 234–60
— 'Livy, Machiavelli and *Coriolanus*', in *Essays, Mainly Shakespearean* (Cambridge, 1994), pp. 136–60

Bate, Jonathan, *Shakespeare and Ovid* (Oxford, 1993)
— 'The Elizabethans in Italy', in Maquerlot and Willems, eds, *Travel and Drama in Shakespeare's Time*, pp. 55–74

Battenhouse, Roy, '*Measure for Measure* and the Christian doctrine of atonement', *PMLA* 61 (1946), 1029–59
— 'The relation of *Henry V* to *Tamburlaine*', *SQ* 27 (1974), 71–9

Bednarz, James P., *Shakespeare and The Poets' War* (New York, 2001)

Beier, A.L., *Masterless Men: The Vagrancy Problem in England, 1560–1640* (London, 1985)

Bellamy, John, *The Tudor Law of Treason: An Introduction* (London, 1979)

Belsey, Andrew, and Catherine Belsey, 'Icons of divinity: portraits of Elizabeth I', in Lucy Gent and Nigel Llewellyn, eds, *Renaissance Bodies: The Human Figure in English Culture, c.1540–1660* (London, 1990), pp. 11–35

Belsey, Catherine, *Critical Practice* (London, 1980)

— *The Subject of Tragedy: Identity and Difference in Renaissance Drama* (London, 1985)

Benjamin, Edwin B., 'Sir John Hayward and Tacitus', *RES* n.s. 8 (1957), 275–6

Bennett, Josephine Waters, *'Measure for Measure' as Royal Entertainment* (New York, 1966)

Berger, Thomas L., and Jesse M. Lander, 'Shakespeare in print, 1593–1640', in Kastan, ed., *Companion to Shakespeare*, pp. 395–413

Berry, Edward, *Shakespeare and the Hunt: A Cultural and Social Study* (Cambridge, 2001)

Berry, Philippa, *Of Chastity and Power: Elizabethan Literature and the Unmarried Queen* (London, 1989)

— 'Woman, language, and history in *The Rape of Lucrece*', *SS* 44 (1992), 33–9

Bevington, David M., *Tudor Drama and Politics: A Critical Approach to Topical Meaning* (Cambridge, Mass., 1968)

Blayney, Peter, 'The publication of playbooks', in Cox and Kastan, eds, *New History of Early English Drama*, pp. 383–422

Bloom, Allan, with Harry V. Jaffa, *Shakespeare's Politics* (Chicago, 1981, rpt of 1964)

Bodin, Jean, *Method for the Easy Comprehension of History*, trans. Beatrice Reynolds (New York, 1945)

— *The Six Bookes of the Commonweale out of the French and Latine Copies, done into English, by R. Knolles* (London, 1606)

Born, L.K., 'The perfect prince: a study in thirteenth- and fourteenth-century ideals', *Speculum* 3 (1928), 470–504

Botero, Giovanni, *Observations Upon the Lives of Alexander, Caesar, Scipio; newly Englished* (London, 1602)

Boutcher, Warren, '"A French dexterity, & an Italian confidence": new documents on John Florio, learned strangers and Protestant humanist study of modern languages in Renaissance England from c.1547 to c.1625', *Reformation* 2 (1997), 39–109

Braden, Gordon, 'Ovid, Petrarch, and Shakespeare's *Sonnets*', in A.B. Taylor, ed., *Shakespeare's Ovid*, pp. 96–112

Bradford, Alan T., 'Stuart absolutism and the "utility" of Tacitus', *HLQ* 46 (1983), 127–55

Bradley, A.C., *Shakespearean Tragedy: Lectures on Hamlet, Othello, King Lear, Macbeth* (London, 1904)

Breight, Curtis C., '"Treason doth never prosper": *The Tempest* and the discourse of treason', *SQ* 41 (1990), 1–28

— *Surveillance, Militarism and Drama in the Elizabethan Era* (Basingstoke, 1996)

Briggs, Julia, *This Stage-Play World: Texts and Contexts, 1580–1625* (2nd edn, Oxford, 1997)

Brown, Paul, '"This thing of darkness I acknowledge mine": *The Tempest* and the discourse of colonialism', in Dollimore and Sinfield, eds, *Political Shakespeare*, pp. 48–71

Bruster, Douglas, *Drama and the Market in the Age of Shakespeare* (Cambridge, 1992)

Buchanan, George, *The History of Scotland written in Latin by George Buchanan; faithfully rendered into English* (London, 1690)

Bullough, Geoffrey, *Narrative and Dramatic Sources of Shakespeare*, 8 vols (London, 1957–75)

Burgess, Glenn, *The Politics of the Ancient Constitution: An Introduction to English Political Thought, 1603–1642* (Basingstoke, 1992)

Burke, Peter, 'Tacitism', in T.A. Dorey, ed., *Tacitus* (London, 1969), pp. 149–71

— 'Tacitism, scepticism, and reason of state', in Burns and Goldie, eds, *Cambridge History of Political Thought*, pp. 479–98

— *The Fortunes of the Courtier: The European Reception of Castiglione's 'Cortegiano'* (Cambridge, 1995)

Burnett, Mark Thornton, *Masters and Servants in English Renaissance Drama and Culture: Authority and Obedience* (Basingstoke, 1997)

Burns, J.H. *The Trew Law of Kingship: Concepts of Monarchy in Early Modern Scotland* (Oxford, 1996), ch. 7

Burns, J.H., and Mark Goldie, eds, *The Cambridge History of Political Thought, 1450–1700* (Cambridge, 1991)

Bushnell, Rebecca W., *Tragedies of Tyrants: Political Thought and Theater in the English Renaissance* (Ithaca, 1990)

Butler, Martin, *Theatre and Crisis, 1632–1642* (Cambridge, 1984)

— 'Ben Jonson and the limits of courtly panegyric', in Sharpe and Lake, eds, *Culture and Politics in Early Stuart England*, pp. 91–116

Calvin, Jean, *The Institution of the Christian Religion*, trans. Thomas Norton (London, 1582)

— *Aphorismes of Christian Religion: Or, a verie Compendious abridgement of M.I. Calvins Institutions, set forth in short sentences methodically by M.I. Piscator*, trans. Henry Holland (London, 1596)

Campbell, Lily B., *Shakespeare's 'Histories': Mirrors of Elizabethan Policy* (San Marino, Ca., 1947)

Carey, John, *John Donne: Life, Mind and Art* (2nd edn, London, 1990)

Carey, Vincent, 'The Irish face of Machiavelli: Richard Beacon's *Solon his Follie* and republican ideology in the conquest of Ireland', in Hiram Morgan, ed., *Political Ideology in Ireland, 1534–1641* (Dublin, 1999), pp. 83–109

Carrier, Irene, *James VI and I: King of Great Britain* (Cambridge, 1997)

Cary, M., and H.H. Scullard, *A History of Rome down to the Reign of Constantine* (3rd edn, Basingstoke, 1975)

Catty, Jocelyn, *Writing Rape, Writing Women in Early Modern England: Unbridled Speech* (Basingstoke, 1999)

Chakravorty, Swapan, *Society and Politics in the Plays of Thomas Middleton* (Oxford, 1996)

Chambers, E.K., *The Elizabethan Stage*, 4 vols. (Oxford, 1923)

Chapman, George, Ben Jonson and John Marston, *Eastward Ho!*, ed. R.W. van Fossen (Manchester, 1979)

Clare, Janet, *'Art made tongue-tied by authority': Elizabethan and Jacobean Dramatic Censorship* (2nd edn, Manchester, 1999)

— 'Censorship and negotiation', in Hadfield, ed., *Literature and Censorship in Renaissance England*, pp. 17–30

Clegg, Cyndia Susan, *Press Censorship in Elizabethan England* (Cambridge, 1997)

— 'Burning books as propaganda in Jacobean England', in Hadfield, ed., *Literature and Censorship in Renaissance England*, pp. 165–86

— *Press Censorship in Jacobean England* (Cambridge, 2001)

Cohen, Stephen A., '"The quality of mercy": law, equity and ideology in *The Merchant of Venice*', *Mosaic* 27.4 (Dec. 1994), 35–54

Coleman, Janet, *A History of Political Thought*, 2 vols (Oxford, 2000)

Collinson, Patrick, *The Elizabethan Puritan Movement* (Oxford, 1967)

— 'The monarchical republic of Queen Elizabeth I', *BJRL* 69 (1987), 394–424

— *The Birthpangs of Protestant England: Religious and Cultural Change in the Sixteenth and Seventeenth Centuries* (Basingstoke, 1988)

— *De Republica Anglorum: Or, History with the Politics put back* (Cambridge, 1990)

— 'Ecclesiastical vitriol: religious satire in the 1590s and the invention of puritanism', in Guy, ed., *Reign of Elizabeth I*, pp. 150–70

Contarini, Gasparo, *The commonwealth and government of Venice. Written by the Cardinall Gaspar Contareno*, trans. Lewes Lewkenor (London, 1599)

Conte, Gian Biago, *Latin Literature; A History*, trans. Joseph B. Solodow, rev. Don Fowler and Glenn W. Most (Baltimore, 1999, rpt of 1994)

Coryat, Thomas, *Coryat's Crudities, Hastily gobled up in five Monethes travells* (London, 1611) (rpt Glasgow, 1905), 2 vols

Cox, John D., and David Scott Kastan, eds, *A New History of Early English Drama* (New York, 1997)

Crick, Bernard, *In Defence of Politics* (Harmondsworth, 1964)

Danson, Lawrence, *Shakespeare's Dramatic Genres* (Oxford, 2000)

Davies, C.S.L., *Peace, Print and Protestantism, 1450–1558* (London, 1977)

Dawson, Anthony B. and Paul Yachnin, *The Culture of Playgoing in Shakespeare's England: A Collaborative Debate* (Cambridge, 2001)

Dekker, Thomas, *The Shoemaker's Holiday*, ed. Anthony Parr (London, 1990)

Desens, Marliss C., *The Bed Trick in English Renaissance Drama* (Newark, 1994)

Dickens, A.G., *The English Reformation* (rev. edn, London, 1986)

Dobin, Howard, *Merlin's Disciples: Prophecy, Poetry, and Power in Renaissance England* (Stanford, 1990)

Dollimore, Jonathan, and Alan Sinfield, 'History and ideology: the instance of *Henry V*', in Drakakis, ed., *Alternative Shakespeares*, pp. 206–27

— eds, *Political Shakespeare: New Essays in Cultural Materialism* (Manchester, 1985)

Donaldson, Ian, *The Rapes of Lucrece: A Myth and its Transformations* (Oxford, 1982)

— '"Misconstruing everything": *Julius Caesar* and *Sejanus*', in Grace Ioppolo, ed., *Shakespeare Performed: Essays in Honour of R.A. Foakes* (Newark, 2000), pp. 88–107

Donawerth, Jane, *Shakespeare and the Sixteenth-Century Study of Language* (Chicago, 1984)

Donne, John, *The Complete English Poems*, ed. J.C. Smith (Harmondsworth, 1971)

Doran, Susan, *Monarchy and Matriarchy: The Courtships of Elizabeth I* (London, 1996)

— 'Why did Elizabeth not marry?', in Julia M. Walker, ed., *Dissing Elizabeth: Negative Representations of Gloriana* (Durham, NC, 1998), pp. 30–59

— '"Revenge her most foul and unnatural murder?": the impact of Mary Stuart's execution on Anglo-Scottish relations', *History* 85 (2000), 589–612

Drakakis, John, ed., *Alternative Shakespeares* (London, 1985)

Duncan, Douglas, *Ben Jonson and the Lucianic Tradition* (Cambridge, 1979)

Duncan-Jones, Katherine, *Sir Philip Sidney, Courtier Poet* (New Haven, 1991)

— *Ungentle Shakespeare: Scenes from his Life* (London, 2001)

Dutton, Richard, *Mastering the Revels: The Regulation and Censorship of English Renaissance Drama* (Basingstoke, 1991)

— *Licensing, Censorship and Authorship in Early Modern England* (Basingstoke, 2000)

— 'Receiving offence: *A Game at Chess* again', in Hadfield, ed., *Literature and Censorship in Renaissance England*, pp. 50–71

Dzelzainis, Martin, 'Shakespeare and political thought', in Kastan, ed., *Companion to Shakespeare*, pp. 100–16

Eagleton, Terry, *William Shakespeare* (Oxford, 1986)

Edwards, Philip, *Threshold of a Nation: A Study in English and Irish Drama* (Cambridge, 1979)

Ellis-Fermor, Una, *The Jacobean Drama* (London, 1965)

Elton, G.R., ed., *The Tudor Constitution: Documents and Commentary* (Cambridge, 1972, rpt of 1960)

— *The Parliament of England, 1559–1581* (Cambridge, 1986)

Erskine-Hill, Howard, *Poetry and the Realm of Politics: Shakespeare to Dryden* (Oxford, 1996)

Ferguson, Arthur B., *The Articulate Citizen and the English Renaissance* (Durham, NC, 1965)

Fiedler, Leslie A., *The Stranger in Shakespeare* (London, 1973)

Fletcher, Anthony, *Tudor Rebellions* (3rd edn, Harlow, 1983)

Foakes, R.A., *Hamlet versus Lear: Cultural Politics and Shakespeare's Art* (Cambridge, 1993)

Forset, Edward, *A comparative discourse of the bodies natural and politique* (London, 1606)

Fortesque, Sir John, *A Learned Commendation of the Politique Lawes of England*, trans. Robert Mulcaster (London, 1567)

Foxe, John, *The Acts and Monuments of the Christian Church (Foxe's Book of Martyrs)* (1563, 1570, 1583), ed. David G. Newcombe and Michael Pidd (facsimile on CD-ROM) (Oxford, 2001)

Franklin, Julian H., *Jean Bodin and the Rise of Absolutist Theory* (Cambridge, 1973)

— 'Sovereignty and the mixed constitution: Bodin and his critics', in Burns and Goldie, eds, *Cambridge History of Political Thought*, pp. 298–328

Fraser, Antonia, *Mary Queen of Scots* (London, 1969)

— *The Gunpowder Plot: Terror and Faith in 1605* (London, 1996)

Freedman, Barbara, 'Elizabethan protest, plague and plays: rereading the "Documents of Control"', *ELR* 26 (1996), 17–45

Fryde, E.B., and Edward Miller, eds, *Historical Studies of the English Parliament, II, 1399–1603* (Cambridge, 1970)

Garrett, Christina H., *The Marian Exiles: A Study in the Origins of Elizabethan Puritanism* (Cambridge, 1938)

Gentillet, Innocent, *A Discourse Upon the Meanes of Wel Governing and Maintaining in Good Peace, a Kingdom, or other Principalitie … Against Nicholas Machiavell the Florentine*, trans. Simon Patericke (1602) (New York, 1969)

Geoffrey of Monmouth, *The History of the Kings of Britain*, trans. Lewis Thorpe (Harmondsworth, 1966)

Gilbert, Felix, *Machiavelli and Guicciardini: Politics and History in Sixteenth-Century Florence* (Princeton, 1965)

Gillespie, Stuart, *Shakespeare's Books: A Dictionary of Shakespeare Sources* (London, 2001)

Gillies, John, *Shakespeare and the Geography of Difference* (Cambridge, 1994)

Goldberg, Jonathan, *James I and the Politics of Literature* (Baltimore, 1983)

Goldie, Mark, 'The unacknowledged republic: officeholding in early modern England', in Tim Harris, ed., *The Politics of the Excluded, c.1500–1850* (Basingstoke, 2001), pp. 153–94

Goodman, Christopher, *How Superior Powers Oght to be Obeyed* (London, 1558)

Gottfried, Rudolf B., *Geoffrey Fenton's 'Historie of Guicciardini'* (Indiana, 1940)

Graef, Ortwin de, '"Sweet dreams, monstered nothings": catechresis in Kant and *Coriolanus*', in Andrew Hadfield, Dominic Rainsford and Tim Woods, eds, *The Ethics in Literature* (Basingstoke, 1999), 231–47

Grant, Michael, *History of Rome* (London, 1978)

Greenblatt, Stephen, *Shakespearean Negotiations: The Circulation of Social Energy in Renaissance England* (Oxford, 1988)

Greene, Nicholas, *Shakespeare's Tragic Imagination* (Basingstoke, 1992)

Griffin, Benjamin, *Playing the Past: Approaches to English Historical Drama, 1385–1600* (Woodbridge, 2001)

Guicciardini, Francesco, *The Historie of Guicciardini containing the warres of Italie and Other Partes* (1579), trans. Geoffrey Fenton (London, 1599)

— *The History of Italy*, trans. Sidney Alexander (Princeton, 1969)

Gurr, Andrew, '*Coriolanus* and the body politic', *SS* 28 (1975), 63–9

— *The Shakespearean Stage, 1574–1642* (Cambridge, 1992)

— *The Shakespearian Playing Companies* (Oxford, 1996)

Guy, John, *Tudor England* (Oxford, 1988)

— ed., *The Reign of Elizabeth I: Court and Culture in the Last Decade* (Cambridge, 1995)

— 'The rhetoric of counsel in early modern England', in Hoak, ed., *Tudor Political Culture*, pp. 292–310

— 'Tudor monarchy and its critiques', in John Guy, ed., *The Tudor Monarchy* (London, 1997), pp. 78–109

Hackel, Heidi Brayman, 'The "great variety" of readers and early modern reading practices', in Kastan, ed., *Companion to Shakespeare*, pp. 139–57

Hackett, Helen, *Virgin Mother, Maiden Queen: Elizabeth I and the Cult of the Virgin Mary* (Basingstoke, 1995)

Hadfield, Andrew, 'The art of fiction: poetry and politics in Reformation England', *Leeds Studies in English*, n.s. 23 (1992), 127–56

— *Literature, Politics and National Identity: Reformation to Renaissance* (Cambridge, 1994)

— *Literature, Travel, and Colonial Writing in the English Renaissance, 1545–1625* (Oxford, 1998)

— 'Was Spenser a republican?', *English* 47 (1998), 169–82

— *The English Renaissance, 1550–1620* (Oxford, 2000)

— 'The Spanish Tragedy, the Alençon marriage plans, and John Stubbs's *Discoverie of a Gaping Gulf*', *N & Q* 245 (March 2000), 42–3

— 'Spenser, Drayton, and the question of Britain', *RES*, n.s. 51 (2000), 582–99

— ed., *Amazons, Savages & Machiavels: Travel & Colonial Writing in English, 1550–1630: An Anthology* (Oxford, 2001)

— ed., *Literature and Censorship in Renaissance England* (Basingstoke, 2001)

— *Shakespeare, Spenser and the Matter of Britain* (Basingstoke, 2003)

Haigh, Christopher, *Elizabeth I* (Harlow, 1988)

Hale, D.G., *The Body Politic: A Political Metaphor in Renaissance England* (The Hague, 1971)

— '*Coriolanus*: The death of a political metaphor', *SS* 22 (1971), 197–202

Hall, Edward, *The Union of the Two Noble and Illustre Famelies of Lancastre & Yorke* (1548) (London, 1809)

Hall, Kim F., *Things of Darkness: Economies of Race and Gender in Early Modern England* (Ithaca, NY, 1995)

Hamilton, Donna B., *Virgil and 'The Tempest': the Politics of Imitation* (Columbus, Ohio, 1990)

Hammer, Paul E.J., *The Polarisation of Elizabethan Politics: The Political Career of Robert Devereux, 2nd Earl of Essex, 1585–1597* (Cambridge, 1999)

Hammond, Paul, 'The argument of *Measure for Measure*', *ELR* 16 (1986), 496–519

— 'James I's homosexuality and the revision of the Folio text of *King Lear*', *N & Q* 242 (March 1997), 62–4

Hankins, James, ed., *Renaissance Civic Humanism* (Cambridge, 2000)

Hapgood, Robert, '*Othello*', in Stanley Wells, ed., *Shakespeare: A Bibliographical Guide* (Oxford, 1990), pp. 223–40

Harvey, Gabriel, *Letter-Book of Gabriel Harvey, A.D. 1573–1580*, ed. Edward John Long Scott (London, 1884)

Harvey, Sir Paul, *The Oxford Companion to Classical Literature* (Oxford, 1984, rpt of 1937)

Haugaard, W.P., *Elizabeth and the English Reformation* (Cambridge, 1968)

Hawkes, Terence, *King Lear* (Plymouth, 1995)

Hayward, John, *The First and Second Parts of John Hayward's 'The Life and Raigne of King Henrie IIII'*, ed. John J. Manning (London, 1991)

Healy, Margaret, *William Shakespeare, 'Richard II'* (Plymouth, 1998)

Healy, Thomas, 'Selves, states, and sectarianism in early modern England', *English* 44 (1995), 193–213

Heinemann, Margot, 'How Brecht read Shakespeare', in Dollimore and Sinfield, eds, *Political Shakespeare*, pp. 226–54

— 'Rebel lords, popular playwrights, and political culture: notes on the Jacobean patronage of the Earl of Southampton', *YES* 21 (1991), 63–86

Helgerson, Richard, *Self-Crowned Laureates: Spenser, Jonson, Milton and the Literary System* (Berkeley, 1983)

Herman, Peter C., '"O, 'tis a gallant king", Shakespeare's *Henry V* and the crisis of the 1590s', in Hoak, ed., *Tudor Political Culture*, pp. 204–25

Herodotus, *The Histories*, trans. Aubrey De Selincourt, rev. A.R. Burn (Harmondsworth, 1972)

Heywood, Thomas, *If You Know Not Me You Know Nobody*, Parts One and Two, ed. Madeleine Doran, 2 vols (Oxford, 1935)

Hill, Christopher, *Intellectual Origins of the English Civil War Revisited* (Oxford, 1997)

Hill, C.P., *Who's Who in Stuart Britain* (London, 1988, rpt of 1965)

Hirst, Derek, *The Representative of the People? Voters and Voting under the Early Stuarts* (Cambridge, 1975)

Hoak, Dale, ed., *Tudor Political Culture* (Cambridge, 1995)

Holderness, Graham, *Shakespeare: The Histories* (Basingstoke, 2000)

— *Cultural Shakespeare: Essays in the Shakespeare Myth* (Hatfield, 2001)

Holinshed, Raphael, *Chronicles of England, Scotland and Ireland* (London, 1587)

Holmer, Joan Ozark, *'The Merchant of Venice': Choice, Hazard and Consequence* (Basingstoke, 1995)

Honan, Park, *Shakespeare: A Life* (Oxford, 1998)

Honigmann, E.A.J., *Shakespeare, The 'Lost Years'* (Manchester, 1998, rpt of 1985)

Houston, S.J., *James I* (Harlow, 1973)

Howard, Tony, 'Shakespeare's cinematic offshoots', in Russell Jackson, ed., *The Cambridge Companion to Shakespeare on Film* (Cambridge, 2000), pp. 295–313

Huffman, C.C., *Coriolanus in Context* (Lewisburg, 1971)

Hulme, Peter, *Colonial Encounters: Europe and the Native Caribbean, 1492–1797* (London, 1986)

Hunter, G.K., *John Lyly: The Humanist as Courtier* (London, 1962)

— *'Othello* and colour prejudice', in *Dramatic Identities and Cultural Traditions* (Liverpool, 1978), pp. 31–59

Jaffa, Harry V., 'The limits of politics: *King Lear*, Act I, scene 1', in Bloom with Jaffa, *Shakespeare's Politics*, pp. 113–45

— 'Nature and the city: *Timon of Athens*', in Alvis and West, eds, *Shakespeare as Political Thinker*, pp. 177–201

James I, *The Workes* (1616) (Hildesheim and New York, 1971)

— *Political Writings*, ed. Johann P. Somerville (Cambridge, 1994)

James, Heather, *Shakespeare's Troy: Drama, Politics, and the Translation of Empire* (Cambridge, 1997)

Jardine, Lisa, *Reading Shakespeare Historically* (London, 1996)
— *Worldly Goods: A New History of the Renaissance* (Basingstoke, 1996)
— and Anthony Grafton, '"Studied for Action": how Gabriel Harvey read his Livy', *P & P* 129 (1990), 30–78
Johnson, Samuel, *Samuel Johnson on Shakespeare*, ed. H.R. Woudhuysen (Harmondsworth, 1989)
Jones, Emrys, *Scenic Form in Shakespeare* (Oxford, 1971)
Jones, Norman, 'Parliament and the political society of Elizabethan England', in Hoak, ed., *Tudor Political Culture*, pp. 226–42
Jonson, Ben, *Sejanus his Fall*, ed. W.F. Bolton (London, 1966)
— *Poems*, ed. Ian Donaldson (Oxford, 1975)
Jordan, Constance, *Shakespeare's Monarchies: Ruler and Subject in the Romances* (Ithaca, 1997)
Jordan, W.K., *Edward VI: The Young King* (Cambridge, Mass., 1971)
Kahn, Coppélia, '"Magic of bounty": *Timon of Athens*, Jacobean patronage, and maternal power', *SQ* 38 (1987), 34–57
Kamps, Ivo, *Historiography and Ideology in Stuart Drama* (Cambridge, 1996)
Kantorowicz, Ernst H., *The King's Two Bodies: A Study in Mediaeval Political Theology* (Princeton, 1957)
Kaplan, M. Lindsay, 'Slander for slander in *Measure for Measure*', in *The Culture of Slander in Early Modern England* (Cambridge, 1997), pp. 92–108
Kastan, David Scott, 'Proud majesty made a subject: Shakespeare and the spectacle of rule', *SQ* 37 (1986), 459–75
— ed., *A Companion to Shakespeare* (Oxford, 1999)
— *Shakespeare and the Book* (Cambridge, 2001)
Keach, William, *Elizabethan Erotic Narratives: Irony and Pathos in the Ovidian Poetry of Shakespeare, Marlowe and their Contemporaries* (New Brunswick, NJ, 1977)
Keevak, Michael, *Sexual Shakespeare: Forgery, Authorship, Portraiture* (Detroit, 2001)
Kelly, Donald R., 'Law', in Burns and Goldie, eds, *Cambridge History of Political Thought*, pp. 66–94
Kendall, Gillian Murray, '"Lend me thy hand": metaphor and mayhem in *Titus Andronicus*', *SQ* 40 (1989), 299–316
Kendrick, T.P., *British Antiquity* (London, 1950)
Kenyon, J.P., ed., *The Stuart Constitution: Documents and Commentary* (2nd edn, Cambridge, 1986)
Kernan, Alvin, *Shakespeare, the King's Playwright: Theater in the Stuart Court, 1603–1613* (New Haven, 1995)
Kettle, Arnold, ed., *Shakespeare in a Changing World: Essays* (London, 1964)
Kewes, Paulina, '*Julius Caesar* in Jacobean England', *The Seventeenth Century* 17 (2002), 155–86

— 'Roman history and early Stuart drama: Thomas Heywood's *The Rape of Lucrece*', *ELR* 32 (2002), 239–67

Kiernan, Pauline, *Staging Shakespeare at the New Globe* (Cambridge, 1999)

King, John N., *English Reformation Literature: The Tudor Origins of the Protestant Tradition* (Princeton, 1982)

— *Tudor Royal Iconography: Literature and Art in an Age of Religious Crisis* (Princeton, 1989)

Kingdon, Robert M., *Myths about the St Bartholomew's Day Massacre, 1572–1576* (Cambridge, Mass., 1988)

— 'Calvinism and resistance theory, 1550–1580', in Burns and Goldie, eds, *Cambridge History of Political Thought*, pp. 193–253

Kintgen, Eugene R., *Reading in Tudor England* (Pittsburgh, 1996)

Kishlansky, Mark A., *Parliamentary Selection: Social and Political Choice in Early Modern England* (Cambridge, 1986)

Knowles, Ronald, ed., *Shakespeare and Carnival: After Bakhtin* (Basingstoke, 1998)

Knutson, Rosalyn Lander, *Playing Companies and Commerce in Shakespeare's Time* (Cambridge, 2001)

Kurland, Stuart M., '*Hamlet* and the Scottish succession', *SEL* 34 (1994), 279–300

Kyd, Thomas, *The Spanish Tragedy*, ed. Philip Edwards (Manchester, 1977, rpt of 1959)

Lacey, Robert, *Robert, Earl of Essex: An Elizabethan Icarus* (London, 1970)
— *Sir Walter Raleigh* (London, 1975)

Leggatt, Alexander, *English Drama: Shakespeare to the Restoration, 1590–1660* (Harlow, 1988)

Levack, Brian P., *The Formation of the British State: England, Scotland and the Union, 1603–1707* (Oxford, 1987)

Lever, J.W., *The Tragedy of State* (London, 1971)

Lezra, Jacques, 'The appearance of history in *Measure for Measure*', in *Unspeakable Subjects: The Genealogy of the Event in Early Modern Europe* (Stanford, 1997), pp. 257–96

Liebler, Naomi Conn, *Shakespeare's Festive Tragedy: The Ritual Foundations of Genre* (London, 1995)

Lindley, David, ed., *The Court Masque* (Manchester, 1984)

— *The Trials of Frances Howard: Fact and Fiction at the Court of King James* (London, 1993)

— *Court Masques: Jacobean and Caroline Entertainments, 1605–1640* (Oxford, 1995)

Livesay, J.L., *The Elizabethan Image of Italy* (Chapel Hill, NC, 1964)

Livy, *The Early History of Rome from its Foundation*, trans. Aubrey De Sélincourt (Harmondsworth, 1960)

Loach, Jennifer, *Parliament under the Tudors* (Oxford, 1991)
— and Robert Tittler, eds, *The Mid-Tudor Polity, c.1540–1560* (Basingstoke, 1980)

Loades, David, *Two Tudor Conspiracies* (Cambridge, 1965)
— *The Reign of Mary Tudor: Politics, Government and Religion in England, 1553–58* (2nd edn, London, 1991)
— *Power in Tudor England* (Basingstoke, 1997)

Lockyer, Roger, *The Early Stuarts: A Political History of England, 1603–1642* (Harlow, 1989)
— *James VI and I* (Harlow, 1998)

Lucan, *Civil War*, trans. Susan H. Braund (Oxford, 1992)

Lucas, F.L., *Seneca and Elizabethan Tragedy* (Cambridge, 1922)

Luther, Martin, *Secular Authority: To What Extent It Should Be Obeyed* (1523), in John Dillenberger, ed., *Martin Luther: Selections from his Writings* (New York, 1961), pp. 363–402

Lytle, Guy Finch, and Stephen Orgel, eds, *Patronage in the Renaissance* (Princeton, 1981)

McCabe, Richard A., 'The Masks of Duessa: Spenser, Mary Queen of Scots, and James VI', *ELR* 17 (1987), 224–42

McCaffrey, Wallace, *Elizabeth I* (London, 1993)

McConica, J.K., *English Humanists and Reformation Politics under Henry VIII and Edward VI* (Oxford, 1965)

McCoy, Richard C., *The Rites of Knighthood: The Literature and Politics of Elizabethan Chivalry* (Berkeley, 1989)

McCullough, Peter E., *Sermons at Court: Politics and Religion in Elizabethan and Jacobean Preaching* (Cambridge, 1998)

McEachern, Claire, *The Poetics of English Nationhood, 1590–1612* (Cambridge, 1996)

Machiavelli, Niccolò, *The Arte of Warre* (1560), trans. Peter Whitehorne (London, 1905)
— *The Prince*, trans. George Bull (Harmondsworth, 1961)
— *The Prince*, ed. Quentin Skinner and Russell Price (Cambridge, 1988)
— *The Discourses*, trans. Leslie J. Walker, ed. Bernard Crick (Harmondsworth, 1970)

McLaren, A.N., *Political Culture in the Reign of Elizabeth I: Queen and Commonwealth, 1558–1585* (Cambridge, 1999)

MacLean, Ian, *The Renaissance Notion of Woman: A Study in the Fortunes of Scholasticism and Medical Science in European Intellectual Life* (Cambridge, 1980)

McMillin, Scott and Sally-Beth Maclean, *The Queen's Men and their Plays* (Cambridge, 1998)

McPherson, David, 'Lewkenor's Venice and its sources', *RQ* 41 (1988), 459–66
— *Shakespeare, Jonson, and the Myth of Venice* (Newark, 1990)

Maley, Willy, '"This sceptred isle": Shakespeare and the British problem', in John Joughin, ed., *Shakespeare and National Culture* (Manchester, 1997)

Maquerlot, Jean-Pierre, and Michèle Willems, eds, *Travel and Drama in Shakespeare's Time* (Cambridge, 1996)

Marcus, Leah S., *Puzzling Shakespeare: Local Reading and its Discontents* (Berkeley, 1988)

Marlowe, Christopher, *The Poems*, ed. Millar Maclure (Manchester, 1968)
— *The Complete Plays*, ed. Mark Thornton Burnett (London, 1999)

Marotti, Arthur F., '"Love is not love": Elizabethan sonnet sequences and the social order', *ELH* 49 (1982), 396–428

Marrapodi, Michele, '"Of that fatal country": Sicily and the rhetoric of topography in *The Winter's Tale*', in Marrapodi *et al.*, eds, *Shakespeare's Italy*, pp. 213–28
— and A.J. Hoenselaars, Marcello Cappuzzo and L. Falzon Santucci, eds, *Shakespeare's Italy: Functions of Italian Locations in Renaissance Drama* (Manchester, 1993)

Marsh, Philip Whaley, *A Handbook of Classical Drama* (Stanford, 1944)

Martindale, Charles, ed., *The Cambridge Companion to Virgil* (Cambridge, 1997)

Marx, Karl, *The Eighteenth Brumaire of Louis Bonaparte*, in *Selected Writings*, ed. David McLellan (Oxford, 1977), pp. 300–25
— and Friedrich Engels, *On Literature and Art* (Moscow, 1976)

Mason, Roger A., 'George Buchanan, James VI and the Presbyterians', in Roger A. Mason, ed., *Scots and Britons: Scottish Political Thought and the Union of 1603* (Cambridge, 1994), pp. 112–37

Masson, Georgina, *A Concise History of Republican Rome* (London, 1973)

Matheson, Mark, 'Venetian culture and the politics of *Othello*', *SS* 48 (1995), 123–33

Mathew, David, *James I* (London, 1967)

Mattingly, Garrett, *Renaissance Diplomacy* (London, 1955)

Mayer, Thomas F., *Thomas Starkey and the Commonweal* (Cambridge, 1989)

Middleton, Thomas, *Five Plays*, ed. Bryan Loughrey and Neil Taylor (Harmondsworth, 1988)

Miller, Shannon, 'Topicality and subversion in William Shakespeare's *Coriolanus*', *SEL* 32 (1992), 287–310

Miola, Robert S., 'Timon in Shakespeare's Athens', *SQ* 13 (1980), 21–30
— *Shakespeare's Rome* (Cambridge, 1983)
— '*Julius Caesar* and the tyrannicide debate', *RQ* 36 (1985), 271–90
— 'Shakespeare and his sources: observations on the critical history of *Julius Caesar*', *SS* 40 (1988), 69–76
— 'Reading the classics', in Kastan, ed., *Companion to Shakespeare*, pp. 172–85

— *Shakespeare's Reading* (Oxford, 2000)

Mirandola, Pico della, *Oration on the Dignity of Man*, in Ernst Cassirer, Paul Oskar Kristellar and John Herman Randall, Jr, eds, *The Renaissance Philosophy of Man* (Chicago, 1948), pp. 215–54

Montaigne, Michel de, *The Essayes of Michel Lord of Montaigne*, trans. John Florio (1603), 3 vols (London, 1910)

Montrose, Louis A., 'A Midsummer Night's Dream and the shaping fantasies of Elizabethan culture: gender, power, form', in Margaret W. Ferguson, Maureen Quilligan and Nancy J. Vickers, eds, *Rewriting the Renaissance* (Chicago, 1986), pp. 65–87

Mortimer, Anthony, *Variable Passions: A Reading of Shakespeare's 'Venus and Adonis'* (New York, 2000)

Morton, A.L., *The English Utopia* (London, 1954)

Moss, Ann, *Printed Commonplace-Books and the Structuring of Renaissance Thought* (Oxford, 1996)

Mossman, Judith, 'Henry V and Plutarch's Alexander', *SQ* 45 (1994), 57–73

Mozeley, J.F., *John Foxe and his Book* (London, 1940)

Muir, Kenneth, 'In defence of the tribunes', *EIC* 4 (1954), 331–3

— 'Shakespeare and Lewkenor', *RES* 7 (1956), 182–3

Mulryne, J.R., 'History and myth in The Merchant of Venice', in Marrapodi *et al.*, eds, *Shakespeare's Italy*, pp. 87–99

— 'Nationality and language in Thomas Kyd's The Spanish Tragedy', in Maquerlot and Willems, eds, *Travel and Drama in Shakespeare's Time*, pp. 87–105

— and Margaret Shewring, eds, *Theatre and Government under the Early Stuarts* (Cambridge, 1993)

Munday, Anthony, *et al.*, *Sir Thomas More*, ed. Vittorio Gabrieli and Giorgio Melchiori (Manchester, 1990)

Murray, Peter B., *Thomas Kyd* (New York, 1969)

Neale, J.E., *Queen Elizabeth* (London, 1934)

— *The Elizabethan House of Commons* (London, 1949)

— *Elizabeth I and her Parliaments*, 2 vols (London, 1953, 1957)

— 'Peter Wentworth', in Fryde and Miller, eds, *Historical Studies of the English Parliament*, pp. 246–95

Neill, Michael, 'Broken English and broken Irish: nation, language and the optic of power in Shakespeare's histories', *SQ* 45 (1994), 18–22

Newman, Jane O., '"And let mild women to him lose their mildness": Philomela, violence, and Shakespeare's The Rape of Lucrece', *SQ* 45 (1994), 304–26

Newman, Karen, '"And wash the Ethiop white": femininity and the monstrous in Othello', in Jean E. Howard and Marion O'Connor, eds, *Shakespeare Reproduced: The Text in History and Ideology* (London, 1987), pp. 143–62

Norbrook, David, '*Macbeth* and the politics of historiography', in Kevin Sharpe and Steven N. Zwicker, eds, *Politics of Discourse: The Literature and History of Seventeenth-Century England* (Berkeley, 1987), pp. 78–116

— '"What cares these roarers for the name of king?": language and utopia in *The Tempest*', in Jonathan Hope and Gordon McMullan, eds, *The Politics of Tragicomedy: Shakespeare and After* (London, 1992), pp. 21–54

— 'The Emperor's new body? *Richard II*, Ernst Kantorowicz, and the politics of Shakespeare criticism', *TP* 10 (1996), 329–57

— '"A liberal tongue": language and rebellion in *Richard II*', in John M. Mucciolo, ed., *Shakespeare's Universe: Renaissance Ideas and Conventions: Essays in Honour of W.R. Elton* (Aldershot, 1996), pp. 37–51

— *Writing the English Republic: Poetry, Rhetoric and Politics, 1627–1660* (Cambridge, 1999)

Notestein, Wallace, *The House of Commons 1604–1610* (New Haven, 1971)

Nuttall, A.D., *Timon of Athens* (Boston, 1989)

Oakshott, Michael J., *Rationalism in Politics and Other Essays* (2nd edn, London, 1981)

O'Callaghan, Michelle, *The 'Shepheardes Nation': Jacobean Spenserians and Early Stuart Political Culture, 1612–1625* (Oxford, 2000)

O'Day, Rosemary, *The Longman Companion to the Tudor Age* (Harlow, 1995)

Orgel, Stephen, *The Illusion of Power: Political Theater in the English Renaissance* (Berkeley, 1975)

Ovid, *Metamorphoses*, trans. Mary M. Innes (Harmondsworth, 1955)

Painter, William, *The Palace of Pleasure*, 3 vols, ed. Joseph Jacobs (Hildesheim, 1968, rpt of 1890)

Parker, Barbara L., '"A thing unfirm": Plato's *Republic* and Shakespeare's *Julius Caesar*', *SQ* 44 (1993), 30–43

Parker, Patricia, 'Fantasies of "race" and "gender": Africa, *Othello* and bringing to light', in Margo Hendricks and Patricia Parker, eds, *Women, "Race", & Writing in the Early Modern Period* (London, 1994), pp. 84–100

Parry, Graham, 'The politics of the Jacobean masque', in Mulryne and Shewring, eds, *Theatre and Government under the Early Stuarts*, pp. 87–117

— 'Entertainments at court', in Cox and Kastan, eds, *New History of Early English Drama*, pp. 195–211

Patterson, Annabel, *Censorship and Interpretation: The Conditions of Writing and Reading in Early Modern England* (Madison, 1984)

— *Shakespeare and the Popular Voice* (Oxford, 1989)

— *Reading Holinshed's 'Chronicles'* (Chicago, 1994)

— *Early Modern Liberalism* (Cambridge, 1997)

Patterson, W.B., *King James VI and I and the Reunion of Christendom* (Cambridge, 1997)

Paul, Henry N., *The Royal Play of 'Macbeth'* (New York, 1948)

Peck, Linda Levy, 'John Marston's *The Fawn*: ambivalence and Jacobean courts', in Smith, Strier and Bevington, eds, *Theatrical City*, pp. 117–36

Peltonen, Markku, *Classical Humanism and Republicanism in English Political Thought, 1570–1640* (Cambridge, 1995)

Perry, Curtis, *The Making of Jacobean Culture* (Cambridge, 1997)

Pettet, E.C., '*Coriolanus* and the Midlands Insurrection of 1607', *SS* 3 (1950), 34–42

Phillips, James Emerson, 'George Buchanan and the Sidney Circle', *HLQ* 12 (1948–9), 23–55

— *Images of a Queen: Mary Stuart in Sixteenth-Century Literature* (Berkeley, 1964)

Plutarch, *Selected Lives of the Noble Grecians and Romans*, trans. Thomas North (1579), ed. Judith Mossman (Ware, 1998)

Pocock, J.G.A., *The Machiavellian Moment: Florentine Political Thought and the Atlantic Republican Tradition* (Princeton, 1975)

— *The Ancient Constitution and the Feudal Law: A Study of English Historical Thought in the Seventeenth Century* (2nd edn, Cambridge, 1987)

Polan, A.J., *Lenin and the End of Politics* (London, 1984)

Ponet, John, *A Shorte Treatise of Politicke Power* (London, 1556)

Poole, Kristen, *Radical Religion from Shakespeare to Milton: Figures of Nonconformity in Early Modern England* (Cambridge, 2000)

Prall, Stuart E., 'The development of equity in Tudor England', *AJLH* 8 (1964), 1–19

Prawer, S.S., *Karl Marx and World Literature* (Oxford, 1976)

Prestwich, Menna, 'Constitutional ideas and parliamentary developments in England, 1603–1625', in Alan G.R. Smith, ed., *The Reign of James VI and I* (London, 1973), pp. 160–76

Pritchard, Arnold, *Catholic Loyalism in Elizabethan England* (London, 1979)

Pugliatti, Paola, *Shakespeare the Historian* (Basingstoke, 1996)

Quint, David, *Epic and Empire: Politics and Generic Form from Virgil to Milton* (Princeton, 1993)

Raab, Felix, *The English Face of Machiavelli: A Changing Interpretation, 1500–1700* (London, 1965)

Rackin, Phyllis, *Stages of History: Shakespeare's English Chronicles* (Ithaca, 1990)

Ray, Sid, '"Rape, I fear, was root of thy annoy": the politics of consent in *Titus Andronicus*', *SQ* 49 (1998), 22–39

Read, Conyers, *Mr. Secretary Cecil and Queen Elizabeth* and *Lord Burghley and Queen Elizabeth*, 2 vols (London, 1955, 1960)

Riche, Barnaby, *Allarme to England, foreshewing what perilles are procured, where the people live without regard of Martiall lawe* (London, 1578)

Riggs, David, *Ben Jonson: A Life* (Cambridge, Mass., 1989)

Rivers, Isabel, *Classical and Christian Ideas in English Renaissance Poetry* (London, 1979)

Roskell, J.S., 'Perspectives in English parliamentary history', in Fryde and Miller, eds, *Historical Studies of the English Parliament*, pp. 296–323

Routh, C.N.R., *Who's Who in Tudor England* (rev. Peter Holmes) (London, 1990, rpt of 1964)

Rowe, Katherine A., 'Dismembering and forgetting in *Titus Andronicus*', *SQ* 45 (1994), 279–303

Rowse, A.L., *The England of Elizabeth* (London, 1950)

Rudd, Niall, 'Pyramus and Thisbe in Shakespeare and Ovid', in Taylor, ed., *Shakespeare's Ovid*, pp. 113–25

Russell, Conrad, *The Crisis of Parliaments: English History 1509–1660* (Oxford, 1971)

Sacks, David Harris, 'Parliament, liberty, and the commonweal', in J.H. Hexter, ed., *Parliament and Liberty: From the Reign of Elizabeth to the English Civil War* (Stanford, 1992), pp. 85–121

— 'The countervailing of benefits: monopoly, liberty, and benevolence in Elizabethan England', in Hoak, ed., *Tudor Political Culture*, pp. 272–91

Salingar, Leo, 'The idea of Venice in Shakespeare and Ben Jonson', in Marrapodi *et al.*, eds, *Shakespeare's Italy*, pp. 171–84

Salmon, J.H.M., 'Catholic resistance theory, ultramontanism, and the royalist response, 1580–1620', in Burns and Goldie, eds, *Cambridge History of Political Thought*, pp. 219–53

Scarisbrick, J.J., *Henry VIII* (London, 1968)

— *The Reformation and the English People* (Oxford, 1984)

Schmitt, Charles B., and Quentin Skinner, eds, *The Cambridge History of Renaissance Philosophy* (Cambridge, 1988)

Schoenbaum, Samuel, *Shakespeare's Lives* (Oxford, 1970)

Seneca, Lucius Annaeus, *Oedipus*, in *Four Tragedies and Octavia*, trans. E.F. Watling (Harmondsworth, 1966)

Shakespeare, William, *Coriolanus*, ed. Lee Bliss (Cambridge, 2000)

— *The First Folio of Shakespeare: A Transcript of Contemporary Marginalia in a Copy of the Kodama Memorial Library of Meisei University*, ed. Akihiro Yamada (Tokyo, 1998)

— *The First Quarto of Hamlet*, ed. Kathleen O. Irace (Cambridge, 1998)

— *King Edward III*, ed. Giorgio Melchiori (Cambridge, 1998)

— *Henry V*, ed. Gary Taylor (Oxford, 1982)

— *King Henry V*, ed. Andrew Gurr (Cambridge, 1992)

— *Macbeth*, ed. Nicholas Brooke (Oxford, 1990)

— *Measure for Measure*, ed. Brian Gibbons (Cambridge, 1991)

— *Othello*, ed. Norman Sanders (Cambridge, 1984)

— *The Tempest*, ed. Stephen Orgel (Oxford, 1987)

— *Timon of Athens*, ed. Karl Klein (Cambridge, 2001)

— *The Tragedy of King Lear*, ed. Jay L. Halio (Cambridge, 1992)

Shapiro, James, *Shakespeare and the Jews* (New York, 1996)

Sharpe, Jim, 'Social strain and social dislocation, 1585–1603', in Guy, ed., *Reign of Elizabeth I*, pp. 192–211

Sharpe, Kevin, '"An image doting rabble": the failure of republican culture in seventeenth-century England', in Kevin Sharpe and Steven N. Zwicker, eds, *Refiguring Revolutions: Aesthetics and Politics from the English Revolution to the Romantic Revolution* (Berkeley, 1998), pp. 25–56

— *Reading Revolutions: The Politics of Reading in Early Modern England* (New Haven, 2000)

— *Remapping Early Modern England: The Culture of Seventeenth-Century Politics* (Cambridge, 2000)

— and Peter Lake, eds, *Culture and Politics in Early Stuart England* (Basingstoke, 1994)

Shuger, Deborah Kuller, *Political Theologies in Shakespeare's England: The Sacred and the State in 'Measure for Measure'* (Basingstoke, 2001)

Sinfield, Alan, '*Macbeth*: history, ideology and intellectuals', *CQ* 28 (Spring/Summer 1986), 63–77

Skinner, Quentin, *The Foundations of Modern Political Thought*, 2 vols (Cambridge, 1978)

— *Machiavelli* (Oxford, 1981)

— *Liberty Before Liberalism* (Cambridge, 1998)

Smith, David L., Richard Strier and David Bevington, eds, *The Theatrical City: Culture, Theatre and Politics in London, 1576–1649* (Cambridge, 1995)

Smith, Thomas, *De Republica Anglorum: A Discourse on the Commonwealth of England* (1583), ed. L. Alston (Shannon, 1972, rpt of 1906)

Smuts, R. Malcolm, *Culture and Power in England, 1585–1685* (Basingstoke, 1999)

Soellner, Rolf, *'Timon of Athens': Shakespeare's Pessimistic Tragedy* (Columbus, Ohio, 1979)

Sohmer, Steve, *Shakespeare's Mystery Play: The Opening of the Globe Theatre, 1599* (Manchester, 1999)

Sokolova, Boika, *Shakespeare's Romances as Interrogative Texts: Their Alienation Strategies and Ideology* (Lewiston, 1992)

Sommerville, J.P., *Politics and Ideology in England, 1603–1640* (Harlow, 1986)

— 'James I and the divine right of kings: English politics and continental theory', in Linda Levy Peck, ed., *The Mental World of the Jacobean Court* (Cambridge, 1991), pp. 55–70

Spellman, W.M., *European Political Thought, 1600–1700* (Basingstoke, 1998)

Spenser, Edmund, *The Faerie Queene*, ed. A.C. Hamilton (London, 1977)

Spurgeon, Caroline, *Shakespeare's Imagery and What it Tells Us* (Cambridge, 1965, rpt of 1935)

Starkey, Thomas, *A Dialogue Between Pole and Lupset*, ed. Thomas F. Mayer (London, 1989)

Steen, Sara Jane, 'The crime of marriage: Arbella Stuart and *The Duchess of Malfi*', *SCJ* 22 (1991), 61–76

Stevenson, David L., 'The role of James I in Shakespeare's *Measure for Measure*', *ELH* 26 (1959), 188–208

Strong, Roy, *The Cult of Elizabeth: Elizabethan Portraiture and Pageantry* (London, 1977)

— *Henry Prince of Wales and England's Lost Renaissance* (London, 1986)

Stuart, Arbella, *The Letters of Arbella Stuart*, ed. Sara Jane Steen (Oxford, 1994)

Suetonius, *The Twelve Caesars*, trans. Robert Graves (Harmondsworth, 1957)

Sutherland, John, and Cedric Watts, *Henry V, War Criminal? & Other Shakespeare Puzzles* (Oxford, 2000)

Tacitus, Gaius Cornelius, *The Ende of Nero and Beginning of Galba: Fower Bookes of the Histories of Cornelius Tacitus. The Life of Agricola*, trans. Sir Henry Saville (Oxford, 1591)

— *The Annales of Cornelius Tacitus. The Description of Germanie* (London, 1598)

— *On Imperial Rome*, trans. Michael Grant (Harmondsworth, 1956)

Tarrant, R.J., 'Aspects of Virgil's reception in antiquity', in Martindale, ed., *Cambridge Companion to Virgil*, pp. 56–72

— 'Poetry and power: Virgil's poetry in contemporary context', in Martindale, ed., *Cambridge Companion to Virgil*, pp. 169–87

Taylor, A.B., ed., *Shakespeare's Ovid: 'The Metamorphoses' in the Plays and Poems* (Cambridge, 2000)

Taylor, Gary, 'Bardicide', repr. in Richard Wilson, ed., *Julius Caesar: Contemporary Critical Essays* (Basingstoke, 2002), pp. 188–209

Tennenhouse, Leonard, *Power on Display: The Politics of Shakespeare's Genres* (London, 1986)

Thomas, William, *The Historie of Italie* (London, 1549)

Thomson, Peter, *Shakespeare's Professional Career* (Cambridge, 1992)

Thorne, Alison, *Vision and Rhetoric in Shakespeare: Looking through Language* (Basingstoke, 2000)

Thucydides, *History. Tr. into Englishe* (London, 1607)

— *The History of the Peloponnesian War*, trans. Rex Warner and M.I. Finley (Harmondsworth, 1972)

Tillyard, E.M.W., *The Elizabethan World Picture* (Harmondsworth, 1972, rpt of 1943)

— *Shakespeare's History Plays* (Harmondsworth, 1962, rpt of 1944)

Trumbull, William, *HMC 75: Downshire Manuscripts, VI, Papers of William Trumbull, Sept. 1616–Dec. 1618*

Tuck, Richard, *Philosophy and Government, 1572–1651* (Cambridge, 1993)

Vaughan, Virginia Mason, *Othello: A Contextual History* (Cambridge, 1994)

Vickers, Brian, ed., *Shakespeare: The Critical Heritage*, 6 vols (London, 1974–81)
— *In Defence of Rhetoric* (Oxford, 1988)
— '*Coriolanus* and the demons of politics', in *Returning to Shakespeare* (London, 1989), pp. 135–93

Virgil, *The Aeneid*, trans. David West (Harmondsworth, 1990)

Walker, Greg, *Plays of Persuasion: Drama and Politics at the Court of Henry VIII* (Cambridge, 1991)
— *Persuasive Fictions: Faction, Faith and Political Culture in the Reign of Henry VIII* (Aldershot, 1996)
— *The Politics of Performance in Early Renaissance Drama* (Cambridge, 1998)

Wallace, John M., '*Timon of Athens* and the Three Graces: Shakespeare's Senecan study', *MP* 83 (1985–6), 349–63

Watt, Tessa, *Cheap Print and Popular Piety, 1550–1640* (Cambridge, 1991)

Wayne, Don E., *Penshurst: The Semiotics of Place and the Poetics of History* (London, 1984)

Webster, John, *The Duchess of Malfi*, ed. John Russell Brown (London, 1964)

Weiner, Carol Z., 'The beleaguered isle: a study of Elizabethan and early Jacobean anti-Catholicism', *P & P* 51 (1971), 27–62

Wells, Robin Headlam, *Shakespeare, Politics and the State* (Basingstoke, 1986)

Wells, Stanley, ed., *The Cambridge Companion to Shakespeare Studies* (Cambridge, 1986)

Welsford, Enid, *The Fool: His Social and Literary History* (London, 1935)

Wendel, François, *Calvin: The Origins and Development of his Religious Thought*, trans. Philip Maret (London, 1963)

Wernham, R.B., *After the Armada: Elizabethan England and the Struggle for Western Europe, 1588–1595* (Oxford, 1984)

Whigham, Frank, 'Flattering courtly desire', in Smith, Strier and Bevington, eds, *The Theatrical City*, pp. 137–56

White, R.S., ed., *The Tempest* (Basingstoke, 1999)

Wilders, John, *The Lost Garden: A View of Shakespeare's English and Roman Plays* (Basingstoke, 1978)

Williams, Neville, *The Life and Times of Elizabeth I* (London, 1972)

Williams, Penry, *The Tudor Regime* (Oxford, 1979)

Willson, D. Harris, *King James VI and I* (London, 1956)

Wilson, John Dover, *The Essential Shakespeare* (Cambridge, 1932)

Wilson, Luke, *Theaters of Intention: Drama and the Law in Early Modern England* (Stanford, 2000)

Wilson, Richard, 'Against the grain: representing the market in *Coriolanus*', in *Will Power: Essays on Shakespearean Authority* (Hemel Hempstead, 1993)

— 'Voyage to Tunis: new history and the Old World of *The Tempest*', *ELH* 64 (1997), 333–57

Wittreich, Joseph, '"Image of that horror": the Apocalypse in *King Lear*', in C.A. Patrides and Joseph Wittreich, eds, *The Apocalypse in English Renaissance Thought and Literature* (Manchester, 1984), pp. 175–206

Womersley, David, '*3 Henry VI*: Shakespeare, Tacitus, and Parricide', *N & Q* 280 (Dec. 1985), 468–73

— 'Sir Henry Saville's translation of Tacitus and the political interpretation of Elizabethan texts', *RES*, n.s. 42 (1991), 313–42

Woolf, D.R., 'The shapes of history', in Kastan, ed., *Companion to Shakespeare*, pp. 186–205

— *Reading History in Early Modern England* (Cambridge, 2000)

Worden, Blair, 'Shakespeare and Politics', *SS* 44 (1991), 1–15

— 'English republicanism', in Burns and Goldie, eds, *Cambridge History of Political Thought*, pp. 443–75

— 'Ben Jonson among the historians', in Sharpe and Lake, eds, *Culture and Politics*, pp. 67–89

— *The Sound of Virtue: Philip Sidney's 'Arcadia' and Elizabethan Politics* (New Haven, 1996)

— 'Politics in *Catiline*: Jonson and his sources', in Martin Butler, ed., *Re-Presenting Ben Jonson: Text, History, Performance* (Basingstoke, 1999), pp. 152–73

Wormald, Jenny, *Court, Kirk, and Community: Scotland, 1470–1625* (London, 1981)

— 'James VI and I, *Basilikon Doron* and *The Trew Law of Free Monarchies*: the Scottish context and the English translation', in Linda Levy Peck, ed., *The Mental World of the Jacobean Court* (Cambridge, 1991), pp. 36–54

Woudhuysen, H.R., *Sir Philip Sidney and the Circulation of Manuscripts, 1558–1640* (Oxford, 1996)

Yates, Frances, *Astraea: The Imperial Theme in the Sixteenth Century* (London, 1975)

Young, Michael B., *James VI and I and the History of Homosexuality* (Basingstoke, 2000)

Zaret, David, *Origins of Democratic Culture: Printing, Petitions, and the Public Sphere in Early Modern England* (Princeton, 2000)

Zeeveld, W. Gordon, *Foundations of Tudor Polity* (Cambridge, Mass., 1948)

— '*Coriolanus* and Jacobean politics', *MLR* 57 (1962), 321–34

INDEX